THE

Frank G. Carrington

ARLINGTON HOUSE·PUBLISHERS
NEW ROCHELLE, N. Y.

Library of Congress Cataloging in Publication Data

Carrington, Frank.
    The victims.

    Includes index.
    1. Criminal justice, Administration of--United
States. 2. Victims of crime--United States.
3. Prisoners--Legal status, laws, etc.--United States.
I. Title.
HV8138.C37   364   74-32208
ISBN 0-87000-302-X

✶ Contents

✟ Foreword

When it comes to matters of law and order, I am very much an average American. I like to go about my business free from the fear that I may be assaulted or robbed. I like to know that my family and friends are safe on the streets and in our homes. I like to go to bed at night secure in the feeling that my life or property is not in danger.

But should my life or property be endangered by a criminal, I want to have a reasonable basis for believing that he will be apprehended, tried, and punished. I want nothing so much, in short, as to enjoy the blessings of liberty unmolested by those of evil heart and malevolent design. And, as is natural to those of us who have been born into this nation, I look to the law as the ultimate foundation of my freedom. But if for some reason the law is unable to protect me, I begin to get worried.

And I must say that in recent years I have begun to worry. I worry because between 1960 and 1973 serious crime rose by 158 percent while violent crime rose by 204 percent—compared to a 15 percent increase in population. I worry because the risk of being a victim of one of these crimes has increased by 120 percent during the same period, and is still on the increase.

I worry because far too few criminals are arrested, far too few convicted, far too few sent to prison. I worry because, when prison sentences are imposed, prison life becomes a breeding ground for yet further crime. I worry because criminal trials are unnecessarily protracted, because appeals are far too open-ended, and because the entire process has been converted from a determination of guilt or innocence into a determination of the propriety of police behavior.

I worry because by such examples, the lawless in spirit are encouraged to become lawless in practice, and because the American people, in growing numbers, have begun to lose faith in their system of criminal justice. And as they begin to lose faith in this system, they also begin to lose faith in and become alienated from the basic structure of law and government established by the Constitution, among the fundamental purposes of which are "to establish Justice, insure domestic Tranquility, . . . and secure the blessings of Liberty to ourselves and our Posterity."

The basic purpose of government in a free society is to protect the lives, liberty, and property of its citizens. But, as Maurice Nadjari, New York State special prosecutor recently stated at a meeting of the International Association of Chiefs of Police, "Our system of criminal justice has broken down. . . . We are no longer capable of securing the people against crime." And, when national polls show that more than 40 percent of Americans are afraid to leave their homes and walk in their own neighborhoods at night for fear of being assaulted, one begins to question whether government is really fulfilling its most basic and important function, and to wonder whether a society can truly be called free if it does not also have freedom from such a fear.

Crime has become as significant a characteristic of modern day America as any other you are likely to name. Its recent rate of increase is startling, and its impact is pervasive. Where once many Americans living in the suburbs and smaller towns correctly felt they were relatively free of crime, now these suburbs and towns are experiencing increases in crime rates of more than two, and as much as four times those occurring in large cities. No longer is serious crime largely the province of big city streets; now it menaces nearly all of us, everywhere.

Reflected in the uncontrolled growth of crime is a relatively new phenomenon: the direct relationship between crime and narcotics addiction. Figures from New York City indicate that something like 50 percent of all robberies and burglaries are narcotics-related, and comparable figures could probably be adduced for most of our other large urban areas. While the availability of hard drugs has been reduced during the last several years, recent evidence indicates that larger amounts of these drugs are again being smuggled into our country, threatening a renewed outbreak and spread of this deadly social cancer.

The 120 percent increase in the per capita incidence of serious crimes during the last thirteen years means that now on the average at least one of every twenty-five Americans will become a direct victim of crime this year. And if you are black and live in the inner city, your chances of being a victim are greatly increased. The late Stanford University criminologist Herbert L. Packer found, through a study he did in 1970, that slum dwellers were at least one hundred times more likely to be victims of street crime as middle class whites living in the suburbs, although the odds are now increasing for suburban whites, too. Black Americans suffer from crime vastly out of proportion to their percentage of the population. Far from being a code word for racism, among what black Americans want most are more law and order in the form of more police protection, better law enforcement, and increased prosecution of criminals, to protect them from the daily terror and suffering of crime.

Figures released by the FBI for 1973 reveal that there were 8,638,400 major crimes *reported* in America, including 19,510 murders, 51,000 forcible rapes, 382,680 robberies, 416,270 aggravated assaults and 2,540,900 burglaries. These figures are so large that they may seem incomprehensible, but they take on some meaning when expressed in the following way: there were 16 serious crimes committed each minute, one violent crime every 36 seconds; a forcible rape was committed every 10 minutes, a robbery every 82 seconds; an aggravated assault was committed every 76 seconds, while a burglary occurred every 12 seconds and larceny or theft, every 7 seconds. These figures are even higher today.

But one cannot fully appreciate the meaning of these figures until they are understood and seen in human terms, in terms of the victims of these crimes: the store clerk murdered in a holdup, the young girl raped on her way home from school, the elderly widow whose purse and monthly social security funds were stolen, the young couple who returned to find their apartment ransacked and all their significant possessions taken, or the body of the slain policeman, ambushed by a self-styled revolutionary. Then too there are ancillary effects produced by crime: the costs, the fears, the suffering and hardships of children and other relatives of those killed or crippled by criminals. But the ultimate reality of crime can only be felt when it reaches out to touch us, or when we see the bodies or look into the faces of the victims of crime. The ultimate human toll that crime takes can never be measured.

It is to his enduring credit that Frank Carrington has, in *The Victims*, trenchantly brought the reality of crime, and the plight of its victims, to the fore and into public focus. All too often the victims of crime have become a vast class of forgotten Americans, overlooked in official proceedings and ignored by the public. Only recently has a sense of "victim consciousness" begun to develop, a sense of outrage over the plight of victims of crime, a concern for their rights, and a growing realization that ultimately we are all victims of crime—for, not only does the growth of violent death taint our whole society, but the increase and spread of crime engenders a fear that constantly overshadows nearly all us, denies us the right to venture forth at night for recreation or necessity, keeps us out of many areas of our cities, and raises the cost of goods and services which we all consume. *The Victims* promises to play a major role in the raising of that consciousness.

But *The Victims* is more than the story of crime and its victims. It is a thorough, extensively researched indictment of the way in which the American criminal justice system currently operates, a system that, in Carrington's words, "erects an elaborate thicket of contrived and artificial protections around the criminal accused, but that is unable to secure the right of non-criminals to go about their business in peace. . . ."

In the last decade or so, a growing zeal for the rights of those accused of crime and an increasing tendency to lay the blame for crime not so much on its perpetrators as on society, have combined to create such a severe imbalance in favor of the rights of those accused of crime over the rights of those victimized by crime and of the public at large, that we have seriously hurt our ability to deal with criminality while only marginally increasing the protection of the innocent. The search for truth and justice, the vindication of the suffering of the victims, the protection of the innocent—these goals have been largely subordinated to a singleminded preoccupation with the rights of the criminal. The system, under its present constraints, appears either unwilling or unable to punish the guilty, vindicate the victim, and protect the innocent.

The result has been, as Carrington demonstrates, that increasingly, crime pays—and pays increasingly well. Professor Gordon Tullock has made some extrapolations on the rationality of crime as a profession, and calculated that, on the basis of 1965 figures, if you commit a crime, your chances of being arrested are only one in seven, and if you are convicted, only one in sixty that you will be sent to prison. Available evidence indicates that one's odds are even better today. The Wall Street *Journal* editorialized on this fact in 1973:

> It pays because the average criminal no longer fears being punished, even if he is caught. Overworked police forces, crowded court calendars, misplaced social concern and a penologist reaction against imprisonment on the ground that it fails to rehabilitate, have given criminals the edge—and given society the short end of the stick.

In a lighter vein, I cannot help recalling in this regard the story of Willie Sutton, the dapper and ingenious bank-robber whose exploits during the Forties and Fifties put him on many a front page. Following what proved to be his final arrest and conviction, the sociologists, criminologists, psychologists, and psychiatrists descended upon him in hordes. They pinched and poked and prodded each and every aspect of his life, from toilet-training on, applying each and every available hypothesis they could contrive to explain his life of crime. Almost without exception, these hypotheses began with the assumption that Willie was somehow "abnormal," that his genetic endowment or environmental experience, or some combination of both, virtually compelled him to pursue a criminal career. After months of exasperating study and conflicting conclusions, it suddenly occurred to an enterprising young interviewer to ask a really intelligent question. "Willie," he inquired, "why do you rob banks?"—and clear as a bell, without so much as a moment's hesitation, Willie shot back: "Because that's where the money is."

That simple and honest explanation is worth a world of learned treatises on the cause of crime. Most of those who commit crime do so because they choose to do so; and they choose to do so because the potential rewards, relative to the risk of being captured and punished, are highly attractive. Their choice, on balance, is really quite a reasonable one.

This situation has developed, to a significant extent, as a result of key decisions by the Supreme Court made in the Sixties: in particular the now famous *Mapp* and *Miranda* cases, as well as several others dealing with the admissibility of evidence. These decisions have created a host of legal requirements and technicalities which have created grounds for endless delay and have permitted the release of countless patently guilty felons. They have established artificial, rigid and impractical requirements on the police and the courts which result in the disqualification of factual evidence that is clearly probative. This has converted criminal trials into trials of the evidence while criminals go free. Senator McClellan's remarks were prophetic when he said in 1969 that the court's rulings threatened "to alter the nature of the criminal trial from a test of the defendant's guilt or innocence to an inquiry into the propriety of the policeman's conduct." The purpose of a trial, of course, is to determine whether the defendant is guilty, which is a question of fact and law. But where a disqualification of evidence on highly technical grounds results in the release of the guilty, we do an injustice to the public that is almost as grave as the conviction of an innocent man. Former Chief Justice Weintraub of the New Jersey Supreme Court aptly summarized the injustice which these rulings cause: "When the truth is suppressed and the criminal is set free, the pain of suppression is felt, not by the inanimate state or by some penitent policeman, but by the offender's next victim for whose protection we hold office." With case after case, *The Victims* demonstrates the absurd and tragic effects of these decisions.

How the idea got itself accepted that the effective application of the criminal law is somehow incompatible with due process for the criminally accused is, I must confess, something of a mystery to me. By the same token, I cannot see why the prosecution of criminals cannot be carried out efficiently, and with justice, without endangering the civil liberties of the innocent, for current statistics make it clear that a law-abiding citizen runs a far greater risk of being victimized by a criminal who has been arrested and later released than he does of being unjustly convicted of a crime. This is not to deny that there are hard cases, or that the line between tolerable and intolerable police behavior is sometimes difficult to draw. We deal so often in the criminal law with what are ultimately questions of prudence, and they do not always lend themselves to mechanical resolution. I take it that we are all in favor of due process for the accused, and that we are all in favor of ordered liberty for society as a whole. Unfortunately, there is no piece of constitutional litmus-paper that we can dip into the circumstantial vat to produce the desired constitutional result. It must be remembered, however, as Sidney Hook has pointed out, that "The potential victim has at least just as much a human right not to be violently molested, interfered with and outraged as the person accused of such crimes has to a fair trial and a skillful defense. As a citizen, most of the rights guaranteed me under the Bill of Rights become nugatory if I am hopelessly crippled by violence and all of them become extinguished if I am killed."

The fact that the commands of the courts have taken on an increasingly rarefied and lenient character has not escaped public attention. Never, I believe, certainly not within my own lifetime, has public esteem for the judicial process been lower; and few factors are so important in this loss of esteem as the widely held opinion that the courts are, as the saying goes, "soft" on criminals. A 1969 Gallup poll indicated that fully 75 percent of the American people felt that the courts did not deal harshly enough with criminals; and in a second poll two years later, in 1971, that sizeable percentage held firm. This is the essence of the crisis.

There are those, I know, who say that we cannot hope to remedy the problem of crime without a thorough overhauling of the nation's social and economic system—the assumption being that poverty, ignorance, and racial prejudice are the ultimate causes of crime. Those who so earnestly advance this argument never adequately explain why so much crime is committed by people who are neither poor nor unintelligent or who have never known a day of racial discrimination in their lives. Even if the assumption were correct, and I do not believe that it is, the ostensible "solutions" that follow in its wake are bound to be viewed by the law-abiding public as at best irrelevant to the immediate realities of crime with which they have to cope. It may be theoretically satisfying to some to explain criminal behavior in terms of inadequate education or economic opportunity, but that is a small comfort to a mother whose 15-year-old daughter is gang-raped on her way to school, as happened recently in Los Angeles. As former Supreme Court Justice Abe Fortas has remarked, we cannot wait until we have rebuilt society according to some utopian, reformist prescription before dealing with the all too commonplace everyday savagery of crime.

There is a peculiar softness to contemporary thought, the defining characteristics of which are the desire to avoid responsibility for the natural consequences of one's own behavior, and the refusal to recognize as legitimate any external constraint on the impulse of one's passions. The strength of this opinion is so great that we behold a widespread avoidance of those things which demand self-sacrifice or discipline, and a seeming unwillingness to impose restraints on others because one is unwilling to impose restraints on himself. This sentiment has had a devastating impact upon the criminal law by robbing society of the conviction that it has the right to demand certain standards of behavior and that it is entirely justified in imposing sanctions upon those who engage in anti-social conduct. This softness, this hesitation to impose rightful sanctions, bespeaks a fundamental lack of conviction in the ultimate foundations of the criminal law—a lack of conviction that the criminals are quick to detect and exploit. If the law is in any way tolerant or indulgent, criminals will be the first to discover the fact. And should they nevertheless run afoul of the law, they cannot help but form a cynical opinion about a legal system in which punishment, precisely because it is employed halfheartedly or irregularly, is thought of as being employed inequitably.

I believe the remarks of Sir Reginald Scholl, a former justice of the Supreme Court of Victoria, Australia, are directly to the point:

> Many years of experience in the criminal jurisdiction have convinced me of two things—that the deliberate wrongdoer . . . will go on planning and committing crimes so long as he thinks the law is weak and yielding enough to give him a chance to evade it, and that he will have no respect for a legal system which is marked by feebleness in the application of its sanctions . . .

While it cannot be conclusively proven that a certain series of decisions by the Warren Court led to a direct, related increase in crime, nonetheless, as Carrington is careful to point out, "it can be argued that the more criminally inclined individuals who are on the streets at liberty to prey upon others, the more crimes will be committed"—and key decisions of the Court "often required the wholesale release of patently guilty criminals and unquestionably made it much more difficult for the police to obtain admissible evidence of crime and for prosecutors to convict those accused of crime." In addition, he argues, with some force, that the liberal majority of the Court were pace-setting leaders instrumental in the creation of a widespread judicial and correctional climate of leniency and permissiveness, which may have encouraged the lawless to believe that they could get away with acts of crime with relative impunity.

Whatever the case may be, permissiveness and leniency seem to have become the order of the day. In every area Carrington documents their pervasiveness and harmful effects: low bail for repeater felons—with a corresponding increase in serious crimes committed by those out on bail; excessive plea bargaining for those charged with serious crimes; grants of time consuming pretrial and trial delays; seemingly endless appeals; overly lenient, short and concurrent sentences for repeater felons; early, permissive paroles for individuals who too often return immediately to crime; and the surrender of discipline in many prisons.

A recent criminal justice study done in Atlanta shows, for example, that of 278 adults arrested for assault, 103 were indicted, and 77 went to trial, 63 were convicted, and only 23 ended up in jail. National statistics indicate that nearly two-thirds of all crimes in our country are committed by "repeaters"—people with previous arrest records who go in and out of our criminal justice system as if it were a revolving door. And upwards of 35 percent of all persons awaiting trial are likely to be arrested again for a new offense while roaming free on bail! Carrington's wide ranging examination leaves little doubt that our criminal justice system is seriously crippled and that in large part this is a result of, in Fred Graham's words, a "self-inflicted wound."

Overcrowded courts, with their large backlog of cases, are an important part of the problem. Criminal cases can often take anywhere from six months to two years to be disposed of, and appeals may further delay or deny justice. Various pre-trial procedures which recent Supreme Court decisions have declared to be constitutionally mandated are significant contributing factors to this problem. As former Chief Justice Stanley Fuld of the New York Court of Appeals has observed, "These new procedures have added tremendously to the caseload of the trial courts and have substantially lengthened the time which elapses between arrest and trial." The courts find themselves in a Catch-22 situation: in order to speed up the disposition of cases, many judges become implicitly willing to allow plea bargaining or assign lenient sentences. As Manhattan District Attorney Robert Morgenthau recently noted. "The bigger the backlog, the lighter the sentences." Yet it is all but certain that excessive leniency and permissiveness throughout the criminal justice system have contributed to increasing crime, if only by placing professional criminals back on the street sooner. But if every criminal defendant demanded a trial, the system would most likely collapse from its own weight. Thus, the courts are caught in a vicious circle of increasing crime. Before he left office, former Attorney General William Saxbe came to the conclusion that "Too many dangerous convicted offenders are placed back in society in one way or another, and that simply must stop. With so few dangerous offenders being jailed, something has got to be wrong somewhere. Much of the fault, as I see it, must rest with prosecutions and the courts." And so, we continue to suffer from the corrosive legacy of official permissiveness and of prejudice in favor of the rights of those accused of crime, as opposed to the rights of the actual and potential victims of crime, which legacy has been bequeathed to us by the Warren Court.

The frequent reversals by the Warren Court, combined with its penchant for rigid procedural requirements, have left many of us disturbed and confused as to what course to follow. The lower federal judges are confused; police officials are confused. Even learned professors are confused. Everyone, it seems, is confused—except the criminal. He knows. He knows that his chances of being arrested are fairly low; he knows that his chances of being convicted are yet lower; and he knows that, even if arrested and convicted, his chances of being imprisoned are lower still. He knows the restrictions which prevent the police from introducing relevant evidence at trial, and he knows that the present state of the law positively encourages the raising of constitutional objections against police behavior. He knows that these objections can be raised before, during or after trial; and, best of all, he knows that such objections are the surest way to obscure the fundamental question of his own guilt or innocence.

The criminal may have a better grasp of the ultimate meaning of the Warren Court's revolution in criminal procedure than all our professors and judges combined. Indeed, the greatest book yet to be written on the subject of present-day criminal law would be the one revealing what criminals actually think of such cases as *Mapp* and *Miranda*, and the way in which their behavior is determined by them.

The right to counsel and the privilege against self-incrimination are noble rights indeed, but only a man of remarkable ideological fervor would insist that they can be protected only by rendering inadmissible virtually all voluntary statements not made in the presence of counsel.

Similarly, only an ideological zealot would insist that the only way to prevent unlawful searches and seizures is to exclude from judicial consideration all evidence, however relevant, obtained by unlawful means.

In this context Mr. Carrington also quotes Sir Reginald Scholl, former Australian Consul General to the United States, whose wise observations I would repeat here:

> My general feeling on these matters [of the criminal justice system], if I may respectfully state it as a foreign lawyer, is that in your enthusiasm for liberalism at all costs you are, perceptibly more than we are in Australia, throwing the baby out with the bath water. It is no good making individual liberty so cast iron, by constitutional guarantees, that one's neighbors can rob one or rape one's daughter with a better chance of escaping justice than in other civilized countries. How stand life, liberty, and the pursuit of happiness in that situation? It is indeed an empty freedom, a vain individual liberty which is accompanied by a significantly increased risk to oneself or one's family of being the victim of crime. What is the real value of greater individual liberty, so called, if it is obtained at the price of making crime harder to detect and punish, and therefore safer to commit. What is the real value to a decent law-abiding citizen of being in less danger of possible abuse of power by the police but in greater danger of fraud, theft, violence, or death from criminals large or small, organized or unorganized?

Clearly, our system of criminal justice is fast reaching an impasse. In light of Maurice Nadjari's opinion quoted earlier, perhaps it has already broken down to the point of abject failure. The proverbial wheels of justice have not merely ground to a half; they have reversed themselves and begun to turn against the innocent victims, and society itself.

In such a situation, it is little wonder that our people are growing increasingly alienated from, and cynical about, their government and its leaders.

What, then, can we do?

Here, as with most of the ills which beset our society, there are no easy answers. But foremost in our efforts, I think, must be what Carrington proposes as our central task: we must develop a "victim consciousness" in our society, and reorient the thinking and the concerns of the criminal justice system towards the rights of the victims of crime, both actual and potential (who are all of us)—thereby restoring a balance to a system that is now weighted heavily in favor of the criminal. If the criminal justice system is once again to fulfill its primary tasks of protecting the innocent and securing justice and safety by punishing the criminal, this is the essential, primary change which must be made.

From such a change will flow many of the sound specific proposals which Carrington puts forward. High on the list, of course, is a substantial modification in the Exclusionary Rule and similar excessive restrictions and requirements imposed on the criminal justice system by the Supreme Court, such as the *Miranda* ruling. Certain recent decisions have already resulted in some minor modifications, and there is reason to believe that the High Court may take significant action along these lines in cases coming before it in the next year or two. In whatever modifications are made, however, it remains important that effective civil means of redress against questionable police actions be available to defendants. In addition, "police crime" is punishable by law. This ought to be protection enough without punishing society through the release of defendants that are clearly guilty.

Changes also have to be made in the system which will make justice more "swift and sure." The truth of the adage "Justice delayed is justice denied" is becoming more and more apparent every day. Judges are increasingly dismissing cases because of excessive delays. The irony is that usually it is not the fault of the prosecutor, but instead a result of the heavy load of court cases, or of legally authorized dilatory action on the part of defense lawyers, such as requests for continuances, postponements, and appeals. Lengthy delays can also result in the unavailability of witnesses and evidence. And when cases do come to trial, they now last an average of two to three times longer than they did little more than a decade ago. Then there is the proliferation of post-conviction remedies, such as *habeas corpus*, that have resulted from Supreme Court decisions expanding the opportunities for appeals from state court convictions to the federal courts. Justice Harlan expressed it well when he wrote in *Mackey* v. *United States*: "No one, not criminal defendants, not the judicial system, not society as a whole, is benefited by a judgement providing that a man shall tentatively go to jail today, but tomorrow and everyday thereafter shall be subject to fresh litigation on issues already resolved." Carrington offers numerous proposals to speed up justice which are deserving of consideration and implementation.

Perhaps even more important than justice that is swift is justice that is sure and certain. Numerous studies have been made to assess the deterrent effect of sentences. Their dominant conclusion is that, far more than the severity of punishment (where the only real deterrent effect has been found in connection with the death penalty for murder—one of several compelling arguments, by the way, for its reasoned reimposition), the *certainty* of punishment has a significant deterrent effect on crime rates. And yet all too often, as Carrington points out with cases and statistics, legal technicalities let off patently guilty felons; light sentences are given for serious crimes as a result of plea bargaining; and convicts with histories of serious criminal activities are given lenient, seldom supervised paroles. For example, during the years 1963 through 1969, the number of persons arrested in New York on felonious narcotics charges (mainly dealers) increased by over 700 percent, while the number convicted more than tripled. At the same time, however, the number going to state prison remained the same and, therefore, the proportion going to prison dropped from 68 percent of those convicted to under 23 percent.

As *The Victims* advocates, we need increasingly to establish mandatory minimum sentences for particular crimes, circumstances, and such categories of criminals as repeater felons. Sentences need not always be long (which can sometimes be counter-productive) in order to be effective, but they do need to be certain.

I have long been a supporter of such legislation at the national level with regard to the use of handguns during the commission of a federal crime.

Carrington proposes that we undertake a careful study of the British criminal justice system, an idea which I also put forward several years ago. The status of civil liberty in England is in no wise poorer than in our own country; and in some respects, it may even be a good deal better. Yet, English criminal law has gotten along quite well without the exclusionary rule, and without a good many other procedural devices that our system in recent years has considered vital to the just resolution of the criminal process. The differences between English and American criminal practice suggest, at the very least, that there is more than one way of dealing fairly and efficiently with those accused of crime. And these differences are worth examining in detail.

A systematic comparative study of British and American criminal jurisprudence could prove of enormous value if conducted by dispassionate scholars. The United States and Great Britain share a common legal heritage. We hold in common fundamental concepts as to what is required to guarantee a fair trial and to safeguard the rights of the accused. And we share a bias in favor of the defendant in a criminal trial. For years after we won our independence our procedures remained virtually indistinguishable. But in time they began to diverge, and in recent years in most significant ways. Today the British are able to find a defendant innocent or guilty within a few months of his arrest; and a certain finality normally attaches upon conviction. In our country, years can elapse between arrest and the conclusion of a trial; and conviction merely marks the beginning of a procedural ballet which can continue virtually indefinitely. In England today, the incidence of crime is small in comparison with ours, and respect for the law and for the legal apparatus remains undiminished.

A comprehensive study of the kind Mr. Carrington and I recommend may suggest any number of improvements which we can make in our own procedures without sacrificing the substantial rights of the accused, and it may also be instructive in telling us what purely *local* developments in American life may have contributed to our current criminality. This study should cover not only such matters as the exclusionary rule, the right to counsel and the application of the privilege against self-incrimination, but also an examination of the ways in which criminal trials might be expedited and appeals streamlined, as well as comparative studies in the area of corrections and penal reform.

Last, but by no means least, I think it would be instructive to study the role of attorneys in criminal trials and to compare the way in which the adversary system affects the conduct and outcome of trials here and in Great Britain. A number of thoughtful observers in our country have expressed their deep concern that the adversary system is becoming an end in itself, that the ultimate goal of justice is being subordinated to political and theatrical gamesmanship. The courtroom in all too many cases has been turned into a kind of theatre of the absurd. Judges are insulted, decorum is scoffed at, and the judicial process held up to ridicule. That such behavior should take place at all is scandalous; but that it should be directed or condoned by members of the Bar is, to me, absolutely intolerable. And I do not see that society is in any way obligated to confer a license to practice upon those whose behavior reveals a thoroughgoing contempt for everything that the law holds dear. Nor do I believe that it would be unjust for the courts or the Bar to remove the licenses of those who make a mockery of the very law whose protection they seek. We could, I believe, profit greatly by British example in this regard, and I commend such a project to the consideration of thoughtful men.

Perhaps central to the effort to create a change in public consciousness, as well as in judicial and other procedures, is Carrington's proposal to establish victims' rights commissions in every state of the Union. Be they publicly or privately supported, such commissions would not only assist the actual victims of crime through various legal and economic thickets in their attempts to vindicate their rights and secure justice, but would also aid the potential victims of crime in the future by proposing and supporting changes in the current criminal justice system which will restore a proper balance of rights within the system and which will discourage future crime, thereby protecting the innocent. I am much intrigued and impressed by this proposal, and I commend its thoughtful consideration to lawmakers and public spirited citizens and organizations across our country.

The Victims shows us the serious state which our criminal justice system and our nation is in, and it issues a call and an agenda for action. The time to act is now. I hope that legislators and justices will not fail to note and take heed of its message. For crime in this nation cannot continue to rise as it has in the recent past; public esteem for the legal process cannot continue to fall. Unless we come to terms with the problem of crime, I fear that almost everything else we attempt to do will come to nought. A free civil society cannot exist where there is widespread fear of criminal assault; it cannot exist where justice is so long delayed that it is, in effect, denied; it cannot exist when the public believes that its legal system cannot protect the lives and liberties and property of the law-abiding. The danger in our time is less that the innocent will be punished than that the guilty will go free. And that, to my mind, is a far more serious injustice than any our system is likely to inflict upon one who may be wrongfully accused. The truth is that an innocent man has very little to fear from our criminal law; the difficulty and danger, if anything, are that the same might be said regarding the guilty man. And I believe that the public will not long tolerate a continuation of our present condition.

Level-headed common sense is required in dealing with the criminal element in our midst. That common sense was summed up with characteristic wit and economy by columnist and professor John Roche, who remarked: "The beginning of wisdom is to know who is going to shoot you if he gets the chance. From there you can go on to Plato and the classics." This is, I believe, essentially the spirit that animates public sentiment on the subject of crime. It is not a very sophisticated view, perhaps; but it is solid. Hard-headed, perhaps; but not necessarily harsh. And what is more, it is fully compatible with the protection of constitutional liberty—that of society as well as that of the accused. Whatever else our system of criminal justice might be thought of as accomplishing, the one thing it can do, the one thing it ought to do, the one thing that the public has a right to expect it to do—is to find out who the criminals are, see to it that they are prosecuted, and discourage them by whatever means necessary from committing crime again. If it is argued that this central function cannot be performed consistently with the requirements of the Constitution, then it will not be long before the public begins to call for a new Constitution.

Which brings me to my final thought. In this day when disrespect for authority of all kinds—religious, parental, legal—is so pervasive; when allegiance to anything other than one's own passions is condemned as illegitimate; when "civil disobedience" is used as a defensive cloak for criminal behavior, let us not forget that, for all its failings, our nation and its rule of law are still robust and strong.

But let us also bear in mind that, for all its strengths, the rule of law can only abide so many attacks and that the delicate webbing of civilization can, like the veil of the temple, be rent, and with it, the world's last best hope for freedom. Let us resolve, then, to seek justice; justice for the accused, but justice also for the victims of crime, and for society. Let us resolve to be fair; but also firm. Let us resolve to stand by the fairest system of law that the world has ever known. And in our resolve, let us call to mind the words of Abraham Lincoln, who said: "Let every American, every lover of liberty, every well-wisher to his posterity, swear by the blood of the revolution, never to violate in the least particular the laws of the country; and never to tolerate their violation by others . . . . let every man remember that to violate the law is to trample on the blood of his father, and to tear the charter of his own and his children's liberty. . . . As the patriots of Seventy-Six did to the support of the Declaration of Independence, so to the support of the Constitution and laws, let every American pledge his life, his property, and his sacred honor."

SENATOR JAMES L. BUCKLEY

✦ Preface

Perhaps the nicest words about this book prior to its publication were said by the editor of the manuscript, who told me that, in the process of editing the manuscript, he could take only a few chapters at a time because he "got so angry at what was happening" to the victims of crime. If the book has this effect upon others then it will have accomplished its purpose. The plight of the victims of crime in the United States—particularly the minorities, the poor and powerless, and the ghetto dwellers—is indeed enough to anger anyone with a decent concern for individual life and liberty.

The thesis of this book—that is, the rights of the victims of crime in this country have been shamelessly disregarded and subordinated to the rights of the lawless and violent—will not, I fear, meet with the approval of the permissivists, the theoreticians, the social tinkerers, and the supercivil libertarians whose sole concern is for the rights of the accused and the convicted criminal. This is really of little consequence because the book was not written for them. It was written, rather, for the average citizen—rich or poor, white or black—in order to emphasize to him just how sorry his status is, as an actual or potential victim of crime, in our criminal justice system. Underlying this thesis is, of course, the proposition that the victim's current sorry status *need not be so* and that something can and must be done to enhance the rights of the victim.

Central to the premise of the book is that the victim's rights can be recognized and protected without doing violence to concepts of fundamental fairness to the accused and of fundamental humanity to the convicted criminal. All that is called for herein is a balance between the rights of the law-abiding and the rights of the criminal accused. Today no such balance exists. Until it does, the victims will continue to be, as they are described in chapter one, "uncertain, unnamed, and unrepresented."

Several additional points should be made about this work and its purpose. First, this book was not intended to be any sort of legal text. I have attempted to keep the text as nonlegalistic as I can, although, of necessity, some legal issues such as court decisions concerning the enforcement of the criminal law must be described.

Second, I do not represent this book to be a scientific "study" along the lines of the countless numbers of "studies" on the criminal justice system, studies which now clutter our libraries from coast to coast. Frankly, I think the average citizen does not need to read innumerable studies to be aware of the fact that crime and violence—and, consequently, the victimization of the innocent—are increasing at a pace unheard of before in our country's history and that none of the scientific studies on the problem has altered the situation one iota.

I believe that far and away the most effective method of making the point that this book seeks to make is by presenting actual examples of cases and situations drawn from every part of this country in order to underscore the incredibly horrible plight of crime's victims. And if anyone should believe that the examples cited herein are atypical, or isolated instances, let him read *any* major newspaper from *any* city or region in the United States and see for himself. This is the real tragedy: the cases I have cited are all too typical. In sum, I have attempted to make my case with examples that deal with the realities of the situation rather than by playing the numbers game with page after page of statistics.

Third, I have been asked by many people, who knew I was writing this book, why I did not further develop the stories of certain victims in order to document the impact of crime upon them. The reason I did not is that I cannot, for a moment, see the necessity of doing so. How do you "document" the grief of loving parents whose four-year-old daughter was kidnapped and murdered? Should you enter the privacy of their home and have them point out to you the room where she slept and the stuffed animals she loved? Should you urge them to verbalize the hurt, loss, and anguish they have suffered?

It seems to me it should go without saying that they *are* grieving, that they *have* suffered their loss, and that most people will have the compassion to recognize and sympathize with them without going into detail about it. In essence, I believe that the *status* of being a victim of crime, particularly of a violent crime, speaks for itself. Most of us who have a decent concern for our fellow human beings know instinctively how deep the hurt can be, and I think not much that is useful can be accomplished by dwelling on the grief of others.

Finally, I am certain that before this book is in print some part of it will be dated; for example, by a change in a given law or by a new court decision. This is the penalty one pays when writing on a subject as volatile as our criminal justice system, where changes occur on a day-to-day basis. Unfortunately, it appears that, unless emphatic action is taken fairly soon, the one element of this book that we can be certain will *not* be dated is that the victims will continue to get the short end of the stick in our criminal justice system.

FRANK CARRINGTON

Wilmette, Illinois
January 1975

Part I
The Victims

1
The Victims

THE SUPREME COURT OF THE UNITED STATES HAD SPOKEN, 5 TO 4, and the victims of crime in this country had sustained a stunning setback. The date was June 13, 1966, and the case was *Miranda* v. *Arizona.*[1] Chief Justice Earl Warren had just announced a ruling that was destined to cause countless murderers, rapists, robbers, thieves, and other assorted criminals to be freed, despite clear and convincing evidence of their guilt; for the *Miranda* decision, by drastically restricting the ability of law-enforcement officers to obtain legally admissible confessions from criminal suspects, had measurably increased the possibility that many of these suspects would escape the consequences of their acts.

Associate Justice Byron R. White wanted no part of the decision, and said so emphatically. In a stormy dissenting opinion, White, speaking for himself, Justice Potter Stewart, and the late Justice John M. Harlan, grimly pointed out that as a result of the majority's decision a good many criminal defendants, who would ordinarily have been convicted, now would be released.* He stated flatly: "I have no desire whatsoever to share the responsibility for any such impact on the present criminal process."[2] He then predicted (correctly, as it turned out) that "in some unknown number of cases the Court's rule will return a killer, a rapist or

*The majority justices in the *Miranda* case were Chief Justice Warren and Associate Justices Douglas, Black, Goldberg, and Brennan. Justices White, Harlan, Stewart, and Clark dissented. The *Miranda* case is discussed in detail in chapter four.

3

other criminal to the streets and to the environment which produced him, to repeat his crime whenever it pleases him."[3] Finally, White stated, with supreme irony, "There is, of course, a saving factor: the next victims are *uncertain, unnamed and unrepresented* in this case."[*][4]

This statement carries with it a profoundly wise and precisely accurate insight into the criminal justice system in the United States: the elementary truth of the matter is that, for the most part, the system has an almost total preoccupation with the rights of the criminal and simply ignores the rights of the victims of crime. There is today in the system a climate of permissiveness that focuses entirely upon the perpetrators of criminal acts. There is no such corresponding concern for the victims of these acts. Insofar as the criminal justice system is concerned, these victims are indeed as Justice White described them, "uncertain, unnamed, and unrepresented."

The victims of crime are most assuredly "uncertain." Although it is reasonably certain that many of us—entirely too many—will become the victims of some lawless and violent act, no one knows just when or where the criminal next will strike. The uncertainty to which Justice White referred can be summed up by the question: "Who's next?" Some of us—primarily the racial minorities and ghetto dwellers—are much more likely to be victimized than others; but no one, no matter how exalted his station in life, in this day and age is immune from the actions of the criminal.

Justice White's description of the victims as "unnamed" is equally accurate. The victims of crime do, of course, all have given names and surnames that appear in police crime reports, hospital records, and sometimes on grave markers. As a general rule, however, in our criminal justice system most of the victims of crime remain a nameless lot, while those who victimized them have often become household words. Who, for example, can recall the name of even one of the eight student nurses whom Richard Speck murdered in their Chicago townhouse? Yet Speck's name is unquestionably a household word. This is so in part because of the spectacularly hideous nature of his crime, and also because his name periodically surfaces in a newspaper headline proclaiming that our criminal justice system has contrived some new "right" for Speck, whether his "right" not to be executed for his crime or his latest "right": eligibility for parole in a matter of four or five years. All of this while his victims have been consigned to obscurity.

---

[*]In the quotations in this book, emphasis is the author's. Where emphasis is in the original, it will be so noted.

4

Finally, and perhaps most significantly, Justice White characterized the victims of crime as "unrepresented." This is, in reality, the key to the entire matter. While many elements within the criminal justice system appear to be bending all of their efforts to contrive novel rights for the perpetrators of crimes, few within the same system are moved to speak up specifically and emphatically for the rights of actual or potential victims of those criminals.

The trial-and-appeal process in criminal cases, for example, long ago turned from being a search for the truth—that is, whether the defendant did or did not commit the crime with which he is charged—to being a microscopic examination to determine whether the defendant's rights have been violated in the slightest manner. If they have, then even the most patently guilty criminal may be freed. Now we all wish our criminal process to be fair. Unfortunately, however, in this country the concept of fairness to the accused has developed to the point that permissiveness toward criminals has entirely obscured the rights of the innocent victims of their crimes.

The victims are likewise unrepresented when highly vocal segments of the criminal justice system continue to call for increased leniency for convicted criminals with not a thought about, or at best mere lip service to, the same criminals' actual or potential victims. This lack of representation was pointed out by California State Senator H. L. (Bill) Richardson in a special report to his constituents concerning the highly permissive report of the National Advisory Commission on Criminal Justice Standards and Goals that was published in mid-1973. Calling the commission's report a "Blueprint for the Felon," Senator Richardson stated ironically:

> The report is the work of professors, bureaucrats and other so-called experts. It might have been improved if the panel had included one victim of assault, one single victim of rape, one victim of mugging. Only the rights of the criminal are considered. Where is equal time for the preyed-upon?[5]

Columnist James Jackson Kilpatrick, commenting on the same report, rather plaintively echoed Senator Richardson's assessment:

> The report is the work of professionals, speaking professional jargon, dreaming professional dreams. Their recommendations are drafted from the criminal's point of view. It would be refreshing to see a report, one of these days, that gave equal time to the victims too.[6]

Perhaps the consummate proof of the current unrepresented status of the victims of crime is to be found in an article by Winston Moore, the black executive director of the Cook County (Illinois) Department of Corrections. Concerned with the problems facing the corrections system, Moore writes:

Last week the American Correctional Association (ACA), at its annual congress in Seattle, added a new affiliate to the organization—"Ex-Offenders."

I have no qualms with the decision to add a new affiliate; my question is why has the ACA not seen fit to add a "Victims" affiliate?

A Midwestern governor this year attempted to place a parolee on the state parole board. Again, I was not as concerned with that decision as I was with the fact that he "kicked off" the parole board a black rape victim to make room for the parolee.[7]

Uncertain, unnamed, unrepresented. This is the sorry status of those who should really be the *primary* concern of our criminal justice system: the decent, innocent, law-abiding citizens who have been victimized, who will be victimized, and who are forced to live in fear of being victimized by the lawless and violent elements in our society. The extent to which this system ignores the rights of the victims of crime in favor of a hand-wringing concern for the "rights" of the foulest criminals can be demonstrated by concrete examples, examples which indict the system for its disdain for the victims.

On July 2, 1972, four-year-old Joyce Ann Huff was playing in the yard of her Lakewood, California, home when a car approached, slowed down, and someone in the back seat took aim and shot the little girl to death with a shotgun. Three men were arrested two days later and charged with this crime. One of the three had an arrest record for attempted murder, assault with a deadly weapon, robbery, burglary, arson, and narcotic offenses.[8]

Now the murder of Joyce Ann Huff is perhaps as horrifying a crime as can be imagined. The pathetic innocence of the victim, together with the calculated and cold-blooded acts of the killers, makes the murder particularly revolting. Those who committed this crime deserve not the slightest consideration or compassion from the law. Surely society, in a case like this, should exact a terrible penance from the murderers. All reason and concern for the victims of crime dictate that those who would kill in such a fashion should pay the supreme penalty.

No such thing will happen, however. Just four days before Joyce Ann was shot to death, a five-justice majority of the Supreme Court of the United States had, in the case of *Furman* v. *Georgia*,[9] declared that the death penalty, as presently applied in the United States, was unconstitutional. If the killers of Joyce Ann Huff were to be convicted, they would face *at most* a life sentence, which under California law means they will be eligible for parole in seven years. This murder presents the clearest possible example of a situation in which the very criminal justice system that did precisely nothing to protect the right to life of an innocent child now guarantees the right to life and the possibility of parole leniency to those who fatally shot her.

Actually, Joyce Ann Huff's killers had a *double* guarantee. No matter what crime they might commit, their right to life would be secure; for the California Supreme Court had in February 1972 anticipated the United States Supreme Court and ruled that the death penalty in that state was unlawful.[10] The California court's decision (which in November 1972 was repudiated by a 2-to-1 margin in a statewide referendum that permitted the reinstatement of the death penalty) held capital punishment to be "cruel or unusual punishment" and therefore violative of the rights of those killers upon whom it might be inflicted. Then, on June 30, 1972, the United States Supreme Court (5 to 4) set its seal of approval upon permissiveness toward murderers by holding the death penalty to be unconstitutional throughout the entire nation.* Thus, at the time Joyce Ann was shot, her killers had been assured by the decisions of two of the nation's highest courts that, even if captured and convicted, they could not be called upon to pay with their lives for hers.

Naturally, these decisions outlawing capital punishment had received the most widespread publicity possible. Newspaper and television coverage was extensive, and national and local media had commented upon the fact that in California such mass murderers as Charles Manson and John Linley Fraser, and political assassin Sirhan Sirhan, were now eligible for parole in seven years. Remember, Joyce Ann Huff was killed *just four days* after the United States Supreme Court had announced its decision in the *Furman* case. Publicity about the decision—and the permissiveness towards criminals inherent in it— was still at its height. It cannot be proved that Joyce Ann's killers, as they drove around searching for a victim, were comforted by the thought that, if they were called to account for their acts, they could never be executed and that they could even hope to benefit from the well-publicized leniency of the California parole laws. Nor can it be *disproved* that such thoughts were not uppermost in the killers' minds. Had Joyce Ann's murderers believed that our criminal justice system put her right to live above theirs and that if they killed her they faced the certainty of execution in the gas chamber, the little girl might well be alive today.

*Ironically, Justice Byron White, whose concern for the victims of crime was so eloquently expressed in his dissent in the *Miranda* case, was one of the five majority justices in the *Furman* case, as was Justice Potter Stewart, who joined in White's dissent in *Miranda*. Justices White and Stewart did not, however, reject the death penalty entirely; they merely held that it was unconstitutional because it was randomly and capriciously applied. Thus their opinions left open the door for a restoration of the death penalty if it were not applied in an indiscriminate manner. But even if capital punishment were restored, Joyce Ann Huff's murderers could never be executed.

Justice William J. Brennan, one of the five majority justices in the *Furman* case, found capital punishment to be unconstitutional because, among other things, it did not "comport with human dignity." Here is yet another attempt to create for the most loathsome criminals a right that is surely denied to their victims; in this case, the right not to be punished in a manner not conforming to the sociological abstraction "human dignity." Whether or not the manner in which the killer's victim died had in it any shred of human dignity is not the slightest concern to Justice Brennan and those who, like him, ignore the victims of crime entirely.

Two of the beneficiaries of Justice Brennan's concern for human dignity are Myron Lance and Walter Kelbach, residents of the Utah State Penitentiary, who in December 1966 murdered six people in and around Salt Lake City. Lance and Kelbach were convicted of these murders and sentenced to die. However, as in all other cases of criminals under sentences of death, the *Furman* case prevented their execution. In August 1972 the National Broadcasting Company aired an hour-long interview with Lance and Kelbach, made while they were still on death row. Entitled "Thou Shalt Not Kill," the program was far more chilling than any of the contrived violence currently on TV, because the murders described in that program actually took place. Grinning and smirking throughout the interview, the killers—Lance and Kelbach—described their crimes in the most graphic detail.

Kelbach, for example, described how he repeatedly stabbed one of the victims, a gas station attendant, while that unfortunate man pleaded that he had a wife. Lance, at this point in the interview, interjected that he and Kelbach thought that the plight of their victim was "kind of funny." He said that one of them remarked at the time: "Did you see the way he squirmed? Wasn't that funny?" At no time in the program did either of the murderers express the slightest contrition for their crimes or concern for their victims—they merely seemed pleased at their own notoriety.[11]

According to Justice Brennan, the execution of these two self-confessed and completely remorseless killers would not comport with human dignity; consequently their lives must be spared. No consideration is given to the fact that human dignity was denied their victim as he lay butchered, crying for his wife, while his killers, in their own words, laughed at "the way he squirmed." Human dignity is apparently a right reserved to the Lances and the Kelbachs. No matter how horribly the victim may have died, the only ones whose dignity is worthy of protection of the law are the killers. *Their* right to live and *their* dignity are secured for them by a criminal justice system that simply ignores the fact that their victims, whose wretched deaths were unaccompanied by human dignity, now have no rights at all.

As noted, the name of Richard Franklin Speck has become a household word in this country because of the almost unbelievably horrible nature of his crime: the methodical, cold-blooded slaughter of eight young student nurses in their Chicago townhouse in August 1966. Speck's victims have long been dead, forgotten by all but family and friends and perhaps a few of the police officers and prosecutors who worked on the case. Speck, of course, continues to live and the criminal justice system, which long ago consigned his victims to oblivion, continues to be the scene of a major battle for Speck's "rights," a battle which has by now pretty much been won—by Richard Speck.

The odyssey of this murderer through the criminal justice system is a classic example of the manner in which various elements of the system combine to create new rights for the Richard Specks while continuing, and even increasing, their lofty disdain for any rights of the actual and potential victims of crime. Speck was convicted in 1967 of all of the eight murders. The evidence against him was overwhelming. The sole survivor of the massacre, Corazon Amurao, one of the student nurses living in the townhouse, who had rolled under a bed while Speck was going about the business of putting the other eight girls to death, positively identified him as the killer. A jury, quite properly, found him guilty and Judge Herbert Paschen, equally properly, sentenced him to die in the electric chair. Speck's execution would not, of course, bring his victims back to life but it *would:* (a) ensure that this worthless individual never killed again, and, (b) indicate clearly that society sufficiently valued the lives of Speck's victims that it would exact from Speck his life for theirs.

Most people received the verdict and sentence with considerable relief. Nothing could mitigate the horror of this crime; the law would take its course and Speck would be permanently removed as a future threat to society. Those who took such comfort from this view reckoned without the Supreme Court of the United States, which in 1971 vacated Speck's death penalty. The Court held that his rights had been violated because those of his prospective jurors who did not believe in the death penalty were excluded from the panel that tried him. This newly created right meant that Richard Speck could not be executed. The man who had, in one evening, calmly strangled and/or cut the throats of eight young women must be resentenced, but he could not legally be resentenced to death. He must be accorded the right to live.

Speck, accordingly, was brought to Chicago in 1972 for resentencing. The killer appeared mildly pleased by the proceedings. He confided to reporters that he could now watch all of the television that he wanted. His attorney had asked the judge to give him a sentence which would give Speck some hope of parole. Judge Richard Fitzgerald, opting for the rights of society, sentenced Speck to 50 to 150 years in prison for each murder, the sentences to run consecutively—a total of 400 to 1,200 years in prison. If he could not be executed, at least society would be assured that Speck would never set foot on the street again.

Judge Fitzgerald, however, also reckoned without the rights of Richard Speck. A new corrections code was to go into effect in Illinois on January 1, 1973. Under this code every prisoner in Illinois, no matter how long his sentence, would be eligible for parole in eleven years and three months— *every* prisoner, including Richard Speck.* And even this was not the end of the story of Speck's rights. Under another provision of the new code, Speck *must* be given credit towards his parole eligibility for the time he had already served. Thus the attempt by Judge Fitzgerald to assure society that Speck would never be released was an exercise in utter futility. The judge could have sentenced him to ten million years with precisely the same result. Under the new and highly permissive Illinois code, Speck, by law, could be paroled in about five years. The rights of one who has never shown the slightest sign of remorse for his murder of eight lives triumphed, as usual, over those of his forgotten victims and of society.

If Richard Speck were to be paroled in a few years, this would be a satisfactory turn of events, according to at least one critic of the American correctional system. Miss Jessica Mitford, author of *Kind and Unusual Punishment* (1973), opined in an interview with a Chicago newspaper that she would rather let Speck out of jail than "maintain the whole huge irrational prison system just to confine him. After all, he probably wouldn't do it again."[12]

Now there are not a great many people who share Miss Mitford's cheerful optimism over the probability that Speck would not kill again. There are those, however, who believe that, as a matter of practical fact, Speck will not be paroled in five years, or even in the foreseeable future. They may very well be correct. But when we consider that Richard Speck has been the beneficiary of a criminal justice system that has so jealously guarded his rights as to lead him from death row to an early parole eligibility in a relatively short period of time, the question arises: May not some new aspect of the permissiveness of the system lead to yet another "right" for Richard Speck, a "right" which will foist him on society, perhaps sooner than anyone expects?

The unpleasant fact that state parole boards engage in almost unbelievable acts of lunatic leniency is illustrated by a case in Iowa in 1972, a case from which Richard Speck, if not society, can take considerable comfort.

*With good behavior.

10

On April 17, 1969, sixty-year-old police chief Earl Berendes of Belle-vue, Iowa, was investigating a break-in at a garage. He was beaten to death with a shovel. The autopsy indicated that Chief Berendes died of massive skull injuries. Two men and a woman were charged with the crime.

On October 3, 1969, after pleading guilty to second-degree murder, one of the trio of suspects, William P. Sweeney, twenty-five, was sentenced to seventy-five years in prison for his part in Chief Beren-des's killing. The other man received the same sentence and the woman was placed on probation. On June 12, 1972, having served two years and nine months of this sentence, Sweeney was released on parole by the Iowa Parole Board.

The citizens of Bellevue were understandably upset over this example of leniency to one convicted of murdering their police chief. According to the *Des Moines Register* of June 14, 1972, Mayor Kenneth Kell and the Bellevue City Council sent letters of complaint to the governor of Iowa and to the Iowa Parole Board.

Mr. Jack Bedell, a member of the parole board, replied to their complaints. According to the *Register*, Bedell airily explained that the board's decision was based on the recommendation of the institu-tional staff. The recommendation stated that the time was ripe to release Sweeney if they "expected a complete rehabilitation," and that "our only excuse for keeping him incarcerated any longer *would have been just to punish him*. And to keep him only to punish him is not in keeping with the attitude of correcting."

The decision of the parole board and the institutional staff that the "time was ripe" to release Sweeney was not, as matters turned out, a particularly accurate one. In December 1972, scarcely six months after his release on parole from the murder charge, Sweeney was arrested for burglary and intoxication after he was found, uninvited, in a woman's apartment. He was given a thirty-day sentence on the intoxication charge pending a hearing to revoke his parole.[13]

Even had Sweeney not been rearrested, his parole, after serving a mere two and one-half years of a seventy-five-year sentence for a truly shocking crime, clearly evidences the complete preoccupation of some—typified by the Iowa Parole Board—with the "rights" of the criminal while the actual and potential victims of the same criminal are ignored. In the case of Sweeney, if Mr. Bedell is to be believed, the Iowa Parole Board discovered that Sweeney had a "right" *not to be punished*. The Iowa corrections staff and the parole board had convinced themselves (erroneously as it turned out) that Sweeney was rehabili-tated, and so, said Mr. Bedell, "our only excuse for keeping him in-carcerated any longer would have been just to punish him." There are those who believe that when someone batters another to death he *should* be punished, but the Iowa Parole Board apparently is not among their number. Hence Sweeney must be released lest further confinement tend to punish him.

The victim of Sweeney's crime, Chief Berendes, apparently did not occupy the thoughts of the parole board to any great extent. Implicit in its decision to release his killer is the idea that Berendes's life and the sacrifice he made are worth about the same amount of prison time that a really persistent check forger would receive on, say, his third offense. The parole board's single-minded desire that Sweeney not be punished quite simply mocks the memory of his victim.

Finally, the Iowa Parole Board totally ignored the question of the impact that its decision might have on potential victims of crimes like Sweeney's, particularly on law-enforcement officers. The board figuratively spat in the face of every law-enforcement officer in that state. It said in effect to Iowa policemen that it was fine for them to lay their lives and safety on the line in the course of their duties, but if one of them was killed, wounded, or maimed, the assailant could, on the basis of the board's rationale in the Sweeney case, feel that he had an excellent chance of serving a very minimal penalty.

The board's contempt for the safety of police officers can be translated into the practical realities of the dangers policemen face daily in their work. Suppose that somewhere in Iowa a policeman has trapped an armed felon inside a house or building. This felon is now faced with two choices: surrender, or attempt to escape by perhaps killing or wounding the policeman. If he is aware of the attitude of the Iowa Parole Board toward convicted cop-killers—criminals read newspapers too—what possible deterrent can there be to prevent him from attempting to avoid capture by perhaps killing the officer? He may well reason that if he should make good his escape he is that much better off, and that should he kill the officer and be caught, he may face only the inconvenience of a few years in prison for the murder. Thus, the Iowa Parole Board's decision has made the already hazardous job of law enforcement infinitely more dangerous.

If the Iowa Parole Board had been sitting in Illinois and a truly repentant Richard Speck had appeared before it, vowing he would never again commit mass murder, would the board's theory of nonpunishment of "rehabilitated" criminals have necessitated the release of Speck also? Perhaps; perhaps not. But in its total disregard for the rights of the victims of crime, the Iowa Parole Board could well have Speck wishing fervently that he had moved one state west and gone about his murdering in Iowa rather than in Illinois.

Parole boards are, of course, not alone in carrying leniency to a degree that leaves the average observer stupified with frustration. In November 1973, in Washington, D.C., a United States district court judge, Aubrey E. Robinson, Jr., released on probation a man who had served four months of a two- to twenty-year term for a second-degree murder. An assistant United States attorney, who objected to the man's being freed, pointed out to the judge that the same defendant had previously been convicted in a child-abuse case that had ended in the death of his five-month-old son. In addition, the prosecutor informed Judge Robinson that the man had previously been charged with attempted sodomy on his daughter, but the charge was dismissed after the suspect sent his daughter out of town the day she was supposed to appear in court. These arguments were to no avail.

The victim in the second-degree murder case, for which Judge Robinson felt a four-month confinement to be sufficient, had been shot in the throat, at close range, with a shotgun. The victim's brother expressed his frustration over the killer's release with an obscenity, and added: "This is very discouraging to our family. I don't feel the man should be crucified, but to kill a person is the greatest crime a person can commit . . . four months is just not justification [for the crime]."[14]

The manner in which some individuals and groups are willing to blind themselves totally to any concern except that over the "rights" of the criminal is well illustrated by the Pavlovian reaction of members of the Chicago affiliate of the American Civil Liberties Union to the arrests of a group of accused terrorist murderers in Chicago. In October 1972 several of the De Mau Mau gang were arrested and charged with a series of nine execution-style murders in the Chicago area. The victims of these crimes included a family of four, a family of three, a student, and a soldier. Each victim was shot to death; the two families were herded together and shot in the head, each in the presence of the others. The slayings were wanton, the victims were chosen at random, and the killers were apparently racially motivated, according to Cook County sheriff Richard Elrod.

A break in the case finally came on a Friday evening, when two of the suspects were arrested in an automobile. Other arrests followed over the weekend, and those arrested were held for forty-eight hours without a bond hearing. The reason for this detention, according to the sheriff, was because of the necessity of interrogating the suspects in order to piece together the incredibly complicated case and to ensure that all of them were rounded up before they could kill again.

The Chicago ACLU hit the ceiling. Not because nine innocent human

13

beings had been murdered but, predictably, because it felt that the "rights" of the accused killers had been abused because of their forty-eight-hour, over-the-weekend detention without a bond hearing. One ACLU legal staffer, William J. McNally, stated darkly: "This is an extremely dangerous practice that approaches a police state, because if they held these men for 48 hours, they might next hold you and me for 72 hours."[15] Another ACLU lawyer, Jerrold Oppenheimer, considered the forty-eight-hour detention "outrageous."[16] If these two outspoken gentlemen had any opinions about whether the crimes the terrorists stood accused of were also outrageous, they kept them to themselves.

The ACLU's one-track concern for the rights of the accused, to the exclusion of any other consideration, brought a scathing response from Robert Wiedreich, the highly respected "Tower Ticker" columnist of the *Chicago Tribune*. He first described the horror of the killings and noted that "in the midst of all this there rises the cry of the civil libertarians quick to condemn police for holding six of the eight men accused of the unprecedented killings for up to 48 hours."[17] Noting the anguish of Messrs. McNally and Oppenheimer over the violation of the suspect's rights, Wiedreich then expressed his own concern:

> We fail, however, to hear one cry from these same lips for the nine innocent victims who were summarily deprived of their civil rights permanently, without due process of law.
> Over the last decade, there has been a growing trend toward protecting the rights of the accused often to the detriment of those entitled [to be] aggrieved.
> Time and again society has stood by helplessly as persons accused of heinous crimes have been freed to commit new crimes while awaiting trial. Others have been set at large through hypertechnical interpretations of the law by the courts.
> And this, of course, has occurred as the tempo of violence in this nation has mounted.[18]

With regard to the detention in this particular case, Wiedreich asked sarcastically:

> Now what, in the judgment of the civil libertarians, was Sheriff Elrod to have done?
> Should Elrod have ignored his responsibility to protect the community from further mayhem by permitting the suspects to continue at large until his men could build the proverbial ironclad case? Police were trying to stick together facts, details, and evidence in an exceedingly complex series of multiple murders that had happened in at least three counties and perhaps two states. At least nine and possibly eleven killings were involved.
> The enormity and gravity of the case was frightening. So was the pos-

14

sibility for continued carnage if prompt action was not taken. Was Elrod expected to sit on his hands, fully aware additional murders might be committed, merely to satisfy the zealous demands of civil libertarians fearful a suspect might be deprived of 48 hours of freedom out of a lifetime.[19]

In his column Mr. Wiedreich expressed genuine concern that the rights of criminals far too often take priority over the rights of the victims of crime and of the law-abiding in our society. As if attempting to prove him right, one of the De Mau Mau suspects, being taken to his arraignment, expressed *his* views on the criminal justice system. Noting the number of cameramen present, the accused shouted to a deputy sheriff: "Richard Speck didn't even get as much publicity as this." He then laughed and continued: "And you know what happened to Speck. Nothin'. And that's what's going to happen to us too!"[20]

With groups such as the ACLU battling for his rights, to the exclusion of those of the victims, this confident young man may well be entirely correct.

On July 10, 1971, the New York Court of Appeals ordered released from prison a young man who was serving a sentence for murdering nine adults and three children by means of a fire he had set. The New York court ruled that a confession, made by the youth to the director of the Yonkers Jewish Community Center, was invalid because the director had cooperated too closely with the police during the investigation. As a consequence, the suspect's rights were held violated, his confession "tainted," and he must be freed. The fact that the defendant had confessed to, and been convicted of, setting the fire in which twelve people had died counted for precisely nothing. The sole concern was with his "rights." According to the *New York Times*, Mrs. Eleanor Jackson Piel, the defendant's attorney, was "elated" by the decision.[21] No doubt the families and friends of the twelve victims share her elation.

Washington, D.C., in 1972 was the scene of a complete travesty of justice, which illustrates how not one but several "rights" of an accused criminal can work together to result in his acquittal despite absolutely overwhelming evidence of his guilt. The crime charged was the rape of a nineteen-year-old coed at George Washington University by a seventeen-year-old youth. The accused rapist had voluntarily confessed the crime to the police and the coed had positively identified the suspect as her assailant. Nevertheless, he was acquitted by a jury.

This incredible result came about as a result of two separate "rights" accorded the accused by the criminal justice system in Washington. First, the jury was not permitted to learn of the suspect's confession because it had not been reduced to writing and it was therefore not admissible as evidence against him. Thus, the "rights" of the confessed rapist prevented the jury from hearing the most probative evidence of his guilt, the suspect's own admission of the crime. Second, so jealous is the law of the rights of rapists that under the District of Columbia Code, no rape conviction is possible unless the victim submitted to "physical force, or . . . threats which put her in reasonable fear of death or great bodily harm." The jury, which almost certainly would have convicted the rapist had it known of the confession, had some doubts as to the amount of force used by the rapist and the amount of resistance put up by the victim. As a consequence, the jury apparently felt it had no alternative but acquittal. The exclusion of the confession together with the terribly difficult requirement of proof of rape in the District of Columbia combined to free one whose factual guilt was patent. The victim was outraged, calling the verdict "preposterous"; she said that the criminal justice system made her feel more like a defendant than a complainant.[22] Few would disagree with her.

The overall permissiveness toward criminals that pervades our criminal justice system is perhaps most marked in cases involving juveniles. Apparently going on the theory that "there's no such thing as a bad boy," state legislatures have, in many cases, created zones of immunity around juveniles that simply cannot be breached by the police or the prosecution. "Rights" have been created for youthful criminals that completely insulate them from the consequences of their acts. And, as usual, the victims are ignored.

In Philadelphia, according to Paul Harvey's news broadcast of January 4, 1973, two young sadists invaded the apartment of an eighty-four-year-old woman and for four days beat, raped, robbed, and tortured her—burning her with matches and a heated steel comb. They were released on probation because, under Pennsylvania law, first offenders under twelve, whatever the offense, cannot be locked up. Someone might try telling their eighty-four-year-old victim that there's no such thing as a bad boy.

In Denver a gang of young men accosted a carload of children and savagely beat their victims, including a twelve-year-old girl, with chains, bricks, and fists. The assailants, when apprehended, turned out to be one eighteen-year-old, two seventeen-year-olds, and a sixteen-year-old. The eighteen-year-old was jailed but the three others had to be released because their parents refused to come to the police station;

under the ultrapermissive Colorado Children's Code, no juvenile can be questioned by the police unless his parents are present.[23]

When the Colorado legislature adopted the Children's Code, there was a great deal of talk about "enlightened views of the rights of children" and "protection of the juvenile offender." Unfortunately, considerations of protection for *innocent* juveniles against sixteen- and seventeen-year-old chain wielders are missing from the code.

A recent case from California illustrates the fact that some courts will, unbelievably, hold that criminals, whose dangerous nature to society is conceded, cannot be detained to protect society from them. In this case the California Supreme Court, in April 1973, specifically held that a lower court could not deny bail to a criminal accused even though the lower court "felt that the safety of the community would be jeopardized by the defendant's release." The facts of the case make this decision all the more outrageous. The defendant had been seen running from a residence on June 20, 1972. He was subsequently arrested while in possession of *two homemade sawed-off shotguns* and two live shotgun shells. On June 22, 1972, he was released on $500.00 bail. On June 24 a "live" pipe bomb was placed in a postal deposit box in Tarzana, California. The defendant was again arrested for this crime and the arraigning court denied bail because it felt that the defendant would be a danger to the community. This judge was, quite properly, attempting to protect society from the future criminal conduct of a palpably dangerous man. Not so the California Supreme Court. It interpreted the California Constitution to prohibit the denial of bail "solely because of petitioner's dangerous propensities." In effect, it told the lower court that the defendant's right to bail was far superior to those of any law-abiding citizens whom he might victimize if he were released. The lower court's laudable efforts to protect society were held to be illegal.

In a caustic dissenting opinion, Justice Lewis Burke, speaking for the rights of society, chided the majority:

> Certainly the California Constitution was not intended to render the courts powerless to control and punish the misuse or abuse of their own process. Any other rule would seemingly permit a defendant, bent on obstructing, harassing witnesses, or causing mischief and mayhem, to make repeated applications for, and receive, bail following successive unlawful criminal acts until his ultimate purpose is finally accomplished. In the hands of persons such as defendant herein, the right to bail would itself become an instrument of crime, a sword and not a shield.[24]

The logic and common sense of Justice Burke's view are, of course, immediately apparent to anyone concerned with the rights of the victims of crime, but not, unfortunately, to his brethren on the court.

The permissiveness of our criminal justice system not only mocks the plight of the victims of crime by freeing the perpetrators, but also frequently results directly in others being victimized because the original violator was freed to return to society or was otherwise a beneficiary of the system's leniency. Perhaps, in the abstract world inhabited by so many of the sociologically oriented exponents of permissiveness, those who agonize over the rights of criminals can convince themselves that A, who has victimized B but who has been released because of a technicality or of leniency in the criminal justice system, will be so grateful to that system for vindicating his "rights" that he will refrain forever from victimizing C, D, and E. In real life, however, this wishful thinking has time and again proven to be utterly nonsensical—and dangerous.

A case in point is George McChan, an early beneficiary of the United States Supreme Court's *Miranda* decision. A Maryland judge was forced to free McChan, an accused robber, because under *Miranda* his confession could not be introduced into evidence against him at his trial. The judge in performing this unpleasant duty stated angrily that he was being forced to "foist a professional holdup man on the public." Five days after he was released McChan murdered a seventy-year-old restaurant owner and critically wounded one of his waitresses with a shotgun.[25] Justice White's prediction that the Court's majority decision in *Miranda* would "return a killer . . . to the streets and to the environment which produced him, to repeat his crime whenever it pleases him," had come true with a vengeance. The "rights" of George McChan, as defined by the five-justice majority in the *Miranda* case, had clearly been vindicated—with one slain innocent victim to show for it.

Another illustration of leniency by courts and parole authorities resulted in two young girls being victimized. In Boulder, Colorado, in November 1972, the two were taking a walk after the eleventh birthday party of one of them. A man in a camper pickup truck forced the girls into the truck, drove them into the mountains, shot them (killing one and wounding the other), handcuffed them together, and left them to die. A passing motorist found the girls and notified the police. The man who was arrested for this crime, according to authorities, had been arrested at least three times in the past four years for lewd and indecent acts, *but had been released on probation each time*.[26]

Again, in 1964 a young Californian, Edmund E. Kemper, then fifteen years old, confessed to killing his grandfather and grandmother and was placed into the hands of the California Youth Authority. In 1971 he was paroled to his mother. On April 24, 1973, the same young man admitted killing his mother, one of her friends, and six coeds whom he had dismembered and decapitated.[27] He was convicted in November 1973 for all eight murders.[28]

In these cases courts or correctional officials had freed potentially dangerous individuals. The objects of this leniency showed their gratitude by murdering ten innocent victims.

The chronicle of cases involving the most wanton, cold-blooded, and remorseless crimes could go on indefinitely, for such crimes have become commonplace on our contemporary scene. Each outrage becomes more terrifying because in our criminal justice system, once the crime has been committed—once an innocent man, woman, or child has been murdered, raped, robbed, or assaulted—the victim becomes no more than a statistic, a forgotten entity in the system.

It is difficult, no matter the subject, to give life to raw statistical data. Yet, if we are to grasp the extent to which the citizens of this country are victimized by criminals, we must look at the statistics of crime. The annual *Uniform Crime Report* of the Federal Bureau of Investigation catalogs the raw figures of *reported* crime in any given year. During 1973 there were 19,510 murders, 51,000 forcible rapes, 382,680 robberies, 416,270 aggravated assaults, 2,540,900 burglaries, 4,304,400 larceny-thefts, and 923,600 auto thefts.[29]

Some studies estimate that the number of unreported crimes may be two to five times greater than that of reported crimes.[30] This may seem strange at first blush, but consider again the case of the Washington, D.C. coed who was first victimized by a forcible rape and then victimized by a criminal justice system that freed her assailant and treated her, the complainant, as if she were the defendant. Let us devoutly hope that this young lady, traumatized enough, never again becomes the victim of violent crime. But if she should, would she report it to the police? Or would she, knowing firsthand the extent to which our criminal justice system disregards the rights of the victims, simply let the matter go unreported? If she chose the latter course, who could blame her?

There are, of course, other reasons why a victim might not report the crime to the authorities. Fear of retaliation by the criminal who committed the crime in the first place; belief that our law-enforcement agencies, desperately overworked in the face of escalating crime and violence, do not have the time or manpower to deal with the particular violation; the almost certain knowledge that even if apprehended and convicted, the criminal would be returned by the courts to the streets—any or all of these factors could dissuade the victim from reporting the crime.

Even apart from the unreported crimes, the statistics of *reported crimes* are staggering. One way to relate these raw figures to reality is to recognize that a given number of reported crimes means an equal number of victims. When we speak of 19,510 murders in 1973, we should think of 19,510 human beings who had every right to life, but who were destroyed because someone else—whether cold-bloodedly, as in the killing of Joyce Ann Huff, or in a fit of passion, as in most domestic killing—decided that his victim no longer had the right to live.

Small things can perhaps focus our attention on this colossal problem, defined only in statistical terms. When his brother was killed in a robbery murder in the Bronx, Peter Schneider wrote a terse and unnerving article in the *New York Times* deploring crime in the streets generally and the murder of his brother in particular. One paragraph spotlights the intolerable homicide situation in our country today. It may help us translate statistics into the suffering of the victims:

> Murder has become commonplace. It has joined the crimes of mugging and rape in occurring with such frequency that newspapers seldom report them. *When I went to the medical examiner's office to identify his body I was given a number to await my turn as we do in busy retail shops.*[31]

Similarly, when we speak of 51,000 forcible rapes, our thoughts should focus on that number of victims—women and little girls traumatized, perhaps for life, by their attackers. And so on, with robberies, burglaries, assaults, larcenies, and auto thefts. If the mental effort is made to translate these crime statistics into their effects upon the victims, some idea of the enormity of the victimization of the innocent will emerge.

We should also attempt to see the victims as people who have suffered grievous physical injury, who have been terrorized, who have had their lives changed forever through a vicious and wanton act. Who, for example, can even begin to imagine the physical and spiritual agony of a seventeen-year-old black girl in St. Louis who had her eyes gouged out by a robber to prevent her from identifying him? She is one statistic in 1971's aggravated assaults, but she is also a human being, a victim. Is she or is she not worthy of our consideration?

If we can put ourselves into a victim-oriented frame of mind; if we can translate the sorry picture presented by dry crime statistics into a decent consideration for the victims of crime and violence in this country, we may then gain some insight into the impact of crime on the innocent victims and, I hope, be ready for the next step—doing something about it.

Our criminal justice system expends billions of dollars annually and absorbs the resources of thousands of police officers, judges, attorneys, corrections personnel, and others from almost every sort of discipline. Yet, when we look at the staggering number of crimes committed yearly the conclusion is inescapable that the system is a total failure. This is so because the primary function of any criminal justice system *must* be to protect the innocent from the lawless. But when we translate the number of reported crimes into the same number of victims, we have an intolerable number of victims of crime, victims whom the criminal justice system should have protected, but didn't.

The failure of our criminal justice system derives directly from ignoring those who should be its primary concern—the actual and potential victims of crime—and from favoring an elaborate apparatus designed to safeguard every conceivable right of the criminal accused and even the convicted criminal. It is axiomatic that if there are two interests in direct conflict in a given system, the greater the preoccupation with one of the interests, the more the other interest will be subordinated. In our criminal justice system the rights of the victims are now subordinated to the rights of the criminal; the system is totally out of balance.

One of our nation's most distinguished scholars, Dr. Sidney Hook, former professor of philosophy at New York University, and now at Stanford University, incisively analyzed this imbalance in our criminal justice system in an article, "The Rights of the Victims: A Reflection on Crime and Compassion," in the March 1972 issue of *Encounter*. In view of the amazing scarcity of literature about the victims of crime—scarcity when compared with the mountain of material about the rights of criminals, both accused and convicted—Dr. Hook's piece is one of extreme importance. If in the future our criminal justice system should take a turn towards the rights of the victims, Dr. Hook's article may well be looked upon as the Magna Carta of the victim's rights. Because Dr. Hook has graciously given his permission to quote copiously from his article, and because of his scholarly and professional credentials, it will be to our profit to describe in detail his thesis.

Professor Hook begins with the observation that domestic violence is increasing at a frightening rate and that there has been an accompanying increase—much of it laudable—in our concern for the rights of criminals. On the question of whether or not there is a cause-and-effect relationship between increased crime and increased concern for the rights of criminals, Dr. Hook suspends judgment. Instead he turns to an examination of "some fundamental questions about the basic ethical and jurisprudential issues involved."

Insofar as the rights of criminals are concerned, Dr. Hook advances two premises with which no rational person can disagree. First, the system must always take care to prevent the danger of "convicting the accused on the basis of plausible evidence, when he in ultimate fact may be innocent." Second, we must remember that no matter how law-abiding we may deem ourselves, someday, through some quirk of fate, we could all end up as a criminal accused.

Dr. Hook then looks at the other side of the coin and weighs the probabilities of his being accused of a crime and his being the victim of a crime:

> Granted that I am a potential criminal. I am also a potential victim of crime. The U.S. statistics of mounting violence show that cases of murder, non-negligent manslaughter, and forcible rape have skyrocketed. It has been estimated that in America's large metropolitan centers, the risk of becoming the victim of crime has more than doubled in the last decade. Since many crimes of violence are committed by repeaters, the likelihood of my becoming a victim of crime is much greater than the likelihood of my becoming a criminal. Therefore the protection of my rights not to be mugged, assaulted, or murdered looms much larger in my mind than my rights as a criminal defendant.
>
> Let us be clear about some things that have become obscured by our legitimate concern with the rights of criminals and those accused of crime. *The potential victim has at least just as much a human right not to be violently molested, interfered with and outraged as the person accused of such crimes has to a fair trial and a skillful defense. As a citizen, most of the rights guaranteed me under the Bill of Rights become nugatory if I am hopelessly crippled by violence and all of them become extinguished if I am killed.*

Thus does Dr. Hook bring into focus the inherent conflict between the rights of criminals and the rights of victims. He expounds his own views for resolution of the conflict:

> I submit that at the present junction of events, because our American cities have become more dangerous to life and limb than the darkest jungle, we give priority to the rights of potential victims. I am prepared to weaken the guarantees and privileges to which I am entitled as a potential criminal, or as a defendant, in order to strengthen my rights and safeguards as a potential victim.

He then takes a long hard look at some of the excesses that have tipped the balance in favor of the criminal:

> But today, a humane concern for the increasing number of victims of violent crimes requires a reinterpretation, another emphasis. When we read that preventive detention at the discretion of the judge (by denial of bail to repeated offenders charged with extremely violent crimes) is denounced by some judicial figures as a "betrayal of elementary justice," as "smacking of the concentration camps of Hitler and Stalin"; when we

22

read that a person jailed for the death of 12 persons is freed from jail and the case against him dismissed because the prosecution's only evidence against him was a voluntary confession to the police who had failed to inform him of his rights; when we read that a man who murdered one of three hostages he had taken had a record of 25 arrests ranging from armed robbery to aggravated assault and battery and that at the time of his arrest he was free on bail awaiting grand jury action on charges in five separate cases in a two-month period preceding the murder; when we read that a man whose speeding car had been stopped [by a motorcycle policeman who, without a search warrant, forced him to open his trunk that contained the corpses of a woman and two children] walks out of court scot-free because the evidence is ruled inadmissible—we can only conclude with Mr. Pickwick that the law is an ass.

Dr. Hook is noted as a libertarian, but a tough-minded one. He scores certain liberals:

Liberalism in social life may be defined as devotion to human freedom pursued and tested by the acts of intelligence. But not all who call themselves liberal understand either themselves or the doctrines they profess. I have called them "ritualistic liberals"—those who think they can be liberal without being intelligent. A particularly conspicuous species of this genus is found among those writers on crime and law enforcement for whom the victims of crime are only incidental rather than central to the problem of crime prevention.

Dr. Hook concludes:

Let us have done with extremists who would mindlessly substitute either toughness or permissiveness for intelligence in their simplistic response to the mounting crime wave. A fruitful way to begin the quest for intelligent solutions is to reorient our thinking in the current period to the rights of the potential victims of crime and the task of reducing their number and suffering. In this way we can best serve the interests of both justice and compassion.

This is the conclusion of an American scholar with well-established credentials as a libertarian and a humanitarian, a conclusion that is inherent in the premise upon which this book is based, namely, that we *must* "reorient our thinking in the current period to the rights of the potential victims of crime. . . ." Lack of concern for such victims is the basic reason for the failure of our criminal justice system, and until that system begins to come to grips with the issue of the rights of the victims of crime—rights which should have been of primary concern in the first place—the failure will continue.

The *Wall Street Journal* was appreciative of Dr. Hook's analysis. In an editorial in the April 11, 1972, issue, the *Journal* endorsed his thesis and reached its own conclusion: "Mr. Hook is right that the best way to serve the interest of justice is to reorient our thinking. To show anguished concern for the criminal but indifference towards his victims is an example not of admirable compassion but of serious ethical confusion.''[32]

The reorientation of our thinking toward the victims must be accomplished without doing violence to the *fundamental rights* that accrue to all of our citizens, whether accused of a crime or not. The concept of fundamental rights can be illustrated quite simply in the context of the law dealing with confessions. If I am accused of a criminal act, I have an absolute right not to be forced to confess to that act by means of physical torture, mental coercion, promises, or trickery that might be calculated to make me confess whether I was guilty or not. Put another way, the state has no right whatsoever to extort an involuntary confession from me. This is fundamental. However, I should not have the right to have a confession, made voluntarily, excluded from use in evidence against me simply because the police officer who was interrogating me neglected to inform me of one or more of my rights. If I have made a confession or admission that is by all appearances voluntary, then a rule that shields me from the consequences of my criminal act entirely—simply because the police made an inadvertent error—is a totally *artificial* protection that benefits me immeasurably as a guilty party, but that is of little use to an innocent party; for if coercive methods have *not* been used, an innocent suspect (unless he is a psychopathic "confessor") will not have confessed to a crime that he did not commit.

Justice and fairness mandate that any involuntary confession not be used against the one from whom it was obtained. Surely no one can dispute this. However, justice and fairness to the victim of a crime to which a suspect has voluntarily confessed (and justice to his potential victims should he be freed) require that the confession, if found to be indeed voluntary, be admitted into evidence against the one who made it.

Equally, even a dangerous criminal, who has been convicted, may have a right to *consideration* of leniency in the courts and processes, but he does not have a *fundamental right* to such leniency if, on balance, the potential danger that he poses to the innocent citizen militates against excessively lenient treatment. Society, rather, has a fundamental right to be protected from the criminal.

This is the sort of balancing test between the rights of the victim and those of the criminal accused which Dr. Hook has so articulately called for and about which this book has been written.

One final and most important point must be made here, one that relates not only to Dr. Hook's thesis about the victims of crime but to the entire thesis of this book. In his conclusion Dr. Hook warns against "extremists" and "mindlessness" in our response to the problem of crime. The answers, he avers, cannot be simplistic. He is, of course, perfectly correct. The answers, however, lie in large measure in the removal of contrived and artificial rights for the criminal, rights emanating from a criminal justice system that protects only the guilty while in no way benefiting the innocent, and in the cessation of excessive and unwarranted leniency towards those accused or convicted of crimes on the theory that society should "take a chance" with the safety of society in the hope that the object of that leniency will not victimize again. This will produce a corresponding increase in the rights of the law-abiding citizen not to be victimized. The question then arises: Is this a mindless, simplistic, or an extremist solution to the problem?

The answer to this question can be stated succinctly. Enhancing the rights of the victims of crime at the expense of the rights of criminals is mindless, simplistic, or extremist only if it can be correctly stated that the attitudes and convictions of the great majority of the population of the United States are mindless, simplistic, or extremist. Beyond any question, the law-abiding majority—rich, middle-class, and poor, black and white, folk who are simply decent and disinclined to prey upon others—is sick to death of living in fear of crime, in fear of being victimized, sick to death of seeing criminals whose *actual* guilt has been established going free because one or more of their "rights" have been violated. Likewise the law-abiding majority is irate over the excessive leniency shown to those who have proven themselves dangerous to society.

This has been proved by every sampling of public opinion in this country in recent years, from polls of professional opinion-research firms such as Gallup and Harris, whose findings are based on scientific samplings of cross sections of our population, to straw polls conducted by national and local newspapers and magazines to learn the views of their readers. Among those sampled, a uniformity of opinion emerges that probably could not be found on any other major issue. Two facts consistently surface: (a) the American people are afraid of crime, violence, and lawlessness and deem such to be one of the major problems facing our nation today; and (b) they want something done about the problem, even though it means that criminals lose a few of their rights, if such will vindicate the rights of the law-abiding to be free from criminal harm.

This point merits consideration of public opinion about the problem of crime and criminals and what should be done about the problem. Therefore, we'll first look at the overriding concern of the law-abiding about crime and then examine how the public wishes its concern translated into constructive action against crime and the criminal.

Public Concern About Crime

The deep and increasing concern over crime in this country can be demonstrated, almost conclusively, by scrutinizing the major public opinion polls in the United States—the Gallup poll of Princeton, New Jersey, and the Lou Harris poll—and other respected polls.

The Gallup organization, from time to time during 1968-72, measured the extent to which crime and violence were the concerns of a cross section of our citizens nationwide, with the following results:

February 1968:

Crime and lawlessness are viewed by the public as the top domestic problems facing the nation for the first time since the beginning of scientific polling in the mid-30's.

The growing concern in this country over crime and lawlessness reflects the actual crime rate which, according to a recent FBI report, is going up nearly nine times as fast as the population.

Crime tops the list when people are asked a subsequent question about problems facing their own community. Even other pressing local problems such as crowded schools, transportation and high taxes, take second place.

Three persons in every 10 (31 percent) admit to being afraid of going out alone at night in their neighborhood. Among women and persons living in the largest cities, the figure jumps to about 4 in 10.[33]

October 1968:

With America's crime rate rising sharply, exactly half of all women in the United States, an estimated 32 million, say that they are afraid to walk alone at night in areas as close as one mile to where they presently live. In the case of men, one in five shares the same fear.

These fears aren't confined to white citizens. An even greater percentage of Negroes say they are afraid to use the streets at night in some of the areas near their dwelling places.[34]

In May of 1971 the Gallup organization polled the leaders ("statesmen, scientists, business executives and others") of seventy nations in the free world, including the United States. Although inflation topped crime and lack of respect for the law among the seventy nations whose leaders were queried, *"Crime is given first place in the United States* by leaders who responded to this special poll, followed by inflation, air and water pollution and race tensions."[35]

In April 1972 the Gallup survey showed an increase of ten percent (thirty-one to forty-one percent) of those who were afraid to walk in their neighborhoods at night. Among women this fear had increased by fourteen percent (forty-four to fifty-eight percent).[36]

In January 1973 fifty-one percent of those responding to the Gallup poll stated that there was more crime in their area than a year ago. Only ten percent responded that there was less crime.[37]

The Harris poll, also a national measurement, parallels Gallup. In November 1970, Harris measured public concern about crime. He compared his findings with those expressed three years earlier in a similar survey of his:

Recently a cross section of 1,300 households across the nation was asked: "In the past year, do you feel that the crime rate in your area has been increasing, decreasing, or has it remained the same as it was before?

	1970 %	1967 %
Increasing	62	46
Decreasing	3	4
Remaining the same	30	43
Not sure	5	7[38]

Thus two of the nation's most widely known public opinion surveys agree about the general concern about crime in America today.

Life magazine, in 1972, took a nationwide sampling of its readers with regard to their fears of crime. Of the 43,000 readers that responded, a surprising seventy-eight percent sometimes felt unsafe in their own homes, and eighty percent of those responding from big cities were afraid in the streets at night.[39]

Finally, and most recently, a *New York Times* survey taken in New York City in late 1973 and early 1974 indicated that sixty-three percent of those surveyed ("rich and poor, black and white, conservative and liberal") regarded crime as the problem of greatest concern. The problem of drugs, in actuality a crime-related problem, was next with twenty-eight percent, and the third area of greatest concern, the "high cost of living, inflation," received a mere twenty percent response.[40]

Beyond any doubt the law-abiding majority is deeply concerned with the problems of lawlessness and violence, and properly so. Yet concern by itself is relatively meaningless. Another element must be added in our analysis of public opinion about crime before the concern expressed can have any sort of constructive result.

A Call for Action—What the Public Wants Done

This section focuses on, again through public opinion polls, reports, and other sources, the hard-line approach toward criminals that has been and is currently being demanded by the law-abiding citizens of this country.

The basic feeling in this area is captured in a special report, "Justice on Trial," that appeared in the March 8, 1971, issue of *Newsweek*. Having commissioned the Gallup organization to take a special poll with regard to crime and lawlessness, the *Newsweek* editors summarized the results of the poll:

> The survey plainly shows that most Americans now want a tougher system of justice—and they are willing to grant the police broad new power to get it. *Fully three quarters of the sample feel that the system's most serious failure is that criminals receive insufficient punishment, and 62 percent find this far more disturbing than the prospect that constitutional rights may be inadequately protected.*[41]

The same survey disclosed that seventy-five percent of those queried believed that convicted criminals were "let off too easily." This is the basic approach taken by the law-abiding majority of our citizens and it appears to be taken by *all* citizens—blacks and whites alike.

Noteworthy are some specific areas in which various aspects of the criminal justice system have been scrutinized through the medium of public opinion polls, together with the results thereof. With regard to the treatment of criminals by the courts, a February 1969 Gallup poll asked 1,471 adults across the country: "In general do you think the courts in this area deal too harshly or not harshly enough with criminals?" Following are "the latest results and trends from similar queries made in past years."

	1969	1968	1965
Not harshly enough	75%	63%	48%
About right	13	19	34
Too harshly	2	2	2
No opinion	10	16	16[42]

The 75 to 2 ratio in favor of harsher treatment of criminals by the courts underlies basically the entire hard-line approach of the law-abiding majority, and the poll noted specifically that in this area the views of Negroes and whites differed very little. More recently, in December 1972, the Gallup poll reported that seventy-four percent of those queried *still* felt that the courts did not deal harshly enough with criminals.[43]

Not surprisingly, the Warren Court, which revolutionized the criminal law during the Sixties with a steady stream of rulings favoring criminal suspects to an extent heretofore unknown in this country (or, for that matter, in any other country), has come in for particular criticism. The Supreme Court under Earl Warren, a June 1969 Gallup poll indicated, received a thirty-three percent favorable rating (eight percent "excellent," twenty-five percent "good") as opposed to a fifty-four percent unfavorable rating (thirty-one percent "fair," twenty-three percent "poor"). Regarding the low esteem in which the Court was held, the poll noted:

> An important factor behind the court's decline in public favor, as judged by the views expressed in surveys, is the growing feeling that the court is "too soft" on criminals. Others complain that the rights of individuals are being protected at the expense of society as a whole.[44]

The implication is clear. The Warren Court (more properly, the liberal majority of the Warren Court) symbolized unconscionable permissiveness towards criminal conduct and the law-abiding majority wanted no part of it.

On other specific issues in the criminal justice system, Gallup found in November 1972, five months after the U.S. Supreme Court had "outlawed" capital punishment, that public support for the death penalty had risen to fifty-seven percent, the highest point since 1963.[45] A Harris poll released in July 1973 revealed that fifty-nine percent favored the death penalty.[46] Similarly, Governor Rockefeller's extremely hard-line proposal for life sentences without possibility of parole for heroin sellers received sixty-seven percent approval, as opposed to only twenty-nine percent disapproval, in a January 1973 Gallup survey.[47] Also significant, in this survey nonwhites approved of the harsh drug laws by a margin of fifty-nine to thirty-six percent.

The vast majority of people of this country want something done about crime and lawlessness. In particular, they demand that criminals, when apprehended and convicted, be punished. Clearly they are sick and tired of the unwarranted leniency shown criminal offenders, leniency which has come to characterize our criminal justice system. This public attitude is based on the common-sense thesis, expressed so eloquently by Dr. Sidney Hook earlier in this chapter, that the victims of crime should have some rights too, but that their rights have become more and more attenuated as our criminal justice system pursues its single-minded concern for the rights of the criminal.

This pursuit of the criminals' rights, to the exclusion of the rights of the law-abiding, has caused a deep and abiding frustration in the minds of our citizens. This is a potentially dangerous frustration for, as it becomes more and more clear that the criminal justice system has broken down and is either unable or unwilling to protect the law-abiding, the temptation arises for the citizen to take matters into his own hands.

This, in turn, can lead to vigilantism, a condition no one, no matter how hard-line his views about crime might be, should desire or tolerate. There is certainly no current epidemic of vigilantism extant in this country, though there are a few scattered signs, which prove that a healthy fear of its specter is not farfetched.

In a three-month period in 1973 there were more than a dozen instances in New York City in which citizens aggressively intervened in street crimes resulting in severe beatings of the suspects. In one case, an armed criminal was set upon by a crowd of some one hundred bystanders and nearly kicked to death before the police finally rescued him.

This syndrome of "bystander intervention" (another name for vigilantism), according to police officials and social psychologists, reflects a growing hostility in the average citizen toward crime, particularly violent crime. In an article describing the rise of vigilantism in New York, William Claiborne quotes Stanford University social psychologist Dr. William Zimbardo on the vigilante mentality: "We can't rely on the formal law-enforcement structure any more, so we'll take care of it ourselves."[48]

The *San Francisco Examiner* reported in early 1974 that citizen posses, branded as vigilantes by law-enforcement officers, were giving the Pacific Northwest "a bad case of the jitters." These posses, groups of citizens who have banded together without the blessing of law-enforcement officers, have created the fear that they might well decide to take the law into their own hands.[49]

This is a disturbing situation, made even more so because it represents the feeling that the criminal justice system has broken down to the extent that only "self-help" methods will offer sure protection.

The system has, in fact, broken down. In most cases the actual or potential criminal gets a far better shake from the system than does his victim. But this does not in the slightest justify the intervention of self-appointed guardians of the law. The answer to the problem, of course, lies in a revitalization of the system so that it is capable of performing its primary function: the protection of the innocent.

No one writing on the subject of crime and lawlessness in 1974 can ignore the Watergate tragedy. Certain liberal pundits have taken the gleeful position that Watergate has, categorically and forever, foreclosed the law-and-order issue to anyone who is deeply concerned over rights of the victims of crime in our society.

This is simply not true. "Law and order" was not a dirty phrase prior to Watergate, nor is it now. An abiding concern over the plight of the victims of crime—most of whom are ghetto dwellers and members of minority races—was not an extremist or racist attitude prior to Watergate, and is not now. Public opinion, as demonstrated by the polls and surveys just cited, was decidedly and increasingly hard-line against crime and criminals before Watergate; there is no reason to believe that the deplorable behavior of a few highly placed men who put politics above the law will bring about a softening of this attitude.

In ever-increasing numbers, people are being murdered, raped, robbed, and preyed upon by criminals. The political criminality of those involved in Watergate cannot change this fact one iota. Perhaps the basic public view about crime and lawlessness is illustrated by three letters received by the *Chicago Tribune* on a single day, April 28, 1973, dealing with the Watergate situation *vis-à-vis* crime in the streets. M. W. Bach of Chicago wrote: "What kind of ridiculous farce is this Watergate business anyway? . . . What the public is worried about is John Doe down the street getting killed or beat up." Echoing this sentiment, Caroline C. Szekeley wrote from Naperville, Illinois: "Too bad the self-appointed sleuths who uncovered the Watergate affair do not turn themselves loose on unsolved murders, kidnappings, muggings, rapes, embezzlements and robberies." Finally, D. E. George of South Bend, Indiana, referred to the entire affair as a "tempest in a teapot" and concluded: "Now we hear that the fellow arrested for shooting Senator Stennis is out on bond. Murderers, muggers, and burglars get by with hardly a slap on the wrist."[50]

Now, Watergate is by no means a tempest in a teapot. The acts unearthed during the investigation of the entire sorry affair are particularly revolting because they were, for the most part, committed for partisan political gain. Nevertheless, the case can be made that the thoughts expressed in the three letters realistically gauge the tenor of public opinion about every kind of crime. And this crime is still as rampant today as it ever was, whereas it was *political* crimes that were basically involved in Watergate and Watergate-related disclosures. The very real crimes involved in the Watergate mess can in no way be condoned, and those involved should be punished.* Hopefully, the entire panoply of Watergate investigations will result in changes in laws and procedures that will prevent such excesses in the future. But, a government totally free of political chicanery and corruption that is unable—or, perhaps more important, unwilling—to protect the least of its citizens from becoming the victims of the depredations of the lawless and violent, is a government that has by definition failed, totally and miserably, in its highest duty. If Watergate creates the attitude in our public officials that, because some who favored a hard-line approach to crime themselves committed criminal

*The question of punishment immediately raises the issue of President Ford's pardon of Richard Nixon. This question is a thorny one and will undoubtedly be debated back and forth for years to come. In the view of this writer, President Ford's decision to pardon Mr. Nixon was unfortunate, but the circumstances of the pardon were so unusual and the factual setting so unique that the pardon really has no bearing upon the far more fundamental question: are we going to do something constructive about the rights of the victims of crime?

acts, we should now ignore the victims of crime, then it will indeed be a tragedy the like of which this country has never seen before.

We proceed, then, upon the assumption that, Watergate notwithstanding, there is a deep feeling in the American public that crime is a major problem and that it is high time something was done about it. Perhaps this attitude is best summed up by an outside observer of the American criminal justice system, an observer with impeccable credentials. Sir Reginald Scholl, Australian consul general to the United States and former justice of the Supreme Court of Victoria, Australia, addressed a meeting of the Philadelphia Bar Association in 1966. His words ring truer today than when spoken:

> My general feeling on these matters [of the criminal justice system], if I may respectfully state it as a foreign lawyer, is that in your enthusiasm for liberalism at all costs you are, perceptibly more than we are in Australia, throwing the baby out with the bath water. It is no good making individual liberty so cast iron, by constitutional guarantees, that one's neighbors can rob one or rape one's daughter with a better chance of escaping justice than in other civilized countries. How stand life, liberty, and the pursuit of happiness in that situation? It is indeed an empty freedom, a vain individual liberty which is accompanied by a significantly increased risk to oneself or one's family of being the victim of crime. What is the real value of greater individual liberty, so called, if it is obtained at the price of making crime harder to detect and punish, and therefore safer to commit? What is the real value to a decent law-abiding citizen of being in less danger of possible abuse of power by the police but in greater danger of fraud, theft, violence, or death from criminals large or small, organized or unorganized?

This book is based on two premises. The first is that until now, the rights of the actual and potential victims of crime have been largely ignored in our criminal justice system, resulting in the almost total failure of that system to accomplish its primary function of protecting the law-abiding from the lawless. The second premise is that the rights of the victims can be expanded and that a reduction of the number and sufferings of the victims of crime can be accomplished, both without doing violence to the fundamental rights of the criminal accused or denying our compassion to the worthy who are caught up in the criminal justice system.

Part II of this book expounds the first premise and describes the ways in which the criminal justice system has failed the victims of crime. Part III deals with the second premise and presents some suggested solutions to the problems. Before proceeding to the second part, however, it is necessary to consider some special classes of victims of crime and how they are victimized.

2
The Special Victims

THERE ARE THREE CLASSES OR GROUPS OF VICTIMS that merit special consideration in any study of the victims of crime: the poor and powerless, because their burden of lawlessness and violence is so disproportionately heavy and because they are in the greatest need of protection; law-enforcement officers, because their occupation requires almost constant contact with the dangerous elements in our society; and, finally, society in general, because the current crime wave in this country—street crime, organized crime, and terroristic crime—has cast a terrible pall of fear over every one of us, in effect victimizing the total society.

The Primary Victims: The Poor and the Powerless

It is an article of faith among certain elitist elements in our society that "law and order" are code words for racism. Likewise, these same individuals—who generally receive their exposure to crime and violence via the six o'clock news on their television sets—constantly charge that those who call for a hard line against crime are merely seeking to repress racial minorities. This reasoning is fatuous. Those espousing such views exhibit either a stunning lack of knowledge or a phenomenal genius for self-deception.

33

The fact of the matter is that the poor and powerless, the racial minorities, and the ghetto dwellers are victimized by all forms of crime far more than is any other group of people in our society. Those who desire to crack down on the criminals are, far from being racist, genuinely concerned that the intolerable burden of crime upon the poor—*especially* among the racial minorities—should be brought under control.

That victims of crime are largely ignored in our criminal justice system is a sorry enough situation in itself. But by far the most shameful failure of the system is its almost total inability—or unwillingness—to provide protection against being victimized for those who most need it: the poor, the minorities, and the ghetto dwellers. If the right to be free from criminal harm is to mean anything, it should surely be accorded to those who are most exposed to lawlessness and violence and who are most dependent upon the system for protection from the criminals.

Precisely the opposite is true, however. The burden of crime upon those who live in crime-infested slums is overwhelming compared with that sustained by residents of affluent suburban and rural areas. The undeniable fact is that the poor pay for crime—at a usurious rate. The problem of crime in America is, without question, a national problem, affecting every citizen in the country. But it is compounded many times over among the poor.

The accusations of racism and repression, made by smug liberals against law-enforcement officers who work in the ghetto, are particularly infuriating because those officers—almost alone in the criminal justice system—see the victims firsthand.

The policeman who has to break the news to a black mother that her fourteen-year-old son has been shot to death because he refused to join a street gang, is just not going to be very much moved by the charge that he and his fellow officers are practicing racism in their efforts to bring the killers to justice, even if the killers happen to be black. Likewise, the detective who has drawn chalk lines around the bodies of an aged Jewish couple gunned down during a robbery of their inner-city delicatessen, will not stay awake nights worring whether his attempts to find the murderers will be deemed repressive by those who have never come face to face with the realities of murder, rape, robbery, and assault against the poor and powerless. Law enforcement in the ghetto is perhaps the most dangerous aspect of police work today; the huge majority of police officers working there are dedicated men who see firsthand the victims of crime and who desire to prevent, to the extent possible, their further victimization.

Vernon Jarrett, the hard-hitting black columnist for the *Chicago Tribune*, remarked the statement by social researcher Robert B. Hill that "the great majority of black families are not characterized by criminality, delinquency, drug addiction or desertion."[1] Precisely. Why, then, should these decent, law-abiding people be victimized so horribly?

Here an important point must be made. As crime in the slums is an utterly intolerable situation, so police brutality there is equally, if not more, intolerable. There is no inconsistency between deploring the victimization of racial minorities by criminals and at the same time calling for a crackdown on a handful of policemen who actually engage in brutality. In fact, the two go hand in hand. If the minority of bad policemen who exacerbate tensions through their wrongful conduct can be weeded out, then the great majority of dedicated officers, who spend their working hours making the streets of the inner cities a little more secure, can do their work more effectively.

There may be a legitimate dispute as to what constitutes brutality. For example, a police officer who is using what he believes to be reasonable force to subdue one assaulting him with a broken bottle (as is the officer's right and duty), may appear to the assailant or to observers to be using excessive force. This sort of instance is unfortunate and often leads to repercussions in the community. The line between reasonable and excessive force is thin and difficult to resolve.

The policeman on the street most assuredly does not have to make himself into a punching bag in order to relieve the frustrations of anyone who happens not to like a blue uniform. And he has every right to use reasonable force to protect himself, or to make an arrest. On the other hand, cases of real brutality—the beating of a handcuffed man or the dragging of an inoffensive motorist from his car for no reason at all—cannot be condoned under any circumstances and the perpetrators of such actions should be brought to book as expeditiously as can be.

Granted, then, that there is police brutality in the ghetto, that it is intolerable, and that it must be halted, the fact remains that there are far more instances of *criminals* brutalizing the ghetto dwellers than there are of *policemen* brutalizing them. And the poor and powerless desperately need protection from the criminal.

The extent to which the poor are victimized in comparison with that to which the affluent are, was documented by the late Stanford University criminologist Herbert L. Packer in a 1970 report. Packer showed that slum dwellers are *at least one hundred times* as likely to be victims of street crimes as are middle-class whites living in the suburbs. According to Professor Packer, one out of seventy of the inhabitants of inner-city slums fell victim to a mugger, rapist, or assailant in 1969, while in the overall population the incidence of these crimes was one in 10,000.[2] Confirming these figures, an Associated Press survey in August 1970 reported that between seventy and eighty percent of big-city crime occurred in Negro or predominantly Negro districts,[3] and *Time* reported in a special study on murder that Negroes, who make up about twelve percent of our population, constitute fifty-five percent of our homicide victims.[4]

These findings, describing the victimization of the poor, were updated in a lengthy article appearing in the December 18, 1972, *Newsweek.* Commenting upon the rising fear of crime among middle-class white Americans, the article rather pointedly noted:

> *What middle-class people frequently forget is that poor people—especially poor black people—have been living with the same fears and worse for a long time.* Parthenia Waters won't venture out after dark from her three-room public housing flat in Chicago's Wentworth police district, *where one out of every 27 persons last year was the victim of violent crime*: murder, rape, robbery or assault.
>
> "Whatever you need and can't borrow from a neighbor just has to wait until the next day," Mrs. Waters explains. All through the night, she stands guard behind the door. "Sometimes I doze off for an hour and then I wake up," she says. "From then till morning I'm walking the floor, listening. I'm so scared somebody might come in here on us. I don't know what I'd do if somebody did." In the morning, she keeps her 12-year-old in the apartment until precisely 8:50 A.M., when the doors of the nearby school are opened, then sees her off from the project's outdoor ramp.
>
> The atmosphere is similarly oppressive in most ghettos. *"It's heartbreaking to see what this city has become," sighs a 70-year-old Harlem woman who was mugged last month.* "I used to enjoy playing bridge with my friends, but we haven't done that in a year. I used to look forward to the evening Lent services, but that's finished." Ironically, even those who break out into middle-class black neighborhoods remain prime targets for black criminals, who realize they can be spotted more quickly in white areas. "I live in constant fear now," says Mrs. Lennon Harris, whose husband just spent $1,000 fortifying their Memphis home after a $3,800 burglary. "You work and save so you can have nice things, then some punk just comes in and takes it away from you."

Statistics on the percentage and the incidence of crime in which the poor are victimized become starkly real when the stories of the victims themselves are told. From the Associated Press report on the extent to which black crime preys on black victims, noted above, come the following instances of what it means to live daily with the fear of ghetto crime:

—A closed pool parlor wears a sign: "Buddy has had his fifth operation because of a holdup by his Soul Brothers." Buddy's Pool Parlor, Newark, New Jersey. Buddy stands outside the shuttered doors flexing his forearm for his friends. The muscles are healing after a shotgun blast tore into his hand and arm. Now, he has a dog, a German shepherd. Still, a late-night break-in postponed his reopening.

—In Detroit's inner city, Wilma Strange works as a secretary at the Grace Episcopal Church, 12th Street and Virginia Park Avenue, where the Detroit riots of 1967 began. On New Year's Eve she stepped off a downtown bus into the early winter darkness, her arms full of parcels. Someone asked her a question. She turned, a male arm locked around her neck. Male fists beat at her face. She fell. When she came to, her purse and parcels were gone. Now she doesn't go out at night, not even to buy groceries she needs for tomorrow.

—Joe McKissick is a private guard . . . and yet he too suffers the impact of ghetto crime. He worked day and night in the Detroit riots as an ambulance driver. When he finally returned to his apartment he found it stripped clean by looters—everything he had saved for, clothes, television set, all of it was gone.[5]

Buddy, Wilma Strange, and Joe McKissick represent thousands of victims of inner-city crime. Their stories, changed slightly for better or worse, adorn the police blotters of every urban center. They represent an entire class of people whose lives are literally dominated by fear. The pathetic story of Wilma Strange concludes: "Now she doesn't go out at night, not even to buy the groceries she needs for tomorrow." That single sentence, by itself, describes an intolerable situation. It is a terrible indictment of a criminal justice system that indirectly imprisons an American citizen in her own home.

Ghetto living conditions are sufficiently deplorable without the added penalty to the poor of being confined to their homes when the sun goes down. *Chicago Tribune* columnist Walter Trohan has written that residents of suburban Washington, D.C., are afraid to go downtown at night for fear of falling victim to criminal violence.[6] What then of those who *live* in downtown Washington, D.C., or any other big-city downtown? The fact that city streets are no longer safe after dark merely limits the choice of where to go for the suburbanite; he can visit restaurants, lounges, and theaters nearer his home. The poor, trapped in the inner city, are not afforded this alternative to the downtown streets.

For most people who live in our city slums, the right to go out at night to the neighborhood grocery store, or on a hot evening to the corner tavern for a beer, simply does not exist unless they wish to run the risk of becoming the victim of violent crime. The lawless elements prowling the streets have made the already wretched existence of the poor a great deal more wretched. Percy Sutton, the black borough president of Manhattan, pointed out, in a speech in November 1972, that the people of Harlem were "virtually imprisoned" by a few people engaged in criminal activity. Mr. Sutton charged the city of New York with "gross neglect" of Harlem, stating that crime against blacks evokes only a "shameful silence" instead of an outcry by the city leaders and a "saturation of the crime area by the police."[7]

The impact of slum crime is not limited to the human misery and fear imposed on the victims by real and threatened criminal acts. The economic effects of lawlessness are particularly harsh in the inner cities and among the black and the poor. A study of crime in Harlem by the Small Business Chamber of Commerce placed the 1970 cost of crime to Harlem residents and property at over two billion dollars. Especially hard hit were the central Harlem businessmen. The study reported that ninety percent of all businesses in that area had been robbed, held up, or pilfered, and fully eighty percent had been the victims of repeated criminal attacks. One man reported that he had been robbed forty times in 1970.[8]

These findings, when one thinks about them, are almost unbelievable. They picture a crime burden on the black businessman of such magnitude that he can be reasonably certain that his business will be victimized in some way. As the businessman is affected, so is the community he serves. His prices are, of necessity, raised to make up for the losses caused by the criminal. The price tag of crime for the poor, the businessman, and the customer spirals upwards.

Often the depredations of the robber, burglar, or shoplifter force white and black businessmen serving the ghetto neighborhoods to close their doors. This results in additional hardships to the residents of those neighborhoods. William Raspberry, a black columnist who writes in terse and tough-minded terms about the problems of urban blacks, described the consequences of the closing, due to innumerable robberies, of High's Ice Cream stores in the Washington, D.C. ghetto:

[It] means that mothers in those neighborhoods [where stores have closed] will have to go a little farther for baby's milk—a major problem when there's no car in the family. It also means the loss of that many open-on-Sunday convenience stores.

And it means too that many of the people who worked in those stores will be job hunting.[9]

This is the miserable situation of the poor in the core cities. The plight of those trapped in our urban ghettos was summarized in an article dealing with the problems of Newark, New Jersey: "In Central

Ward, perhaps the worst ghetto in the East, decent black families live as virtual prisoners, afraid to let their children out even to play."[10] Until something is done to alleviate these unbearable conditions and to guarantee to decent blacks, browns, and whites the right to be safe, no matter where they live, our criminal justice system will continue to register its biggest and most tragic failure.

One certain fact emerges in every study of ghetto crime: the law-abiding but poor blacks are sick and tired of being the perpetual victims of crime. They demand law and order and the vindication of their rights to be safe. This attitude was documented in a May 1970 survey by the *National Observer*, which sent correspondents to twenty-one major American cities to interview inner-city residents, community leaders, and police officials on the subject, "Black Law and Order." The findings of these surveys were summarized in an article by Edwin A. Roberts, Jr.:

> There is increasing, visible evidence that the nation's inner-city blacks— the principal victims of urban crime—are becoming militant supporters of law and order. Not only are they taking new steps to protect themselves and their property, they are organizing in a variety of ways to assist their old nemesis, the police.
>
> This dramatic turnabout, which is partly the result of more enlightened police department policies, is the best news city crime fighters have had in years. Because when the community pitches in to make neighborhoods safer, the odds against the criminal climb fast.[11]

Embodying the blacks' desire for law and order in the ghetto was Selma Whownes, who is active in Brooklyn's Bedford-Stuyvesant ghetto. Interviewed by *National Observer*, Mrs. Whownes said:

> Our big problem in black areas is the lack of police. You know, we used to hate cops, but those days are gone. The people who used to call cops pigs are also gone. Now you see people in the street abusing cops for not showing up in time to prevent an incident, and you see cops yelled at because they're never around.[12]

Further evidence of this hard-line attitude towards crime is found in a report issued in December 1968 by the Anti-Crime Committee of the New York NAACP. The report calls unequivocally for a law-and-order crackdown to end "the reign of criminal terror in Harlem."[13] This document, issued after four months of study by the committee, is a dignified and forceful statement by the residents of a ghetto community that is continually victimized by crimes of every sort. The Harlem blacks are, quite properly, demanding that the right of being safe apply to them.

The committee's recommendations warrant examination, as the following excerpts indicate:

POLICE PROTECTION

We are in full agreement with those who state that there should be a substantial increase in the number of policemen on the beat. We are also in full agreement with those who believe that more effective use should be made of the police strength already available. We shall continue to fight police brutality through litigation, exposure and public protest, *but we favor the use of whatever force is necessary to stop a crime and to apprehend the criminal.*

NARCOTICS AND ADDICTS

The minimum penalty for the sale of narcotics should be ten (10) years in prison. We hail the action of the New York State Legislature which would impose a maximum sentence of life imprisonment upon those who sell marijuana to minors. The same penalty should be applied to those selling any other kind of narcotics to anyone.

It is a fixed policy of educational authorities in New York State to conduct a physical examination of school children at regular intervals. We favor, as part of this examination, a test to ascertain whether dope in any of its forms has been introduced into the systems of children.

PROTECTION FOR HOUSES

We call for the placing of armed guards in every house in all public housing projects. We call for action towards the same end under suitable arrangements in all private housing. We favor such legislative and administrative action as is necessary to reduce the time for processing gun permit applications for such guards. *No guard should be compelled to risk sacrificing his life on the altar of red tape.*

THE PENALTY FOR FIRST DEGREE MURDER

If capital punishment is not to be restored, *we demand the passage of a law forbidding the release of first degree murderers until at least thirty (30) years have been spent behind bars.*

THE PENALTY FOR "MUGGING"

We demand that the *minimum penalty for "mugging" be five years in prison with no time off for good behavior and no eligibility for parole during that period.* This penalty should be meted out to *first offenders* as well as others.

THE MENACE OF VAGRANCY

Homeless people are dangerous because their very need for food and shelter is a powerful incentive to rob and maim. Hundreds come from other cities. Hundreds are evicted for non-payment of rent. Hundreds more are alcoholics and drug addicts who for the time being cannot keep jobs and meet expenses. Tickets back home should be provided for those who come from other cities. Adequate temporary shelters should be provided for the homeless of our own city. *Anti-vagrancy laws should be vigorously enforced. At all events, the people of this community should not be compelled to live under the threat of depredation by derelicts.*

In all this, however, we should be compassionate and helpful. Some vagrants have fled from the hopelessness and oppression of the Deep South to the disillusionment of New York. They should be a major concern of social agencies.

PROBATION, BAIL AND PAROLE

We are shocked to learn of the large number of persons charged with or convicted of crimes who are *permitted to roam the streets and hallways without hindrance.* Hundreds of crimes are committed by those against whom criminal charges are already pending and by those only recently paroled. We learned of one case in which a young man committed three murders after being placed on probation for a previous crime.

Our inquiries into probation, bail and parole are only beginning. Subsequent reports will contain detailed recommendations; but one very disturbing situation has been brought to light. We learned that one reason for leniency in releasing accused persons temporarily is that court calendars are so clogged that they might well remain in jail for months, if not years before trial.

We hail the creation of one hundred and twenty-five (125) additional judgeships, but we are also aware that late starts in the morning, long recesses, and early adjournments demonstrate that full use is not being made of present judges. In addition, lawyers make a practice of stalling until a judge favorable to their wishes is on the bench. This is understandable, but it does not serve the public interest. *We therefore serve notice that we shall keep a record of the dispositions made of cases by all judges sitting in criminal courts; that we shall make that record public from time to time; and that we shall publish it widely, be it good or bad, when such judges come up for re-election or re-appointment.* For this purpose we shall enlist the aid of other organizations.

Such reforms as are initiated in this field should make the all-important distinction between the convicted and the accused.

CITIZENSHIP AND CRIME

No matter what public officials and policemen do, there is no substitute for the concern of the average citizen. In the Harlem community, the attitude toward crime and criminals must change. *There is nothing cute about a juvenile snatching a pocketbook. There is nothing heroic about preventing a legitimate arrest. There is nothing smart about buying stolen property.* But a wholesome attitude must lead to constructive action. Citizens who are aware of illegal operations in their communities should report them to the proper authorities. We must observe here that these authorities must not be so stupid as to cause the name of the citizen to be known to those against whom the complaint is made. A citizen who sees a crime in progress should call the police at once. A neighbor who hears a suspicious noise or movement in someone's apartment when the occupant is home should call the police. The person who sees one or more persons loitering in a hallway for no apparent reason should call the police. The victim of a burglary or mugging should always report it even if he believes that "nothing will be done." Sometimes criminals are apprehended by piecing things together and every little bit helps. In short, in a democracy either the people enforce the law or it is not enforced.

This is probably as hard-line a document as has ever been written. Yet, in reality, the only individuals who should register any surprise at these demands are those liberals—mostly white, mostly suburban— to whom ghetto crime is by definition a natural state of affairs and to whom anyone attempting to curb the lawlessness must be, *ipso facto*, racist. One of the cornerstones of liberal dogma is that only liberals know what is good for the objects of their concern. Thus, the liberals have determined unilaterally that "law and order" are code words for racism and that law enforcement in the ghetto is *a fortiori* repressive. The fact that the blacks (who experience crime firsthand rather than through TV in safe suburban living rooms) may earnestly desire some law and order and some repression of the criminal terrorists who are victimizing them, is not to be considered in the liberal credo.

The attitude that crime is a sort of natural condition for blacks and other minority people was castigated by the aforementioned Winston Moore. Moore, a black man and the executive director of the Cook County (Illinois) Department of Corrections, stated brutally: "The bleeding liberals who have so much guilt that they can justify blacks killing blacks because we're immature [are] the ones who want to keep you immature. Quit justifying why I kill my buddies on Saturday night and try to stop me from doing it."[14]

Moore's scorn for liberal concern over black criminals was echoed in a November 1972 article in the *Washington Post*, "It's Blacks Who Must Control Crime," by Orde Coombs, who teaches black literature at New York University. Describing the mugging by blacks of a friend of his who lived in the ghetto, Mr. Coombs stated that that crime "must compel those of us who are black to put an end to the epidemic of crime which is raging through our urban communities and threatens to stunt our growth unless we quickly do something about the menace."[15] Pursuing this thesis, Coombs correctly pinpoints narcotics addiction as a major factor of ghetto crime. He calls for removal of addicts from the streets and life imprisonment for drug pushers, and "if the liberals cry about constitutional rights, chase them back to Scarsdale, for they do not quake every time they saunter out of doors."[16]

Likewise, those who find racism in a call for a hard line against the criminals who constantly victimize the law-abiding ghetto dwellers should consider the following thoughts from Roy Wilkins, the respected executive director of the NAACP, writing in a syndicated column:

> A Negro chief of police, Charles Boone, of Gary, Indiana, has finally said what had to be said if crime by blacks is to decrease and city life is to be made tolerable for both black and white citizens. Boone accused two judges of leniency in cases of black burglars and of giving Negro criminals "license to steal." A study by his department showed that 90 percent of the Negroes charged with robbery and other crimes in his county are "back on the streets committing the same crimes they were arrested for."
>
> Except for a few voices, Negro citizens have given consent to robbery, muggings, assaults and murder by their silence. They have been intimidated by a curious twisting of the "us blacks together" philosophy which holds that complaining of black criminals is somehow "betraying the race." This is nonsense. One can be proud of being black without embracing every black mugger, rapist and auto thief.
>
> Negro communities need to speak out and act against Negro criminals. They need to cease trotting out the same old excuses for black wrongdoings: "broken homes," "prejudice," "inferior schools," "joblessness," ad infinitum. Negro Americans should not cease fighting against those evils, but they should cease using them to excuse Negro criminality.[17]

As recently as May 1973, Richard Hatcher, Gary's black mayor, urged a gathering of 2,000 Gary residents, mostly black, to help us get rid of the "vermin and scum that profit here"—the drug pushers in the Gary area. According to the *Chicago Tribune,* Mr. Hatcher got his biggest hand "when he said he had little respect for high-priced attorneys who defend drug pushers and then return to suburban homes."[18] Now Mayor Hatcher is a certified liberal, but the distinction between him and the suburban liberals is that Mr. Hatcher, as chief executive of a major city with a majority black population, is faced with the *reality* of crime, and he clearly wants something done about it. On this issue at least, he is not overly sympathetic with those whose experience with violence and lawlessness is purely vicarious.

In November 1973, Coleman Young was elected the first black mayor of Detroit. At his inaugural celebration on January 2, 1974, he was called upon by the United States district judge Damon Keith, a black, to urge black people to cooperate with the police. Judge Keith addressed the new mayor:

43

The crime problem, which has won for our city an unprecedented degree of adverse publicity, is essentially a wave sparked by black criminals preying upon black victims.

Tragically, this crime wave is aided and abetted by black people who say, "It's no business of mine." When police come, nobody is there who remembers seeing anything.

Your call, loudly given and responded to, can reverse the crime trend in this city and prove more than any other one thing that a black man can run a city in an outstanding manner and bring it new honors.[19]

Mayor Young responded:

I issue a warning now to all dope pushers, rip-off artists and muggers. It is time to leave Detroit. Hit the road!

I don't give a damn if you're black or white, if they wear Superfly suits or blue suits with silver badges.[20]

Mayor Young pointedly warned both the would-be criminal and the potentially brutal or corrupt policeman to stay out of Detroit. This again underscores the fact that victimization of the poor and powerless by *either* criminal abuse or police abuse is equally intolerable. Thus we see some fairly intransigent and intolerant language by black leaders— none of whom could by any stretch of the imagination be called an Uncle Tom or a creature of the establishment—directed at those criminals who prey upon the minority groups for whom they speak.

Anyone harboring lingering doubts about the impact of crime in the ghetto and about the call from the ghetto for protection from criminals should read *What the Negro Can Do About Crime.** The authors—Jay A. Parker, a black, and Allen Brownfeld, a white—have set forth, in the starkest terms possible, the manner in which crime of all sorts affects the daily lives of racial minorities, particularly those who are trapped in the inner city. The authors state flatly:

While a great deal is said and written about the fact that Negroes are responsible for the majority of serious crimes in our urban areas, less is said about the fact that they are also the predominant victims—that the all-black inner city areas of New York, Chicago, Washington, Los Angeles and other cities are more dangerous than white areas within those cities, or in the surrounding suburbs. If white Americans fear crime and violence, that fear is even more overwhelming for black Americans, since most of them live in the midst of it.

This book refutes categorically the notion that "law and order" are merely code words for racism. Moreover, it proves that ghetto dwellers

*New Rochelle, N.Y.: Arlington House, 1974.

44

are demanding, and are deserving of, far more protection from the lawless than they are currently getting.

The foregoing leads to three inescapable conclusions: (1) the principal victims of crime are the urban poor who bear an unconscionably large share of violence and lawlessness; (2) they are sick and tired of bearing it; and (3) they want protection from the criminal—not when the liberals come to realize the extent to which the poor and racial minorities are victimized, but right now.

The elitists who carp at the policemen and others who advocate a hard line against ghetto crime might be well pleased if the police leave the ghetto entirely. The result of such a turn of events has been described by an eminent legal scholar, James R. Thompson, former professor of law at Northwestern University and currently the United States attorney for the Northern District of Illinois. Writing in a friend-of-the-court (*amicus curiae*) brief filed by Americans for Effective Law Enforcement, Inc., before the United States Supreme Court in the 1968 case of *Terry* v. *Ohio*, Mr. Thompson stated:

> The police could, of course, withdraw from the ghetto. . . . This alternative might be somewhat tolerable if only criminals lived in the ghetto; at least *their* interferences with human liberty in the form of murder, rape, robbery and other crimes would be practiced on each other. But others live in the ghetto as well—innocent, law-abiding American citizens, by far the overwhelming majority. They are entitled under the . . . Constitution of the United States to live their lives and experience the safety of their homes and their streets without fear of criminal marauders. They have suffered enough—discrimination, poverty, lack of education, appalling conditions of alienation. Must they also be deprived of the protection of the law as well?[21]

Mr. Thompson's eloquence in behalf of the racial minorities as victims of crime may have played a large part in the fact that the Warren Court in the *Terry* case approved, 8 to 1 (Justice Douglas dissenting), the police practice of "stop and frisk" as a means of curbing urban crime.

The last line of Mr. Thompson's appeal for protection of those in the ghetto provides a succinct summation of this section. The ghetto dwellers—primarily racial minorities—have suffered enough from "discrimination, poverty, lack of education, appalling conditions of alienation." That the present criminal justice system, in its preoccupation with the rights of the criminal and its blindness to the plight of the victim, has failed to protect those who most need the deserved protection is the bitterest indictment of the system imaginable.

Target: Law-Enforcement Officers* As Victims

The title of this section raises the question: Why should law-enforcement officers be singled out as special victims of crime? I had thought that such a question would never be asked until several years ago, when I was with the Denver Police Department. At that time a friend asked me why police officers "took it so hard" when one of their number was killed or wounded by criminal violence. Now this lady was no knee-jerk liberal. She was in fact a political conservative, the daughter of a respected former police commissioner in the East, and a staunch supporter of law enforcement. She simply could not understand why the killing of a police officer should be regarded as *more* heinous than the killing of an ordinary citizen.

Now she was quite correct in believing that killing any human being is a horrible thing, and that elevating law-enforcement officers to special-victim status when they are killed or injured does not mean that the murder of the ordinary citizen is less serious. There are, however, important policy arguments, from the point of view of public protection, regarding law-enforcement officers as a special class of victims.

First of all, consider what we ask the policeman, and no one else in our society, to do. The policeman alone is required, by occupation, to respond to calls for assistance against the criminal element and to take aggressive action should he come into contact with acts of lawlessness. But more, he must actually look for trouble—he must seek out confrontations with lawbreakers. For example, the ordinary citizen is under no legal obligation whatever to respond to a cry for help on a city street. Nor is he required, in any legally enforceable manner, to take action even if he should see a crime in progress. The policeman, of course, is expected to respond and take action in situations such as these. Should he willfully fail to do so, he could—and should—be immediately disciplined for neglect of his duty.

The policeman's duty, however, goes even further than taking action when he is called upon, or when he chances upon a crime in progress. We expect our law-enforcement officers to attempt to stop crime before it happens through aggressive street patrolling. Again, a citizen is privileged to avoid dark alleys and shadowy hallways in

*For purposes of this section, "law-enforcement officers" and "police officers" will be used interchangeably to cover all officers engaged in law enforcement: police officers, sheriffs' deputies, highway patrolmen, federal agents, etc. Corrections officers, who are required by their jobs to come into daily contact with the penitentiary inmates, likewise should enjoy special status, at least insofar as they might be killed or injured by inmates. Their problems are discussed in chapters five and six.

46

which a potential criminal may be lurking. Not the policeman. Alleys and hallways are where rapists, robbers, and muggers are most likely to be found and we expect the policeman to go there looking for them. A significant part of his duty is to seek out confrontation with the criminal before that criminal can act, in order to prevent violence from befalling the rest of us.

We expect all of this for a salary that most day laborers would laugh at. Our law-enforcement officers are, for the most part, grossly underpaid. They certainly do not become police officers, with all of the dangers and frustrations the job entails, for the money it pays. While there are, unquestionably, bad cops—corrupt, brutal, sadistic, bigoted—far and away the preponderance of our law-enforcement officers are truly dedicated men and women, committed to the protection of society from the lawless and to doing a dirty and hazardous job that few others would do for three times the salary.

The fact is, our society owes a great debt to the men and women who compose the "thin blue line" between victim and criminal. When one of these officers becomes himself a target for criminal violence, society should take special note of it. If the thin blue line is broken, the law-abiding in our society will be at the mercy of every lawless and violent element.

These, then, are the reasons we should regard policemen who become victims of crimes as a special class: first, because of the nature of the job we expect our law-enforcement officers to do; and, second, because an attack on the safety of a policeman is, indirectly, an attack on every law-abiding individual in our society.

Even the *New York Times,* usually no friend of law enforcement, had the sense to realize this latter point. Editorially condemning a wave of ambush attacks on the police in late 1972 and early 1973, the *Times* became worried that increased ambushes would cause the law-enforcement establishment

> . . . to abandon law-abiding community residents—the overwhelming majority—to the desperadoes.
>
> Unfortunately, this is what has happened in some sections of the cities. On occasion, when police have been gunned down in slum housing projects, they have simply withdrawn from those areas, allowing the rule of law to be replaced by the rule of the knife and the gun. In such cases, no one's property or person can any longer be considered safe. Terror takes over.[22]

This "withdrawal syndrome" on the part of the police was graphically underscored in a recent article, "On Becoming A Crime Statistic," by Mr. Lewis M. Phelps, in the September 9, 1974, issue of the *Wall Street Journal.* Mr. Phelps, a member of the Chicago Bureau of the

Journal, had been a burglary victim. The Chicago police officer to whom Mr. Phelps reported the burglary gave as his opinion that sooner or later the police would catch the burglars in the act, *but* he continued:

> I'm not even going to make much of an effort to chase them. Because if I do, and I catch them, they probably will resist. I'll have to hit them with my gun or my club to subdue them, or else I'll get hurt myself. Then I'll have a brutality charge on my hands even if he hits me first. So I'll just go through the motions of chasing him, just enough to make it look right. And that's just exactly the way most cops in this city feel.

Indeed. Reason enough to regard attacks on law enforcement officers as in fact attacks upon a special class of victims.[23]

Today's law-enforcement officer lives with danger as he goes about his duties. The number of assaults against policemen has increased to the point where a brick thrown from a rooftop at an officer on foot patrol or a bullet hole through the window of a squad car is commonplace. Far too often another badge is pinned to the "Killed in the Line of Duty" board in the police chief's office. The policeman today is a target. And he knows it.

The target status of the law-enforcement officer and the increasing danger of police work are starkly and dramatically illustrated by the numbers of policemen killed by felons in the past few years. From 1967 to 1973, 691* officers have been murdered in line of duty:

1967	76
1968	64
1969	86
1970	100
1971	126
1972	112
1973	127[24]

These statistics tell a sorry story indeed. Clearly, murdering police officers is on the upswing, dramatically so. The number of officers killed in 1973 is double the number murdered in 1968.

In addition to the murders of law-enforcement officers, there were in 1973 an estimated total of 62,300 assaults on police officers, a ratio of fifteen assaults for every hundred officers.[25]

One particularly shocking aspect of the killing of police officers in recent years has been the overall increase in ambush slayings. While *any* murder of a law-enforcement officer is intolerable and the perpetrators of all such killings should be dealt with as harshly as the law permits—including imposition of the death penalty—there remains, nevertheless, a distinction between killing an officer while he is performing his duties (that is, pursuing a robber or investigating a suspicious person)

*This figure does not include accidental deaths.

and slaying one from ambush. The latter takes place for no other reason than that the victim is a police officer. Those who ambush police officers by bullet, bomb, or other means are surely the most dangerous and depraved elements in our society. They must be rooted out for the protection not only of the individual police officer but also of society itself.

Ambush killings have shown a marked increase in recent years. During the period 1964-68, thirteen police officers were slain in ambush attacks. During the period 1969-73 the number of officers killed in such attacks increased to fifty-six, a rise of over 400 percent.[26]

The significance of these statistics simply cannot be ignored. A police officer must accept, as part of his job, the chilling prospect that he may be killed or wounded by a felon caught in the act of perpetrating one crime or by a fugitive fleeing from another. No policeman, however, should be expected to risk sudden death from ambush simply because he represents the peace forces of society. No claim of "social alienation" or "striking out at a sick society" should ever shield the ambusher from the consequences of his acts, and those convicted of such attacks should receive no possible consideration of mercy or leniency.

A series of incidents that transpired in San Francisco in 1970 vividly illustrates both the dangers inherent in police work and the depraved nature and sheer viciousness of the cop-hater who ambushes policemen.

On Monday, October 19, 1970, San Francisco patrolman Harold L. Hamilton was shot to death while responding to a robbery alarm at a bank. He thus became another tragic statistic in the growing toll of police officers killed in line of duty. The killer was captured and it appeared that the case, insofar as Officer Hamilton was concerned, was closed. All that remained for him was burial by his widow and his colleagues.

Someone whose innate depravity staggers the imagination had a different idea. Reasoning that a large number of police officers would attend the funeral of their murdered comrade, this mental pervert conceived the idea of bombing the church at which the funeral was being held. The bomber's plan almost succeeded. A nail-filled bomb exploded outside St. Brennan's Church shattering the church windows and sending fragments of shrapnel flying through the air. Fortunately, the bomb exploded shortly before Mrs. Hamilton and the funeral party entered the church and no one was injured. That none was injured does not even slightly detract from the unspeakable nature of the attack. The bombing was obviously an ambush-type assault against the police *as such,* and the effect of the act on the grieving widow and on the feelings of Hamilton's fellow officers can only be imagined.[27]

These two attacks—the killing and the bombing—are examples of

49

direct physical attacks against the police. Each time a law-enforcement officer is killed, wounded, or assaulted, a direct attack takes place. Such attacks, however, do not tell the entire story of the current wave of attacks on police officers and on law enforcement generally. The problem is more complex and deserves at least some brief consideration here.

The police, as representatives of law and order in our society, are currently the victims of three types of attacks: direct attacks, targeting attacks, and collateral attacks.

Direct Attacks

Direct attacks are those in which law-enforcement officers are physically assaulted by individuals or groups. The outrageous way our law-enforcement officers are thereby victimized has just been described.

Targeting Attacks

Occasions often arise in which certain individuals or groups engage in activities that *of themselves* do not constitute direct attacks against law-enforcement officers, but that do increase significantly the dangers faced by police officers. Targeting attacks are so called because they enhance the target status of the officer—that is, his vulnerability to direct attacks by others.

Targeting attacks arise when some individual or group takes a position in the name of some abstract concept, such as "free speech," "right to privacy," "compassion," or "gentleness and tolerance," that materially increases the danger to a police officer. The targeting attacker may, in fact, realize that his actions increase the risks to a law-enforcement officer (and, incidentally, to society as a whole), yet he will rationalize that the abstract concept he espouses is worth the risk to the officer. On the other hand, the targeting attacker simply may not concern himself over the extent to which his activities increase the chances that a policeman will become a victim.

Targeting attacks take many forms:

1. *Rulings by judges which expose police officers to enhanced danger*

Every law-enforcement officer in this country knows—many from bitter experience—that one of the most dangerous aspects of police work is the so-called routine traffic stop. This is so because an officer who approaches a motorist whom he has stopped on a street or highway has no way of knowing whether he is dealing with the typical—and perhaps inadvertent—traffic-law violator, or with someone fleeing a major crime who will attempt to kill the officer in order to get away.

The inherent danger of traffic stops is borne out by statistics. In the three-month period from January through March 1973, for example, thirty-five law-enforcement officers in the United States were murdered— *eleven of them in traffic-stop situations.*[28]

Despite the proven hazards of traffic stops, two appellate courts in 1972 held that officers making traffic stops were not permitted for their own protection to search for weapons on the persons whom they had stopped. Both the United States Court of Appeals for the District of Columbia Circuit[29] and the California Supreme Court[30] held that the "right of privacy" of the traffic offender outweighed the right of the police officer to protect himself by searching for weapons. The decisions indicated an almost complete disdain for the danger to law-enforcement officers involved in traffic-stop situations.

The decision of the District of Columbia appeals court was overruled in December 1973 by the Supreme Court of the United States,[31] but the attitude of the lower court, that constitutional abstractions outweigh the safety of law-enforcement officers, is nevertheless significant. The California decision was not affected by this Supreme Court ruling and is still the law there. In fact, so jealous is the California Supreme Court of the privacy of traffic offenders that an officer may not even make a protective "frisk" or "pat down" for weapons unless he can show "specific facts or circumstances giving the officer reasonable grounds to believe that a weapon is secreted on the motorist's person."[32]

If a law-enforcement officer in California is gunned down by a fleeing felon who has been routinely stopped for a traffic offense, it is the killer who has made the *direct* attack. However, it is the justices of the California Supreme Court who, by imposing such unrealistic restrictions upon that officer's right to protect himself, have made a *targeting* attack against the victim.

2. *Judges who impose inordinately lenient sentences on actual or would-be assailants of the police*

Judges who show unwarranted leniency to those who attack the police condone by implication such attacks and advertise in effect that in their courts at least it is "open season" on the police. Their failure to punish those who actually attack or conspire to attack police officers thus carries a one-two punch.

On February 5, 1971, a Chicago Circuit Court judge granted probation to a seventeen-year-old "dissident." The judge, deplorably, did not believe that incarceration was warranted after the young man pled guilty to setting fire to a police car, striking a policeman, leading a charge against police lines in which he and others threw rocks and bottles at policemen, and grabbing a policeman's pistol while resisting arrest.[33]

In June 1971 Justice Arnold G. Fraiman of the New York State Supreme Court granted probation to two men who had been indicted for conspiring to "kill a cop a week" and who had been convicted of illegal possession of guns and homemade bombs. Patrick V. Murphy, former commissioner of the New York Police Department who was regarded as one of our most liberal law-enforcement executives, bitterly assailed the grants of probation:

> I categorically deplore that disposition and I want to express my frustration and regret that even after a jury has found men guilty of heinous crimes—in this case the illegal possession on guns and homemade bombs—a judge finds it appropriate to place two of the convicted men on probation.
>
> The sentences were apparently influenced by the protests from certain community leaders and journalists arguing that the two defendants are intelligent men and resourceful leaders who, while awaiting trial, conducted themselves well.
>
> I find it hard to understand how men convicted of possessing bombs and guns can be exonerated as responsible community leaders.
>
> This is especially surprising in light of the clear testimony evidently accepted by the jury, that one of the two men receiving probation actually made the bombs himself and the other man originated the idea of killing one policeman a week.
>
> It is especially tragic to be confronted by this type of judicial action when policemen in this city and elsewhere are being wantonly shot, stabbed and fire-bombed.[34]

Judge Fraiman, and the Chicago judge who showed such compassion for those who attacked policemen, would probably recoil in horror at the idea that they were making a targeting attack against law-enforcement officers generally. Yet if their misguided lenient treatment of the defendants resulted in even one additional attack on policemen because other would-be attackers were encouraged by the judges' failure to punish, then a targeting attack would surely have been made.

3. *Those who would disarm the police*

Of the 722 policemen killed between 1962 and 1971, 690 were killed with handguns, shotguns, and rifles. Still, unbelievable as it may seem, there are elements in our society who would disarm our policemen.

Some calls to disarm the police can only be characterized as sheer lunacy. For example, this proposal from one Gerhard Falk, a university professor:

> The use of firearms, restricted in England to only those who absolutely need them in the course of their duties, should be equally restricted in American jurisdictions. By not carrying a gun, the traffic officer, for example, who has more extensive contact with the public than any other policeman, would instill greater confidence in the public and remove a psychological barrier between himself and the public which firearms inevitably produce. Most officers never handle dangerous persons, and therefore do not need a gun. In fact, it is likely that the carrying of weapons imparts a false sense of

pride in police officers and gives them a poor excuse for continuing a lack of education and training.[35]

Law-enforcement officers on our city streets today may surely be excused if they harbor considerable doubts over Professor Falk's assurances from academe that "most officers never handle dangerous persons."

Other attempts to disarm policemen have been more sophisticated. On June 5, 1970, Mayor Frank Fasi of Honolulu issued a directive forbidding the members of the Honolulu Police Department from arming themselves while maintaining law and order at colleges and universities in Honolulu. In a rather pompous telegram to President Nixon, congratulating himself on this action, Mayor Fasi stated: "This policy was initiated today on the premise that law and order should be tempered with justice and not with force."[36]

Honolulu police chief Francis Keala, who opposed the order, was less enthusiastic: ". . . as chief of police I have a sworn duty to protect all the citizens of this community. I also have a moral and legal responsibility for the safety of my men."[37]

David K. Trask, head of the union to which most Honolulu policemen belonged, was even more outspoken: "I'll be damned, as a responsible union leader, if I'll let my people's lives be gambled with at the whim of a politically elected official such as Fasi."[38] The union sought an injunction in court to nullify Fasi's order and fortunately it was granted. But had an unarmed policeman on a Honolulu campus been killed or assaulted in a situation in which his side arm could have protected him, the result would clearly have stemmed from Mayor Fasi's headline-grabbing targeting attack.

In 1969 the San Francisco Neighborhood Legal Assistance Foundation sought to disarm off-duty San Francisco policemen. It filed an action in court seeking to overturn a departmental regulation that off-duty officers should carry side arms.[39] The lower court refused to overturn the regulation and the California Court of Appeals agreed, stating in a unanimous opinion: "There is nothing on the face of the regulation which shows that it is intended for anything but the protection of the public, including possible victims, of whatever race, and of the officers too."[40]

Had this action succeeded, it would have been a glaring example of a targeting attack; off-duty policemen would have been infinitely more vulnerable to direct attacks. We expect our police officers to perform their duties twenty-four hours a day, and we would surely criticize an off-duty policeman for failing to take action should he come across a crime in progress. From 1962 to 1971 sixty-five officers were killed while attempting to prevent crimes and apprehend criminals in off-duty hours. Had the busy lawyers of the San Francisco Neighborhood Legal Assistance Foundation succeeded in disarming off-duty policemen, they would likely have been responsible, sooner or later, for the death of an unarmed off-duty officer acting to stop a crime. No clearer example of a targeting attack can be found.

4. *Apologists for those who advocate killing the police*

In Baltimore, in 1970, the Black Panther Party engaged in a terror campaign against the Baltimore Police Department. Tactics included distributing hate literature that called for the killing of policemen and that explicitly instructed how to ambush and murder them. At the height of this campaign, one officer was killed and another wounded in such an attack. The activities of the Black Panther Party constituted a direct attack against the police. The Baltimore Police Department, quite properly, went to court to seek an order prohibiting further distribution of the hate literature. The police department won its suit and the Black Panthers were, at least temporarily, enjoined from distributing their poison. The judge in the case pointedly compared the Panther's antipolice activities to those used by Hitler against the Jews in the 1930s.[41]

Incredibly, however, the Baltimore affiliate of the American Civil Liberties Union entered the case on the side of the Panthers. Characteristically, the ACLU defended, under the guise of "free speech," the right of the Panthers to advocate and instruct in the murdering of policemen. This was clearly a targeting attack. As the ambush murder of the Baltimore policeman had proven, the pernicious literature materially increased the danger of attacks on other policemen. By defending the distribution of this literature, the ACLU clearly increased the danger to the lives and safety of Baltimore's law-enforcement officers.

The foregoing examples of direct and targeting attacks against law-enforcement officers demonstrate that the policeman may be victimized by criminals, or by noncriminals whose activities give, intentionally or not, significant aid to criminals at the expense of the policeman's safety.

Collateral Attacks

Whereas both direct and targeting attacks involve the question of actual physical danger to the police, collateral attacks do not. Collateral attacks are activities that are designed to demoralize, discredit, neutralize, or control individual police officers or law-enforcement agencies.

Such attacks can take many forms: agitation for the creation of civilian review boards, advocacy of community control of the police, false allegations of police misconduct, frivolous harassment-type civil suits against individual officers and agencies, and scholarly attacks by academicians, theoreticians, and, on occasion, mediamen. Few, if any, of those involved in these attacks have ever experienced, or have the slightest knowledge of, the realities of police work.

Collateral attacks will not be further discussed here because this section is primarily concerned with the policeman as the victim of physical violence. Moreover, the questions raised by collateral attacks pose so grave a threat to law enforcement generally and are of such importance to the victims of crime that I've devoted an entire section in chapter seven to them.

From the foregoing we see the police officer as a victim of direct and indirect (targeting) attacks against his personal safety. The law-abiding have a real stake in seeing that such attacks do not succeed. If the majority of our policemen should fail to do their jobs because of the physical dangers threatened, the innocent will be at the mercy of the lawless. The response of the law-abiding public should be outrage at both physical attacks and targeting attacks against law-enforcement officers, and constructive action to counter these attacks.

Society as a Victim

A little girl is gunned down as she plays in the yard of her California home. A young woman is raped in Washington, D.C. A man is beaten and robbed of his weekly pay in a Chicago subway. Each of these is a crime and each has one or more victims. The innocent individual who had been murdered, raped, or robbed is surely a victim; so too the family and friends of the rape and murder victims, and the wife and children of the robbery victim, whose paycheck would have fed the family.

Each of these crimes also tends to diminish our society a little. As each act of barbarism takes place, it proves that our society, particularly our criminal justice system, has once more failed to protect the innocent and the law-abiding from the criminally inclined.

This diminishment of society must of necessity be couched in theoretical terms. There are, however, more concrete areas in which it can be shown that our current crime explosion victimizes not only the individual who has been preyed upon, but also every one of us—society as a whole.

The Dollars-and-Cents Cost of Crime

Consider, for example, the rather practical aspect of the dollars-and-cents cost of crime. Crime is enormously expensive. In a 1970 report, *U.S. News & World Report,* long respected for its painstakingly accurate research and comprehensive reporting, estimated the annual monetary cost of crime in this country to be over fifty-one *billion* dollars.*[42] Of this, said the report, organized crime took $19.5 billion through such activities as gambling, dope selling, loan sharking, hijacking, trafficking in illegal liquor, and prostitution.

The impact of organized crime affects all of us. Welfare costs, for example, already threatening to bankrupt city and state governments, continue to rise as organized crime, gambling, narcotics, and loan-sharking rackets siphon millions of dollars out of our urban ghettos. In addition, street crimes, especially thefts by drug addicts seeking the wherewithal to maintain their habits, add immeasurably to the price tag of lawlessness.

Crimes against property and business, the *U.S. News* report estimated, cost an additional $13.1 billion in the form of business kickbacks, shoplifting, burglary, and larceny. Again, society is the victim, as the cost of these business crimes is routinely passed along to the consumer in the guise of higher prices. As usual, the primary burden falls upon the poor. For example, inventory shortages, seventy percent of which are attributable to employee thefts, add approximately fifteen percent to the cost of goods to compensate for the shortages. To the affluent housewife, this "theft assessment" may be only a minor annoyance. To the inner-city mother attempting to support three children on her welfare allotment, such a price rise is disastrous.

Law-enforcement costs were estimated by *U.S. News* at $8.5 billion annually for the police, courts, and corrections. This is, in effect, the money we pay to vindicate the right of the law-abiding to be free from criminal harm. It is at best a bad bargain, when we ponder our crime picture today.

Additionally, according to the report, Americans pay out yearly about $5.5 billion for private-protection costs *over and above* federal, state, and local law-enforcement costs. The fear of crime has in recent years sparked a tremendous demand for tear-gas guns and other instruments of self-defense: watchdogs, the bigger the better; locks and burglar alarms; and security-guard services. The private-protection business is one of the fastest-growing industries in the country. The undeniable fact is that lawlessness has reached such dimensions that government alone cannot cope with it. Consequently, those seeking not to be victimized have turned to the private sector. But the price is high. It may take the form of the direct expense to a home owner of installing an expensive burglar-alarm system in his house (prices range from $2,000

*An update of this figure, in its issue of December 16, 1974, indicated that total crime expenses at that time had risen to $88.6 billion.

on down). Or the cost may be indirect: increased prices because businesses and industry have been forced to employ one or more of the available private-protection services for added security. Whichever, another exorbitant crime expense falls upon the already burdened honest citizen.

The *U.S. News* analysis presented, finally, a sort of catchall classification of the remaining types of crime expense. Included in this category, which adds up to an estimated $4.2 billion annually, are such expenses as the loss of earnings, medical costs and property damage caused by homicides, assaults, and drunk driving. Of all the costs of crime discussed, these are the ones which are the most closely related to the human misery which is felt by the victims of crime—particularly violent crimes. While the public as a whole is victimized by such things as higher prices and increased taxes, other costs such as uninsured medical expenses and loss of work fall squarely on the victims of the crimes involved—particularly the ghetto dwellers whose chances of being victimized by violence are infinitely greater than are those of affluent suburban residents, and whose chances of obtaining insurance against such depredations decrease in proportion to their chance of being victimized. A day laborer or a domestic who, as a result of a robbery embellished by a pistol whipping, must spend two weeks in a hospital, and two more weeks recuperating, unable to work, will, more likely than not, feel the economic impact of the crime—the loss of money taken in the robbery, loss of earnings and medical bills—long after the physical scars of the assault have healed.

Society is victimized by the economic impact of crime, but we pay in other ways besides dollars and cents.

The Environment of Fear—The Impact of Crime on Our Daily Lives

We live in an environment of fear, and our entire society is consequently victimized. The spectre of criminal terror has become such an integral part of our lives that many, if not most, of us have consciously or unconsciously accommodated our day-to-day activities and living routines to it. We accept a state of constant fear as the norm, and conform to that norm.

The most opprobrious example of this pervasive fear is to be found in the fact that sizeable numbers of our citizens, who undoubtedly consider themselves to be living in a free country, become, in effect, voluntary prisoners in their dwellings when the sun goes down. This is clearly indicated by the public opinion polls, cited in chapter one, indicating that nearly half of all Americans fear to walk in their neighborhoods at night.

The polls, as one might expect, also reported that those who live in the central cities experience a greater fear of going out at night than do residents of suburbia. This finding squares with reality. Our urban centers are now, in many cases, little more than crime-ridden slums. Entire areas of our inner cities—Central Park in New York City, for example—have, as William F. Buckley, Jr. phrases it, been "more or less formally ceded to criminals." Urban dwellers, with the exception of a few fortunate denizens of well-lighted, well-policed "gold coast" areas, are forced to accommodate their habits to the dictates of their fears: when dark comes—stay home.

Of all of our cities, nowhere else has the fear of violence swept the streets cleaner than in the nation's capital. Washington, D.C., resembles a ghost town after dark, a silent witness to the sorry fact that muggers, armed robbers, rapists, and other felons have in effect declared the nighttime capital streets off limits to the law-abiding citizen.

Walter Trohan, the Washington-based columnist for the *Chicago Tribune*, reported that in one month in 1971 he received invitations from four of D.C.'s top-flight restaurants offering him a free dinner for two simply in hopes of swelling their patronage.[43] In the same vein, Mr. Trohan noted that the night-life situation in Washington has become so critical that one restaurateur sent letters to former patrons inquiring if they were dissatisfied with his food or service. *Over two hundred replied that they no longer visited downtown Washington at night.* The joys of dining at some of the first-rate restaurants were just not worth the risk of violence. The restaurant's former patrons had accommodated their dining and entertainment habits to their fears.*

In other, more subtle ways, we acknowledge our fear of the criminal. Bus passengers in almost every major city in the country must prepare themselves with the exact fare before boarding because the drivers, to discourage robberies, no longer carry any change with them. Similarly, riders in taxicabs are no longer regaled with expert opinion on matters national and international by their drivers because they cannot hear through the one-inch bulletproof plastic that separates them from their cabbies. Although this insulation from taxi drivers' loquaciousness may not evoke an overwhelming sense of loss in many, the fact remains that the plastic shield starkly symbolizes the high incidence of violence that has befallen urban cabdrivers.

The foregoing examples are illustrative of how we adapt our lifestyles to the threat of crime and violence. To accommodate the criminal, we reshape our lives. Fear masters us. Such capitulations to our ap-

* I should in fairness note that currently, thanks mainly to aggressive and tough-minded, yet innovative crime-fighting techniques adopted by police chief Jerry Wilson, inroads are being made into the crime problems of the nation's capital. Nevertheless, as of this writing its streets are still deserted at night.

prehensions are a far cry from realizing the right to be safe, a right the law-abiding individual should be able to expect the government to secure for him.

The exact-fare requirement on most city buses provides perhaps as graphic an example as can be found of our accommodation to our environment of fear: (a) bus drivers, being generally unarmed and easy targets, are robbed with increasing frequency; (b) instead of coping with the problem by apprehending, convicting, and incarcerating the robbers for long terms, we adapt to the problem by requiring that all passengers deposit the exact change in a locked fare box so that the driver has no money for would-be robbers to take; thus (c) the situation is accommodated to the robbers, who will now select another class of victims. But it is society that is victimized by this capitulation.

Until our society rebels at such accommodation to criminal activities, until we begin to strike at the robbers themselves rather than out of fear accommodating our lives to them and all they represent, our right to be safe will continue to be illusory and society as a whole will continue to be victimized by our environment of fear.

Society As a Victim of the Terroristic Crime

During the late 1960s and early 1970s society was also victimized by the revolutionary criminal. During this period, we Americans witnessed uncounted acts of terrorism and revolutionary crime—primarily from the radical Left—including hundreds of bombings, arsons, attacks on law-enforcement officers, forced closings of colleges and universities, riots, and attempts to "close down" various institutions, even the government of the United States.

It must be emphasized that these were, purely and simply, *crimes.* Efforts were made then, and are still being made, to rationalize the acts of the terrorists and revolutionaries as mere examples of "political expression" by "dissidents" exercising their "constitutional rights" to protest various government policies with which they happened not to agree.

Nothing could be further from the truth. There is nothing in the Constitution of the United States that gives anyone the right to blow up a building, shoot at policemen, or deny by force the right of others to use public buildings or streets. Yet each of these illegal acts took place time and again.

There were, to be sure, individual victims. For example, Robert Fassnacht, a graduate student, was murdered in the bombing of the mathematics building at the University of Wisconsin in 1970. But to a far greater extent, society was victimized by this era of revolutionary crime. Tens of thousands of law-abiding citizens and students who were not permitted to go about their business in peace because small but vocal and violent groups resorted to violence to further their aims became victims of the terrorists.

Nor is terroristic crime on a national scale a thing of the past. In 1973 the New York City Police Department linked a group known as the Black Liberation Army, reputedly responsible for killing policemen in the New York area, to robberies and ambushes in St. Louis, North Carolina, and California.[44]

In the San Francisco Bay area the Symbionese Liberation Army kidnapped the daughter of newspaper publisher Randolph A. Hearst. This same organization claimed credit for the murder of Marcus A. Foster, the superintendent of schools of Oakland, and has been connected with the seemingly random murder of four white persons in San Francisco.[45]

The wave of bombings in this country is far from over. The FBI reported that from January through September 1973 there were 1,430 bombing incidents in the United States, Puerto Rico, and the Virgin Islands: 704 incidents involved explosive devices, 726 involved incendiary devices. Eleven persons were killed and 138 persons were injured in these attacks. Targets included: 428 residences, 353 commercial operations and office buildings, 133 school facilities, and 65 law-enforcement personnel, buildings, and/or equipment.[46]

Thus society continues to be victimized by the lunatic fringe, which believes it has some sort of God-given right to employ tactics of violence, terrorism, and intimidation to gain its ends.

In this chapter I have singled out three "special" classes of victims, advancing reasons why each class should be deemed special. This categorization is not at all meant to negate the plight of the other victims of crime. Basic to the thesis of this book is the proposition that when anyone is victimized—whether in a "special" category or not—the criminal justice system has failed in its duty to protect the law-abiding from the lawless. We'll look now at just how, and to what extent, the law-abiding are in fact victimized.

Part II
The Criminal Justice System vs. The Victims

3
Overview:
A Faltering System

A CRIMINAL JUSTICE SYSTEM MUST HAVE ONE, and only one, primary function: the protection of the innocent. Certainly the means by which this protection is accomplished should be basically fair to those who become embroiled in the system; the fundamental rights of our citizens, guaranteed by our Constitution, must be preserved. But in attempting to balance the rights of victim and criminal, the system, first and foremost, should be geared to seeing to it that decent, law-abiding people are not left to the mercies of the lawless and violent elements in our society.

A criminal justice system that prides itself upon the scrupulosity with which it safeguards the rights of the criminal suspect, *and* that is able to safeguard the rights of the law-abiding to be reasonably free from criminal harm, has achieved the necessary balance and can regard itself as an unmitigated success. However, a system that erects an elaborate thicket of contrived and artificial protections around the criminal accused, but that is unable to secure the right of noncriminals to go about their business in peace, is totally out of balance and is in fact a complete failure.

If a perfect criminal justice system existed, it would accomplish its primary function by preventing *all* criminally inclined individuals from victimizing the innocent. Such a system, however, does not exist. Even the best police force—the preventive arm of the criminal justice system—cannot be everywhere at once and prevent every criminal act.

No one in his right mind, then, can fault the system for being unable to effect a perfect crime-prevention program.

Conceding this, I contend that the system still has an overriding obligation to protect the law-abiding. When the preventive function fails, which by definition is every time someone is victimized by a criminal, the system still has a basic duty to perform. It must make every effort to apprehend the criminal, bring him to justice, and punish him for the crime he has committed in order: 1) to vindicate the rights of his victim; 2) to isolate him and therefore prevent him from victimizing others; and 3) to deter others from following his example.

Even this obligation cannot, as a practical matter, be fulfilled in every case. The police simply cannot make an arrest every time a crime is committed. There are more criminals than there are policemen; the latter can no more make an arrest for every crime than they can prevent every crime from happening in the first place. Additionally, some crimes are impossible of solution: cases in which the victim has been killed and there are no other witnesses; cases in which the victim is unable or unwilling to identify his assailant; cases in which the criminal has been smart enough—or lucky enough—not to leave any clues; and, finally, cases in which the perpetrator has fled the jurisdiction or gone into hiding. (Of course, if the police willfully or corruptly fail to investigate a crime or refuse to apprehend a known perpetrator, then the victim has a valid complaint against them for neglect of duty; cases such as this, however, are the exception rather than the rule.)

Conceding then that we can neither prevent all crimes nor bring every criminal to account for his misdeeds, the system still has the obligation to do what it can to protect the innocent. Once a suspect in a criminal case has been apprehended and formally accused, the system —recalling its overriding duty to secure the rights of the law-abiding— should isolate that suspect from society before trial if he appears to pose a threat to others. It should then proceed to try the accused as speedily as it can and in such a manner as to ensure the likelihood that the truth regarding his guilt or innocence will be brought out.

Finally, if the accused is convicted, the system should deal with him expeditiously, by reasonable and speedy postconviction processes. This done, we may hope that he will not repeat his crime because: a) he has been made aware that the risks of committing further crimes are too great; or b) he has been isolated from all other potential victims; or c) he has been rehabilitated. Further, the manner with which he has been dealt by the criminal justice system should serve to deter others from committing crimes themselves.

What this all boils down to is that a criminal justice system, to be effective, must guarantee to the law-abiding that the criminal law will be *swiftly and surely* enforced against the lawless. This way, and only this way, the system can perform its protective function.

The criminal justice system that has just been described in theoretical terms is characterized by the fact that its primary concern is the rights of actual and potential victims of crime. Unfortunately for the law-abiding citizens of the United States, such a victim-oriented system bears not the slightest resemblance to the system under which they now live.

As noted, our criminal justice system directs almost the entire protective apparatus inherent in it towards the criminal accused and the convicted criminal. Other nations whose systems of law are similar to ours—that is, the common-law countries: England, Scotland, Wales, Canada, Australia, and New Zealand—have criminal justice systems that do concern themselves with the rights of the innocent. This happy state of affairs does not, to be sure, totally exclude the rights of the accused; it does, however, represent a better balance between the rights of the criminal and those of his victim. In these countries, for example, the criminal process is a search for the truth and the suspect is not permitted to escape the consequences of his acts by taking advantage of a maze of legal technicalities designed for the sole purpose of suppressing the truth. If his guilt is indicated, he is called to account.

Our system, in comparison, does not even begin to search for the truth or for a balance between the victim's rights and the violator's. If one wishes to know the full extent to which our system is out of balance, the entire system must be described as a unified whole; each imbalance, in favor of the criminal and against the victim, forms a part of that whole. This chapter, then, presents an overview of the system, so that each imbalance may be put into this perspective. In the following chapters the details of the antivictim imbalances inherent in the system will be analyzed.

Consider the path of the criminal through the criminal justice system; view it through the eyes of his victim. Assume that a given individual has committed a serious crime—murder, rape, robbery, or theft. First of all, the statistical chances are great that the perpetrator of the crime is a repeater. Here the imbalance begins, for it is obvious that if the criminal has victimized before, the criminal justice system in dealing with him has failed to deter him, or to isolate him, or to rehabilitate him. Hence he was at liberty and of a mind to victimize again.

Now an innocent citizen is victimized. What is his immediate reaction? If the crime is violent, then there will be the physical outrage and pain inflicted by the assailant. There will be monetary loss from medical bills, loss of work, etc. Even if the crime is non-violent—say the burglary of a house or an apartment while the occupants are away —there will surely be the monetary loss of what was stolen along with the outrage of being victimized.

Pain, outrage, loss—these are emotions every victim feels, and quite justifiably. Yet there are many victims who, despite their feelings, simply do not report the crimes. Again, the failure of the criminal justice system is demonstrated when those who have been victimized have so little faith in the ability of the system to vindicate their rights that they don't even bother to report the crime. One reason for this may be that of the coed in Washington, D.C. (see chapter one) who was the victim of a rape but whom the system treated as a defendant. Another could be fear of reprisals if the crime is reported, particularly if it was committed in the ghetto. For example, in an in-depth article on crime in a Los Angeles ghetto, the *National Observer* quotes a "middle-aged black mother" on street gangs:

> The gangs brag about it and threaten us: "You tell the pigs and you're next." A lady here had just painted her house and some kids really messed it up with spray paint. She told the police, and the day before she was to go to court against them her house was burned down. The gang told her if she talked she'd be next. She's moving. I don't blame her. I would be. I can't afford nothing but this big dog I just got.[1]

Persons unfortunate enough to be in the position of this black mother have a real incentive not to report a crime, especially if it is likely that nothing will be done to prevent further terrorization.

The failure of victims and witnesses to report a crime or to identify the perpetrators is now fairly common. Even if a crime is reported, and the perpetrator is identified and apprehended, the victim (and any witnesses to the crime in support of the victim) may yet have much to fear, because in our system the criminal accused will likely be released on bail or upon his own recognizance—that is, his personal promise to appear. As we saw in chapter one, the California Supreme Court ruled, with lofty disdain for the victims of crime, that a court could not deny bail to an accused no matter how dangerous he might be to society. This attitude is prevalent in the criminal justice system. Criminals who are patently dangerous to society are released, time and again, on little or no bail to continue their criminal careers or to terrorize those who might be witnesses against them.

Had the young arsonists, described above in the *National Observer* article, actually been arrested by the Los Angeles police and charged with the crime, it is a virtual certainty that they would have been released prior to trial, enabling them further to terrorize or kill their victim.

Fear of reprisal dominates the lives of the victims and witnesses.

Superintendent James M. Rochford of the Chicago Police Department has described an incredible case history:

> Let me relate a factual history of [a] gang leader as an example of the present system. While incarcerated in Stateville penitentiary, he recruited a gang of robbers and murderers. Four weeks after his release, he and his gang held up a tavern. Two days later, the gang decided that the bartender could identify them, so four of the robbers returned to the tavern and shot the bartender ten times. Later, in an attempt to intimidate an undertaker who had witnessed one of their robberies and who was under police protection, the gang exhumed a body and threw it through the window of the undertaker's establishment.
>
> Their viciousness reached a peak following their apprehension for the robbery of a drug store. The druggist, despite their threats, testified against them. Four weeks later they kidnapped the 51-year-old druggist and a 71-year-old female assistant, shot them, doused them with gasoline and set them afire.
>
> Our neighboring community, Evanston, also felt the effects of this gang when they stabbed and shot to death the manager and assistant manager of a restaurant during the commission of a robbery. The identity of one of the perpetrators was established, so his own gang shot and burned him beyond recognition.
>
> These six murders were committed within a two month period.
>
> Within the next four weeks, their infamous record also includes the shooting and killing of another robbery victim. Plus, they shot and wounded a police officer who interrupted their attempt to commit still another robbery . . . the leader of the gang now is free on bail and roaming your streets.[2]

The following case forcibly illustrates the failure of our criminal justice system to protect anyone except the criminal. Mrs. Georgia Carradine, who lived in a Chicago ghetto housing project, was unfortunate enough to witness a murder. After identifying the perpetrator to the police, she was threatened by gang members. Told that if she testified she and her children would be killed, Mrs. Carradine refused to testify. Our criminal justice system, as exemplified by the courts of Illinois, promptly responded, forcibly. It locked up Mrs. Carradine. Had Governor Richard Ogilvie not intervened and granted her executive clemency, Mrs. Carradine would have had to serve a six-month sentence for her refusal to testify, despite the fact that it was conceded that she was in very real terror of her life.[3]

Now this is unbelievable. Mrs. Carradine's fear was well founded. The Chicago gangs are among the toughest in the world and gang murders in the Chicago ghetto are daily occurrences. Additionally, gang members have been known to receive exceptionally lenient treatment from the Chicago courts. For example, in 1972 a trial judge in

Chicago granted probation to a youth who shot to death a sixteen-year-old girl in a random sniper slaying.[4]

The case of Mrs. Carradine is a classic example of the failure of our criminal justice system. The system 1) failed to get tough with those who terrorize the ghettos; 2) admittedly could not offer her anything realistic in the way of protection from those who had threatened to kill her; yet, 3) sought to send her to prison for refusing to testify, despite the acknowledged threat on her life and her children's lives. Perhaps if she had testified and had been killed, the killer would have wound up before the same Chicago judge and received probation also.

Prior to trial, the accused may take advantage of delaying tactics such as continuances and postponements, which in some courts are allowed to the defense almost indefinitely. These tactics are used, often successfully, in the hope that the victim and any witnesses against the accused may eventually give up in disgust; after losing many days of work, they show up one day for trial only to be told that the case "has been continued again."

Then, as the trial date approaches, the accused may be permitted to plead guilty to a much lesser offense. Our courts are now so clogged that prosecutors are put in the unhappy position of having to negotiate guilty pleas to charges that have been reduced out of all proportion to the seriousness of the offense. If every criminal accused demanded a trial, the system would simply collapse of its own weight; therefore, the defendant is in a bargaining position to get the best possible "deal" in return for not forcing the prosecution to go to trial. The blame for the clogged criminal dockets belongs, at least in part, to the system, which has set up so many time-consuming procedural "safeguards" around the accused that a criminal trial to determine guilt or innocence may last for months. The prosecutor, then, is not at fault for having to engage in plea bargaining. But this is small comfort to the victim of a robbery and pistol whipping who is forced to spend a month in the hospital where he learns his assailants have received six-months probation in return for their pleas of guilty to simple assault.

Finally, the accused is brought to trial. Now, as has been stated, a criminal trial in other countries with legal systems similar to ours is a search for the truth. The question is: Did the defendant commit the act of which he stands accused? Evidence that is relevant to the issues and probative of his guilt or innocence is presented to the judge or jury by the prosecutor. Defense counsel presents the case for the accused. If the evidence of the prosecution indicates guilt beyond a reasonable doubt, then the defendant is usually found guilty.

No such system exists in the United States today. In the 1960s, decision after decision of the United States Supreme Court, under Chief

Justice Earl Warren, turned the criminal trial, which should be used to search for the truth, into a charade. In case after case now, a criminal defendant, whose factual guilt is patent, is able to keep the most overwhelming evidence of his guilt from the knowledge of those who are sitting in judgment as to his guilt or innocence. All he need do is prove that the police or prosecution, in securing the evidence, infringed his "rights" in the slightest manner.

For example, the Warren Court fashioned and refined a handy device for the defendant called the "Exclusionary Rule," which serves one single purpose: the suppression of the truth. Under our criminal justice system—unlike any other system in the world—if a defendant can convince a judge or a majority of an appeals court that evidence of his guilt was obtained in a manner that violated any of an ever-growing body of contrived rights, then the defendant is entitled to have that evidence suppressed. This means it cannot be considered by a judge or jury in weighing his guilt. In cases in which the evidence, which must be suppressed, is necessary to prove the guilt of the accused, the application of this rule can have but one of two results. Either the prosecutor will be forced to dismiss the charges for lack of evidence that he can use in court, or, if the trial has begun, the judge will be forced to dismiss the case and watch the accused walk out of court a free man, while his victim sits there wondering what our criminal justice system is all about.

Now in the great majority of criminal trials there are three principal ways to prove the guilt of the accused: physical evidence, statements of the accused, and eyewitness identification of the accused. These are the same three areas in which the Warren Court acted to keep the truth from being heard. Because the scope of such rulings of the Warren Court will be covered in some detail in the next chapter, it is only necessary to deal with them briefly here in order to gain an overview of the lengths to which the contrived rights of defendants have been extended, via the suppression of the truth, in our criminal justice system. Here, surely, the imbalance between victim and criminal is most marked.

1. *Physical Evidence* Under the exclusionary rule, physical evidence cannot be admitted against an accused if this evidence was procured by an "illegal" arrest or search and seizure by law-enforcement officers. Physical evidence—a pistol, a bloodstained T-shirt, money taken in a robbery, a fingerprint, a blood sample, or narcotics—is the most reliable evidence available and in many cases the only kind available to police officers in criminal cases. Thus, if a police officer investigating a criminal case makes an arrest or conducts a search and seizure that is later found to be "illegal," the fruits of the arrest or search and seizure—that is, physical evidence that may overwhelmingly indicate the guilt of the

accused—must be suppressed. The stated (but never proven) purpose of the exclusionary rule is to "punish" the police for their "illegal" conduct. The victim of the crime is, of course, also punished by having the criminal freed by the suppression of the truth; as are future victims of that criminal, should he continue his criminal habits. The only one who is not punished is the one who should be—the criminal.

The ridiculous lengths to which the concept of "illegal" search and seizure is taken is illustrated by a case described in an article emanating from California and reprinted here in its entirety from the *Denver Post* of January 30, 1970:

> A baby has the same rights as anyone else and therefore forcible searches of his or her diapers without the infant's consent are unconstitutional.
>
> The ruling came in Municipal Court Friday in the pretrial hearing of a man and woman who were arrested after detectives found heroin in the diapers of a 9-month-old baby girl.
>
> Ramona Padilla and her companion, Robert G. Cordova, both of Colton, California, were arrested Dec. 29 after the drug was discovered in the diapers by narcotics detectives.
>
> The defense argued at Friday's hearing that the search of the baby was illegal because the baby didn't give her consent and there was no evidence justifying a forcible search.
>
> However, Deputy District Attorney Joseph A. Burns argued that the Fourth Amendment, which protects against unwarranted searches, didn't apply to a baby.
>
> "It's ridiculous to say that a baby has a right to a speedy trial or the right to counsel," Burns said. "A baby would have no occasion to demand such rights." Since a baby doesn't have the capacity to do so, he argued, it shouldn't have the right to protection from the amendment.
>
> In the end, however, Municipal Court Judge Theodore G. Krumm disagreed. A baby has the rights of a person, he said, and therefore must be afforded the protection of the Constitution. The case was dismissed.
>
> Later, Burns told reports, "By legal standards, it is an interesting case. But practically, the ruling could cause lots of trouble. Now everyone will know that's the place to hide narcotics—in their baby's diapers."

Complicating the problem for policemen is the fact that very few judges can agree upon what precisely constitutes an illegal search and seizure. Hence, a policeman, untrained in the law, yet acting in good faith, as were the officers who searched the baby's diapers, may find himself "second-guessed" by a judge and suffer the frustration of watching an obviously guilty defendant go free.

2. *Statements by the Accused* When a criminal suspect voluntarily confesses a crime or makes a statement that implicates him in a crime, the jury should be entitled to know this. Until 1966 this common-sense rule was the law of the land—once a judge ruled that a con-

fession or admission was voluntarily made, apart from force or threats or promises of leniency, then it was admissible in evidence.

A five-man majority of the Warren Court changed all of that in *Miranda* v. *Arizona*,[5] mentioned in chapter one. Whether the statement was voluntarily made no longer mattered. If a defendant could show that the police interrogators erred in the slightest in giving him a required litany of warnings of his rights, then he was entitled to have his confession or admission excluded from the jury. In case after case, because of the *Miranda* decision, confessed murderers, rapists, robbers, and other criminals walked out of court free men, sometimes to kill, rape, rob, or otherwise victimize again. Their "rights" had been violated so they must be freed; the rights of actual and potential victims simply did not enter into the picture.

An actual case illustrates this. On February 27, 1970, U.S. Customs agents in Milwaukee intercepted a package of hashish sent from Nepal and addressed to a young Milwaukee attorney. With the permission of the senior partner, the agents staked out the law office where the addressee of the package worked, and observed the young lawyer receive the package. After the lawyer left work for the day he was arrested on the street and immediately advised of his rights, pursuant to the *Miranda* ruling. He admitted to a customs agent that the package was in his lock box at the law firm. Later a U.S. district court judge ruled that this voluntary confession, *made by an attorney*, was inadmissible in evidence against him because he had not sufficiently waived his rights. The judge also ruled that the hashish seized from the defendant's lock box was inadmissible, in part because the agents learned of the lock box through an "illegal" interrogation. Again, the truth was suppressed in a tortuous attempt to protect the "rights" of a practicing attorney knowingly engaged in narcotics smuggling.

3. *Eyewitness Identification*   Often during the commission of a crime the victim or a witness will get a good enough look at the perpetrator to identify him in court. The police, in order to make sure that the identification is accurate, usually conduct a lineup. Prior to 1967, if the trial judge was satisfied that the lineup was conducted reasonably fairly and the witness's identification was reliable, the witness or victim was permitted to testify that he had identified the suspect in a lineup and then to identify the suspect in court. The Warren Court changed all of this. In a three-case series the Court ruled that "fairness" to the suspect required that the accused have an attorney present at every lineup and if the attorney was not present (or his presence was not waived), the witness could not testify in court about having identified the suspect in the lineup. In some cases, the witness or victim was not even permitted to testify as to the identity of the suspect in open

court, even though the victim or witness had stated that he could positively identify the suspect.[6] Thus, if there was no evidence against the suspect except the identification of the victim or witness, then he must be released.

The particular series of "lineup" cases decided by the Warren Court was significantly modified in 1972 by the "new" Supreme Court under Chief Justice Warren E. Burger.[7] Nevertheless, some of our state courts still adhere to the rigid rule of the earlier decision and in these states the truth continues to be suppressed.

The foregoing examples portray the manner in which the defendant in a criminal trial can take advantage of minor, even highly technical, errors by the police and, as a result, can have relevant and probative evidence of his guilt excluded from his trial. Should a criminal proceed to trial, and should evidence of his guilt be admitted against him, many criminals still have a fall-back position in the insanity defense. The basic question is: Should a criminal go free because he claims that he was "crazy" at the time of the offense? In far too many cases—particularly in cases involving sex crimes—this is precisely what happens.

A *Washington Star-News* editorial reprinted in *Human Events* cites, as an example of this, the case of a marine stationed in Virginia who kidnapped a waitress at gunpoint and took her on a ten-day trip. After he was caught and brought to trial he was found not guilty by reason of insanity and a federal judge concluded that he had no choice but to release this dangerous man into society.

This happens far too often. The safety of society, of victims such as the kidnapped waitress, and of potential victims is clearly involved. No one seriously contends that those who are really insane should be jailed. But neither should they be released. Nevertheless, our system now, completely preoccupied with the accused, does release people found to be dangerously insane to prey again upon the innocent.

Thus, we see major advantages to the criminal from the commission of the crime through the criminal trial. The same advantage lies with a defendant, should he have been convicted, on appeal. He can ask the appellate courts to review every aspect of his conviction. If he can convince one or more appellate judges that the trial judge improperly admitted evidence against him such as a confession, items of physical evidence, or a courtroom identification, then the entire proceeding begins anew. He may be awarded a new trial with the evidence suppressed or, in some cases, the appellate court may dismiss the charges against him.

The appellate system in the United States in criminal cases is cumbersome beyond belief and works to the definite advantage of the criminal defendant. Under recent court rulings every convicted person must have access to the appellate courts. If one cannot afford the costs of appeal, free legal counsel must be provided. The process is never ending. A person convicted in a state court, for example, may appeal through each state appellate level to his state supreme court. This process, because of crowded appellate court dockets, may take years, during which time the criminal may be free on appeal bond. Should he lose in the courts of his states he can ask the Supreme Court of the United States to review his conviction. Should the Supreme Court refuse, that would seem to be the end of it. But it is not. The convict may then go to the federal courts and start over, claiming in a petition for habeas corpus that his state conviction violated his constitutional rights. In the federal system the state defendant can then go through the U.S. District Court and the U.S. Court of Appeals back to the Supreme Court once more.

What this appellate merry-go-round amounts to is that there is simply no finality to a criminal conviction in our system. An Oregon case, decided by the U.S. Supreme Court in June 1972, presents an example of this cumbersome process.

In August 1967 in Portland, Oregon, Mrs. Doris Murphy was murdered. Her husband Daniel Murphy was arrested, tried, and convicted for the crime. During the investigation, the police took from Murphy, without a warrant, fingernail scrapings that were admitted into evidence against him. He appealed his conviction, alleging in part that the taking of his fingernail scrapings was an "illegal search and seizure." The Oregon Court of Appeals ruled that the taking of the fingernail scrapings was proper and upheld Murphy's conviction. The Oregon Supreme Court refused to review his conviction as did the Supreme Court of the United States. Murphy then sought review in the federal court system via a petition for habeas corpus in the U.S. District Court in Oregon. There he again alleged that his state conviction violated his constitutional rights. The U.S. District Court upheld his conviction and he appealed to the U.S. Court of Appeals for the Ninth Circuit. There a three-judge panel, *five years and nine months after the crime*, in an unsigned one-page opinion, ruled that the taking of his fingernail scrapings was an "illegal search and seizure"; it ordered a new trial for Murphy with the fingernail scrapings suppressed. The state of Oregon appealed the case to the U.S. Supreme Court, which ruled in June 1973 that the taking of Murphy's fingernail scrapings was proper and that his conviction should be affirmed.[8]

To a layman, and to many lawyers, this case is almost unbelievable. Prior to the final U.S. Supreme Court decision, five courts, including the highest courts in Oregon and the United States, had upheld Murphy's conviction or refused to review a lower-court decision upholding the conviction. Yet three judges, almost six years after the crime, with one stroke of the pen were able to overturn the holdings of the five previous courts. Now, no knowledge of the law of search and seizure superior to that of all the judges of the other courts that had reviewed the case lies in the three judges of the court of appeals that reversed Murphy's conviction. Yet such are the rights of convicted criminals in our criminal justice system that they permit a convicted murderer to shop around until he can find a court sufficiently liberal to discover suddenly that his "rights" were violated and his conviction must be reversed.

Murphy was convicted of the brutal strangling of his wife. She, the victim, naturally received no thought from the appeals court that found a violation of Murphy's "rights." But consider now the position of the state of Oregon prior to the U.S. Supreme Court's reversal of the court of appeals. If the court of appeals decision had been upheld, Oregon would have had to try Murphy again, without the fingernail scrapings that helped convict him, or it would have had to release him. Oregon would have faced the very difficult position of being forced to retry a man for a crime committed six years ago. Witnesses might well be unavailable, evidence might have been disposed of, and the prosecutor who handled his case, and who would know more about its trial strategy than anyone else, might no longer be with the prosecutor's office. A realistic decision might have to be made that it would now be impossible to retry Murphy successfully at this late date. On the other hand, the state of Oregon had a very legitimate interest in seeing that wife murderers are not simply set free. The state of Oregon took the proper step of appealing the court of appeals decision to the Supreme Court of the United States; as matters turned out, it was successful. Obviously, however, the Supreme Court cannot review *every* case in which a federal court chooses to nullify the considered decisions of state courts, so the problem presented by the *Murphy* case—that of permitting a convicted criminal to shop around until he can find a court to agree that somehow his rights were violated—still remains.

The *Murphy* case illustrates another aspect of the criminal justice system: judicial nit-picking, whereby appellate courts in a series of mental gymnastics search out a "violation of rights" that requires a patently guilty and previously convicted defendant to be freed. Judicial nit-picking in this case is found in the absolute refusal of the court of appeals to consider any of the practicalities involved in the police investigation. The Portland police had ample reason to believe that Murphy strangled his wife. Because her body had deep scratches on it, there was additional reason to believe that traces of her skin and blood would be under the fingernails of the murderer. When Murphy came to police headquarters, later to be joined by his attorneys, the police, over Murphy's protests, took the fingernail scrapings from him. The U.S. court of appeals ruled that the police should have secured a search warrant to scrape his fingernails—a classic example of judicial nit-picking.

Consider the position of the police: they had already asked Murphy for permission to take the scrapings and had been refused. So it is clear that he knew what they wanted to do. If he was not aware that there might be damning evidence under his fingernails *before* he came to the police station, he certainly was aware of this fact after he was asked to consent to the scraping. If the police had taken the time to get a warrant to scrape his fingernails, what would Murphy have done? The Oregon Court of Appeals, which first upheld Murphy's conviction, answered:

> Unless the defendant were bound, manacled, guarded or by some other means placed in a position where he could not clip his fingernails, scrape the nails of one hand with the nails of another, put his fingers in his mouth or go to the lavatory from the time the police asked him for permission to take fingernail scrapings until the time that they sought and obtained a warrant, it was entirely likely that the evidence would have been destroyed in the interim.[9]

Thus, we see two courts reaching diametrically opposite conclusions on the same fact situation. The Oregon appeals court took the common-sense approach that had the fingernail scrapings not been taken when they were, the evidence would have disappeared. The U.S. court of appeals refused to consider the practical aspects of the case and considered only the defendant's "rights"—one of which would have been the "right" to rid his person of evidence of murder before the police were able to seize it. When a criminal is permitted to cast about until he finds a court that will create a newly conceived "right" to destroy evidence against him, then that court system is far over-balanced in favor of the criminal. In a word, trials and appeals in our system are, quite frankly, weighted in favor of the accused and against the victim.

We turn now to examine, in this overview, the corrections function of the system including the sentencing function of the courts, which function is the path into the corrections system. If, ideally, the primary and overriding concern of the criminal justice system were for the innocent and the victims of crime, then it seems clear that the general premise underlying the sentencing and the corrections functions should be to deal with both the convicted criminal to be sentenced and the sentenced criminal entering into the corrections system in a manner that would ensure the greatest safety to the law-abiding. Then and only then should sentencing judges and corrections officials turn to the offender and say: "Now we shall see what we can do to help *you.*"

Without doubt, sentencing and corrections are two of the most difficult problems facing the criminal justice system today. It is a fact that most of our prisons are not very pleasant places for the criminal to be and that they do not do much that is useful in the way of rehabilitating the criminal. It is also a fact that hospital emergency rooms and morgues are not very pleasant places for the victims of crime to be. Finally, it is a fact that until we learn how to rehabilitate offenders so that they will not return to a life of crime after leaving prisons, we are going to continue to have a rearrest record of fifty percent or more. Unfortunately, as our recidivism rate glaringly indicates, we are nowhere near to the solution of the rehabilitation problem. The sorry state of the science of rehabilitation in this country was described with admirable candor by Leonard Orland, professor of law at the University of Connecticut and a former member of the parole board of that state. Writing in the *New York Times* about the Attica prison revolt, Mr. Orland stated flatly: "In point of fact, we are not even sure how to go about the task of rehabilitation."[10]

Basically then, given the fact that prisons are not the finest of places and that rehabilitation is a goal more often sought than obtained, the question facing sentencing judges and corrections people is whether the primary object of their concern is going to be the safety of the law-abiding public or what is best for the offender with whom they have to deal.

A case that arose in Rochester, New York, presents the sentencing question squarely. Judge David O. Boehm of Monroe County Court in Rochester had before him for sentencing a homosexual who had been convicted of first-degree assault. In fact, the defendant had stabbed his victim repeatedly, causing him to require some 150 stitches. Judge Boehm placed the defendant on probation rather than send him to Attica because, as a homosexual, he might be "dehumanized if not killed" there. Judge Boehm also told him to stay away from his victim.[11]

This incident vividly portrays the victims of crime as being only incidental in the criminal justice system. The defendant, judging from his act of violence, is a dangerous man. He may stay away from his former victim as ordered by Judge Boehm, or he may not. He may refrain from cutting somebody else up, he may not. This is a factor that Judge Boehm, not being clairvoyant, cannot know. And it is *precisely this fact* that makes this case so disturbing. The judge has opted *for the risk to society rather than the risk to the criminal.*

76

When someone commits an act of violence—murder, rape, robbery, or assault—it can be fairly assumed that in the greatest majority of such cases the criminal is a dangerous man. When a sentencing judge, like Judge Boehm (or the Chicago judge who placed on probation the young murderer who shot a girl to death in a sniper attack), elects to return such people to the streets through the devices of suspended sentences or probation, he is, beyond question, placing the rights of the criminal above the rights of 1) the actual victim, 2) the potential victims of the person released, and 3) potential victims of other criminals who are comforted by the fact that if they are brought to justice for their crimes, they may also be the beneficiaries of similar leniency. The law-abiding citizen has a tremendous stake in such dispositions.

A similar rationale applies to parole boards that are confronted with the decision to release upon society those who may or may not victimize again. In chapter one we saw the case of the Iowa Parole Board releasing William Sweeney, the murderer of a police chief, after he had served but two and a half years of a seventy-five-year sentence. This decision not only mocks the memory of the slain officer, but might result in more murders of Iowa law-enforcement officers by felons encouraged by the leniency shown to Sweeney. Additionally, the Iowa Parole Board's starry-eyed conclusion that Sweeney was rehabilitated was erroneous. He was arrested for burglary just six months later.

The questions that the homosexual case in Rochester and Sweeney's case raise are fundamental. Granted that incarceration is likely to do a convict very little good and may indeed harm him, to whom is the first consideration due: the convicted criminal or the law-abiding citizen? If leniency shown to an individual who has already demonstrated a capacity for violence results in the victimization of another, then has not the system that produced such leniency failed completely in its duty to the law-abiding? In such cases should there not be some accountability by the source of the original leniency?

This chapter is merely an overview; questions such as these will be discussed in detail in chapter five. The cases of the homosexual and William Sweeney are not isolated instances; it is obvious that even in the sentencing and corrections aspect of the system, far too often the victim of crime is relegated to the forgotten-man status.

The *Wall Street Journal*, in an editorial deploring the 1973 shooting of Senator John Stennis, voiced a similar concern with the rights of society *vis-à-vis* the criminal. The editorial noted that one reason we have so much crime is that, frankly, crime pays. It concluded ruefully:

It pays because the average criminal no longer fears being punished, even if he is caught. Overworked police forces, crowded court calendars, misplaced social concern and a penologist reaction against imprisonment on the ground that it fails to rehabilitate, have given criminals the edge— and given society the short end of the stick.[12]

In sum, the criminal justice system is incredibly permissive towards the wrongdoer. From crime through trial, appeal, sentence, and corrections, forces in the system heavily favor the violator; the victim . . . who cares?

4

The Warren Court* vs. the Victims: Suppression of the Truth

THE UNITED STATES SUPREME COURT under the chief justiceship, and to a large extent under the personal leadership, of Earl Warren during the

*"Warren Court" is in essence a shorthand phrase that recognizes both the chief justiceship and the liberal leadership of Earl Warren. Of course, Black, Douglas, Brennan, Goldberg, and Fortas were also part of the liberal block of the Court and in some cases their leadership eclipsed their chief's. Additionally, any comments on "liberal" and "conservative" justices are not unvarying because justices varied in their feelings. Black, for instance, believed that First and Fifth Amendment guarantees were absolute while on Fourth Amendment issues there was no more hard-line member of the court. Finally, any characterizations made herein deal only with the criminal-law area. The following is the general lineup of the Warren Court from 1960 to 1969.

Liberal Block	*Conservative Block*
Earl Warren (retired 1969)	Potter Stewart (sitting)
William O. Douglas (sitting)	Tom Clark (resigned 1967)
William J. Brennan (sitting)	Byron White (sitting)
Hugo Black (died 1971)	Felix Frankfurter (resigned 1962)
Arthur Goldberg (resigned 1965)	Charles Evans Whittaker (resigned 1962)
Abe Fortas (resigned 1969)	John M. Harlan (died 1971)
Thurgood Marshall (sitting)	

During the most active years of the Warren Revolution the lineup was:
Liberals: Warren, Black, Douglas, Brennan, Goldberg, Fortas, and Marshall.
Conservatives: Stewart, White, Clark, and Harlan.

79

Sixties left this country a very definite legacy in the field of criminal law. Sometimes the 1960-69 period of jurisprudence is referred to as the "Warren Revolution," and not without reason. The criminal law, or, more properly, the enforcement of the criminal law, was indeed revolutionized. Surely there is no other more controversial issue facing this country than the extent to which the revolution was a good thing or a bad thing.

Liberals and civil libertarians, at least those to whom *any* state or federal power *per se* infringes personal liberties, believe that the Warren Revolution was the greatest thing in the world. They praise the Court in ringing tones for enforcing the Constitution for all by vindicating the individuals' rights against abuse by the government, and by protecting the poor and the powerless. To a point those who praise the Warren Revolution are correct. Certain of the Court's decisions dealt with and to a large extent improved the *fundamental fairness* of the criminal justice process. It is difficult to see how anyone, no matter his outlook on law and order, could quarrel with such rulings as those guaranteeing the right to counsel to indigent defendants, requiring the prosecution to provide the defense with information in its possession favorable to the defendant, and guaranteeing to all defendants the right to a fair trial free of prejudicial publicity.

Critics of the Warren Court, however, believe that the Court, in many other decisions, went far beyond the basic principles of fundamental fairness and created by judicial rulings a body of law structured to protect only the guilty criminal from the consequences of his acts. Such decisions, the critics argue, result in a situation in which the rights of the law-abiding—particularly the poor and the powerless—against abuse by the lawless and violent are not vindicated at all. For example, as noted, many today are afraid to leave their homes at night for fear of criminal violence. Just how much good does it do these people to know that their rights against government interference are so zealously guarded if they are made virtual prisoners in their homes by the criminals?

One of the chief exponents of the theory that the Warren Revolution went too far is Senator John L. McClellan, Democrat of Arkansas. As chairman of the Criminal Laws and Procedures Subcommittee of the Judiciary Committee of the United States Senate, Senator McClellan, in the legislative branch, is almost as powerful a figure in our criminal justice system as is the chief justice of the United States. The senator is a hard-liner on crime. He is also aware that the pendulum can swing too far in either direction and has been vigilant to ensure that bills before his subcommittee do not violate elements of essential fairness to the accused.

In a Senate speech in August 1969, Senator McClellan said the impact of the rulings of the Warren Court threatened "to alter the nature of the criminal trial from a test of the defendant's guilt or innocence to an inquiry into the propriety of the policeman's conduct."[1] To back up his statements, the senator presented the following summary of the activities of the Warren Court: "Between 1960 and 1969 the Court's record of reversals of criminal convictions was: 63 of 112 federal criminal convictions were reversed—a figure of almost 60 percent; 113 of 144 state criminal convictions were reversed—a figure of almost 80 percent."[2]

These staggering reversal rates led Senator McClellan to comment: "I simply cannot believe that our federal circuit judges are so incapable and lacking in qualifications or that our state supreme courts are so incompetent and prone to error as to warrant such an overwhelming record of reversals by the Supreme Court."[3] He also noted that since 1960, verdicts of not guilty had increased by twenty-three percent in robbery cases and by fifty-three percent in burglary cases.[4]

A more indirect criticism of the Court's movement away from the rights of society as a whole and toward those of the accused, was enunciated by Chief Justice Weintraub of the New Jersey Supreme Court in a 1971 case involving the Exclusionary Rule: "The first right of the individual is to be protected from attack. That is why we have government as the preamble to the federal Constitution plainly says."[5] He also stated: "The Bill of Rights was not intended to deny that primary mission. This is not to belittle the inestimable rights thus consecrated but rather to say that these rights may not be read to defeat the very reason for government itself."[6]

Many people, however, believe that by its solicitude for the accused, to the exclusion of any other considerations, the Warren Court did in fact use the Bill of Rights to defeat the primary purpose of government, the protection of the innocent. This is clearly demonstrated by the responses to those surveys (noted in chapter one) in which seventy percent felt that the courts were too lenient on criminals and specifically gave the Warren Court a fifty-three to thirty-five percent unfavorable to favorable rating, in large measure because of "the growing feeling that the Court is too soft on criminals. Others complain that the rights of individuals are being protected at the expense of society as a whole."[7]

Public reaction to the Warren Court has also been expressed indirectly, via the democratic process, by legislative enactments. Our legislators, from United States senators and congressmen, through state legislators, down to county and city councilmen, are responsible, and must be responsive, to their constituents. The successful politician is successful precisely because he is attuned to the wishes of those whom he represents. In the area of law and order, this is especially true for, unlike certain special-interest laws such as a farm bill or legislation regarding drainage canals, crime is a problem that affects all of those whom he represents.

Illustrative of this attuned response is the Omnibus Crime Control and Safe Streets Act of 1968. This act, drafted primarily by Senators John McClellan and Roman Hruska of Nebraska, is one of the most significant pieces of legislation in the annals of the criminal law. One provision was particularly controversial: Title II, which, in effect, overruled the Supreme Court in two areas where the Court had pushed the rights of criminal suspects to the outer limits of unreality—confessions by, and eyewitness identification of, the perpetrators of crimes.

Basically, Title II states that in federal courts the *Miranda* decision of the U.S. Supreme Court does not control; rather, confessions a judge finds to be otherwise voluntary will be admissible in evidence even though the *Miranda* warnings were improperly given to a criminal suspect. Likewise, Title II overruled the Supreme Court's pronouncements on the lineup cases; results of a lineup would be admissible in evidence, even though the suspect's attorney was not present at the lineup, provided that the judge hearing the case finds that the lineup was conducted fairly and that the eyewitness identification was reasonably accurate.[8]

This provision was bitterly opposed by the American Civil Liberties Union and other liberal groups, and it was opposed as well by then President Lyndon Johnson and his attorney general, Ramsey Clark. Indeed, to listen to the opponents of Title II, the passage of these "repressive" provisions would usher in the great American police state. Congress, however, responsive to the wishes of the law-abiding majority of our citizens, passed the 1968 act, including the controversial provisions of Title II, by the margin of 72 to 4 in the Senate, and 368 to 17 in the House of Representatives. The import of this is patent. When legislation like the Safe Streets Act of 1968, which purports to revise liberal, procriminal Supreme Court decisions, passes so overwhelmingly, it is because the legislators are well aware that action to curb some of the excesses of the Supreme Court is desired, if not demanded, by equally overwhelming majorities of the voters.

The fact is evident: the Warren Revolution in the criminal law was not the same source of unmitigated joy to significant majorities of our citizens as it was to ardent civil libertarians, keen-eyed young law students, and the defense bar. The law-abiding citizen has a predilection for practicality in his views of things and it is too much to ask him to become ecstatic over Constitutional abstractions of due process that necessitate freeing an accused murderer, robber, mugger, or burglar when that citizen is in fairly constant apprehension of being murdered, robbed, mugged, or burgled.

Just how well grounded are the fears of the law-abiding citizen is shown by the rate of increase in crime between 1960 and 1970, roughly the years of the Warren Court. While our population increased by thirteen percent during that period, serious crimes—murder, forcible rape, aggravated assault, burglary, larceny of $50 and over, and auto theft—increased by 176 percent. And violent crime—murder, forcible rape, robbery, and aggravated assault—increased by 142 percent. In 1971 serious crimes rose an additional seven percent and violent crimes rose fourteen percent. In 1972 serious crime declined by two percent while violent crime increased by two percent, and in 1973 serious crime increased by six percent while violent crime increased by five percent.

The fear of crime is a very real element in our daily lives and, as has been pointed out, the greatest burden of both the fear of crime and the crime itself falls upon our poor and the racial minorities. One question remains of pressing importance, yet one that is not possible of an answer with any exactitude: How much, if any, of the rise in crime generally and violent crime in particular in the United States is attributable to the Warren Court's revolution of the criminal law?

Some say none or very little. Fred P. Graham, a lawyer, the former Supreme Court reporter for the *New York Times*, and an extremely knowledgeable person about the criminal justice system, in his book *The Self-Inflicted Wound*, calls the increase a "cruel coincidence."[9] Mr. Graham is basically sympathetic to the Warren Court, although in his book he does conclude that it went too far, too fast (hence *The Self-Inflicted Wound*). His coverage of the Court was highly professional; therefore, his opinion should count for a good deal. Additionally, it is undoubtedly true that other factors such as population growth, the alienation of certain segments of the population, social and economic upheaval, and racial unrest contributed directly to the increase in violence and lawlessness in the Sixties. Finally, it has been pointed out that crime continued to increase through 1971 and only took a small, two percent, decrease in 1972, in the years since the Warren Court ceased to be, that is, since Warren left the Court and those who were once a part of the liberal majority on the Court have now become a minority (Douglas, Brennan, and Marshall).

Perhaps the answer to the question lies, at least in part, in the fact that while it cannot be mathematically proven that any particular decision or series of decisions of the Warren Court led to a direct and corresponding increase in crime, it can be argued that the more criminally inclined individuals who are on the streets at liberty to prey upon others, the more crimes will be committed. The Warren Court's decisions favoring criminal suspects often required the wholesale release of patently guilty criminals and unquestionably made it much more difficult for the police to obtain admissible evidence of crime and for prosecutors to convict those accused of crime. Thus, each time that the Court's decisions required the freeing of guilty men and women, a criminally inclined individual was returned to his environment to engage in criminal acts as it pleased him. Additionally, it can be stated with certainty that the liberal majority of the highest court in the land took the lead in creating a *climate of permissiveness* toward criminals that in many cases actually encouraged the lawless and violent to believe (in some cases quite correctly) they could go about their criminal activities with relative impunity.

The climate-of-permissiveness theory explains why we continue to have a problem of rising crime: it is obvious that ten years of permissive jurisprudence of the Warren Court will not be dissipated by three years of a relatively hard-line stance against crime taken by the Burger Court. Since October 1969, when Warren Earl Burger succeeded Earl Warren, the Burger Court has actually overruled relatively few of the Warren Court's decisions, although it has, in several cases, cut back the overbroad scope of key Warren Court decisions and appears on a course to end the permissiveness of the predecessor Court. Still, the greatest part of the Warren Court's liberal, pro-criminal-suspect law is still in existence; until a great deal more of it is changed, we will continue to have a body of Supreme Court law that favors the criminal accused.

So long as our law-enforcement officers are compelled to enforce our criminal laws under the dictates of the Warren Court (and this *must* be done—disagreement with the Warren Court's decisions and active work for their change provide not the slightest justification for refusing to adhere to them until they are changed), we will continue to have criminals, whose factual guilt is patent, set free. The Burger Court is moving to correct the imbalance currently found in the criminal law, but with certain exceptions, it has not evidenced the same tendency of the liberal-activist Warren Court for wholesale reversal of prior decisions. Thus we still have to a large extent, and particularly in the critical area of the suppression of the truth in a criminal trial, a situation in which all of the lower courts, prosecutors, and law-enforcement officers are bound by the dictates of the Warren Court.

The Warren Court, beyond question, created a climate of permissiveness towards lawbreakers in our criminal justice system. However, in all fairness, it must be stated that certainly not all of the current climate of permissiveness can be laid at the feet of the Warren Court. That Court did not create the Iowa Parole Board that freed the murderer of a police chief after a mere two and one-half years. Nor can the highly permissive decision holding the death penalty unconstitutional in June 1972 be laid at the feet of the liberal majority of the Warren Court, for in that case the two remaining "conservative" justices from the Warren Court, Byron White and Potter Stewart, swung over to vote with liberal justices Brennan, Douglas, and Marshall to form a five-justice majority.

To take yet another example, the Warren Court contributed immeasurably to the climate of permissiveness in its 1968 decision that held that persons opposed to the death penalty could not be routinely excluded from juries in capital cases.[10] This ruling resulted eventually in the Court's vacating hundreds of death sentences, including that of Richard Speck—about as outrageously permissive an act as one can imagine. But it was the Illinois legislature that enacted into the law the provision that *any* prisoner, no matter how serious his crime and no matter how long his sentence, *must* be considered for parole in a maximum of eleven years and three months, thus making Speck (with credit for time already served made mandatory in the same law) eligible for parole in five years. This is pretty permissive stuff too, but you can't blame the Warren Court for it.

Thus, it would be unfair to blame all our crime problems on the Warren Court. Permissiveness is a fact of life in today's society and our criminal justice system is top heavy with those who still cannot get it through their heads that crime is caused by criminals rather than by some sort of collective societal guilt. There are, however, certain areas of law, made by the Warren Court, generally by wholesale overruling of years of previously valid laws, in which the rights of the criminal were made paramount to the rights of the law-abiding. These areas, briefly described in the preceding chapter, concern one of the most critical aspects of the breakdown of the criminal justice system: the suppression of the truth. The three main areas in the system in which—thanks to the Warren Court—the truth must be suppressed are 1) the Exclusionary Rule; 2) the *Miranda* ruling on confession and admissions; and 3) the lineup cases and other cases dealing with the admissibility of evidence. This chapter will deal with the first two in detail. The third area is, generally speaking, being modified considerably by the Burger Court and requires less extensive analysis as a practical matter but is still relevant as indicative of the attitude of the Warren Court that formalism comes ahead of the truth.

The Exclusionary Rule

The Exclusionary Rule is a legal doctrine that was made a part of our Constitutional criminal law and imposed upon all of the states by the

Warren Court in the 1961 case of *Mapp* v. *Ohio.*[11] In *Mapp,* and subsequent cases, the Court ruled that no evidence of the guilt of the criminal accused could be used against him if it was obtained in the course of, or as a result of, an illegal arrest or search and seizure.

In practical terms the application of the Exclusionary Rule works pretty much like this: if the police have seized physical evidence of crime from an accused, either through the search-and-seizure process or incident to an arrest, the accused may move to "suppress," and exclude from use against him, the evidence on the grounds that either the arrest or the search and seizure or both were "illegal"—that is, that they violated his rights under the Fourth Amendment. If the accused can convince the court hearing the motion to suppress, that the arresting or seizing officers have run afoul, *in any manner,* of an incredibly complicated body of state or federal search-and-seizure law, then he is entitled to have the evidence excluded no matter how relevant, probative, or even conclusive of his guilt it might be.

If the accused is successful in his efforts to suppress evidence, then that evidence cannot be used against him at his trial. If there is other admissible evidence of his guilt, the state may proceed to trial on that evidence. However, if there is insufficient evidence to go to trial without the suppressed evidence, then the most likely result will be that the prosecutor will be forced to dismiss the case for lack of evidence; or if the motion to suppress was made during the trial, the judge will be forced to dismiss the case. In any event, when a successful motion to suppress evidence has been made, the truth will, by definition, also have been suppressed.

As already noted, physical evidence is often the only evidence of guilt in a criminal case. One hypothetical example of this will suffice. Three men wearing ski masks rob a store; they are subsequently arrested by the police in their car and a search of the car turns up the ski masks, the weapons used, and the loot from the robbery. Assuming that none of the suspects confesses and that the holdup victim can identify none of them, since each was masked, the *only* evidence against the suspects would be the physical evidence seized in the car. Now, if on a motion to suppress a judge should find that the police did not have probable cause—that is, reasonable grounds—to make the arrest and search the car, then the guns, loot, or ski masks could not be introduced into evidence against the robbers. Almost without question they would have to be freed because the Exclusionary Rule, as applied to the states by the *Mapp* decision, requires that the only evidence of the crime be suppressed. Of course, the truth of the matter would also have been suppressed.

Prior to the *Mapp* case each state was free to adopt the Exclusionary

Rule or not as it chose; after *Mapp*, the rule, because the Court based its ruling on the United States Constitution, became binding on every law-enforcement officer and agency in the country.

Chief Justice Burger, dissenting in a 1971 case, has stated the premise upon which the rule was adopted as a part of our criminal law: "The rule has rested on a theory that suppression of evidence in these circumstances was imperative to deter law-enforcement authorities from using improper methods to obtain evidence."[12]

Reduced to its simplest terms, the rule was adopted to "police the police" in order to prevent them from engaging in illegal searches and seizures. The theory was that an officer who engaged in an illegal search and seizure would be "punished" if the fruits of his illegal act (that is, the evidence) could not be used in evidence against the person from whom they were seized.

The theory of policing the police simply has not worked. Logic would seem to dictate this result if the realities of police work are considered. Law-enforcement officers are constantly confronted with search-and-seizure problems; if they know or have reason to believe that evidence, contraband, weapons, or the fruits of a crime are at a given location or in the possession of a given individual, their job requires them to get the evidence. In the case of detectives and federal agents, their function is investigative and they usually have some sort of advance notice of the necessity to search, whereas with patrolmen, deputy sheriffs, and highway troopers the search-and-seizure problem usually comes upon them unexpectedly via a personal observation, a sudden confrontation with a suspect, or receipt of information from an informant, victim, or witness. Whatever, the police officer, usually untrained in the law, must make a fairly hasty decision whether or not to make a search and seizure.

Now the officer can have three mental states when confronted with a search-and-seizure problem: 1) he knows that a search and seizure would be clearly unlawful; 2) he knows that a search and seizure would be clearly lawful; or 3) he knows the search is not clearly unlawful but is not sure that it is clearly lawful.

These contingencies can be illustrated. First consider cases in which the police know that a search would be clearly unlawful. Detective Jones knows that Smith is a dealer of narcotics, having arrested him on previous occasions and found him in possession of narcotics. On a certain day he receives information from a reliable informant that he has seen a large supply of narcotics at Smith's house. The informant further states that to the best of his knowledge Smith has no intention of moving and Detective Jones knows that Smith has lived at his residence for years. It is 10:00 A.M. on a weekday and Jones knows from experience that it will take him about two hours to type up a search warrant, get a prosecutor to approve it, and get a judge to sign it. Jones, however, either through laziness or contempt for the rules that circumscribe his conduct, proceeds to Smith's house without a warrant, breaks in, arrests Smith, searches the house, and finds narcotics.

Patrolman Harris is assigned to patrol a high crime area on the 4:00 P.M. to midnight shift. Through boredom with routine patrol or sheer perverseness towards his duties he decides to search everyone he sees who is wearing a green shirt. He does so, basing each search on nothing but the color of the shirt of the suspect and the fact that he is in a high crime area. He searches nine people, finding nothing on six, illegal weapons on two, and narcotics on one.

These searches are clearly unlawful and both officers know it, or should know it. In the case of Detective Jones, the law is settled that, unless there is an emergency situation involving danger to police officers or others, or loss or destruction of evidence, a search warrant must be procured to search a residence. In the case of Patrolman Harris, the law is equally well settled; randomly searching persons for no reason except some sort of hunch, or because the officer just feels like it, is an illegal search. The narcotics seized from Smith's house and the guns and narcotics seized by Patolman Harris must, under the Exclusionary Rule, be suppressed and neither Smith nor those searched by Harris can be successfully prosecuted.

But what of the Exclusionary Rule? It was worthless here as a deterrent. Both Detective Jones and Patrolman Harris *knew* when they made their searches that they would be clearly illegal and there was not the slightest possibility of the evidence being admissible. Jones and Harris should, indeed, be punished for their illegal acts, through a civil suit or departmental discipline. They certainly are not punished by the application of the Exclusionary Rule. Since they disregarded the rule in these cases, they would certainly not be deterred by it from conducting other illegal searches and seizures.

Jones and Harris are examples of the minority of "bad cops": police officers who choose to disregard the rules through laziness, corruption, or willful misconduct. They should be punished—for one reason because they make life harder for the good policemen. But the Exclusionary Rule is not the device to do it.

The Exclusionary Rule in this set of cases has neither resulted in punishment for nor deterred the offending officers. But it has resulted in the certain freeing of four suspects whose guilt for narcotics and weapons offenses is clear, and has provided no relief for the six innocent green-shirted individuals who were illegally searched by Patrolman Harris.

Now consider searches that are clearly lawful. Assume the same facts as in the first case except that Detective Jones obtains a search warrant for Smith's house based on information from the reliable informant (a procedure the law permits), has the prosecutor approve it, and the judge sign it. He proceeds to Smith's house with fellow officers, searches the house pursuant to the search warrant, and discovers narcotics.

Patrolman Harris, patrolling his area at 3:00 A.M., is told by his radio to meet a party at a certain intersection. He responds and meets an informant, whom he knows personally and who has given him information before. The informant points out to Harris a man sitting in a car across the street and tells Harris that the man has a gun in the waistband of his trousers and is in possession of heroin. Harris goes to the car, opens the door, and removes the gun from the suspect's trousers. Harris tells the suspect that he is under arrest for carrying a concealed weapon, searches him further, and finds narcotics.

Both of these cases are examples of proper police work, cases which have been upheld by the Supreme Court of the United States. The Exclusionary Rule would not apply here and the evidence would be admissible.

Often borderline cases arise in which the officers cannot be certain whether their actions will be held lawful. Detective Jones receives information from a reliable informant that he, the informant, has just been offered a chance to buy a truckload of stolen shoes from Phillips. Jones tells the informant to attempt to complete the transaction. The informant calls at about 4:00 P.M., on a weekday, and tells Jones that Phillips has agreed to the deal, that the truck containing the shoes is at Phillips's parking lot, and that it may soon be moved to a rendezvous out of town to complete the deal. Jones proceeds to the parking lot with several men. Fearing that if the truck is moved he may lose it in rush-hour traffic, and knowing that it will take him hours to procure a search warrant, Jones seizes the truck, searches it, and finds the shipment of stolen shoes.

Patrolman Harris is again on patrol in the early-morning hours in a high crime area. He sees a broken window in the back of an appliance shop and upon investigation finds that the shop has been broken into. He also notices blood at the site of the broken window. Harris puts this information out over the radio. Some six miles away Patrolman Wilson, who has heard the broadcast, observes a car with two men in it going at a high rate of speed. He stops them and asks the driver for his license and registration. When they are handed to him he notices a spot of fresh blood on one of them. Wilson then shines his light into the back of the car and observes some bulky objects on the back seat covered by a blanket. He orders the suspects out of the car, lifts up the blanket, and finds several appliances in unopened boxes. He arrests the men for burglary and, after help arrives, without a warrant searches the car, finding burglar tools under the front seat and more appliances in the trunk.

Both of these cases are very close cases involving warrantless searches, and judges might well differ as to whether each search was legal. But consider the cases in the context of the Exclusionary Rule. If the searches are found to be legal, there would be no problem. But if the searches were found to be illegal and the Exclusionary Rule must be applied to the fruits of the search, so that the stolen shoes in the first case and the stolen appliances and burglar tools in the second would be inadmissible in evidence, what would be the result?

First, of course, the accused in both cases would have to be freed, for without the evidence seized there would be no case.

Next consider the officers themselves. In neither case was the officer's conduct outrageous or done with a willful intent to violate someone's rights. In both cases the officers were faced with situations in which they had ample reason to believe that stolen property was concealed in movable vehicles and would disappear if not seized.

What of the supposed deterrent effect suppression of the evidence would have? It is perhaps arguable that if the evidence in each case were suppressed at the trial, officers Jones and Wilson, being present, would learn that their actions were deemed "illegal" searches and seizures and if faced with *exactly* the same situation again, might not make the same mistake. However, it is unlikely that precisely the same fact situation would recur involving the same officers; further, if such did recur, the officers could not be expected to test all of the ramifications of the decision in the described cases against their decisions on the street. So again, in borderline instances they would just have to follow their judgments, made in good faith.

If the evidence seized in these borderline cases was upheld at the trial and the searches found to be illegal only at the appellate level years later, it is likely that the officers involved might never learn of the decision at all, thus reducing the deterrent effect of exclusion of the evidence to zero. Finally, even if the officers who were actually involved were aware that their searches were deemed illegal, it is highly questionable that any true deterrent effect would be felt by other officers in Jones's and Wilson's departments or in police departments in other cities or states. Unless the case is particularly notorious, most police officers are not made keenly aware of each and every trial and appellate decision in search and seizure. There can be no real deterrence if the party to be deterred is not aware of what is to deter him.

Chief Justice Burger summed up this aspect of nondeterrence:

> Whatever educational effect the rule conceivably might have in theory is greatly diminished in fact by the realities of law-enforcement work. Policemen do not have the time, inclination, or training to read and grasp the nuances of the appellate opinions that ultimately define the standards of conduct that they are to follow. The issues that these decisions raise often admit of neither easy nor obvious answers, as sharply divided courts on what is or is not reasonable amply demonstrate. Nor can judges, in all candor, forget that opinions sometimes lack helpful clarity.[13]

The Chief Justice also concluded that, as noted above, the time lapse between a given search and seizure and an opinion is an important factor in nondeterrence:

> The presumed educational effect of judicial opinions is also reduced by the long time lapse—often several years between the original police action and its final judicial evaluation. Given a policeman's pressing responsibilities it would be surprising if he ever becomes aware of the final result after such a delay.[14]

Thus, the logic of the deterrent effect of the Exclusionary Rule is rather shaky. It clearly will not deter the officer who acts in bad faith, knowing that his conduct is unlawful; only direct penalties—which the Exclusionary Rule in no way provides—will accomplish that aim. Likewise the Exclusionary Rule will not deter officers who act in good faith, for by definition the good-faith officer will act because he thinks, albeit mistakenly, that he is acting within the law. And the idea of any long-range after-the-fact deterrence imposed upon the police profession as a whole has been pretty well laid to rest by Burger's reasoning that the majority of policemen simply do not have the "time, training, or inclination" to read and grasp the nuances of appellate opinions—particularly in such a complicated area as search and seizure and especially in view of the usually long time lapse between police action and judicial decision about that action. In short, a police officer is scarcely going to be deterred by a decision of which he is unaware or only hazily aware.

It is a pity, and quite surprising, that the question of deterrence of illegal police conduct, upon which the Exclusionary Rule is based, has not been the object of much meticulous empirical study—but such is the case. In fact, only two such studies have been made, both in Chicago, and in neither study was empirical evidence found to indicate that the Exclusionary Rule does in fact deter unlawful police conduct.[15]

The freeing of the patently guilty in order to punish the police exacts an extremely high price from society and in particular from the victims of crime. As Chief Justice Weintraub of the New Jersey Supreme Court has phrased it: "When the truth is suppressed and the criminal is set free, the pain of suppression is felt, not by the inanimate state or by some penitent policeman, but by the offender's next victims for whose protection we hold office."[16]

The high price to society of the Exclusionary Rule has also been noted by Chief Justice Burger: "Some clear demonstration of the benefits and effectiveness of the Exclusionary Rule is required to justify it in view of the high price it extracts from society—the release of countless guilty criminals."[17]

Just how high a price this is can be seen from the following cases in which the Exclusionary Rule has been used to suppress evidence and reverse the convictions of murderers, robbers, rapists, burglars, narcotics dealers, and others found guilty of serious crimes. In each case the guilt of the accused was clear, yet minor errors of search and seizure—errors which certainly showed no willful or flagrant violations of constitutional rights by the police—required that evidence vital to the case against the accused be suppressed.

Coolidge v. New Hampshire, 403 U.S. 443 (1971)

On January 13, 1964, Pamela Mason, a 14-year-old schoolgirl, left her house on a babysitting assignment. Eight days later her frozen body was discovered in a snowdrift just a few miles from her home. Her throat had been slashed, and she had been shot in the head.

The defendant's car matched the description of a car that had been seen on the night Pamela disappeared and at the spot where her body had been found. The defendant, by his own admission, frequently visited a launderette where she posted her babysitting notice, and a knife belonging to the defendant was found there. The defendant's wife voluntarily produced two shotguns and two rifles that belonged to the defendant and offered them to the police. A subsequent examination of the guns revealed that one of the rifles had fired the bullet that was found in the murdered girl's brain.

Upon the basis of this evidence, the state attorney general, who was authorized under New Hampshire law to issue warrants, issued an arrest warrant for the defendant and a search warrant for his automobile. Sweepings of dirt and other fine particles taken from the car matched like particles taken from the clothes of the murdered girl. These items were introduced into evidence at trial.

After studying the case for more than five months, the Supreme Court held (5-4) that the search of the automobile was unreasonable. Although five justices in the majority could not agree as to why the search was illegal, they did find that the search warrant was invalid on the basis that the attorney general was not a neutral and detached magistrate. Conviction reversed.

Bowers v. *Coiner*, 309 F. Supp 1964 (S.D. W.Va., 1970)

The defendant Bowers was convicted in state court for the armed robbery of a savings and loan company.

FBI agents with a warrant for Bowers's arrest went to the apartment of one William Eagle where Bowers was a frequent guest and attempted to arouse the occupants. The lights were on but no activity was seen. An agent went to a pay telephone across the street and telephoned Mr. Eagle, the lessee of the apartment. The agent told him that FBI agents were outside the apartment and that they wanted to talk to him. The agent could hear the other agents knocking on the door through the telephone. Mr. Eagle opened the door, and the agents entered and subsequently arrested Bowers, who was sleeping in the bedroom. The agents seized two revolvers, .38 and .25 calibers.

The court held that because the agents had announced neither their authority nor their purpose, the entry and subsequent search and arrest were in violation of the Fourth Amendment.

People v. *Trudeau*, 187 N.W.2d 890 (Mich., 1971)

On November 6, 1967, during an attempted burglary of a vault at a synagogue in Southfield, Michigan, the night watchman was killed by blows to his head from a crowbar. One of the few leads was a heel print left at the scene. On November 19, 1967, the defendant was arrested inside a United States post office, where he had attempted to break and enter a vault.

Because of the similarity between the two jobs, the detective assigned to the murder case attended a preliminary hearing on the post office case in order to view the defendant's shoes. His shoes were subsequently removed by two police officers without a warrant and given to the detective.

At trial, the shoes, the imprint, and their comparison by an expert were introduced into evidence and the defendant was convicted of second-degree murder. The court held that the removal of the shoes without a warrant violated the Fourth Amendment. The case was reversed and remanded for a new trial.

United States v. *Davis*, 423 F.2d 974 (5th Cir., 1970)

FBI agents in a rural area of Alabama arrested Davis and his son pursuant to warrants charging them with the unlawful flight to avoid prosecution for the larceny of an automobile. Before the arrest procedures were completed, the elder defendant bolted from the house. He ran toward his house with the agents and his son in hot pursuit. He stopped at the steps, turned and brandished a .38-caliber pistol. In the gunfire that followed, the defendant's son was wounded. When order was finally restored, the agents cared for the son until an ambulance arrived. They then took Davis to Montgomery.

About three and one-half hours later, the agents returned to the scene to retrieve Davis's weapon. Although it was after dark, they discovered the pistol immediately upon alighting from the car because of the reflection of the porch light on the surface of the gun. The gun was recovered from the yard, and the agents left.

The court held that the entry into the yard without a warrant was unreasonable.

Root v. Gruper, 483 F.2d 361 (8th Cir., 1971)

The victim, Lonny Sutton, called the telephone operator saying that his wife had shot him and to call an ambulance because he was dying. The ambulance driver and his assistants found Sutton unconscious from a shotgun wound. On the way to the hospital they passed the marshal, who was on his way to the scene of the shooting. Sutton was dead on arrival.

The marshal waited at the residence, which was empty, until the sheriff arrived. Together they entered the house and proceeded to the kitchen where they found a shotgun and shells, which were introduced into evidence at trial. The defendant's conviction was reversed on the basis that the warrantless search of the house was unjustified.

United States v. Colbert, 454 F.2d 801 (5th Cir., 1972)

In Birmingham, Alabama, on the evening of October 24, 1970, two officers, who were on call to another destination, noticed the defendants Colbert and Reese standing empty-handed in front of a nightclub. One of the officers noted that Colbert fit the description of a man wanted by the Birmingham police for assault with attempt to commit murder.

After making their call, the police officers observed the defendants carrying expensive briefcases near the same location where they had previously been seen. The defendants began walking towards a parked automobile. The driver of the automobile, spotting the police officers, made a motion toward the defendants and sped off. When the officers got out of their car, the defendants placed their briefcases on the sidewalk and walked away. The defendants denied ownership of the briefcases and refused to identify themselves. One of the officers opened the briefcases and found that each contained a sawed-off shotgun of illegal length. The defendants' conviction for possession of an illegal firearm was reversed. The Court held (2-1) that the search of the briefcases and the seizure of the guns without a warrant were unreasonable.

United States v. *Soriana,* Case No. 72-25-CR-JE (S.D., Fla.)

On December 23, 1971, a reliable informant advised agents of the Bureau of Narcotics and Dangerous Drugs (BNDD) that one Anna Betancourt, who resided at 3520 S.W. 4 Street, Miami, was expecting the delivery of a large quantity of narcotics. Previously, on December 16, 1971, the informant and Anna Betancourt had purchased a large amount of milk sugar and Christmas wrapping that were to be used to cut and wrap the narcotics. On January 4, 1972, the informant went to the Betancourt residence and was asked to leave because narcotics were on the premises. Agents then observed a white male and female enter the house empty-handed and exit a short time later with a large paper shopping bag. They then drove to another location, deposited the shopping bag in a trash receptacle, and drove off. The bag, which was retrieved by BNDD agents, contained numerous glassine bags and Christmas wrapping paper, which by chemical analysis proved to contain traces of heroin.

The agents prepared an affidavit that recited these facts. The affidavit was then presented under oath to a United States magistrate, who issued the search warrant and handed it to the BNDD agent who had presented the sworn testimony. Unfortunately, the magistrate had failed to insert the name of the agent to whom it was directed.

Upon a motion to suppress, the court found that probable cause existed for the search but the failure to insert an agent's name on the search warrant was a fatal error. Result—the suppression of 238 pounds of pure heroin.

Whiteley v. *Warden of Wyoming State Penitentiary,*
401 U.S. 560 (1971)

In 1965 a hardware store and a bar located in Saratoga, Wyoming, a remote part of that state, were the subject of a breaking and entering. The sheriff for that area received a detailed description of the car belonging to the bandits as well as part of the license number. In addition, the sheriff received a tip that Whiteley and a companion had probably committed the burglary. The sheriff obtained an arrest warrant and then issued a radio alert. Whiteley and his companion were stopped less than twenty-four hours later in Laramie, Wyoming, in a car fitting the description of that involved in the burglary. Whiteley gave the arresting officer a fictitious name, but the officer recognized the companion. The two were arrested, and objects that had been stolen from the hardware store and the bar were found in the car.

At trial, the companion testified in vivid detail how he and Whiteley had accomplished the burglaries. The stolen items were introduced into evidence. Whiteley was convicted and the case was affirmed on appeal. Six years and several habeas-corpus petitions later, the U.S. Supreme Court held that the search was unreasonable. Conviction reversed.

Whiteley had previously been convicted of three felonies and had served six terms in the state penitentiary.

Von Utter v. *Tulloch*, 426 F.2d (1st Cir., 1970)

A confidential informant known to the police as a user of narcotics, advised that Von Utter would arrive in Provincetown, Massachusetts, between March 8 and 10 driving a white Volkswagen two-door sedan with Connecticut registration JJVU, and that the car would contain marijuana and LSD.

Police officers, who had obtained a search warrant for the automobile, approached the defendant as he emerged from a drugstore and advised him that they had a warrant to search his car. The defendant stated that there would be no need, that he would do it himself. He then reached into the glove compartment, seized some contraband, and fled on foot. The officers gave chase, apprehended him, and placed him under arrest. They then searched the car and found a quantity of narcotics. His 1968 conviction in state court was overturned more than three years later on a habeas-corpus petition to the federal court. The court held that (1) the affidavit for the search warrant was inadequate since the informant's tip was too vague to be of any value, and (2) the search could not be justified as being incident to a lawful arrest.

United States v. *Sokolow*, 450 F.2d 324 (5th Cir., 1971)

A police officer, investigating the theft of cigarettes, observed the suspect's car backed up to Sokolow's garage. The officer saw the cigarettes in the back seat of the car and arrested the suspect. He then noticed a large number (29) of room air-conditioners located in the garage and proceeded to an adjacent motel to question Sokolow about the air-conditioners. After being advised of his rights, Sokolow stated that he had purchased the air-conditioning units from a local appliance dealer and produced receipts to that effect. The officer examined the receipts and noticed some discrepancies. Sokolow and the officer then walked to the garage where the officer recorded the serial numbers on two of the units.

A National Crime Information Center check of the serial numbers revealed that the units had been stolen, and the appliance dealer advised that Sokolow's "receipts" were estimates and not receipts. Sokolow was arrested and subsequently convicted. The court of appeals, however, ignored many of these facts and held that the taking of the serial numbers without a search warrant was an unreasonable search and reversed the conviction.

United States v. Kaye, 432 F.2d 647 (D.C. Cir., 1970)

Agents of the FBI, who were investigating the theft of government property, searched the defendant's premises pursuant to a search warrant and seized several items that were later admitted into evidence.

The affidavit asked for a search warrant for "the entire premises of 3618 14 Street, N.W., Washington, D.C., a two-story brick building used for the sale and service of TV's, stereos, and records, and with a large sign reading 'Fredrick L. and Company'." The search warrant issued by the court was captioned "[E]ntire premises, 3618 14th Street, N.W." and authorized the search of "the premises known as 3618 14th Street, N.W."

The entire building was leased to the defendant. The defendant's store and shop occupied the first floor and basement, and the second floor was occupied as the defendant's living quarters. Although there was no question about the existence of probable cause to search, the court held that the search warrant did not authorize the search of the second-floor apartment regardless of the language in the supporting affidavit, which might be construed more broadly. The language was the same except for the description "a two-story brick building," which was included in the affidavit and not in the warrant.

State v. Madden, 465 P.2d 363 (Aug. 1970)

James Beck was riding his bicycle along Camelback Road in Phoenix shortly after 3:00 A.M. on October 18, 1967, when a Cadillac pulled alongside and forced him off the road. Several assailants emerged from the car, grabbed Beck around the neck and body, forced him into an irrigation ditch, and robbed him of his watch, wallet, checkbook, money, and keys. The victim called the police and an emergency bulletin was sent out on the police radio.

At 3:18 A.M. the Cadillac was seen and stopped by the police. The defendants were taken into custody and the car was garaged. About a half hour after the defendants were arrested, the vehicle was searched and the stolen items found.

The court held that the warrantless search of the automobile was not justified. Reversed.

State v. Brown, 260 A.2d 716 (R.I., 1970)

A police officer observed a red Ford convertible, occupied only by the driver, turn into the driveway of an office building and extinguish its lights. The automobile was strange to that area. The officer next observed the automobile occupied by four persons backing out onto the highway. The driver stopped, alighted from the automobile, and approached the officer. When the other occupants started to advance on the officer, the latter made them get back into the car. At that time he observed a duffel bag stuffed with objects, a pry bar and a check-making machine.

The occupants were taken to the police station for questioning. Approximately thirty minutes after they were initially stopped, the police chief walked out to the car where in addition to the above objects he saw two pairs of gloves on the front seat and a walkie-talkie protruding from under the seat. In the interim the police had received a report of a breaking and entering of the office building at the location where the car had been stopped.

The Rhode Island Supreme Court complimented the police officer for good police work and stated that although a search of the car would have been permissible when the suspects were stopped, the search thirty minutes later was not. Conviction reversed.

Hair v. *United States*, 289 F. 2d 894 (D.C. Cir., 1961)

In *Hair*, police officers were called to investigate a housebreaking, robbery, and rape. During the course of this investigation, the victim made a photographic identification of Hair and Burroughs, and a tentative identification of Blakeney. The police immediately went to Hair's house to place him under arrest. As they approached the house, about seven or eight feet from the door, Blakeney opened the door, began to step out, then turned and ran up the stairs. The officers, without giving notice of their identity or purpose, immediately entered and gave chase. Blakeney dived through a window and escaped. He was subsequently apprehended and identified by the victim. While passing through Hair's house, the officers observed several items that matched the description of the stolen goods. Based upon this observation, they obtained a search warrant and seized these items, which were introduced in evidence at Hair's trial. On appeal, the United States Court of Appeals for the District of Columbia reversed Hair's conviction on the ground that the failure by the police to stop and announce their identity and purpose before entering Hair's house tainted the evidence seized and therefore it was improper to admit those items in evidence at Hair's trial.

Woods v. *State*, 466 S.W. 2d 741 (Texas, 1971)

A woman who lived alone was awakened in her bedroom by the defendant. He threatened her with a knife, robbed her, and raped her while she was forced to lie on her stomach with a pillow over her head.

With the aid of a nightlight she saw the knife and also noticed that the defendant was wearing leather boots.

As soon as the defendant left, the woman called the police, who searched the area and found boot tracks outside the house. The police traced the tracks from the woman's house to the vicinity of the defendant's house. After knocking and entering, the officers observed the defendant standing with his boots on. He was questioned and told to go outside and place his boots in the boot tracks. Later, the boots were confiscated and the defendant was taken before a magistrate. One of the officers returned to the defendant's house, conducted a warrantless search, and found the knife used in the rape.

The defendant's rape conviction was reversed with the court holding that the arrest and search, without a warrant, were illegal.

State v. *Barwick,* 483 P. 2d 670 (Idaho, 1971)

A man was returning to his camper when he was attacked by two men. He was struck to the ground, jumped on, and choked by a man whom he later positively identified. The defendant took the man's billfold and ran off.

The victim notified the police. While cruising the area, the officers noticed a car traveling with a flat tire. They proceeded to follow the vehicle as it rapidly accelerated and then slowed down. The officers stopped the vehicle and the defendant got out and walked back to the patrol car. While the defendant was attempting to find his driver's license, the officer noticed blood on his hand. The defendant was then arrested for vagrancy. The defendant was advised of his *Miranda* rights, after which the policemen asked him if they could search his automobile and he consented.

While defendant was out on bond for the vagrancy charge, he was arrested for robbery. The defendant's conviction was subsequently overturned and the evidence was suppressed by the Idaho Supreme Court, which found the initial arrest illegal.

These examples, it should be noted, are appellate cases. Countless other cases in which the suspect's guilt was evident have had to be dismissed before or at the time of trial because the prosecution's case could not be made without the suppressed evidence.

Another area of criticism of the exclusionary rule is that it is applied indiscriminately to all search-and-seizure violations no matter how technical or minor they may be. Likewise it makes no difference, insofar as the application of the rule is concerned, if the officer is acting wantonly and willfully to violate the rights of another or if he is acting in good faith—even if a number of judges have ruled in other cases or in the same case, that his actions were proper. Chief Justice Burger phrased the issue this way:

> Although unfortunately ineffective, the Exclusionary Rule has increasingly been characterized by a single, monolithic and drastic judicial response to all official violations of legal norms. Inadvertent errors of judgment that do not work any injustice will inevitably occur under the pressure of police work. These honest mistakes have been treated in the same way as deliberate and flagrant . . . violations of the Fourth Amendment. For example, in *Miller* v. *United States*, . . . reliable evidence was suppressed because of a police officer's failure to say a "few more words" during the arrest and search of a known narcotics peddler.[18]

This sort of across-the-board application of the rule, invoking it against the good-faith errors of the police as well as against true police misconduct, is another cogent argument for modifying the rule or doing away with it completely.

Another major criticism of the Exclusionary Rule is that it contributes significantly to the delays that are crippling our criminal courts. Such is the view of Justice George Brown of the California Court of Appeals:

> I have no doubt that it has led to a glut of cases in the courts caused by a multiplicity of challenges to the methods by which evidence was obtained at every stage of the criminal proceedings. While most of these challenges are unsuccessful, I am convinced that the amount of court time consumed in the consideration and disposition of such contentions is so large as to be one of the principal causes of our current backlog and our overworked courts.[19]

Logic and common sense support Justice Brown's position. In a criminal justice system that is not saddled with the Exclusionary Rule, a person who has been arrested knows that at his trial he will face any relevant physical evidence introduced against himself. An armed robber, for example, who knows that the police have found the items taken in the robbery, the gun used, and the clothes he wore in his house or automobile, will also know that these items will doubtless be used in evidence against him. He can, of course, claim that they were "planted" on him or that he was merely holding them for safekeeping for a friend or put forth some other explanation—but he is flatly faced with the fact that the judge or jury in his case will know that they were indeed found in his possession. Such evidence would, in a great many cases, convince him to plead guilty.

Not so in the United States. Here, in the same situation, the Exclusionary Rule permits the suspect, through his attorney, to move at the trial court level to suppress this vital evidence. Hours, perhaps days, of court time—which in other systems is spent in determining the truth of the matter, whether the defendant is guilty or innocent—will be spent in minutely scrutinizing the actions of the police in obtaining the items pointing toward the suspect's guilt. Did the police obtain a search warrant? If so, was the warrant based upon sufficient probable cause? Was the warrant free from technical defects? If no warrant was obtained, was there time to obtain one? Did the police knock at the suspect's door? And on and on. Recall the preceding examples of cases in which every sort of technicality was used by appellate courts to suppress evidence. Each such technicality is available to our hypothetical defendant in his attempt to suppress the evidence against him; a tremendous burden is thus placed on the courts, which must hear literally thousands of such motions to suppress a year.

Now, if the motion to suppress is denied at the trial court level and the evidence is held to be admissible, the suspect may decide to plead guilty. On the other hand, he may decide to go to trial—even though the evidence may be used against him—in the hope that if he is convicted, he can utilize the interminable appellate processes (described in chapter three) to have an appeals court reverse the trial court's ruling on the evidence, and thereby have his conviction reversed.

Should the trial court suppress the physical evidence against him, the suspect would now have every reason to go to trial rather than plead guilty because obviously the case of the prosecution will be seriously weakened without the use of such evidence—if enough evidence is left to bring the case to trial at all.

Thus, the Exclusionary Rule, in addition to suppressing the truth and benefiting the guilty, places an enormous burden upon the court system, both at the trial and the appellate court level. Our court dockets are so crowded, the backlog of cases so staggering, that in many parts of the country "speedy justice" is a mockery. The Exclusionary Rule has contributed no end to this situation.

It is highly significant that the United States is the only country among those with similar systems in which relevant and probative evidence is excluded from the criminal trial. Not one other common-law country has the Exclusionary Rule as a part of its jurisprudence. Lawyers, judges, policemen, and ordinary citizens from Great Britain, Australia, and Canada look with wonder—but without admiration or envy—at its use in this country. In a recent case the Supreme Court of Canada held that a judge had no discretion to exclude relevant evidence on the grounds that it was improperly obtained. Justice Martland stated succinctly: "The admission of admissible evidence before the Court and of substantial probative value may operate unfortunately for the accused, but not unfairly."[20] As noted in chapter one, Sir Reginald Scholl, Australian consul general to the United States and former justice of the Supreme Court of Victoria, told the Philadelphia

Bar Association in 1966 that in Australia and England probative evidence of guilt obtained by illegal means could not be excluded. He then asked: "Can you any longer afford the highly technical and expensive, but quite recently acquired, luxury of excluding it?"[21]

Many distinguished individuals, including the chief justice of the United States, legal scholars, judges and lawyers, law-enforcement officials, and the man in the street, wonder if indeed we can "any longer afford" such a device as the Exclusionary Rule. Several proposals have been made that would eliminate or modify the Exclusionary Rule while at the same time punishing the policeman who willfully violates another's rights through an illegal search and seizure. These proposals and others will be discussed in Part III.[22]

The Exclusionary Rule then, the first legacy of the Warren Court designed to suppress the truth, has taken a heavy toll upon the law-abiding and upon the victims of crime. Each time the Exclusionary Rule is utilized to free a criminal, the victim's rights remain unvindicated: the guilty one goes unpunished. Further, the number of re-arrests for crimes—whether violent crimes with individual victims or crimes such as the sale of narcotics with both addicts and society as victims—indicates that a criminal, once released, will likely commit his crime again.

The suppression of the truth embodied in the Exclusionary Rule rarely, if ever, punishes the policeman; it does nothing to redress the grievances of those innocent persons who have been subjected to truly unlawful searches and seizures; it does punish the past and potential victims of the freed lawbreaker; and it rewards the criminal because the officer has blundered. Very simply, when the truth is suppressed, justice is mocked.

The Freed Confessors:
Miranda v. *Arizona* and Its Aftermath

Following the adoption of the Exclusionary Rule in 1961, the Warren Court's next major contribution to the climate of permissiveness and the suppression of the truth came in 1966, in *Miranda* v. *Arizona*.[23] This case, decided by a five-justice majority (Warren, Black, Brennan, Douglas, and Goldberg in the majority; White, Stewart, Harlan, and Clark dissenting), revolutionized the process of obtaining, by the police, and the use of, by the prosecution, confessions and admissions, made by a criminal suspect or accused, as a means of enforcing the criminal law. The majority justices held that the Fifth Amendment to the Constitution of the United States requires that, unless the police give certain specific advisement of his rights to a criminal suspect prior to interrogating him, no statement made by that suspect will be admissible in evidence against him.

Prior to *Miranda* the law had recognized that voluntary admissions or confessions of a criminal accused were admissible in evidence against him. *Miranda* ended that. Prior to *Miranda* the law was clear. No confession would be received in evidence unless it could be shown to be voluntarily made. Quite properly, any confession that appeared to be a result of torture, physical coercion, mental coercion, threats of force or reprisals, or promises of reward must be excluded. The reason for this was quite simple—a confession obtained in this manner might not be true. A suspect may, for example, know that he is innocent of a given crime but if he is told by an interrogator that if he doesn't confess his sick wife will also be arrested and charged with the crime, then he may confess to save her from being arrested. Likewise he might confess rather than risk a beating by the police. In short, if such pressures were placed upon him, they might render his confession, as such, untrustworthy.

But, if it could be proven to the trier of law—the judge sitting in a criminal case—that under *all* the circumstances a confession, admission, or other statement was in fact freely and voluntarily made, then that statement could be used in evidence. *Miranda* ended all of that. It created a new and totally artificial body of law that can only be described as having as its purpose the discouragement of the use of any criminal's confession and the suppression of the truth contained in voluntary confessions. The *Miranda* majority ruled that any time a suspect is in police custody for the purpose of interrogation, that person, "prior to any questioning, . . . must be warned that he had a right to remain silent, that any statement he does make may be used as evidence against him, and that he has a right to the presence of an attorney, either retained or appointed."[24] Further, if the suspect indicates that he wishes an attorney or that he desires not to talk, then he must not be questioned.[25] Insofar as the requirement of the presence of a lawyer is concerned, this is an almost complete bar to interrogation for it would be a rare case indeed in which an attorney, who believed that there might be the slightest chance that his client was guilty, would permit him to talk to the police.

What this boils down to is that a five-justice majority in *Miranda*, while conceding that the use of third-degree tactics was extremely rare, decided that *any* police custody was so compulsive of an involuntary confession that it would violate the suspect's rights under the Fifth Amendment if the warnings of rights were not given. (*Miranda* arose out of the police's questioning a suspect at the police station; in 1969 the Court held that it also applied to police questioning a man even in his own home.)[26] Now, the notion that a man cannot give a voluntary confession without an elaborate waiver of all of his rights, just because he is in police custody, simply has no basis in fact. People have been making free and voluntary confessions while in police custody for years and the practice had not been questioned. The *Miranda* majority of the Warren Court apparently wanted to do all it could to prevent the making of legally admissible confessions.

In *The Self-Inflicted Wound* Fred Graham describes the decisions made during the 1960s in the area of the criminal law by the Warren Court. Although liberally oriented and basically sympathetic with the *Miranda* decision, Graham writes:

> This was the core of the Supreme Court's difficulties over *Miranda*—in order to abolish the abuses that cropped up in some but by no means all police investigations, it would have to condemn the "voluntariness" approach which the Court itself had always approved before and which the police saw as a reasonable way to do their job. If the Court were to frame a prophylactic procedure rigid enough to rule out all of the abuses that the voluntariness approach could permit, *it would also outlaw many instances of reasonable, noncoercive police inquiry about crime.* . . . Also, where the previous landmark decision had imposed rigid but narrow restrictions on state officials' conduct, *Miranda* was to lay down a statute-like code of procedure consisting of four commandments, some of which included subcommandments. . . . Despite the Court's zigzag course, its trend was clear; it would continue to cast about for an objective standard by which police questioning could be regulated *and if the standard proved so rigid that the police could not interrogate effectively at all, that would be a tolerable outcome in the (the majority of) the Warren Court's eyes.*[27]

In short, as Mr. Graham's incisive analysis points out, the *Miranda* majority was willing to suppress the truth.

The majority opinion in *Miranda* is as crystal clear an example as it may be possible to find of an utter, abysmal, and complete contempt by a judicial body for the rights of the victims of crime. In *Miranda* the entire emphasis was upon the rights of the criminal with such useful clichés as "the inviolability of the human personality" put forth to justify the decision. The human personality may be inviolable but the human body happens to be violable, by bullets, knives, sticks, stones, fists, and all sorts of other weaponry. The victims of crime whose bodies had been violated were contemptuously ignored.

Not by Justice Byron White, however. In one of the most penetrating defenses of the rights of victims of crime in Supreme Court jurisprudence, he stated:

104

The most basic function of any government is to provide for the security of the individual and his property. . . . These ends of society are served by the criminal laws which for the most part are aimed at the prevention of crime. Without the reasonably effective performance of the task of preventing private violence and retaliation it is idle to talk about human dignity and civilized values.

The modes by which the criminal laws serve the interest in general security are many. First, the murderer who has taken the life of another is removed from the streets, deprived of his liberty and thereby prevented from repeating his offense. In view of the statistics of recidivism in this country and of the number of instances in which apprehension occurs only after repeated offenses, no one can sensibly claim that this aspect of the criminal law does not prevent crime or contribute significantly to the personal security of the ordinary citizen.

Secondly, the swift and sure apprehension of those who refuse to respect the personal security and dignity of their neighbor unquestionably has its impact on others who might be similarly tempted. . . .[28]

Justice White then described the third function of the criminal law—rehabilitation. Returning to the majority opinion, he stated:

The rule announced today will measurably weaken the availability of the criminal law to perform in these tasks. It is a deliberate calculus to prevent interrogations, to reduce the incidence of confessions and pleas of guilty and to increase the number of trials. . . .

There is, in my view, every reason to believe that a good many criminal defendants, who otherwise would have been convicted on what this court has previously thought to be the most satisfactory kind of evidence, will now under this new version of the Fifth Amendment, either not be tried at all or be acquitted if the State's evidence, minus the confession, is put to the test of litigation. . . .

I have no desire whatsoever to share the responsibility for any such impact on the present criminal process.

In some unknown number of cases the Court's rule will return a killer, a rapist or other criminal to the streets and to the environment which produced him, to repeat his crime whenever it pleases him. As a consequence there will not be a gain but a loss in human dignity.

There is, of course, a saving factor: the next victims are uncertain, unnamed, and unrepresented. . . .

Nor can this decision do other than have a corrosive effect on the criminal laws as an effective device to prevent crime. A major component in its effectiveness in this regard is its swift and sure enforcement. The easier it is to get away with rape and murder, the less the deterrent effect on those who are inclined to attempt it. This is still good common sense. If it were not, we should posthaste liquidate the whole law enforcement establishment as a useless, misguided effort to control human conduct.[29]

The "unknown numbers of cases" in which animals were returned to the street soon began to mount up. Many confessed murderers, rapists, robbers, and other violent criminals were freed because law-enforcement officers had not anticipated the *Miranda* decision. In a case soon after *Miranda*, the Supreme Court ruled that anyone who had *confessed*, but not been tried, before June 13, 1966 (the date of the decision), must receive the benefit of the new rules laid down, so that many confessed criminals who were fortunate enough to fall into this category had to be freed.[30]

Then, the lower courts started interpreting *Miranda* in cases arising after it was decided. Justice White's fears that many defendants, who would have been convicted before *Miranda* was decided, must now have their convictions reversed came true with a vengeance. The following cases are merely a *few* examples of the manner in which *Miranda* has been interpreted, in cases arising prior to and after the decision, to require that otherwise voluntary confessions be thrown out and that convictions be reversed or confessed criminals freed. Some of the cases illustrate the fact that some courts apparently *want* to free confessed criminals, or at least reverse their convictions, by holding the confessions to be illegal and by requiring a new trial for confessed criminals. As in the cases dealing with the effects of the Exclusionary Rule, the single thread running through the cases is the total preoccupation with the criminal's rights. The victim's rights are held completely incidental to those of the violator, or they are not even considered at all. Additionally, in each of the cases, the confession from all appearances was voluntarily made. Thus, when the confessions were held invalid, the truth was most assuredly suppressed.

The following cases are appellate cases in which *Miranda* has been applied in the years since it was decided, resulting in almost unbelievable miscarriages of justice:

Commonwealth v. *Singleton*, 266 A.2d 753, 439 Pa. 185,
Supreme Court of Pennsylvania (1970)

Defendant confessed to and was convicted of murder in the beating death of his mother, sister, and grandmother. The court noted that the commonwealth's case consisted primarily of defendant's incriminating statements; however, his statements were nullified and his conviction was reversed. The defendant had been given the proper *Miranda* warnings in every respect except that he was advised that anything that he said could be used "for or against" him. The court held that the use of the single word "for" vitiated the entire confession under the *Miranda* holding.

Commonwealth v. *Davis*, 270 A.2d 199, 440 Pa. 123,
Supreme Court of Pennsylvania (1970)

Again the court reversed a first-degree conviction for robbery-murder because the word "for" was included in otherwise satisfactory warnings.

Biggerstaff v. *State*, Okla. Cr., 491 P.2d 345, Court of
Criminal Appeals of Oklahoma (1971)

The defendant—convicted of first-degree murder—had been given *Miranda* warnings which were satisfactory in all respects except that he was advised that he was entitled to an attorney "at any time." The court found this warning to be insufficient advice to the suspect that he had a right to the presence of an attorney during questioning. It cited a similar holding by the United States Court of Appeals for the Fifth Circuit in *Atwell* v. *United States*, 398 F.2d 507 (1968). The court in *Atwell* rejected the use of the words "at any time," stating: " 'Anytime' *could* be interpreted by the accused in an atmosphere of pressure from the glare of the law enforcer and his authority, to refer to an impending trial or event other than the moment the advice was given and the interrogation following" (398 F.2nd 510).

The court in *Biggerstaff* also noted that, absent the defendant's confession, which had been ruled inadmissible, the evidence was not sufficient to sustain a conviction for the crime of murder.

In the foregoing cases the courts apparently felt compelled by the rigidity of the language in the *Miranda* decision to engage in extremes of semantic gymnastics in order to hold the confessions of three convicted murderers inadmissible, despite the clear intention of the police to comply with *Miranda*. The courts in these cases completely disregarded any objective standard that would demonstrate that the confessions were voluntarily made. Instead, they delved into the murky area of what the suspects *might* have understood from otherwise sufficient warnings.

Franklin v. *State*, 252 A.2d 487, 6 Md. App. 572, Court
of Special Appeals of Maryland (1969)

Defendant was convicted of several armed robberies. He was given full and proper *Miranda* warnings on September 4, 1967, at which time he made incriminating statements about certain of the armed robberies. On September 6, 1967, he was interrogated about the armed robbery involved in his appeal. Upon this latter occasion he made statements that were used to impeach him when he testified at trial. Defendant was not readvised of his rights under *Miranda* at the September 6 interrogation. The court held that the September 6 statements were inadmissible because of the two-day hiatus since the original warnings had been given. The court gave no reason for this decision except to state that the two-day delay "would fall short of compliance with the dictates of the *Miranda* decision" (252 A.2d 487 at 491).

People v. *Milton,* 75 Calif. Rptr. 803, Court of Appeals of
California (1969)

Defendant, when arrested for the murder of his wife, was given the proper *Miranda* advisements by the arresting officer, at which time he stated that he did not wish to make a statement. Some two hours later a detective, who was apparently unaware of the previous warning and refusal to make a statement, again properly advised the defendant of his rights, whereupon the defendant made admissions which were inconsistent with his later trial testimony. The appellate court held that the admissions should have been excluded. Defendant's murder conviction was thus reversed, *despite the fact that the second interrogator was unaware of the first refusal and that the admissions made at the second interrogation were apparently voluntary.*

Scott v. *State,* 475 S.W. 2d 699,
Supreme Court of Arkansas (1972)

In reversing the defendant's conviction for the rape of a two-year-old girl, the court noted in this case that there were no eyewitnesses to this crime as the victim was too young and the only other witness, her father, had been killed in an automobile accident. Defendant was properly advised and refused to make a statement. Then, according to the court: "About three months later a deputy sheriff who was passing the cell where Scott was confined asked him, in the course of what appears to have been a bantering conversation, if he had raped the little girl. Scott replied, 'Yeah' " (475 S.W. 2d).

This statement was held invalid as not being voluntarily made under *Miranda* and the rape conviction was reversed.

The preceding cases are examples of lower courts engaging in some fairly energetic second-guessing of law-enforcement officers, because of the compulsion of the inflexible dictates of *Miranda.* Although in each case there is no evidence of coercive questioning, and although the statements appear to have been made voluntarily, the courts saw fit to reverse the convictions on such close issues as the timing of questions asked, the prior refusal to talk even though this may well have been unknown to the second questioner, and, as in *Scott*, the lack of any attempt at interrogation at all. In each case it clearly appears that *only* the inflexibility of *Miranda* dictated the reversal.

Commonwealth v. *Goldsmith*, 363 A.2d 322, 438 Pa. 83, Supreme Court of Pennsylvania (1970)

Defendant, wanted for murder and manslaughter, surrendered to police accompanied by his attorney. The attorney left and defendant was interrogated by the police, at which time he made incriminating statements. Prior to his interrogation he was asked seven questions concerning whether or not he understood his rights, to which he replied: "I will give you an oral statement. My lawyer said I could make one without giving you the motive of what happened." The court held that his was an invalid *Miranda* waiver and it rejected the inference that defendant had knowledge of his rights from the fact that he came to the station with his attorney.

DuPont v. *United States*, 259 A.2d 355, District of Columbia Court of Appeals (1969)

A Washington, D.C. police officer received information that defendant had a machine gun concealed in his bed in a girl's apartment. After receiving from the girl a valid consent to search her apartment, the officer seized the machine gun from the defendant's bed. Defendant was arrested. At the police station the arresting officer called defendant's attention to a large sign on the wall containing the *Miranda* warnings. Defendant refused to look at it. Later a Sergeant Evanoff interrogated defendant. He attempted to give defendant the *Miranda* warnings, but defendant cut him off stating, "I know my rights, man," and, according to the court, defendant indicated that "Sergeant Evanoff didn't have to go into that." Again defendant did not look at the card on the wall.

Thereafter, defendant made inculpatory statements exonerating the girl in whose apartment the gun was found, called his attorney, and then made further inculpatory statements. The court suppressed all of the defendant's statements as violative of *Miranda*.

Chief Judge Hood, dissenting, stated that under these facts:

> I think *Miranda* must be interpreted in a realistic and reasonable manner, and that the officers did all that reasonable men could do.
> What more could the officers have done? Should they have forced appellant to read or listen? Should the detectives have continued to read when it was obvious that appellant was not listening?
> It is my opinion that when officers make a good faith effort to inform an arrested person of his *Miranda* rights and that person refuses to pay any at-

tention to the officers, such person has no standing to claim that he was not informed of his rights. [259 A.2d 359, 360.]

In the two preceding cases the investigating officers gave, or attempted to give, the *Miranda* warnings. They had every reason to believe that the defendant was well aware of his rights, yet in each case the rigidity of the *Miranda* rule compelled the courts to suppress the statements made. Any common-sense analysis would dictate that one who states he knows his rights, or one who arrives at the police station with an attorney would be aware of his rights and that their statements were voluntary. Such a common-sense approach was disregarded by the courts, however, and the inflexible *Miranda* standards were applied.

These cases are not isolated instances. They were collected from well over 150 appellate cases, decided during the years 1968-73 in which law-enforcement officers ran afoul of the inflexible standards of *Miranda*, even though there was a good-faith attempt to comply with *Miranda* and no coercive tactics had been used. And these are only appellate cases. There is simply no way to determine how many cases have been dismissed at the trial level, or simply have not been brought to trial, because of asserted *Miranda* violations. At a conservative estimate, such cases, nationwide, number in the hundreds, perhaps the thousands.

Eugene H. Methvin, a senior editor of *Reader's Digest,* in a 1970 article in *Human Events* entitled "Let's Restore the Fifth Amendment," catalogued a series of cases in which *Miranda* required the freeing of extremely dangerous individuals. These cases reveal the terrible burden that *Miranda* and cases like it have placed upon law-enforcement officers. In each case the suppression of the truth is evident:

In Seattle, Harry Van DeVenter went free because police omitted one sentence before he confessed a robbery-murder: "If you can't afford a lawyer, we will get you one." The officers had carefully warned him he had a right to a lawyer and to refuse to answer their questions. Van DeVenter willingly admitted killing an elderly hotel night clerk, Paul Wightman, and taking $30 from his cash register. He even led police to the two guns he had thrown into Puget Sound, and ballistic tests verified that they were indeed the lethal weapons. Stormed the *Seattle Post-Intelligencer:* "Harry Van DeVenter is a free man because no attorney was present when he confessed a killing. Paul Wightman is a dead man, robbed and shot without benefit of legal counsel. Whose rights were violated?"

After Los Angeles police read a robbery-murder suspect his *Miranda* rights, the man said, "I want to have an attorney present." The officers called in a Legal Aid Society lawyer and let the two talk alone. Invited back in, the officers asked their first question. The suspect started to answer. The lawyer interrupted, ordered the officers out, and after another conference invited them back in. Again the suspect started to answer. Again the lawyer interrupted. "I'm tired and I don't want your help," the suspect objected. Again the lawyer ordered the officers out. The third time they started to question, the lawyer curtly told them his client would have "nothing to say." That ended the case, since police could not obtain sufficient evidence to prosecute.

In Denver a rape victim tentatively pointed to one of several photographs of known sex offenders she "thought" resembled her attacker. Detectives brought him to headquarters, and following the new Supreme Court rules read the *Miranda* warning. "I would like to talk to my lawyer," the man said, and was shown to the office phone. The lawyer was not home, and after a short wait the man blurted, "I might as well tell you about it." He did so—in detail that left no doubt that he was indeed the rapist. Yet because Chief Justice Warren had placed the burden on police to prove a confessed criminal waived his rights voluntarily, the rapist went free without prosecution.

A 14-year-old Oklahoma boy killed his mother with ten rifle shots. His father with two policemen questioned him, and he admitted it. But Judge Merle Lansden threw out the confession and found the boy not guilty, declaring he had "no alternative" under Chief Justice Warren's *Miranda* opinion even though "I feel he was amending the Constitution." "This is the worst miscarriage of justice I've ever seen," declared Prosecutor Loys Criswell. "It means you can't even question your own child if he breaks a window without getting a lawyer. This is ridiculous."

In Miami one Sunday night three young men dragged a woman off the street into a vacant lot and brutally gang-raped her. From her hospital bed she identified a photograph of a young neighborhood man with a criminal record and later picked him out from a lineup. But neighborhood informants told police, "You've got the wrong man," naming three others. Caught fleeing the state, the three declined to answer questions. "If we followed what the Supreme Court believes is fair play, we would have had to let the man in jail take his chances with a jury," says Det. Sgt. Bill Shepherd. "But we were afraid an innocent man's freedom was in jeopardy, so we decided to violate the *Miranda* decision and interrogate anyway. For an hour Sgt. Shepherd talked to one of the three, carefully explaining his rights: "If this fellow is in jail for something you did, why don't you clear him?" he said. The suspect confessed, led police to the precise rape scene, and even detailed incidents the victim had neglected to mention—such as how the three had pinned her to the ground, muffling her mouth, when an automobile drove into a nearby driveway. The innocent man went free— but so did all three rapists, because under the new rules the confession was deemed "involuntary." "I've been a policeman for 18 years, and I don't know any other way we could have handled this case fairly," Sgt. Shepherd told me. "How would you have done it?"[31]

These cases also illustrate the very important point that often there

111

is simply not enough evidence to convict defendants apart from their voluntary confessions. Two noted authorities on the law of confessions and admissions have expressed the problem clearly:

> A man is hit on the head while walking home late at night. He does not see his assailant nor does anyone else. A careful and thorough search of the crime scene reveals no physical clues. Then take the case of a woman who is grabbed on the street at night and dragged into an alley and raped. Here, too, the assailant was unaccommodating enough to avoid leaving his hat or other means of identification at the crime scene, and there are no other physical clues. All the police have to go on is the description of the assailant himself. She describes him as about six feet tall, white, and wearing a dark suit. Or consider this case, an actual one, in Illinois. Three women are vacationing in a wooded resort area. Their bodies are found dead, the result of physical violence, alongside a foot trail, and no physical clues are present.[32]

To complicate the problem for the police, the *Miranda* decision also held that any "fruits" of a confession obtained in violation of the *Miranda* rules must also be excluded. Therefore, if a suspect makes a confession that includes telling the police where physical evidence such as a murder weapon or the proceeds of a robbery are, such physical evidence cannot be used if the confession is later found to have been obtained in violation of *Miranda*. Thus, in cases like these, the truth is doubly suppressed.

The *Miranda* majority airily dismissed the problem that in case after the case the voluntary confession is an absolute prerequisite: "Our accusatory system of criminal justice demands that the government seeking to punish an individual produce the evidence against him by its own independent labors, rather than by the cruel simple expedient of compelling it from his own mouth."[33] By this simplistic statement the majority appears to believe that all criminals leave glaring trails of other evidence behind them, and that all the police have to do is pick it up. This is simply not the case, as we have seen.

The Court's attitude brings to mind a statement made by Justice Black in another context: "It is always easy to hint at mysterious means available just around the corner to catch outlaws."[34] The "mysterious means" by which the police are to apprehend criminal offenders are quite easy to talk about from the ivory tower of the bench. But for the working officer, charged with the job of actually catching criminals, such bland hints at mysterious means are frustrating indeed. This perceptive statement did not, however, prevent Justice Black from being a majority justice in *Miranda*.

Finally, decisions such as *Miranda*, which are couched in the broadest language imaginable, give permissive courts a sort of *carte blanche* to stretch the restrictions on the police far beyond even what *Miranda* envisioned. For example, the California Supreme Court, without question the most permissive court in the country, reversed the conviction for two murders of a sixteen-year-old confessed killer named Burton. There was no question in the *Burton* case that the police acted properly in questioning the youth. The court itself admitted that "a police officer carefully explained to defendant his *Miranda* rights" and that "he understood such explanation and . . . waived these rights." Nevertheless, the court held the confessions to be inadmissible because Burton was not allowed to see his *mother*. Now, there is not the first word in the *Miranda* decision concerning the right of a suspect to see his mother, yet the California court, in its apparent zeal to loose confessed murderers upon society, stretched the rights of the youthful killer to this surrealistic length.[35]

In all of the cases described herein, there is not the slightest question of rack or thumbscrew treatment. Nor is there any indication of what Chief Justice Warren, in *Miranda,* chose to refer to as "the simple, cruel expedient of compelling [evidence of guilt] from [the accused's] own mouth." In fact, in each case described, the confession was so patently voluntary that a pre-*Miranda* court would not have thought twice about admitting it into evidence. This is because, prior to *Miranda*, the courts in this country had a realistic and common-sense standard for judging the voluntariness of confessions.

Miranda has, of course, changed all of this. Now the common-sense standards have been replaced by an artificial litany of warnings that stand alone, austere, and implacable; if even *one* of the warnings is not drummed into the head of the suspect or if an officer deviates by a few words from the artificial standard, any confession, no matter how conclusive the evidence that it was voluntarily made, must be excluded and often the perpetrators of the most heinous crimes are freed.

Such travesties of justice may have been in the mind of Henry Friendly, a highly respected justice of the United States Court of Appeals for the Second Circuit, when in 1968 he called for a reexamination of the privilege against self-incrimination because of *Miranda* and other similar decisions of the Warren Court. Judge Friendly stated: "At the end of the 1960s it is necessary to vindicate the rights of society against what in my view has become a kind of obsession with the privilege against self-incrimination which has stretched it far beyond its language and history . . ."[36]

As with the Exclusionary Rule, the United States stands alone in requiring the exclusion of voluntary confessions. The rule in Great Britain, Canada, and Australia is the same as the pre-*Miranda* rule in this country, that the confession must be proven to have been voluntary in the legal sense. In 1970 an attempt was made to impose *Miranda*-like restrictions on the Canadian police. A bill had been introduced in Parliament which provided that no statement of an accused could be used in evidence against him if he did not have a lawyer upon request at questioning. The bill was defeated by Prime Minister Pierre Trudeau's Liberal Party. Speaking against the bill, D. Gordon Blair (Lib., Ont.) stated: "I think our concern should be about justice, not only to the persons who are suspected of committing crimes but to all other members of society."[37] In an obvious thrust at the criminal justice system in the United States, he added:

> I hope that never in this country will we be caught up in the kind of debate they have been conducting south of the border on the subject of law and order.
> Law and order can only truly be based upon justice and upon the realization by all people that their criminal law is administered in a just way.[38]

With decisions like *Miranda* resulting in the freeing of obviously guilty criminals, it is very difficult, if not impossible, for law-abiding citizens in this country to believe that our criminal justice system is being "administered in a just way."

For those to whom *Miranda* is an abomination before all law, logic, and justice, there is considerable hope that relief may be in sight. Congress has purported to "overrule" *Miranda,* at least in the federal courts, through legislation, and the "new" Supreme Court under Chief Justice Warren Burger has indicated a willingness to reconsider the entire issue. Further, in 1971 the Burger Court, in the case of *Harris* v. *New York,*[39] somewhat limited the scope of *Miranda;* it ruled that while statements taken in violation of *Miranda* could not be used by the prosecution in *its* case, if the defendant took the stand such statements could be used to challenge the truth of the defendant's testimony. *Miranda*, said Chief Justice Burger, speaking for a five-justice majority, did not grant the right to commit perjury with impunity.

Finally, the Supreme Court now has before it a case that will test the scope of the *Miranda* decision. The case involves a Michigan man, Thomas W. Tucker, convicted of the brutal rape and beating of a forty-nine-year-old woman. To the police the defendant made a statement that was voluntary in all respects but that failed to meet the requirements laid down by the Court in *Miranda;* therefore, his statement could not be used against him. In this statement, however, the suspect had given the police the name of one Henderson as an alibi witness. Unfortunately for the defendant, Henderson not only did not corroborate his alibi but gave extremely damaging testimony against Tucker at the trial in which he was convicted. The Michigan Supreme Court upheld Tucker's conviction but, typically, the federal courts reversed the conviction after Tucker brought a habeas-corpus petition.

The federal court ruled that Henderson's testimony was the "fruit" of Tucker's "illegal" confession and ordered a new trial for Tucker without the use of Henderson's testimony. In agreeing to review the case, the U.S. Supreme Court, for the first time since *Miranda,* has before it the question whether *Miranda* should be overruled or modified.[40]

Until such time, it is the law of the land, and law-enforcement officers, prosecutors, law-abiding citizens, and victims alike must live with it. Even if *Miranda* should be overruled, that decision will stand a monument to the permissiveness of the Warren Court and a memorial of the way our system slights victims of crime and suppresses truth.

The Legacy of Permissiveness: Other Decisions of the Warren Court and Their Impact

Certainly the Exclusionary Rule and the *Miranda* decision were the two greatest blows that the Warren Court struck against law enforcement and the victims of crime. By the Exclusionary Rule and *Miranda,* two of the most relevant and probative types of evidence of guilt—physical evidence and voluntary confessions—were made extremely difficult to obtain in a usable form. In other areas, however, the Warren Court appeared to be equally disdainful of the rights of the law-abiding. We will now briefly examine some of these.

The "lineup" cases (*U.S.* v. *Wade*; *U.S.* v. *Gilbert*—hereafter referred to as *Wade-Gilbert*) were noted briefly in chapter three. This was the series of cases in which the Court ruled, in 1967, that a victim or witness who had identified the perpetrator of a crime in a lineup could not testify in court as to the lineup identification unless the suspect had had an attorney present at the lineup or had waived his right to have the attorney present. The Court also ruled that if the suspect's attorney had not been present at the lineup, then the victim or witness could not even identify the suspect to the jury *in open court* unless the prosecution could prove that the in-court identification was not "tainted" by the lineup that was held minus an attorney.

Prior to the lineup cases it lay with the trial judge whether or not to allow an identification of the suspect in court. If the defendant convinced the judge that his identification by a victim or witness had been obtained by illegal police practices—like suggesting to the witness that he identify the suspect in a lineup, or conducting a "rigged" lineup so that the suspect stood out like a sore thumb for easy identification—then the judge, in fairness to the defendant, could suppress the identifica-

115

tion. If not, the jury would be permitted to hear all of the circumstances of the identification of the defendant and make up its own mind as to whether the identifying victim or witness was telling the truth.

In the lineup cases the Warren Court did precisely what it had done in *Miranda:* (1) it removed the prior common-sense standards for admissibility of evidence—voluntariness in the case of confessions, fair procedures for the identification in the lineup cases; and (2) it substituted rigid and artificial standards—the litany of warnings in confession cases, the presence of an attorney in the lineup cases—thereby entirely removing the discretion of the trial judge to admit the evidence if the Court's newly conceived standards were not met.

As with the Exclusionary Rule and *Miranda* decisions, the lineup cases often resulted in a direct suppression of the truth. If the police through inadvertence, lack of an understanding of the new rule, or because no attorney was available or would agree to show up conducted a lineup without an attorney present (or waived), the bewildered victim of, say, an armed robbery, who had positively and accurately identified the robber in a lineup, might find himself forbidden by the judge from testifying about the lineup and even from identifying the robber in court at trial.

Many suspects had to be freed because forbidden, albeit positive and accurate, eyewitness identification was the only evidence against them. In one case, a Denver police detective had made a positive identification of a hoodlum who had assaulted him, yet this identification was suppressed because no attorney had been present at the lineup and the assailant was freed. This is a glaring example of the rigidity with which this rule was applied.

Fortunately, in 1972, in the case of *Kirby* v. *Illinois,*[41] the Supreme Court under Warren Burger greatly restricted the impact of the lineup cases by ruling that the attorney-at-the-lineup requirement applied only to lineups held *after* the suspect had been indicted. Since most lineups are conducted to identify the suspect in order to make a case for indictment, this decision greatly curtailed the adverse effects of the decision on law enforcement.

Now one important point must be made regarding *Kirby*. It was decided by a five-justice majority (Burger, Stewart, Blackmun, Powell, Rehnquist), yet none of the majority justices would for a moment countenance unfair police practices. Should a defendant be able to show that his identification was procured improperly, such as a suggestive lineup in which he was in effect pointed out by police officers to the witness, then he might still have such identification suppressed. The key difference between the Court's rationale in *Kirby* and its reasoning in *Wade-Gilbert* is that in *Kirby*, the standard for admissibility was returned to the common sense of fundamental fairness, whereas in the *Wade-Gilbert* series of cases, the standard had been the inflexible one of the presence of an attorney. No suspect really aggrieved by oppressive police tactics in the identification area will *lose* any rights because of *Kirby*—and far fewer guilty persons will be freed.

The Warren Court on occasion seemed of the attitude that once it had made evidence obtained by an "illegal" search and seizure inadmissible in court, it would then attempt to make it as difficult as possible for the police to make a *legal* search and seizure—or even to know what one was. The Court, for example, set up highly technical and very difficult legal requirements for obtaining proper search warrants by the police.*[42] Then three months later, in a reversal of some twelve years of law, it held that, with very limited exceptions, police officers making searches of buildings must have search warrants in almost every case. Thus, the problem confronting a conscientious police officer, not trained in the law, could be summed up: "I know that the evidence is in a given house. I know that I must have a warrant to search the house. Yet the requirements for a valid warrant are such that I cannot really be sure that if I secure a search warrant, it will be held valid."

In another ruling the Court held that a criminal suspect's fingerprints that had been taken after an arrest and subsequently held to be "illegal" could not be used in evidence against him.[43] This ruling often placed the police in a damned-if-you-do, damned-if-you-don't position. For example, shortly after this decision was announced, a young girl was beaten to death in Denver. The only clue to the identity of the murderer was a set of fingerprints, not those of the victim, found on a beer glass in her apartment. The police had several suspects—boyfriends of the victim—but did not have sufficient evidence to arrest any of them. None of the suspects' fingerprints were on file. Had the police arrested the suspects for the purpose of fingerprinting them, the fingerprints, even if they matched those found at the crime scene, would have been inadmissible in evidence. Thus the officers were stymied. They had fingerprints at the crime scene and suspects in the crime, but the Court's recent ruling prevented them from being able, legally, to connect the two. The murder was never solved.

The Warren Court also engaged in second-guessing of law enforcement officers. Officers who in good faith did not give the *Miranda* warnings to a suspect because they were questioning him in his own home, found that this was improper and the conviction of a confessed murderer was reversed. In another case federal agents, without a warrant, placed a recording device on a telephone booth to overhear a

* In a 1971 decision by the Burger Court, this case was made much less restrictive upon the police.

bookie calling in bets. This had been deemed a perfectly proper technique until the Warren Court discovered that the bookie was entitled to a "reasonable expectation of privacy" in the phone booth to carry on his illegal activities. The evidence of the overheard bets was suppressed.[44]

Particularly in the law of search and seizure, policemen were expected to conduct themselves as if they had mastered a body of law which appeared to change almost daily and upon which the lawgivers themselves could not agree. Splits of 5-4 and 6-3 among the justices appeared to be the rule in search-and-seizure cases, with each side telling the other how wrong it was. In deciding cases, the justices have months to agonize over whether a given search was legal. Yet the officer, who has to decide whether or not to act, is expected to make a correct decision in about thirty seconds, or have his entire case fail.

Thus we see the major Warren Court rulings as suppressors of the truth. I should in fairness state that not all of the rulings of that Court went against the peace forces. For example, the Court permitted police officers to "stop and frisk" those reasonably suspected of crime;[45] to protect the identity of confidential narcotics informants;[46] and to search a house that they had entered in "hot pursuit" of a suspect.[47]

These cases were, however, exceptions rather than the rule. As noted earlier in this chapter, the Court in ten years reversed 176 of our 256 criminal convictions. That is a reversal rate of sixty-nine percent, or almost seven in ten. This reversal rate indicates an extremely high rate of permissiveness towards criminals and a correspondingly low rate of concern for the law-abiding. Additionally, in most of the cases of reversals, the Court laid down new and restrictive guidelines for police conduct. These created new difficulties for the police and prosecutors in preventing crime and apprehending and convicting criminals.

Almost all of the Warren Court's decisions reversing convictions in criminal cases refer in lofty and, on occasion, rather smug terms to individual rights, liberties, and freedoms. Every murderer, rapist, robber, thief, and drug pusher whom the Court's holdings have freed, or whose criminal career has been encouraged by the Court-inspired climate of permissiveness, by definition denies his victim, without due process of law, the right to life or liberty or property or to go about his business in peace. This simply was not considered by the Warren Court. Permissiveness for the violator and suppression of the truth of a criminal's guilt were the watchword of the Warren Revolution. Consideration for the victims was ignored.

Ideally the victims of crime and their families should rejoice that our legal system stoutly protects the liberties of those who victimize them. When the father of a rape-murder victim, at the trial of the killer,

118

watches the defense table suddenly break out in an orgy of handshaking and laughter because, as a result of some minor violation of the killer's rights by the police, the judge has just suppressed both the defendant's confession and all of the physical evidence against him, thus freeing him, the father should theoretically be ecstatic that our system jealously guards the rights of all, even murderers. But he probably won't be.

He just may feel that our permissive system is preoccupied with the rights of rapists and murderers, whereas his rights and those of his daughter before she died have been ignored, even denied. And he will be right.

5
Permissiveness
Continued:
Courts and
Corrections

Introduction

IT IS AN ELEMENTARY PROPOSITION that if there were fewer criminally inclined individuals at liberty to victimize the innocent, there would be fewer victims of crime. It takes no exploration of the field of logic to realize this. If criminal A has robbed and assaulted B, and if A has been apprehended and convicted for this crime, then the criminal justice system is faced with the known fact that A is an individual with a propensity for violent crime. He has victimized an innocent citizen *at least once*. Now if A is released into society with no more inconvenience to himself than the transitory annoyance of arrest and trial (or guilty plea), then he is, beyond question, at liberty to victimize again. The lenient treatment accorded him not only will not serve as a deterrent to others similarly inclined, but will act as a definite incentive to potential criminals who have seen that crime is simply not punished.

Our hypothetical example is, sadly, all too actual in our criminal justice system, as countless cases and studies demonstrate. Mr. James Q. Wilson, professor of government at Harvard University, wrote in 1973 an article in the *New York Times Magazine* entitled "If Every Criminal *Knew* He Would Be Punished If Caught. . . ."[1] A masterful, scholarly, and incisive call for common sense in our criminal justice process, this article, cites several studies graphically illustrating the system's penchant for setting criminals, often repeaters, at liberty:

● In the Common Pleas Court of Pittsburgh in 1966 "well over one half of the white males convicted of burglary, grand larceny, indecent assault, or possession of narcotics *and who had a prior record* were placed on probation; nearly half of the two-time losers convicted of aggravated assault were placed on probation as were more than one fourth of those convicted of robbery."[2]

● In Wisconsin, between 1954 and 1959, sixty-three percent of the adult males convicted of a felony and who had one prior felony conviction were granted probation, as were forty-one percent of those who had *two or more* prior felony convictions.[3]

● In New York State, between 1963 and 1969, the proportion of those convicted of felony narcotic offenses (many dealers, not merely users) who were sent to prison fell from sixty-eight percent to twenty-three percent. As Professor Wilson pointed out with regard to this sharp drop-off, since dealing in narcotics is essentially a business crime, the businessmen and women, who were *not* jailed for plying this particular trade, must surely be convinced that crime does indeed pay.[4]

At the other end of our continent, a study by the California Governor's Select Committee on Law Enforcement Problems, released in 1973, reported that between 1960 and 1971, prison sentences in that state decreased from twenty-five percent to five percent, probation cases increased from twenty-five percent to seventy-five percent, *while overall crime in California increased by 122.5 percent.*[5]

The conclusion is inescapable: our law-abiding citizens are being victimized to an intolerable extent by convicted criminals who have been returned to the streets. Additionally, other criminally inclined individuals are convinced that if they too wish to prey upon others, their chances of being punished are at best minimal.

This is an absolutely horrible state of affairs, made even worse by the fact that the remedy is so very simple: the swift and certain apprehension and punishment of those who commit crimes—"punishment" meaning incarceration in the greatest majority of cases, at least for some period of time.

In his dissenting opinion in the *Miranda* decision (see chapter four), Justice Byron White discussed the theory of deterrence by swift and certain justice:

The swift and sure apprehension of those who refuse to respect the personal security and dignity of their neighbors unquestionably has its impact on others who might be similarly tempted. That the criminal law is wholly or partly ineffective with a segment of the population or with many of those who have been apprehended or convicted is a very faulty basis for concluding that it is not effective with respect to the great bulk of our citizens or for thinking that without the criminal laws, or in the absence of their enforcement, there would be no increase in crime. Arguments of this nature are not borne out by any kind of reliable evidence that I have seen to date.[6]

Professor Wilson, in his article on the certainty of punishment as a deterrent to crime, concludes that it is precisely this certainty that acts as the deterrent, and he cites recent studies to back up his conclusion. The basic inference to be drawn from the studies cited seems to be that, while the *severity* of a given punishment has little proven deterrent effect, the fact that a criminal knows that he *will* be punished acts as a substantial deterrent.[7]

Isaac Ehrlich published in 1973 a study that analyzed the specific relationships between crime and punishment. He found that "the rate of specific felonies is . . . positively related to estimates of relative gains [the more money to be gained by stealing, the more attempts made to steal it] and negatively related to estimates of costs associated with criminal activity." Hence, the "rate of specific crime categories, with virtually no exceptions, varies inversely with estimates of the probability of apprehension and punishment . . . and with the average length of time served in prisons. . . ."[8]

The aforementioned California Select Committee on Law Enforcement Problems reached a similar conclusion in its study regarding the certainty of punishment: "Prison can contribute to public protection against all felonies by punishing offenders who are convicted and deterring those who are potential offenders. For this purpose, it is more important that the punishment be swift and certain rather than be severe" (p. 67).

The concept of punishment as a deterrent to crime has been articulated by some individuals who certainly should know: the criminals themselves. In August 1973 Herbert Mullin was convicted of the murder of thirteen persons in Santa Cruz, California. Mullin testified at his trial, where he admitted the killings, that had he received prison sentences for earlier crimes he would not have committed the murders.

He told of receiving a suspended sentence for possession of marijuana in 1968 and, then, of being sentenced to a mere ten days in jail for resisting arrest. He continued: "If I had gotten one year for resisting arrest I would never have killed anyone because jail is a deterrent. What were they waiting for? Until I broke a big law so I would spend the rest of my life in jail? . . . If I had spent five years in jail I never would have killed anyone because jail is a horrible experience.[9]

In a similar vein, a convicted bank robber wrote to Mike Royko, columnist for the *Chicago Daily News*, about lenient sentencing disposition as applied to his own case:

> The judge in sentencing me stated that I was indeed "a dangerous offender" and that he expected me to rob another bank at the first opportunity.
>
> Then he sentenced me to 8 years out of a possible 20 years and inserted immediate parole eligibility.
>
> This, although he knew I had been confined 15 of the past 20 years for 13 felonies and 4 misdemeanors.
>
> Had I known that I would have received a mandatory 25 year sentence for bank robbery, without any opportunity to negotiate a plea, there would have been no power on earth strong enough to force me to rob the bank that I robbed.

We have, then, reasonably good authority, based in large measure upon common-sense principles, for the proposition that swift and certain punishment is in fact a deterrent to the potential criminal. While this proposition admittedly cannot be mathematically proven, it *can* be stated with every assurance that if we do not punish convicted lawbreakers, we have no hope at all of deterring other potential lawbreakers.

Swift and certain punishment would reduce the number of criminals at liberty to victimize the innocent by: (1) isolating those dangerous to society, particularly violent criminals, and those who have committed serious crimes, and (2) deterring would-be criminals because of the absolute certainty that they will be punished for all but the most trivial of crimes.

Unfortunately, this is simply not happening in our criminal justice system today, thanks largely to the permissive attitude of too many judges, correctional officials, and social theorists involved in the system. This chapter focuses on unwarranted permissiveness, from the victims' point of view. It is most assuredly *not* a wholesale indictment of our court and corrections systems. There are, of course, many, perhaps a majority, of our judges and corrections officials who are deeply concerned with our rising crime rates and with the plight of the victims. This chapter deals with the abuses within the system, those many instances in which permissiveness is carried to such lengths that the concept of swift and certain punishment of criminals is abandoned.

In recent years the lines have been drawn generally into two schools of thought regarding the treatment of those accused, or convicted, of criminal acts. The first of these is the hard-line or victim-oriented viewpoint; the second is the permissive or criminal-oriented approach.

The victim-oriented view is more closely related to traditional and historical observations regarding crime and punishment, with the protection of the public being the primary concern. Insofar as crime itself is concerned, this view holds the criminal responsible for his crime (except in those cases in which he was obviously insane; that is, unable to tell right from wrong) and expresses the moral outrage of the law-abiding element of society against the criminal. It also takes the very realistic attitude that some criminals commit crimes simply because it pleases them to do so, or that they like to see people hurt. An apt description of such criminals was made by Ridgely Hunt of the *Chicago Tribune* in a series of stories dealing with robbers and robbery victims in Chicago: "It appears that many robbers lack any shred of compassion or sympathy for their victims—and probably for anyone else. They are alienated from the rest of mankind and thus indifferent to human suffering."[10]

With regard to the punishment of criminals, the hard-line theory calls for criminal sanctions for the following purposes: (1) punishment, to vindicate the rights of the victim and to express society's outrage; (2) isolation, to protect the public; (3) deterrence, to discourage others similarly inclined by the example of the criminal; and (4) rehabilitation—if the criminal is amenable to the rehabilitative process. The emphasis here is clearly on the rights of the law-abiding, with the protection of society from the lawbreaker being the first consideration. This is not to say that help for the criminal offender is ignored under the hard-line view; it is merely a question of priorities. In most cases two options are presented regarding the disposition of an offender: the first involves taking a chance that the release of a criminal, while perhaps beneficial to him individually, may create a decided risk to society; the second is that incarceration of a criminal will protect society, while not being of particular benefit to the offender. Those who are victim-oriented will generally opt for the second. Once the second option has been chosen, then such rehabilitative efforts as may be feasible can be attempted. But the priority is clear: society comes first.

The permissive philosophy towards criminals was summarized brilliantly by the California Governor's Select Committee on Law Enforcement Problems:

> Some 15 years ago, a number of vocal critics of the criminal justice system attacked [the purposes of punishment of the criminal embodied in the hard-line view] on various grounds. They said that punishment or retribution was immoral, barbaric, and uncivilized. They said isolation for public protection was not justified except in extreme cases like homicidal maniacs who should be restrained only long enough to be treated. They said that punishment did not deter others from committing crimes, and even if it did, it was immoral to punish a criminal to deter others from crime. In their view crime was not so much a matter of individual responsibility as it was a failure of society. As a consequence they felt that the only justifiable goal of the criminal justice system was to rehabilitate the offender so he would be able to avoid criminal behavior in the future. And finally, they claimed prisons did not rehabilitate but actually caused crime, and that prisons which did not rehabilitate should not exist.[11]

This, in a nutshell, is the philosophy of the permissivists. Is it, perhaps, overstated? One concrete example will answer this question, in the negative. In 1973 Representatives Barbee and Ward, members of the Wisconsin legislature, introduced "An Act to Create 973.18 of the Statutes, Relating to Prohibiting the Use of Imprisonment as Punishment and Requiring the Sale of State Prisons." The legislative analysis of this incredible bill is reprinted here verbatim, with emphasis supplied:

ANALYSIS BY THE LEGISLATIVE REFERENCE BUREAU

This bill *prohibits the state from imprisoning anyone for the violation of a statute,* unless his record, as reviewed by the sentencing judge or by the department of health and social services in the case of a person committed to its custody, indicates there is an *imminent* danger of *substantial* physical harm to himself or others if he were released on probation. Persons confined in institutions must receive prevailing wage rates for services rendered during confinement. *Any person in prison at the time the bill takes effect* (January 1, 1975) *must be released* except any prisoner committed to the custody of the department of health and social services who may:

1. Have conditions imposed on his release where necessary to assist in the person's rehabilitation; or
2. Be confined if, after a hearing, the department determines that his release would pose an *imminent* danger of *substantial physical harm* to himself or others.

Finally, the bill requires the department of health and social services to dispose of its prison property. After a minimum fair market price is established, prison property must be offered for sale to minority groups, but if an offer to buy a given piece of property is not received from any minority group within 90 days, the property will be offered for sale at public auction, with proceeds going to the general fund.[12]

It is reasonably safe to say that never has there been a more sheerly nonsensical example of permissiveness propounded. Under this bill criminals simply cannot be imprisoned to punish them for their crimes. Further, it requires that all prisoners be released except those who pose an imminent danger of substantial physical harm to themselves or others. Under this wording a man who had cold-bloodedly murdered his wife, say by poisoning, solely to benefit financially from her estate, but who had never been a threat to anyone else, could not be imprisoned; or if he was in prison when the act took effect, he must be released.

Likewise, the *only* condition upon which a criminal may be confined is the threat of "imminent danger of substantial physical harm" to himself or others. How, one wonders, could a police chief or district attorney, fighting to keep a criminal who had been convicted in his jurisdiction from being returned, *prove* that a violent individual, sent to prison for a robbery-murder two years before, poses an "imminent" and "substantial" threat of harm? Also, the requirement that a prisoner must present an imminent and substantial threat of "physical" danger in order not to be released is patently ridiculous. Pursuant to the specific words of the statute, every burglar, thief, swindler, forger, and other nonviolent criminal would have an automatic ticket to the outside, with a guarantee of freedom from future incarceration, unless he physically assaulted his victim.

Finally, the bill requires the sale of all of the state's prisons. Under the wording of the statute, even those few "imminently" and "substantially" dangerous individuals who must remain confined "shall be placed in institutions offering such treatment, education and training as is necessary and available to provide for the violator's rehabilitation and to prepare him for release." Any idea of the isolation of even conceded dangerous criminals in secure institutions in order to protect the law-abiding citizens of Wisconsin has been abandoned in this amazing piece of legislation.

Considered in its worst light, the proposed bill is a piece of permissive lunacy designed to foist an entire criminal population upon the good people of Wisconsin. Even giving the bill the benefit of every doubt and considering it as a sincere (albeit misguided) attempt at rehabilitation of criminals, one is constrained to deem it a classic example of the syndrome of permissiveness. It clearly is willing to "take a chance" with the safety of the law-abiding in the hope, and it is only a hope, that the wholesale release of Wisconsin's criminals will not result in an equally wholesale victimization of the law-abiding.

Subscribers to the victim-oriented view of the treatment of criminals would consider the foregoing bill to be anathema, embodying,
as it does, a complete contempt for the idea that society has a right to
punish its lawbreakers and to protect the potential victims of crime.
Unfortunately, however, there are far too many permissivists who are
only too willing to risk the safety of society.

Those willing to take a chance with the security of the law-abiding
are generally social tinkerers who view the problems of crime and
criminals from relatively safe, ivory-tower positions: the courts, the
higher echelons of the corrections establishment, the quiet meeting
rooms of special commissions and study groups, and the college cam-
puses. Those who view the realities of crime firsthand and who live in
constant fear of being victimized are precisely the individuals with
whose safety the permissivists are so willing to take a chance through
leniency to the criminal. The potential victims have a giant stake in
whether or not this social tinkering is wise, much more than do those
who from safe distances actually *do* the tinkering.

This may be illustrated by the recent highly permissive report of the
National Advisory Commission on Criminal Justice Standards and
Goals. One of the recommendations of this commission was that
probation should become the standard sentence in criminal cases,
with confinement retained chiefly for those offenders who could not
safely be supervised in the community.

Now there may be many residents of these communities who do
not want their lawbreakers returned to them via probation, which the
commission recommends as the "standard sentence in criminal
cases." Yet this is the recommendation. The commission is eager to
experiment with the safety of the community, by taking a chance that
criminals placed on wholesale probation will not victimize again. And
the residents of the community—upon whom the risks will actually
fall—will not likely be asked how they feel. It wouldn't matter anyway.

Punishment for the criminal, then, is neither swift nor sure because
of permissivism. We turn now to specifics, to demonstrate just how
those who are willing to take a chance with public safety cause an inordinate amount of victimization.

The Courts: Justice Neither Swift Nor Sure

1. Bail Abuses

The first stage of the criminal justice process at which the rights of
society and the rights of the accused come into conflict occurs when a
suspect is arrested and charged. At that time the decision must be

127

made by some court or committing magistrate whether or not to release him on bail.

The law-abiding citizens of this country react with an ever-growing frustration when daily they learn of some new outrage committed by a criminal. The frustration is compounded when it is discovered that the criminal involved was at liberty because of the permissiveness of our criminal justice system regarding bail for suspected criminal offenders. Often we learn that X, arrested for some particularly vicious bit of lawlessness, was at the time of his arrest free on bail pending his trial for one, two, three, or more previous offenses.

The questions of the right to bail and the amount of bail to be set are among the thorniest problems facing our criminal justice system. Cogent arguments can be made that fairness dictates that the right to bail should be limited only with the greatest care. It is quite obvious, for example, that the suspect's ability to prepare an effective defense will be greatly enhanced if he is free to assist his attorney and to seek out witnesses in his behalf. A criminal accused, furthermore, is presumed innocent until proven guilty and his confinement prior to trial appears to fly in the face of this presumption, particularly if he should later be acquitted or the charges against him dismissed.

In addition, pretrial confinement takes him from his home and family, disrupting his family life, an unhappy situation, common to all inmates. Finally, it is a statistically proven fact that suspects released on bail are more likely to be acquitted than those who are confined; however, in this context it can be argued that, by definition, those who are admitted to bail are the "better risks" or are those against whom the evidence is less overwhelming in the first place, thus making a favorable determination as to their cases more likely.

On the other hand, there are reasons equally cogent, at least from the point of view of the safety of society, that the right to bail, if carried to excess, can seriously prejudice the rights of the actual and potential victims of crime. The most telling of these arguments is the fact that our criminals are, for the most part, repeaters. Those free on bail for one crime may well be prone to commit others, either for the same reasons that prompted their first crime, or to raise the money to pay attorney's fees, fines, and other costs associated with the original charge. Similarly, a person free on bail is also free to attempt to terrorize or otherwise dissuade the victim or witnesses from testifying against him. Finally, the temptation is always present, especially for those whose crimes are serious, not to show up for the trial at all.

Obviously, then, there exists a conflict of rights, with the necessity for a just balance between fairness to the criminal accused and safety for society. Typically, in the area of the right to bail, as in most other areas, our criminal justice system has resolved the conflict in favor of the criminal and against the interests of the victim. It refuses to consider any sort of a just balance; the rights of the victims are, in most cases, totally subordinated to the rights of the suspect. The right to bail has now become so absolute that in many jurisdictions no consideration whatever is given to the rights of the law-abiding.

This has come about because most courts and legislatures across the nation have decreed that there is one and only one purpose for setting bail: to insure the appearance of the defendant in court. This in turn has been interpreted by some courts as allowing them free rein to release whom they please, despite the probability that the suspect will commit more crimes, terrorize victims and witnesses, or engage in other illicit activities while free on bail. Danger to the community and the innocent victims of crime is not contemplated.

A case in New York City in late 1972 and early 1973 illustrates this. One Joseph Gruttola was charged by the police with robbing a restaurant and shooting a patron of the restaurant and a policeman who had attempted to arrest him. Gruttola was captured by other police officers after a running gun battle in which the suspect was slightly wounded.[13]

Gruttola was arraigned before Judge Bruce McMarion Wright of the Criminal Court of New York City. Judge Wright, nicknamed "Turn-'em-Loose-Bruce" by New York policemen because of his ultralenient bail policies, set bail for Gruttola at $5,000, which meant that Gruttola would be freed upon posting $500 cash. The district attorney's office had asked that bail be set at $100,000. However, Gruttola's attorney asked for a low amount of bail because his client was "a good man and owns a business" and because it was Christmas. Judge Wright agreed with the defense attorney.

This superlenient treatment of a suspect accused of armed robbery, felonious assault, and attempted murder brought an immediate outcry from city officials. Even liberal mayor John Lindsay stated that he was "dismayed" at the low bail, and that he understood the "outrage" of the police over the incident because "the perpetrator was a cold-blooded gunman if there ever was one."

Patrick V. Murphy, then New York's liberal police commissioner, was even more outspoken:

> This is a disgrace. It points out once again how difficult it is for policemen to be effective when the judiciary, for whatever reason, doesn't do its job. As things stand now, a would-be murderer of a policeman is at large, while his victim, a young patrolman, lies wounded in a hospital. This cannot go on for much longer.[14]

Robert McKiernan, president of New York City's Police Benevolent Association, telegraphed his outrage to Chief Judge Stanley Fuld of the New York State Court of Appeals:

Corruption in the judiciary takes more than one form. Judge Wright corrupts the meaning of the word justice. His action mocks the public interest. The PBA asks you to institute proceedings to remove Judge Wright from the bench.[15]

Despite the proper indignation of these officials, the worst was yet to come from Judge Wright. The next day an attorney for the police department appeared before Judge Alfred Kleiman and requested that Gruttola's $500 bail be revoked because Gruttola had threatened, while in the hospital, to kill the policeman who had wounded him. Judge Kleiman revoked Gruttola's original bail and he was rearrested—only to be immediately released again on $500 bail by Judge Wright. The latter theorized that bail is designed "to assure appearance in court and if the accused has roots in the community then there is no bail."

This was too much for Edward M. Blagden, a patron of the restaurant, who, with the police officer, had been shot. The wounded witness against Gruttola released to the newspapers an open letter to Judge Wright:

> Your Honor: I understand that you released the holdup man who shot me and Patrolman Dowd early on Thursday morning. I also understand that you released him on $500.00 bail. The man tried to kill several people and threatened the lives of many others.
>
> The police risked their lives to catch him and you turned him loose. That does not seem to make much sense. He is dangerous. In view of what he did with a loaded gun Thursday morning, can you assure Patrolman Dennis Dowd and myself that he is going to be a model citizen from now on?
>
> Do you think he would like to pay our hospital bills? Is he planning to show up and stand trial? Is there no chance of his shooting someone else? Is there a good reason for him to go home for Christmas while we can't?
>
> The bail system has a purpose in life but you just made a joke of it. I think you owe me and my fellow New Yorkers an explanation. I await your reply with interest. Very truly yours, Edward M. Blagden.[16]

As a matter of fact, Gruttola did show up for trial and was convicted. But the issue remains: the laws of New York and other states, which purport to make the assurance of a suspect's appearance the *only* condition for bail, have been, and will continue to be, interpreted by lenient judges as a device by which they may foist the most patently dangerous criminals upon the community in the guise of setting little or no bail.

This sort of interpretation of the right to bail has prompted the most serious abuses in case after case. Criminal suspects, freed because of lenient bail policies, fail to show up for trial, commit other crimes, terrorize or kill victims and witnesses, and generally engage in lawless conduct that mocks the rights of their past and future victims.

BAIL JUMPING

If the purpose of bail is to assure the presence of the accused in court, then in many instances it is a failure from the start. In November 1971 the New York State Joint Legislative Committee heard witnesses testify that in New York City ten percent of all felony cases had to go unprosecuted because the defendants, released on bail or upon their promise to appear, did not show up in court.[17]

The committee heard other startling statistics. Between February and November of 1971 the defendants in 75,000 cases, ranging from minor housing violations and nonpayment of rent to felonies, had jumped bail, violated parole, or failed to appear at arraignment. One bail jumper had his bond set at $500 even though he had a record of seventeen previous arrests and fifteen convictions. Another bail jumper had his bond set at $200 although he had a record of five convictions and was wanted on two other charges at the time that bail was set.

One bizarre case, again in New York, involved a bail jumper who telephoned the judge before whom he was to appear to advise him that he was "on his way to Puerto Rico." After apologizing to the judge for his nonappearance, the suspect, facing charges of attempted murder involving the shotgun shooting of three policemen, told the judge that he was thinking of "shooting it out with the cops if he had to." The suspect had been freed on $5,000 bail because he had not received a speedy trial.[18]

New York is, of course, not alone in facing the problem of bail jumping. In 1971 the Washington, D.C., Bail Agency reported that twenty-five percent of those released under the ultrapermissive federal Bail Reform Act failed to show up for trial.[19] In Illinois the Cook County clerk of courts reported that in 1969 nearly 25,000 individuals freed on bond failed to appear.[20]

Two cases illustrate just how loose an interpretation some judges give the concept of "assuring" that the defendant will be present for trial. In Denver in 1971 a previously convicted armed robber was one day freed on $96,000 bonds in eight cases filed against him in Denver federal, district, and county courts. The suspect and three others had been arrested a few days earlier at Denver's Stapleton International Airport. They were about to board a flight to Las Vegas with a suitcase containing $20,000 worth of furs and jewelry taken in the burglary of a Denver realtor's house. Nevertheless, a county judge reduced the suspect's bail on the burglary charge from $25,000 to $12,000 and he was freed.[21]

In Springfield, Illinois, an eighteen-year-old accused rapist, whose first trial had resulted in a hung jury, escaped from the county jail in which he was being held pending a new trial. Rearrested, he was again released on $20,000 bail upon the payment of $2,000 cash bond for him by the Illinois Department of Children and Family Services, out of state funds.[22]

Now, in these two cases, there is evidence that the idea of flight was clearly on the defendants' minds, and both had been charged with serious crimes. Nevertheless, judges in each case set relatively low bail despite the fact both defendants had given every indication that they might well take flight again.

Of course, if the defendant is determined not to appear, either because he knows that his conviction will result in a pretty steep sentence or because he simply takes the easy way out by fleeing the jurisdiction, then *no* amount of money bail is going to assure his appearance. For example, in July 1973, a major narcotics supplier in New York jumped a $325,000 cash bond that had been posted on a $2.5 million bail amount. The cash amount was supplied for him the previous April by friends and relatives who put up their real estate holdings as collateral for the bonding company. One businessman in North Carolina had put up his entire business, valued at $100,000, as part of the collateral. As a result of the defendant's failure to appear, the entire bond was forfeit. The bonding company could then obtain foreclosures against those who put up their property to secure the bond.[23]

Bail jumping, then, is clearly a problem. However, the fact remains that most people, when released on bail or upon their promise to appear, *do* show up for trial. Thus, if nonappearance by the defendant were the *only* problem, then the adverse impact of this on the safety of society would be primarily the expense and manpower of the police being utilized to round up the bail jumpers when the same expense and manpower allocations could better be used in the basic protective function of the police. Unfortunately, bail jumping is far from being the only problem connected with bail abuses. A far more critical aspect of the issue is the problem of further crimes by those free on bail.

CRIMES BY THOSE ALREADY ON BAIL

When an individual has been arrested once for a serious crime, then there is every likelihood, at least where there is strong evidence of his guilt (for example, if he were caught in the act, if he has been positively identified as the perpetrator, if he has confessed, or if competent physical evidence against him has been seized), that society is faced with a dangerous individual. As has been noted, there are strong policy considerations, based on concepts of fairness to the accused, for enforcing his right to bail. But, must these considerations be the *only* bases for the decision whether or not to free him? Should not the threat that he may pose to future innocent victims be considered in addition to the defendant's rights? Must society be required to "take a chance" with the safety of the law-abiding, a chance it surely does take if the potential danger of the suspect to the community is ignored when bail decisions are made?

There is simply no doubt about the fact that many criminal defendants free on bail do in fact commit other crimes. Some authorities have put the recidivism rate for those released on bail at over fifty percent in some locations. Even such a conservative figure as ten percent recidivism, which would be accepted by most writers, is a major cause for concern.[24]

In any event, it is impossible to know just how many additional crimes are committed by those free on bail, because only in those cases in which a) crimes are reported to the police, and b) the police make an arrest or otherwise identify the suspect can we know whether that suspect was free on bail from another crime. Thus, as is true of most other statistics on crime, there is an element of the unknown based on the fact that much crime is unreported and many crimes are not solved.

One statistical analysis that gives some idea of the problems of crimes committed by those free on bail was made by the Metropolitan Police Department of Washington, D.C. A survey was made of rearrest data concerning those individuals who were on some form of "release status" for the months of April, May, and June 1972.

Before discussing this survey, we should note that the District of Columbia is governed, in the area of release on bail, by the federal Bail Reform Act of 1966.[25] This act, applicable in all jurisdictions covered by federal law, is perhaps the most permissive bail legislation in this country. The Bail Reform Act established a policy of pretrial release for as many defendants as possible on their *personal promise to appear in court or on an unsecured personal appearance bond*. Money bail was to be the last resort for a judge in assuring the appearance of the defendant at trial.[26] Basically, this law prevented judges from even considering whether the individual released would commit other crimes. This situation led U.S. District Court judge George L. Hart of the District of Columbia to note, rather pointedly, "If a defendant promised me that he was going to murder three persons, I would have to let him go."[27]

Against this background we turn to the report of the Metropolitan Police Department for the second quarter of 1972. During that period the department made 2,517 arrests for major crimes. Of these arrests 247 were made of persons currently free on their personal recognizance—that is, on their promise to appear in court. The breakdown of the 247 rearrests is as follows:

Homicide	10
Rape and Sex Crimes	11
Robbery	82
Burglary	29
Auto Theft	29
Narcotics	86
TOTAL	247

Thus, in almost 10 percent of the major crimes for which arrests were made in the District of Columbia in a three-month period, those charged had been freed under the District's permissive bail laws. In terms of the victims of crime, at least 167 (not counting the narcotics offenses) innocent individuals had been victimized because of that permissiveness.[28]

The report gives the details of several typical cases that demonstrate specifically the types of crimes for which the suspects were originally arrested and the types of crimes for which they were rearrested while on bail:

CASE #1 TWP, Age 19 years

Charges: Armed Robbery/Homicide and Rape

TWP was arrested by the police on August 17, 1971, and charged with armed robbery (holdup). In this case, TWP and another male subject entered a dairy store, in the northwest section of the city, on June 4, 1971, produced a pistol, and robbed the store operator of $20.00 in bills from the cash register.

TWP was released on personal recognizance, pending trial in this robbery case.

On June 27, 1972, while awaiting trial and while on his personal recognizance, TWP was arrested and charged with first-degree murder, second-degree murder, burglary, robbery, and rape. Investigation relative to these offenses, which occurred on October 25, 1971, in the northwest section of the city, revealed that an eighty-two-year-old female citizen was robbed, raped, and then suffocated to death in her apartment. Information developed in the case implicated TWP, who was subsequently arrested and is now currently residing in the D.C. Jail awaiting trial.

CASE#2 JER, Age 23 years

Charges: Armed Robbery/Fugitive from Justice (Maryland Homicide)

On May 27, 1972, JER was arrested for armed robbery (gun), on the basis of a warrant, charging him with the May 24, 1972, robbery of a thirty-nine-year-old northwest resident. This charge alleges that JER and an unknown subject gained entrance to victim's apartment, while armed with a handgun.

They then tied the victim up with a telephone cord, ransacked the apartment, and left the victim bound in his bathtub. JER was placed on personal recognizance in this matter.

On June 21, 1972, JER was rearrested in the District of Columbia, as a fugitive from justice. This arrest was made after it was learned that JER was wanted for the homicide of his wife, that occurred on that date, in Capital Heights, Maryland, and while he was on personal recognizance in this city.

JER is currently in D.C. Jail waiting extradition to Maryland.

CASE#3 BJE, Age 20 years

Charges: Armed Robbery (2)/Armed Robbery

On October 4, 1971, BJE was arrested and charged with two armed robberies of northwest service stations.

#1 BJE was identified as the lone armed subject, who on November 29, 1970, robbed a service station, while armed with a sawed-off gun. Identification was accomplished through photographs and a subsequent court-ordered lineup.

#2 During the previously mentioned lineup, BJE was also identified as one of two suspects who entered a service station (two blocks from the first case) and at the point of a pistol, robbed the attendant of $53.00 and during a struggle with the victim, discharged several shots.

On October 15, 1971, BJE was released on personal recognizance for both offenses.

April 17, 1972, BJE pleaded guilty to both armed robberies and was authorized to remain on personal recognizance until sentence was pronounced.

During these particular proceedings, in this jurisdiction, BJE was additionally placed on personal recognizance release in Rockville, Maryland, as a result of his arrest in that state on September 29, 1971, for another armed robbery.

On April 25, 1972, on the strength of a superior court warrant, charging burglary II, that had occurred on April 7, 1972, BJE was rearrested, while still on personal recognizance for the previous robbery offenses.

His identification in this case was achieved through the recovery of stolen property, arrest of a second suspect, and ultimate implication by that individual.

BJE is currently being held under $10,000 bond in D.C. Jail.

CASE#4 JM, Age 19 years
Charges: Armed Robbery/Armed Robbery

On March 8, 1972, JM was arrested, for armed robbery after having been identified by a female victim as having robbed her on the previous day. At the time of his arrest, patrol officers recovered a fully loaded .32-caliber pistol from his waistband, and the proceeds of the crime. JM was placed on his personal recognizance, pending trial.

On May 15, 1972, sixty-six days later, while still on personal recognizance, he was rearrested and charged with the armed robbery of a fifty-eight-year-old female, that occurred on April 26, 1972. This crime is alleged to have been perpetrated while JM and a second subject were both armed with handguns. Both JM and the second suspect were arrested on the basis of U.S. magistrates' warrant and after they were identified through photographs.

JM is currently confined in D.C. Jail, under $10,000 bond, pending trial.

CASE#5 JAC, Age 19 years
Charge: Burglary/Obstructing Justice/Armed Robbery

On March 24, 1972, JAC was arrested and charged with burglary of a northwest apartment, that occurred on March 5, 1972. His identification was accomplished through information furnished by a witness, that observed JAC leaving the premises carrying the proceeds of the crime. JAC was placed on personal recognizance, by the superior court, under the supervision of the D.C. Bail Agency, for this offense, pending trial.

While on personal recognizance, on April 4, 1972, JAC is alleged to have approached the sixty-five-year-old female witness, in the above described burglary, and threatened her life if he went to jail for that offense. On April 5, 1972, he was rearrested on strength of a superior court warrant, charging him with obstructing justice. JAC was then ordered to jail in lieu of $10,000 bond, pending grand jury action.

On April 14, 1972, while confined in D.C. Jail, JAC was identified and charged with armed robbery (gun), which is alleged to have been committed on April 3, 1972, while he was on personal recognizance, for burglary. In this matter, JAC is alleged to have entered the victim's residence with two other subjects, one of whom was armed with a rifle, and after pushing the fifty-seven-year-old victim to the floor and covering him with a coat, ransacked the apartment. The victim subsequently reported property valued in excess of $400.00 stolen, and one .38-caliber handgun.

JAC is currently in D.C. Jail, under $10,000 bond, charged with burglary, obstructing justice, and armed robbery that occurred while he was on personal recognizance.

The problem of repeat offenders—those arrested for one crime, released on bail, and then rearrested for another crime—is perhaps as critical in Dallas, Texas, as in Washington, D.C. Former police chief Frank Dyson reported in 1973 that in three months in 1971 (January, April, July), the Dallas Police Department filed cases against 1,076 individuals for major crimes. Of these, he noted, *over half* were repeat offenders and he cited examples:

> RFK, a burglar, was freed on eleven outstanding bonds which totaled $51,000. His oldest offense had occurred seventeen months before.
>
> TJM, also a burglar, had been free for thirteen months after posting a total of $30,000 in bonds in seven cases.
>
> BGR, a thief and forger, was free on seventeen outstanding bonds amounting to $23,000. His oldest crime had occurred thirty months previously.[29]

A series of cases, in Chicago in 1971 and 1972, involving one suspect demonstrates the excesses of the "right" to bail. On March 18, 1972, a man was arrested for the rape and beating of a twenty-three-year-old woman. The suspect, who had previously served seven years in prison for two rapes, was at the time of his arrest free on $50,000 bond on charges of seventeen sex-related crimes. A grand jury, with the usual good sense shown by the average citizens who make up grand juries, had set bond at $1,050,000 for the sex crimes, but the criminal justice system, exemplified by the Chicago courts, knew better. The suspect's bond was reduced by a million dollars to the $50,000 figure and he was, typically, freed to rape again.[30]

The foregoing demonstrates that there *are* a significant number of criminally inclined individuals who use their freedom on bail to victimize again. Unfortunately, far too many judges are perfectly willing (some appear almost eager) to loose these dangerous individuals on society.

In chapter one the disdain of the California Supreme Court for the rights of the law-abiding was demonstrated by its decision prohibiting a lower court from denying bail in order to protect society from a concededly dangerous man. The lone dissenting judge accused the majority of turning the right to bail into an instrument of crime. This accusation also applies to other judges, who time and again release on the lowest possible bail, or no bail at all, individuals whose dangerous nature is apparent.

DANGER TO VICTIMS AND WITNESSES BY THOSE ON BAIL

The danger to society from those released on bail is a generalized danger to the entire community into which the defendant is freed. More specific dangers often await the victims of or witnesses to the crime for which a given suspect has been arrested and freed on bond. The suspect has every motivation to persuade them not to testify against him. If persuasion does not work, he can always resort to terror. Since there is very little, as a practical matter, that the police can do to protect the victims and witnesses in every case, the likelihood of the defendant utilizing his freedom on bond to defeat the ends of justice is real.

A recent study conducted in Washington, D.C., by the Institute for Law and Social Research found that forty-two percent of the criminal cases in that city failed to go to trial because prosecution witnesses refused to cooperate. The study further indicated that thirty-seven percent of the prosecution witnesses surveyed said they refused to cooperate because they feared what might happen to them; they wanted better protection.[31]

Obviously, if a suspect is free on bail, he is in a much better position to terrorize or even kill witnesses against him. This can, and does, happen far too often. In New York City a murder defendant was released on $15,000 bail over the vigorous protest of the district attorney. Three days later the suspect was charged with an unprovoked attack on one of the prosecution's witnesses in which he put out a cigarette on the witness's face and beat him with a metal pipe, fracturing his nose.[32]

In Chicago, an ex-convict, free on bail for aggravated assault, was charged with soliciting and conspiring with another man to murder the two witnesses against him in the assault case.[33]

In Connecticut, four men were charged with the dynamite slaying of a witness against them in connection with the theft of automatic weapons from an armory. Two of the men charged with the death of the witness had been released on $50,000 bail from federal charges stemming from the same crime.[34]

It is, of course, difficult to estimate just how many victims and witnesses are terrorized by criminal defendants freed on bond, because, obviously, if the victims or witnesses are so afraid of the defendant that they refuse to testify against him about the original crime, they will be equally afraid to tell about the tactics he has used on them in order to make them afraid. If, in any given case, it can be shown that the defendant utilized his freedom on bail to intimidate potential witnesses against him, then no clearer abuse of the bail process can be shown. The right of the accused to be admitted to bail will have become perverted into a "right" to obstruct justice as it pleases the criminal.

APPEAL BONDS

The discussion of the right to bail, and its abuses, has heretofore dealt with the right to bail prior to the trial of the accused. Regarding this, a theoretical case can be made based on the argument that the defendant should be admitted to bail because he is presumed innocent until proven guilty. This argument, of course, ignores the rights of the past and potential victims of the defendant, but it can be made.

No such argument can be made, however, for those who have been *convicted* by a court or jury and sentenced to prison but who then seek release on bond pending an appeal. In some such cases, where the crime charged is a "white-collar" or nonviolent crime, society is not much harmed if the convicted perpetrator is allowed to remain free until his appeal is heard. But in cases of violent crime, narcotics trafficking, and organized crime, the rights of the law-abiding are definitely trampled on if a convicted offender is permitted to remain at liberty during the months or years that it takes our courts to decide his appeal. Justice is neither swift nor sure if that offender is free on bail to continue the activity for which he was convicted.

One of the most egregious examples of abuse of a court's power to allow bail pending an appeal arose in Cook County, Illinois. In June 1973 crime syndicate figure Mario DeStefano was convicted by a jury of the 1963 torture murder of loan shark Leo Foreman. A syndicate hit man, Charles (Chuck) Crimaldi, who had participated in the murder, testified that DeStefano had butchered Foreman with a knife as he lay dying on the floor. DeStefano had previously been convicted of another murder and had served a fourteen-year sentence for that crime.

On June 26, 1973, Cook County Circuit Court judge Robert A. Meier sentenced DeStefano to twenty to forty years in prison for the Foreman killing, but on November 15 of the same year he ordered him freed on an appeal bond. The Illinois Court of Appeals and the Illinois Supreme Court, over the vigorous protests of Cook County state attorney Bernard Carey, upheld Judge Meier's release of DeStefano and, at the time of this writing, he remains free.

Robert Wiedreich, the top-flight daily columnist for the *Chicago Tribune*, who wages with his pen a one-man campaign against the Chicago Cosa Nostra, took exception to the freeing of a twice-convicted murderer.[35] He castigated Judge Meier for unleashing "on the streets of

139

Chicago a murderous animal so vicious it is like a throwback to the dark ages," and he even-handedly assailed the appeals courts for upholding the release.

More to the point, Mr. Wiedreich was able to contact Charles Crimaldi, the killer-for-hire-turned-witness against DeStefano, who is now living in hiding and in constant fear. Crimaldi bitterly pointed out that now he, who cooperated with the prosecution, must hide out while DeStefano was free to look for him. Crimaldi stated flatly to Wiedreich: "I wouldn't do it again under any circumstances."

Setting aside for a moment the feelings of revulsion and frustration that most law-abiding citizens must feel at the leniency shown to this convicted killer, Crimaldi's statement indicates the more serious practical impact that Judge Meier's decision to free DeStefano will have on the investigation and prosecution of organized crime figures. Organized crime is a cancer in our society; it flourishes because of its enforced code of secrecy. Only by breaching the wall of secrecy can law enforcement hope to eradicate this menace.

The freeing of DeStefano, who almost assuredly will direct a manhunt for the hapless Crimaldi, will, equally assuredly, make any witness against an underworld figure think twice before he agrees to cooperate with the criminal investigative forces. As Mr. Wiedreich rhetorically queried: "How can society ever expect another witness to testify in open court against the underworld? How can it demand that a man lay his life on the line, well knowing that his tormentor may be set free regardless of his crime?"

Individuals at the top levels of organized crime or the narcotics traffic do not stop their illicit activities simply because they have been arrested for or convicted of a crime. If they are free on bail, either before or after trial, they will continue to ply their trade. Ironically, it is precisely those in the lucrative fields of organized crime and narcotics who can afford the generally large amounts required for appeal bonds. There is something perverted in the logic of a system that permits the real money-makers of crime to buy their freedom, *even after conviction,* to continue in the enterprise that resulted in their convictions in the first place.

Shortly after DeStefano's release, I was on one of those radio talk shows during which people call in their opinions and questions. I was asked by a black man how DeStefano could be released on bail after his second murder conviction when a black who was convicted of, say, robbery would be shipped off to the penitentiary without delay. I couldn't answer him.

The right to bail is a precious right, one that should be accorded without question to those offenders who evidence being a reasonably good risk for release. But when common sense clearly indicates that the defendant presents a danger to the law-abiding, then we should think twice before gambling with the rights of his past and potential victims and free him on little or no bail.

2. The Problem of Court Delays

In 1970 the chief justice of the United States, Warren Earl Burger, was interviewed by the editors of *U.S. News & World Report.* The questions put to the chief justice involved various aspects of our legal system, primarily the criminal justice system.

With regard to the critical issue of delays in the system, *U.S. News* asked: "Would you say that delay has been a major contribution to the rise of crime over the last decade? Would you pin it on the court system that closely?" The chief justice responded:

> I cannot think of any judicial factor more important than delay and uncertainty. It's always difficult to assign priorities in this sort of thing, but *I know of none I can think of more important than the absence of the sure knowledge that a criminal act will be followed by a speedy trial and punishment.*
>
> And that's why I have said that if we could have every criminal trial ready to be presented within 60 days after the arrest or the charge, I think you'd see a very, very sharp drop in the crime rate. It would surely put an end to the large number of crimes committed by men out on bail waiting six to 18 months to be brought to trial.[36]

Chief Justice Burger, as the highest judicial officer in the nation, speaks with authority, and he is precisely correct in his views. Justice, to be effective, must be swift and sure. The corrosive effects of interminable delays mock the concept of swift and sure justice.*

The criminal gains from the lack of speedy justice. As Burger noted, he may remain free on bail to perpetrate other crimes during the months or years before his case is presented for trial; witnesses against him may move away, otherwise disappear, or simply forget what they saw or heard; the victim may give up in disgust at the snail-paced way his own rights are vindicated; court congestion may place the suspect in an advantageous bargaining position to negotiate for a reduction of the charge to one carrying little or no punishment; he may be able to claim that he has been denied a speedy trial and that the charges against him must be dismissed; and, finally, in many cases he may take advantage of our interminable appellate system to remain free for years even after his conviction.

*This section deals with our failure to ensure swift or speedy justice. The next section, on sentencing, tackles our failure to provide *sure* justice.

141

The other side of the coin is that court delays work to the extreme disadvantage of the victim. As each aspect of the delay problem benefits the criminal, the rights of his actual and potential victims are correspondingly diminished. Suppose that an innocent citizen is robbed and pistol-whipped and the robber is apprehended and charged with the crime. Now the victim has every right to expect that society will move swiftly to vindicate his rights by dispensing justice to his assailant. By the time the case reaches its termination, however, the victim will likely have a jaundiced view of our system's interpretation of the word "justice." For he will soon know firsthand that justice delayed is justice denied—at least to *him*.

In December 1971 Patrick V. Murphy, then police commissioner of New York City, spoke before the Association of the Bar of that city and decried in scathing terms the impact of court delays. He first pointed out the natural reaction of crime's victims: "There is more crime today than ever before. But too many criminals are not going to jail and their *victims* scream that the criminal justice system has broken down, and they are right. . . ."[37]

Commissioner Murphy likened the criminal justice system to a funnel. The police pour in the criminals whom they have arrested at the wide end, but there occurs a blockage at the narrow end—the courts. As a result, as more and more criminals are arrested, the criminals spill over the wide end of the funnel back into society. The comparison is appropriate. Court delays, for a variety of reasons, cause the congestion that blocks the narrow end of the funnel. The courts then must do everything they can to clear their dockets. And, ironically, the criminals benefit from the very congestion caused by so many criminals committing crimes.

Mr. Murphy backed his analogy with facts:

> In 1960, the New York City Police Department made 35,629 felony arrests. Last year [1970] we made 94,042, an increase of 165 percent over a ten-year period. You ask what happened to last year's 94,000 felony arrests? Exactly 552 out of the 94,000 went to trial. The rest of them were "disposed of." "Disposed of" means dismissed outright, reduced to misdemeanors via plea bargaining, reduced to much lesser felonies via plea bargaining.[38]

To a greater or lesser extent, problems of court congestion and delay are common to every criminal jurisdiction in the nation. Chief Justice Burger, in his interview with *U.S. News & World Report*, noted that in criminal cases in the federal courts during the past ten years, the time lapse from the date of charge to the date of trial had doubled, as had the amount of time it took to try a criminal case.[39] A March 1974 report by the Institute for Court Management indicated that the average length of time from charge to trial in Cook County, Illinois, was nine months, and that there was a backlog of 2,500 felony cases.[40]

Court delay, with its many benefits for the criminal and all of its disadvantages for the victim, is one of the most corrosive aspects of our criminal justice system. Let us now demonstrate this with actual cases.

On March 28, 1970, a woman was sitting in a tavern in Oak Park, Illinois, minding her own business. Five members of a motorcycle gang walked in. They knocked the woman off the bar stool, then tore off her clothes and whipped her with a chain across her breasts and stomach. A factory worker from the night shift unsuspectingly entered the tavern. He, in turn, was beaten with a chain, breaking his nose, and was forced to commit unnatural sex acts with the woman. The gang then robbed the man of $85, the woman of $18, and fled.

The members of the gang were arrested the same day and three were positively identified by the two victims as their assailants. The three were charged with robbery and deviate sexual assault.

On April 3, 1970, the three were brought before Judge Norman A. Korfist of the local municipal court and released without bail on their promise to appear. The case was continued to May 15 and then to June 19, 1970. On July 10, 1970, the assistant county prosecutor, to avoid the long, drawn-out process of pretrial hearings, grand jury proceedings, and trial testimony that a felony charge necessitates, agreed to reduce the robbery charges to petty theft and the deviate sexual assault charges to reckless conduct. Both of the reduced charges were misdemeanors.

Judge Korfist dismissed the petty-theft charges, found the trio guilty of two counts each of reckless conduct, and *fined each of the three $500.* They paid their fines and walked out of court free men. One of them was later convicted of the attempted murder of a police officer and a citizen.[41]

The victims were disgusted at the "justice" they received from the system. The mere *threat* of the delays involved in the criminal justice proceedings in Illinois had caused the prosecutor to reduce the charges to misdemeanors. The victims have filed a $50,000 civil suit against their tormentors. Perhaps the civil courts will dispense a brand of justice different from that of the criminal courts.

On August 13, 1973, a Chicago man was arrested for the fatal stabbing of a young housewife in Chicago's Grant Park. Two days later he confessed to the murders of three other women in 1970, 1972, and 1973. At the time of the 1973 murder the defendant was free on $5,000 bond on a September 1972 charge of attempted rape and aggravated battery in the beating of a woman with a concrete block concealed in a bag. The suspect, at the time bond was set for the 1972 crime, had a record of arrests for indecent exposure, robbery, larceny, unlawful use of weapons, attempted armed robbery, battery, and murder; he had been convicted eight times for various crimes.

Between the September 1972 assault and the August 1973 murder the suspect's case was continued nine times, six at the request of the defense and three by agreement between prosecutor and defense attorney. During these months, he had by his own admission murdered at least one innocent victim. Through its dilatory criminal process, the system put a very dangerous man on the streets, free to victimize at will. He did.[42]

In Washington, D.C., in January 1974, robbery charges against six men were dismissed because an appeals court held that they had been denied a speedy trial. Judge George L. Hart of the U.S. District Court had ordered the dismissal because four years had elapsed since the six men had been arrested and they had not yet been brought to trial. The appeals court upheld Judge Hart's ruling.

The case began four years before when six men—some armed with sawed-off shotguns—robbed the Commerce Department Federal Credit Union of $128,000 in cash. A week later the FBI arrested six suspects and simultaneously recovered what appeared to be some of the stolen money and several of the guns used in the robbery. The prosecution felt it had a pretty solid case.

Then began a series of appeals by the defendants and rulings by the courts over the question of some missing grand jury minutes. The appeals caused one delay after another. A panel of the U.S. Court of Appeals took *over a year* to decide an argument over the grand jury minutes, then took ten months more to reconsider the case and reverse itself. In addition, an illness of Judge Hart himself caused a four-month postponement of the original trial date.

The U.S. attorney's office opposed the dismissal of the charges, pointing out with undeniable logic that it was not the fault of that office for the delay. Judge Hart conceded this, but nevertheless ordered the dismissal of charges: "The U.S. Attorney, as such, is not responsible [for the delay], the government, as such, is."[43] What this appears to mean is that if a criminal defendant causes enough delays by raising questions on which it will take the trial and appellate courts months or years to rule, or if by good fortune his trial judge becomes ill, then he is entitled to a dismissal of charges, even though the prosecutor is not even remotely responsible for the delay.

The ruling reduces to absurdity the problems of delay in the criminal justice system. It permits the accused to manipulate the criminal justice process to cause lengthy delays before he goes to trial, and then to seek a dismissal of the charges against him based on the delays *he himself has caused*. As it is, the problem of delays mocks the rights of society. This refinement by the District of Columbia courts makes the situation ludicrous.

There are, of course, countless cases in which the delays in the system have greatly prejudiced the rights of the law-abiding, but the three preceding illustrations suffice to demonstrate the problem. In the first case, the mere threat of the cumbersome process required to initiate felony proceedings against the three young sadists resulted, after an *initial* four-month delay, in serious felony charges being reduced to minor misdemeanors, which in turn resulted in their freedom upon payment of a minimal fine. The second case illustrates the effect of actual delays. The defendant, charged with a violent felony, and owning a long record of arrests and convictions for violent crimes, was permitted to remain free for almost a year while the charges against him were continued time and again. During this period of freedom, he murdered two innocent persons. Finally, the District of Columbia case simply requires that the suspects be freed because of court delays, caused at least in part by the defendants' own activities.

One common thread runs through each case: the rights of the law-abiding were treated with incredible callousness. The actual victims in these cases were two individuals tortured and degraded, two women brutally murdered, and several credit-union employees menaced by shot-gun-wielding bandits. Nothing has been or will be done by the criminal justice system to vindicate their rights. But the delays in the system—caused mostly by the system's obsessive concern for the criminal's rights—have been lifesavers to the murderers, robbers, and torturers.

Turning now from the general *effects* of delay in our criminal justice process, let us consider more specific reasons for the causes of its congestion, hence its delays.

The first and supervening reason for congestion and delay is that we have reached a point where, truthfully, the benefits of crime are increasing while the costs of crime (to the criminals) are decreasing. In a word: crime pays. And, as more individuals realize this simple fact, more individuals will commit crimes. Hence the vicious cycle: more crimes are committed, more criminals are arrested by the police and enter our criminal justice process, more delays result from the congestion, more criminals benefit. . . . So the costs of crime to criminals continue to decrease. There is so little deterrent now in our criminal justice system that the only truly surprising thing is that *more* people have not turned to crime.

At the trial level delays are caused at the outset by crowded court calendars; by an insufficient supply of judges, prosecutors, defense attorneys, and backup personnel; and by even too few courtrooms. In Cook County, Illinois, for example, an in-depth study found that there are

134 circuit court judges but ninety percent of them were assigned to non-criminal cases.[44] This shortage of personnel is compounded by the fact that our current concepts of procedural safeguards for the rights of the accused have placed in the hands of defense attorneys an almost limitless armory of weapons of delay.

One of the most effective of these weapons is the device of asking for and receiving continuance after continuance. There is no surer way of aiding a criminal defendant, at least one free on bail (as most are), than by postponing his appearance before the bar of justice time and again.

A recent study in Cook County, Illinois, focused on this problem and unearthed some pointed data. The study was conducted for the Chicago-Cook County Commission on Criminal Justice by the Institute for Court Management, a private nonprofit corporation headquartered in Denver. One key conclusion of the study of Cook County courts was that private defense attorneys who work on more cases than they can handle are causing trial delays through the device of continuances, and these delays are eroding the efficiency of the courts. Ernest C. Friesen, executive director of the Institute for Court Management and former head of the administrative office of the United States courts, noted that much delay "is built around retained counsel [who are] basically paid for keeping their defendants on the street. That's their art."[45]

And an art it is. Nothing can weaken the resolve of victims and witnesses more quickly than to be required to appear at the criminal courts building time after time only to be told that the case has been continued again. In addition to the delay and aggravation, the victims and witnesses often lose many days of work. Even the most conscientious of them may finally decide that the simple economics of the situation finally dictates that they can no longer afford to show up in court.

Another major advantage to the defendant in continued postponements is that in today's mobile society witnesses may move away, either not to be found or unwilling to return to testify. Too, as time elapses after a given event, the shorter the human memory becomes about that event. Little wonder then that the continuance merry-go-round is the best of all possible worlds for the criminal defendant.

Another major cause for delay is that decisions by our appellate courts on all levels require or permit all sorts of procedural motions in behalf of the defendant. These consume tons of time for courts, prosecutors, and defense attorneys. Motions to suppress evidence, to challenge the admissibility of a confession, to discover and examine evidence, for a change of venue, for joinder or severance of defendants—to list only a few—are often required to protect the defendant's rights under recent interpretations of the Constitution.

Some of these motions can be dealt with by oral argument, but many others require written briefs and memoranda of authorities from both parties and, not infrequently, written rulings by the judge. A motion may require a "mini-trial" prior to the trial on the merits, with testimony from policy officers and other witnesses often taking many hours or even days of court time. All of this is enormously time-consuming and accounts for a good deal of the delay.

On occasion, you find instances where judges simply do not devote the proper amount of time to criminal trials. For example, a survey taken by the Chicago Crime Commission on two days in September 1973 revealed that forty to sixty percent of the 124 courtrooms in the Civic Center were idle between 10:00 A.M. and 11:30 A.M. and between 2:00 P.M. and 3:30 P.M.[46] A similar survey taken in Manhattan, cited by Senator Sam Ervin (D.-N.C.) in a 1973 speech on the floor of the Senate, found that in one typical week, state supreme (that is, trial) court justices in criminal cases were on the bench an average of only three hours and twenty-one minutes a day.[47]

This does not mean that all of the judges are not working. Many of them are undoubtedly meeting in chambers with attorneys, working on written opinions, or carrying on other judicial business. But in those instances in which judges are simply not working at all, the delays caused are intolerable.

There are, of course, other causes of pretrial delay: problems involved in notifying witnesses and assuring their appearance in court; the lengthy process of presenting every case involving a felony to the grand jury in those states, like Illinois, requiring a grand jury indictment for felony prosecutions; defendants failing to appear—to name only a few.

The point is, in our system the period from arrest to trial is fraught with possibilities for delay: motions to suppress and other procedural motions for the protection of the defendants' rights are required by law and court decisions; in other instances, tactics are utilized solely for the purpose of causing delay for its own sake. While these tactics may benefit the criminal accused greatly, they accomplish very little that is useful to the safety of the law-abiding.

When a criminal case finally comes to trial, the trial process itself is often utilized for lengthy periods of delay. The jury selection process itself is prone to abuse in this regard. In many trials today, particularly those in which the news media have taken an interest, jury selection may take days, weeks, or even months, tying up the courtroom, court personnel, attorneys, and all other parties involved. No less an authority than Edward Bennett Williams, perhaps the foremost criminal defense attorney in the nation, has scored the practice of lengthy jury selection procedures. In an interview published in U.S. *News & World Report*, September 21, 1970, he stated:

I think that the method of selecting jurors in many states is one of the most archaic things about our criminal justice system at the trial level. The Manson case is an excellent illustration of this. They put the jurors in the witness box and practically tried the whole case in interrogating each juror.

It's an outmoded and useless practice, and I think it is one of the things that is bringing the whole system into disrepute. You don't need six weeks to get a jury. You can get a jury to try fairly any case that you can conceive of in one day or less. I've tried some cases that have gotten a lot of attention in the press and never have I taken more than a day to get a jury.[48]

Unfortunately, there are far too many attorneys, of considerably less stature than Mr. Williams, who utilize the process of jury selection to draw out the proceedings, often to a ridiculous extent, thus adding their share to the ever-growing backlog of criminal cases.

Likewise, the criminal trial itself often becomes something of a farce so far as the time consumed is concerned. Again, a case in point is the trial of Charles Manson and his tribe for the revolting murders they committed in California. This marathon took seven months to try before the jury convicted all of the defendants; seven months in which, obviously, no other cases could be tried by the judge sitting on the case. This, of course, added immeasurably to that court's backlog.

It is currently fashionable to attempt to politicize the criminal justice system. A crime that would have been deemed solely a murder, rape, or robbery ten years ago, now becomes a *cause célèbre*; the perpetrators defend themselves on the grounds that they were merely "striking back at an oppressive society," or "killing the pigs as an act of liberation." Radical attorneys have been flocking to such cases. Often egged on by a news-hungry media, these attorneys can extend a fairly straightforward criminal trial indefinitely and transform it into a forum for all sorts of irrelevant political gnashing of teeth. Such showcase trials may provide a perfectly splendid ego trip for the defendants and their attorneys, but they deny to many others awaiting trial their opportunity for a speedy hearing.

Another factor contributing to inordinate trial delays is that some appellate courts have become so supremely concerned with the rights of the criminal defendant that the trial judges appear timid to brake the defense in any manner for fear of being reversed on appeal. Thus, evidence that should be excluded as irrelevant to the central question of the guilt or innocence of the accused is now ruled admissible, no matter how time-consuming it may be, to prevent a reversal—and a new trial— by a superlenient appellate court.

Thus, pretrial proceedings, and the criminal trials themselves, promote congestion and delay in our criminal justice system. In addition to these two stages, the incredibly complicated system of criminal appeals in this country constitutes a major delay factor; perhaps worse, it is one of the more prominent reasons for public distrust of and disillusionment with the criminal justice system.

Most of our citizens, of whatever political persuasion, wish our criminal justice process to be fair to the accused. It is, however, extremely difficult for an intelligent layman to understand how a defendant, *after* conviction by a court or jury, can avail himself of a seemingly inexhaustible series of appellate tribunals hoping, at some stage, to find an appeals court that will reverse his conviction in a process that may take years.

The backlog of criminal appeals is now causing excessive delay, which in turn adversely affects one of the most important aspects of the entire system—the finality of a conviction. With few exceptions, any convicted person can appeal his conviction; further, because the right of free appeals has been granted to the indigent, the case load of our appellate courts is simply staggering. As the case load increases, delays in deciding the cases must also increase.

Criminal appeals are lengthy affairs. The defense and the prosecution must submit written briefs to the court; in all but a few jurisdictions the courts must hear oral arguments, and then one or more members of the courts must file written opinions. Often months pass before the courts' decisions are announced. If this procedure is followed from one appellate court to the next, the final resolution of a given case may, indeed, be a matter of years.

One writer has termed the crowding of federal appellate dockets a threat to the national law.[49] Washington State Supreme Court judge Robert C. Finley stated flatly that in cases at the appellate level, "Present delays of from six to twelve to twenty-four months are inexcusable."[50] In short, the burden of criminal appeals constitutes a major threat to the criminal justice system.

One of the reasons for the appeals problem is that the convicted criminal has so many courts to appeal to. In most jurisdictions at least the following appellate avenues open to him. First are direct appeals, that is, appeals to the courts in the jurisdiction in which he was convicted. Thus, a person convicted in Illinois can appeal to the Illinois Court of Appeals and then to the supreme court of that state. From the Illinois Supreme Court he can ask for review of his case by the U.S. Supreme Court. A federal defendant, convicted in federal district court, can appeal directly to the U.S. Circuit Court of Appeals; from there, he too can petition the U.S. Supreme Court for review.

In addition to direct appeals, recent court decisions provide that the federal courts are open to the defendant for "collateral attacks" on his conviction. This means that an individual convicted in a state court, who has appealed his conviction through his state's intermediate and supreme court appellate levels and who has been denied review by the U.S. Supreme Court, may now, through the device of a writ of habeas corpus, appeal to the U.S. District Court, the U.S. Court of Appeals, and even back to the U.S. Supreme Court, on the grounds that his state conviction in some manner violated his rights under the Constitution.

The problems involved in such collateral attacks were illustrated in chapter three by the case of Daniel Murphy, who unsuccessfully appealed his conviction for the murder of his wife to the Oregon Court of Appeals, the Oregon Supreme Court, and the U.S. Supreme Court. He then sought to make a collateral attack, via a writ of habeas corpus, on his state conviction in the Federal District Court for the District of Oregon. Again he lost, and it was not until the next step in his appeal, the U.S. Court of Appeals for the Ninth Circuit, that he struck pay dirt. That court reversed his conviction, five years and nine months after his trial, on the grounds that the police violated his rights by taking scrapings from under his fingernails without a warrant.

Now it was the turn of the state of Oregon to appeal, and it did so successfully. The U.S. Supreme Court in June 1973 reversed the decision of the Ninth Circuit and Murphy lost at the final stage. The important point of Murphy's odyssey through the appellate system is that by law he was permitted to make six appeals to five different courts before the U.S. Supreme Court sealed his conviction. The entire process took over six years.

Some extent of the impact of collateral attacks on state criminal convictions in federal courts may be assessed by the fact that twenty years ago there were 541 such petitions for such a review. Today there are nearly 10,000.[51]

In addition, most states have provisions for state habeas-corpus proceedings whereby various extended hearings must be afforded the defendant, no matter how much time they may consume. A classic example of this situation was described by Judge Julian Hanley of Wyoming County, New York, whose jurisdiction includes Attica Prison. Noting that habeas-corpus writs from Attica alone total almost 800 petitions a year, Judge Hanley described the case of Milan Radunovich's orange.[52]

Milan Radunovich is characterized by Judge Hanley as Attica's "writ champion," having filed eleven habeas-corpus petitions in eighteen months. One morning he did not get his orange for breakfast and filed the following document (the translations are Judge Hanley's):

> Milan Radunovich for his petition alleges on the on day of 2-11-72 in the mess hall in Attica Prison that he did not resved (received) orang

150

(orange) which was not on the teble (table) and Radunovich did call the salgen Kakaron (Sgt. Corcoran) but the salgen (sergeant) did not come over to hear me.

(2) That in the mid of the teble (middle of the table) toll (told) the officer to call salgen that one orange was missing from the teble.

(3) That the officer did praper (proper) job called the salgen but the salgen did not come to hear Mr. Radunovich the inmeds (inmates) was hengry (hungry) for the fact.

(4) When the salgen did come to the side of the cauntr (counter) Mr. Radunovich did call him by name and salgen did come then I tell him sar (sir) one orange is missing from teble I did not get orange the salgen anser was so fur as I consern you did get the orange.

(5) That Milan Radunovich has ben act properly by the rools & regulation and that salgen has been act unproper to me which this fact the inmeds see bring to the court & testefid about the fact.

(6) That salgen have doot a fection on me & I am ceapt lock (keep locked) in the present time 2-15-72.

(7) If is any other charge against me I would like this fact to be esplained to this court & the inmeds to testefid what I have been done wrong.

(8) This fact is giving to the prisoners that they look for nother trouble of the fact that they gave me 5 days lock on.

(9) That Mr. Karkaren has atemt bifor to do same thing when he have been informed that I have poot awrit (put a writ) against Mr. Cuur.

(10) In this fact officer Mr. Deny cantesifize (can testify) when my dor was not ope for the hobby shop & Mr. Deny did informed me that I was keapt lock then I did fine later that I was only lock until I go to the court which this order was made by salgen Kakaren.

Milan Radunovich prays that this court to hear him and bring the facts by law of the state of New York for justification but not by the individuals in the prison wher they have grit dial of disagration against the individuals inmeds.

(Signed and sworn to MILAN RADUNOVICH)

(Wyoming County Docket #4774)[53]

Beginning with a cautionary note, Judge Hanley then described the amount of time and personnel required to deal with this writ.

Let not either the humor or the pathos of this situation carry you away. Consider the actual effects from this filing.

First, on February 22, 1972, a hearing order was signed by this court. The Attorney General's office then prepared a formal return (four copies). A superior court hearing was held in Attica Prison with counsel for petitioner supplied from Legal Aid (taxpayers' expense). The writ was denied March 17, 1972, requiring the preparing, signing, and filing of a formal court order.

This is only act one. Next, comes act two. An appeal notice is filed and Radunovich's orange now goes up to the Appellate Division of the New York Supreme Court. Counsel is assigned there, too. Briefs and transcripts are filed, the appeal is argued and five judges solemnly render a decision affirming the original dismissal.

Act three. Radunovich applies to New York's highest court, the New York Court of Appeals for leave to appeal. One of their learned justices considered the entire matter and filed a written opinion denying the right to appeal.

End of play? Not really. No real drama ends without an epilogue and Radunovich has one. Having now exhausted his state remedies, he is free to take his orange to the federal courts and can carry his case all the way to the Supreme Court of the United States, if they will hear him. Without counting any possible federal personnel, Radunovich's orange has been considered to date, by a variety of judges, court reporters, clerks, criers, and assorted court employees whose combined annual salaries greatly exceed a quarter of a million dollars.[54]

Can there be any wonder that our trial and appellate courts are being slowly choked to death? Neither the state appellate courts nor the federal courts can sustain such a burden. Nor can the victims of crime sustain the burden of a court system wherein delays at every level—pretrial, trial, and appeal—prejudice their rights so severely. And in so many ways.

3. The Sentencing Process

Justice, to be effective, must be swift and sure. An individual arrested for a crime must know that he will be brought speedily before the bar of justice, and if convicted, punished. As noted, justice in the United States if far from swift. Nor is justice sure.

The certainty of punishment has become a farce. Judicial leniency in the sentencing process, where punishment is, or is supposed to be, meted out, is now epidemic in many locations. This stems in part from the personal philosophy of individual judges; also, from an enormous amount of pressure generated by highly articulate and vocal individuals and groups, connected with every conceivable facet of the criminal justice system, who are calling for little or no punishment for those convicted of crime. The 1973 report of the National Advisory Commission on Criminal Justice Standards and Goals, a high-level, government-funded commission, specified that most criminals should be treated as leniently as possible and that many criminals should go free.[55]

Another institutional exponent of leniency is the National Council on Crime and Delinquency (NCCD), a citizens group, which has likewise recommended that only "dangerous offenders" should be imprisoned.

The NCCD defines a dangerous offender as one "who has committed a serious crime against a person and *who shows a behavior pattern of assaultiveness* based on serious mental disturbances."[56] The italicized portion should be a little scary for the potential victims of crime. One who has assaulted and raped a woman for the first time, and against whom a "behavior pattern of assaultiveness" could not be proved, would, under this definition, not be imprisoned. It would take a second, or perhaps a third rape before the behavior pattern could possibly be established. Meanwhile, two or more rape victims would see their assailant go unpunished. Additionally, should the NCCD have its way, every burglar, thief, shoplifter, embezzler, forger, and confidence man could ply his trade in peace, knowing that, so long as he does not commit a crime against a *person*, he is not a "dangerous offender" and therefore could *never* be imprisoned.

In any event, the criminal can rest fairly well assured that if he is caught and convicted there is every likelihood that he will not be punished—at least not by incarceration. Who suffers from this trend? Surely not the criminal who, having calculatedly victimized some innocent citizen, walks out of court a free man with only the rather minor inconvenience of probation or supervision to check his future activities. It is, of course, the victims who suffer: the actual victims who are in effect told that *their* rights to be free from criminal harm are of so little consequence that those who have trampled on their rights are likely to go unpunished; and the potential victims of the criminal who, rather than being isolated from society, is set at liberty by a system that is perfectly willing to take a chance—often a completely unrealistic chance—that he will not victimize again.

The victims also suffer because other criminally inclined individuals, who would almost certainly have been deterred had they *known* they would be punished if caught and convicted, now not only are not deterred, but may well be positively encouraged by the climate of leniency they see.

This permissiveness, which culminates in the theory that only rarely should we punish the criminal, is absolutely inexplicable when we consider that it is being fostered and advocated at a time when rising crime rates have reached crisis proportions. The crime-rise problem itself, public concern with the problem, and the fact that the law-abiding public wants something done about the problem have been discussed in chapter one and need no repetition here. One further point, however: in no area of the criminal justice system are the permissivists more adamant in their opposition to punishment than in the area of the juvenile criminal. The Commission on Standards and Goals, for example, recommended flatly that states should refrain from building any more state institutions for juveniles.[57]

It is interesting, if not very comforting for the victims of crime, to ponder this recommendation in light of the facts that nearly one half of all of our crimes are committed by juveniles, and that from 1960 to 1970, adult arrests for violent crimes rose sixty-seven percent while juvenile arrests for the same crimes rose *167 percent.*[58]

Thus, we live in a climate of violence, yet the response many would make is increased permissiveness. There is more violent crime in the United States today than at any time in history, and *still* the permissivists insist that punishment should fit not the crime but the criminal. All in the hope—and a forlorn hope it is—that we can rehabilitate the criminal. And if, as so often, those felons to whom leniency is granted refuse to be rehabilitated and commit more and more crimes, the permissivists are perfectly willing to pass this intolerable burden along to the law-abiding.

This attitude was remarked and rejected by no less an authority than Norman A. Carlson, the respected director of the Federal Bureau of Prisons. Responding to those who advocate "treatment" for convicted criminals rather than jail, he stated: "Attempts to turn the majority of criminals loose on American society are well intentioned but badly misguided. They represent a desperate effort to find an overnight solution to some of the admitted failures of correctional institutions in the past."[59]

The theory that considers only the question of the criminal's welfare and his rehabilitation must, by definition, be opposed to the concept of the certainty of punishment as a deterrent to the potential criminal. It is perhaps here that the permissivists most violate, through their social tinkering, the rights of the victims of crime. For while there is little doubt that the certainty of punishment is a deterrent to the would-be criminal, the exponents of leniency persist in ignoring any such common-sense rationale as this.

Justice Byron White of the U.S. Supreme Court has recognized that the certainty of punishment deters crime. Studies cited in the introduction to this chapter buttress his views. Chief Justice Burger, in his aforementioned interview with *U.S. News & World Report*, stated flatly that he knew of no factor in the criminal justice system more important than the sure knowledge that a criminal act will be followed by a speedy trial *and punishment.* Prosecutor William L. Cahalan of Wayne County (Detroit), Michigan, respected national authority on criminal-law problems, stated with reference to the need for mandatory minimum sentences for criminals: "I am convinced that our system of law enforcement and criminal justice would then accomplish its primary purpose—certainty of punishment will deter crime."[60] A recent study by the Public Systems Research Institute of UCLA found that an increase in higher levels of *both* the severity and the certainty of sanctions (punishment) was associated with lower crime levels, although it also found that social factors had greater effect on crime levels than criminal justice.[61]

In truth, the best case for the certainty of punishment as a deterrent is found not in writings and studies but in a little pure common sense. Setting aside the psychopaths and sociopaths, who won't be deterred from committing crimes by much of anything (but who should be isolated from society), we know from common sense that if an individual is *certain* he will be punished if convicted of a crime, then he will think twice before committing that crime. Prisons and jails are, by all reports, not pleasant places to be. Human nature rebels at confinement. If the potential criminal knew that he would be locked up if convicted, the same common sense dictates that he would hesitate before committing whatever crime he had in mind.

The common-sense approach is equally applicable to the corollary of the certainty of punishment as a deterrent: if the potential criminal believes that there is a reasonably good chance, or even a certainty, that he will *not* be punished, then there is no deterrent whatsoever to his criminal conduct. In fact, it is precisely this corollary that characterizes the abuses in the sentencing aspect of the criminal justice system today. Crime rates are intolerably high and in many jurisdictions still rising. At the same time, leniency in the punishment phase of the system is also on the rise, with a concomitant failure of deterrence.

The ringing call today for increased leniency is based, at least in part, upon the notion that the "tough approach" has failed. To this, one is tempted to reply: *What* tough approach? Have we really been taking a tough approach in our dealings with the criminal offender? Or has judicial leniency, fostered by the nonpunishment, "rehabilitation-for-all" theoreticians, been a major factor in our rising crime rates?

One way to examine the question whether or not we have taken a "tough" approach to the punishment of crime is to compare the number of persons in prisons with both the number of crimes committed and the rise in crime. The results are simply astonishing. Between 1960 and 1971, according to the Uniform Crime Reports of the FBI, violent crimes—murder, forcible rape, robbery, and aggravated assault—crimes for which the perpetrator *should* be sent to prison, increased 180 percent. The national prison population for the same period remained almost exactly the same and some twenty-nine states actually showed a *decrease*.[62] For example, in three of our high-population and high-crime states, the change in prison population was:

STATE	1960	1971	DECREASE
New York	17,027	14,544	2,653
Pennsylvania	7,802	6,422	1,380
Illinois	9,064	7,206	1,858[63]

In February 1973, New York State corrections commissioner Russell G. Oswald told a committee of the New York legislature that in that state there was space for 6,300 more offenders "without doubling in any cells."[64]

Now these statistics can only lead to one conclusion: while crime has been on the increase at a truly alarming rate, far fewer of the perpetrators of these crimes are going to prison for them. The certainty of punishment has been reduced to a minimal risk to the criminal, and the deterrent effect of such punishment has, proportionately, been reduced.

Other examples of the practice of the nonpunishment theory in jurisdictions across the country can be cited. In statistical terms:

● In a recent year, fifty-four percent of the persons convicted in federal courts got fines or probation in lieu of prison terms.[65]

● In California between 1960 and 1971, prison sentences dropped from twenty-five percent to five percent; cases in which probation was granted rose from twenty-five percent to seventy-five percent, and during this period crime increased by 122.5 percent.[66]

● In 1973 Assemblyman Alfred Delli Bovi from Queens released statistics covering July 1, 1972, to June 30, 1973, which indicated that New York City family courts had freed sixty-four percent of its convicted murderers and ninety-two percent of those convicted of rape and arson, without imposing any form of detention or punishment.[67]

● In Wayne County (Detroit), Michigan, in 1972, sixty-five percent of all of those convicted of a felony did not go to jail or prison.[68]

● In St. Louis ninety-one percent of the confessed drug pushers who appeared in county courts in 1972 were given probation and released.[69]

● In January of 1973, Deputy Chief Inspector William T. Bonacum, head of Narcotics Division, New York City Police Department, reported that of 20,726 persons arrested by his division for serious narcotics offenses, only 418 were sent to state prison.[70]

● In a study made by the *Philadelphia Inquirer*, thirty-nine percent—almost four out of ten—of the defendants convicted of murder, rape, aggravated robbery, or aggravated assault and battery were placed on probation. Of those convicted of rape, the study found, fifty-six percent were placed on probation.[71]

From this data it is clear that, in the sentencing process today, there is little or no certainty of punishment, and yet the permissivists seek to reduce what little certainty there is.

They wish to continue and even expand the granting of probation, even where the criminal has been convicted of violent or dangerous crimes. In such instances, those who grant or urge leniency, besides reducing the deterrent effect of the certainty of punishment, are clearly taking a chance with the safety of the law-abiding. When a decision is made not to isolate the criminal from society, but rather to release him in the hope that he will be rehabilitated, and when that decision, as it often does, results in an innocent person being victimized by the probationer, then that victim must bear the full burden of the single-minded concern of the permissivists for what they deem the best interest of the criminal. That this exclusive concern for the well-being of the criminal frequently is misplaced seems not even to dent the mental armor of the exponents of total leniency.

From April 1, 1972, to June 30, 1972, in the District of Columbia, 297 persons on probation from the superior court were rearrested. Of those rearrested for *serious* crimes, the breakdown is as follows:

Homicides	5
Rape and Sex Cases	10
Robbery	25
Burglary	23
Auto Theft	9
Narcotics	39
TOTAL	111

The following case summaries indicate the types of crimes committed by those shown leniency by being placed on probation.[72]

CASE #1 TCR, Age 20 years
Conviction: Carrying a Gun
New Charge: Homicide

On October 28, 1970, TCR was arrested and charged with carrying a deadly weapon. In this case, two plainclothes officers observed TCR carrying an object wrapped in a towel and when they approached TCR to investigate, he fled from them on foot dropping the towel, which contained a .44-caliber pistol. TCR was apprehended after a foot chase and charged with weapons offense.

TCR was convicted, on the weapons charge, on October 26, 1971, and was referred to the Youth Center for evaluation. On February 15, 1972, TCR was sentenced under the Federal Youth Corrections Act and placed on Superior Court probation for an indefinite period commencing on February 17, 1972.

Two months later, on April 16, 1972, while on Superior Court probation for illegally carrying a pistol, TCR was arrested and charged with homicide. In this case, investigation disclosed that TCR shot and killed the operator of a gasoline service station during the commission of an armed holdup. TCR was arrested at his home one day after the holdup murder and he is now being held in D.C. Jail without bond on the homicide charge.

CASE #2 JDG, Age 21 years
Conviction: Attempt Unauthorized Use
New Charge: Rape

On October 5, 1971, JDG was arrested and charged with unauthorized use of a vehicle and possession of a prohibited weapon. In this case, JDG was arrested while operating an auto that had been stolen from Arlington, Virginia. At the time of his arrest, he had a prohibited weapon and a B-B gun in his possession.

The criminal charge of possessing a prohibited weapon was not papered and the charge of unathorized use of a vehicle was changed to attempt unauthorized use of a vehicle.

On December 6, 1971, JDG was sentenced to ninety days, under the Federal Youth Corrections Act, or the attempt unauthorized use of a vehicle. This sentence was suspended by the court and JDG was placed on Superior Court probation for a term of six months to run from December 6, 1971, to June 5, 1972.

On May 10, 1972, while still on Superior Court probation, for attempt unauthorized use of a vehicle, JDG was arrested for the offense of rape. In this case, JDG stopped a fifteen-year-old female on the street, misrepresented himself to her as a police officer, and told her to accompany him to his apartment or he would have to arrest her. She attempted to run from him, but he forcibly pulled her into a parking garage, in the Capitol Park area, and beat her about the head and face causing her to lose consciousness. He then removed part of her clothing and raped her. Upon completing his assault, he advised the complainant to remain on the ground and he fled the scene on foot running.

JDG was subsequently arrested a short time later, a few blocks from the scene of the offense.

JDG was released from D.C. Jail on $5,000.00 bond in this offense, on May 13, 1972.

CASE #3 LWJ, Age 26 years
Conviction: Petit Larceny
New Charge: Armed Robbery/Narcotics

On April 14, 1971, LWJ was arrested and charged with petit larceny.

On May 21, 1971, LWJ was sentenced to six months, imposition of the sentence, suspended, and placed on two years probation under the supervision of the Superior Court Probation Office.

On June 3, 1971, while on the above probation, LWJ was rearrested and charged with armed robbery. In this case, LWJ along with a second subject entered a store, in the northwest, displayed a gun, and announced a holdup. Both subjects removed an indeterminate amount of money from the cash register. LWJ was arrested a short time later, several blocks from the scene, and with the money from the holdup still in his possession.

On February 11, 1972, LWJ was released on personal recognizance for the above robbery.

On April 5, 1972, while on the above Superior Court probation and personal recognizance, LWJ was rearrested and charged with the Uniform Narcotic Act. In this case, LWJ was observed in a northwest department store, removed a belt from the rack, and left the store. LWJ was arrested a short time later and upon being searched, had in his possession three brown envelopes containing marijuana.

LWJ is currently in D.C. Jail awaiting trial.

CASE #4 JEW, Age 22 years
Conviction: Assault
New Charges: Sodomy

JEW was arrested, on September 9, 1971, and charged with simple assault. In this case, JEW approached a female citizen, in the southwest section of the city, grabbed her, and stated that he would hurt her if she didn't come with him. The complainant broke away from JEW, went directly home, and called the police, who subsequently arrested JEW on a description given them by the complainant.

JEW was convicted on the simple-assault charge on May 16, 1972, and was placed on one-year probation under supervision of the Superior Court.

On June 18, 1972, while on Superior Court probation, for a little over one month, for simple assault, JEW was arrested by the police and charged with rectal and oral sodomy. In this case, a female citizen reported that on June 15, 1972, she was approached by JEW at a bus stop and forced to accompany JEW by bus to the northeast section of the city, where JEW is alleged to have committed these unnatural sex acts.

The subject JEW was identified by the complainant, a warrant was issued, and he was arrested. JEW is currently residing in the D.C. Jail, awaiting trial.

CASE#5 HLR, Age 19 years
Conviction: Carrying a Gun
New Charge: Armed Robbery

On November 10, 1971, HLR was arrested for robbery (fear) of a northeast resident. He was released from custody in lieu of a ten percent bond of $1,000, under the supervision of the D.C. Bail Agency.

Nine days later, on November 19, 1971, HLR was rearrested while in possession of a .38-caliber handgun on public space and charged with carrying a dangerous weapon, was convicted in Superior Court, and placed on probation from March 10, 1972, until March 9, 1973, with the previous robbery charge still pending.

Sixty-nine days later, on May 18, 1972, while on bond and Superior Court probation, HLR was rearrested for the armed robbery (with a gun) of $235.00 from a fifty-nine-year-old northeast resident. At the time of his arrest, he was identified by the victim and had a .22-caliber handgun in his possession.

HLR is currently being held in D.C. Jail in lieu of posting a $10,000 surety bond.

CASE#6 JLJ, Age 21 years
Conviction: Carrying a Gun
New Charge Pending: Narcotics
New Rearrest Charge: Armed Robbery

On May 12, 1971, JLJ was arrested by the police and charged with carrying a deadly weapon and possession of an unregistered firearm and ammunition. In this case, a citizen pointed out a man to the police that was alleged to be carrying a gun on his person. Investigation by police officers revealed that JLJ was in fact carrying a fully loaded .38-caliber revolver on his person and that he had no permit to do so.

JLJ pleaded guilty to carrying a pistol without a license and was given a 180-day sentence, which was suspended and he was placed on Superior Court probation, until November 5, 1972.

On January 7, 1972, JLJ was arrested, by police for violation of the Uniform Narcotic Act, while he was still on probation, on the weapon charge. In this case, JLJ was observed by police to place a suspicious packet into an auto and investigation disclosed the packet to contain an opium substance. JLJ was placed on personal-recognizance release, under the supervision of the D.C. Bail Agency, pending trial on the narcotics charge.

JLJ failed to show up for trial and a bench warrant was issued for his arrest for failure to show up, for trial as scheduled on March 8, 1972. Trial is still pending in this case.

On June 26, 1972, while on probation and personal-recognizance release, JLJ was arrested on a United States magistrate's arrest warrant, for armed robbery. In this case, two subjects robbed a male citizen on the street at gun point, beat him with a pistol, and robbed him of $652.00 in bills. JLJ was identified by the complainant in the case.

JLJ is now confined in the D.C. Jail, pending trials.

A study by the Chicago Crime Commission and the *Chicago Tribune* of the probation system in Cook County summed up its findings succinctly in one headline: "Critics Hit Probation System Here—But Criminals Think It's Great." The study found that many convicted probationers in Cook County commit other crimes while on probation—sometimes several times over; that probation department supervision was so lax that the threat of revoking probation and jailing errant probationers scarcely existed; and that the courts handled errant probationers about the same way that it handled those not on probation.[73]

The *Chicago Tribune* rather dryly noted that it was impossible to document how many crimes were charged to those released on probation because the probation department did not keep such records. It did give as examples two cases in which the probation system not only did not work but resulted in the commission of other crimes. In one case, prior leniency resulted in a murder:

> An example of how the system doesn't work is seen in the case of Ernie Slaughter, the probationer whom police have charged with slaying 23-year-old Susan Hebel during a burglary attempt in a South Ellis Avenue home last Aug. 17.
> Slaughter previously was arrested twice on burglary charges.
> In May, 1972, the first charge was reduced to theft in return for a guilty plea, and he was placed under court supervision—a lesser form of probation.
> In April of this year, a month before his supervision was to expire, Slaughter was again arrested for burglary.
> On May 11 he pleaded guilty to burglary and was placed on probation for two years. Only a few months into his new probation term, police charge that he tried to commit another burglary and that it resulted in the death of Miss Hebel, a graphic artist.[74]

In a second case the utter fatuity of the concept of nonpunishment of criminals is demonstrated:

> Jerome Reese, 33, is a case study of how probation violators are frequently handled in Cook County.

161

In 1971, after serving a year in the House of Corrections, Reese was released on probation for the next four years.

During the first two years of his probation, Reese, whose criminal record goes back to 1959, was arrested four times—twice for burglary, once for theft, and once for criminal damage to property.

Though each arrest was a potential violation of probation, no effort was made to revoke probation and send him to jail. Instead, that state went to the trouble of trying him for each separate crime.

For theft Reese spent 30 days in the House of Corrections, thus spending time behind bars while still on probation.

For criminal damage to property he was put under court supervision—a type of probation—for a year. Thus he was put on probation for a crime committed while on probation.

For one burglary he was convicted and sentenced to prison. The other burglary charge resulted in a mistrial when the jury couldn't reach a verdict.

It was only after this material that Reese's probation was revoked.

Reese is currently behind bars, but only after the state spent a lot of time, money and energy to convict him anew.

Experts say that under a well-run probation system, Reese, after his first arrest on probation, could have been taken before a judge who had the power to sentence him to spend the remainder of his probationary period in prison.[75]

The California Governor's Select Committee on the Problems of Law Enforcement made a study of the number of crimes committed by persons placed on probation under California's "model" probation subsidy program. Under this program the state pays the county $4,000 for each person placed on probation under intensive supervision rather than being committed to prison. Of 122 sample cases studied by the committee, sixty-seven probationers or 54.9 percent had one or more arrests while on probation, and as many as twelve had six or more arrests while on probation.[76]

The California commission went one step further. It found that a significant number of defendants who had been granted probation and had then been convicted of felony while on probation, *were granted probation again.* For example, twenty-nine percent of those convicted of rape, thirty-three percent of those convicted of robbery, and sixty-eight percent of those convicted of assault, *while on probation*, were again placed on probation.[77] This is frightening news for the potential victims of crime in California, where one third of those who commit rape and robbery while on probation for another crime are nevertheless placed on the street to victimize again.

Leniency in the sentencing process through the abuse of granting probation or other form of release without incarceration thrice ignores

162

the rights of crime's victims: (a) it reduces the deterrent effect on would-be criminals of the certainty of punishment; (b) it places upon the streets, through failure to isolate the criminally inclined, those who can and will victimize others; and (c) it fails to vindicate the rights of the law-abiding by punishing those who have violated *their* right to go about their business in peace.

In yet another manner such leniency ignores the rights of the victims: by sentencing the violators to relatively short prison terms. Now, it is arguable that the *certainty* rather than the *severity* of punishment is the key factor in deterring crime. But this does not mean that, when the crime is serious or previous crimes have been committed by the defendant, punishment should not be severe as well as certain. The survey (noted earlier) of sentencing practices in Philadelphia conducted by the *Philadelphia Inquirer* found that thirty-nine percent of those convicted of violent crimes—murder, rape, aggravated robbery, and aggravated assault and battery—received probation leaving sixty-one percent of such criminals who were sent to jail or prison. *But*, of those sent to prison, fifty-four percent, or over one half, received terms of only one year or less. Only ten percent received terms of more than five years.[78]

Now, the crimes involved in these cases are those in which the victim is injured by or *at least* threatened with deadly force. They are crimes that most clearly demonstrate the dangerous nature of the perpetrator. Yet for every 100 persons convicted of such crimes, 39 were not locked up at all; and of the 61 sent to jail, over 30 received sentences of only a year or less. A mere six received more than five years.

The victims in Philadelphia and other cities, of vicious forcible rapes, unprovoked beatings, or armed robberies, perhaps accompanied by a pistol whipping or a shooting, will not feel particularly secure if they know that seventy percent of the criminals who victimized them will either serve no time at all or be on the streets again in less than twelve months.

The concepts of the certainty and the severity of punishment must be combined to be effective. Certainty of punishment should be the rule for almost *all* crimes. As the seriousness of the crime escalates or if the crime is the second, third, or fourth in a series, then severity should be added to certainty. If a first-offense auto thief knows that, in all but the most extenuating circumstances, he *will* serve thirty to ninety days, this certainty will likely serve as a deterrent to his crime. The certainty of the same sentence obviously will *not* serve as a deterrent to a young hoodlum who takes a loaded pistol with him on his way to rob a local liquor store, or to a rapist who, perhaps for the second or third time, sets out to relieve his libido. They *must* know that not only will their punishment be certain but it will fit the seriousness or repetitious extent of the crime.

In view of the foregoing, what are the counterarguments of those whose creed is nonpunishment for the criminal? Their basic argument runs something like this:

1) Prisons and jails do not rehabilitate criminals.
2) Therefore, society will be better served if we abolish the concept of incarceration of criminals in prisons and jails and, in all but the most extreme cases, opt for their freedom, in the hope that some sort of "supervision" in the community will rehabilitate them.

The logic of the first point is impeccable. Prisons do not rehabilitate criminals, at least in most instances. The logic of the second point, however, leaves something to be desired. Its basic flaw is presuming that all, or most, of the criminals permitted to remain at liberty will, with "supervision," commit no more crimes. This presumption places the burden of hoped-for rehabilitation squarely upon the innocent, law-abiding members of the community, who must now share their streets with those who have proven themselves unable to respect the rights of others.

This is a lot to ask. We are told, in effect, that if we are sufficiently kind to our criminals at large, they will reform themselves, and that the aberrant behavior of those who do not reform and who murder, rape, rob, or steal again, is the penalty we the law-abiding must pay to further the rehabilitative theories of our social tinkerers.

Despite the Pollyannaesque assurances of these social tinkerers, it is high time finally to realize that some criminals will *never* be rehabilitated. They are just no good. They *like* to hurt others. They *like* to victimize others. And they will continue to do so despite all of the attempts at moral resuscitation the permissivists dream up.

Most people, at liberty because they do *not* kill, rape, rob, or steal, are unwilling to become the guinea pigs for a system where the safety of the law-abiding is based in large measure upon the good will of our convicted criminals, legally on the loose, not to commit further crimes —and the good will of our potential criminals, undeterred by nonpunishment of previous criminals, not to enter upon the paths of crime themselves.

The question the law-abiding citizen quite properly asks is: Why should I risk my safety and the security of my family and my possessions by permitting most of the dangerous elements of society to be at liberty to victimize me? Especially so since locking them up will:

1) deter potential criminals,
2) isolate criminals from me, and

3) vindicate the rights of those whom they victimized.

The permissivist would answer, first, that society has no right to "punish" them and, second, that by placing them in prison we only make them worse.

The response to this first point is that society has an absolute right, indeed a duty, to punish the lawless. Without this right, we would exist in a state of chaos. Our lives and safety would be at the mercy of those who would victimize us at will.

The response to the second argument is that crime has reached such dimensions that we can no longer afford to let fear of the unrepentant criminal, released after serving a prison sentence, dictate our policies. At least while they *are* incarcerated, criminals are not able to victimize others. Further, if certainty of punishment were the rule rather than the exception, their punishment would serve to deter others.

If convicts do come out of prison unrehabilitated, as they probably do, society then has two duties. The first is to the law-abiding: we should make it absolutely clear to the unrehabilitated and unrepentant prisoner that if, after leaving prison, he commits another crime, he will go right back to prison, this time for a considerably longer period. If he comes out again and commits still another crime, society will isolate him for a still longer period. And so on. In other words, society should make the cost of continued crime so high that the criminal will be deterred by the certainty of an increased penalty.

Then, and *only* then, can society begin to perform its second duty, this one to the convict: bending every effort and sparing no expense to learn how to rehabilitate those offenders we have isolated to safeguard the community and to deter others.

The two duties are not inconsistent. Once we have assured the safety of the law-abiding community, we can turn the considerable resources of this country toward finding the proper therapeutic techniques to help the criminal. We should premise this therapeutic effort upon helping the prisoner to rehabilitate himself—he must play a part in the process.

In effect, we should say to the criminal: if you commit a crime there is every likelihood you will be incarcerated. Once done, we will do everything we can *to help you help yourself*, and we will continue to help you after your incarceration. *But*, if you are unwilling to help yourself, if you commit further crimes, then we will continue to incarcerate you for longer and longer periods of time, simply for our own protection.

This proposal for the treatment of convicted criminals will not, I fear, meet with much approval from the permissive elements. A basic philosophical difference deeply divides us. To the permissivists, concern for the criminal is primary, the safety of society only secondary. Their single-minded desire to return the criminal to the community and hang the consequences to that community demonstrates as much. The theory of nonpunishment disdains the concepts of deterrence, isolation, and punishment, by which concepts alone society can, and must, protect itself. The permissivists are entirely too willing to risk the safety of society, but whether society is equally willing to take such a chance is a matter of the most serious doubt.

On the other hand, the concepts of deterrence, isolation, and punishment place the rights of the law-abiding on a much higher level than the rights of the criminal. Those holding such concepts are unwilling to play with the safety of the noncriminal community. The rights of the vast majority of law-abiding citizens in this country should not be subordinated to the rights of the minority of criminals.

The basic differences in the two philosophies are perhaps best spotlighted in a paragraph from the study of the National Commission on Criminal Justice Standards and Goals regarding juvenile criminals:

> There are a number of studies which suggest that many children mature out of delinquent behavior. If this is true, the question is whether it is better to leave these persons alone or put them in the formal juvenile justice system. Because there are no satisfactory measures of the effectiveness of the juvenile justice system, there is a substantial body of opinion which favors "leaving alone" all except those who have had three or four contacts with the police.[79]

Now, this "substantial body of opinion" that advocates "leaving alone" all juvenile criminals is permissivist theory refined to the nth degree. The sole concern is with the interests of the juvenile criminal in the rather bizarre hope that he will mature out of his criminal conduct. Under this theory, a sixteen-year-old criminal who assaults and snatches the pocketbook from a hard-working domestic on a ghetto street should not, if captured, *even be brought into the juvenile justice system*. He should be left alone. If the same juvenile next steals a car and wrecks it, he should, according to this theory, still be left alone. Upon this third crime, say a robbery, he *might* be brought into the juvenile justice system, although the "substantial body of opinion" might recommend noninterference until he has had "four contacts" with the police.

What of the lady who was assaulted and robbed, the owner of the car which was wrecked, or the victim of the second robbery? Nothing, of course. They, as law-abiding citizens, will simply be required to sustain their losses in order to vindicate the maturing-out-of-crime proposals propounded by the ivory-tower theroreticians. All that we are

166

asked to be concerned with are the interests of the juvenile criminal. His victims are ignored. Since most estimates indicate that at least one half of our crime is committed by juveniles, countless victims would be forced to watch the spectacle of those who had victimized them being left alone.

The society-oriented theory of the certainty of punishment would do just the opposite. For the first crime—assault and purse snatching—some penalty would be meted out. Perhaps a thirty-day sentence with all but one weekend in jail suspended, but there would be some deprivation of liberty with a promise of further and more substantial deprivations if additional transgressions occurred. The youth would most certainly *not* be permitted to go and brag among his friends that, as under the former theory, he had committed three serious crimes and had been left alone.

None of the foregoing is meant to suggest for a moment that such rehabilitative devices as probation, supervision, counseling, diversion from the criminal process, and community-based corrections should be abandoned. They should not, for there are those who are amenable to rehabilitation—that is, they have some desire to rehabilitate themselves.

But all of these devices, which the advocates of nonpunishment insist should be the *rule*, must be placed in a position secondary to the safety of society. Far too many innocent people in this country have been victimized because of nonpunishment. These victims have every right to regard our criminal justice system as an absolute failure.

Corrections Problems and the Victims

No single group of individuals in this nation has a more difficult or thankless job than our corrections administrators and those who work for and with them. They are charged not only with the custody of the worst elements in our society but also with the almost impossible task of doing something constructive for them. They are bombarded from all sides with conflicting demands. The public demands a secure facility. The courts demand changes, which may be necessary but which will drastically reduce their administrative discretion. The militant Left demands that prisoners run the prisons.

Some of the problems confronting prison administrators have been described by Warden Russell Lash of the Indiana State Prison:

Inmates now have rights that were unknown even five years ago.
Recent court decisions seem to indicate that inmates' mail cannot

be censored and that he can write to whomever he wishes. This includes his victims and women and children whose names and addresses appear in newspapers. Should the inmate break the prison rules—for example, assault an officer—the inmate must be afforded a hearing. At this hearing the inmate may confront his accuser, call witnesses, and cross-examine. At this prison, we also have extended him the right to have an attorney represent him at this hearing. One inmate recently sued and won $500 in compensatory damages against the assistant warden and custody supervisor in a prison in Pennsylvania because he was not given a hearing. Incidentally, there is no insurance company in the United States which will insure me or any employee at this prison against civil liability.

From the past, certain insights can be found into today's problems.

—Most of the old Auburn system, which consists of close supervision and hard work, has been phased out and little has been put in its place. Idleness, and all the problems it creates, is now a way of life behind the prison wall.

The work ethic aspect of the Auburn system is important and should be retained. However, I agree with the contemporary social view that a prisoner should be given extensive freedom within the walls so long as this freedom does not jeopardize the security of the prison.

—The power over and control of inmates have been diminished to the point where the prison could not operate for one day without the cooperation of 95 percent of the inmates.

—Substantial power has been removed from the prison and diffused throughout state government, but the responsibility still remains at the prison. Should a disturbance occur today, the prison administration would probably be blamed, but the causes that precipitated the disturbances may be beyond the prison's control.[80]

Even more scathing are the comments of Winston Moore, executive director of the Cook County Department of Corrections:

Many correctional administrators are in a quandary about what to do about the intensity of violence in their institutions. Some administrators unwisely have fallen victim to self-appointed "experts" who lack pragmatic knowledge about and experience with inmates or institutions. But these "experts" have obtained monies from foundations, government, and private sources to conduct "social experiments" with inmates.

These opportunists deal from an idealistic and undisciplined perspective. When their "experiments" fail, they are the first to blame correctional staffs for allegedly sabotaging their projects. These are the same people who were helpless in attempts to control campus unrest in recent years.

In jails and prisons, they create havoc and instill false hopes in inmates. Their short-term programs, most often introduced as simplistic, instant solutions for rehabilitation, only detour an inmate from legitimate rehabilitative progress.[81]

168

Problems such as these and others faced by those involved in the corrections field are so monumental that one section of a book can barely scratch their surface. In fact, hundreds of books, studies, articles, and monographs have been written about corrections problems and still not much light has been shed on the subject. Consequently, this section will concentrate on only one facet of the problem: how the current state of chaos in the area of corrections affects the victims of crime—both the law-abiding citizens on the outside and the residents within the prison walls, corrections officers as well as inmates.

No sane person is against the concept of prison reform, least of all our correctional administrators. They have for the most part taken the lead in treating inmates in a fair and humane manner. If the actual running of prisons had been left to their hard-earned expertise, these administrators would probably have brought about the basic requirements of prison reform while maintaining due concern for the security of the community.

Unfortunately, the past few years have seen the rising of an army of self-appointed corrections "experts" who have taken it upon themselves to dictate to professional corrections administrators how to run their institutions. A few have been successful. Almost without exception these experts have expressed a hand-wringing concern *only* with the "rights" of prisoners—usually those prisoners who resort to violence against their fellow inmates, guards, and other innocent victims.

What might be called the "Attica syndrome" illustrates this: prisoners resort to the worst sort of violence—murders, homosexual rape, riots, assaults, arsons—and the result from many is an anguished wail that the violence was surely not the fault of those who perpetrated it. Rather, society is somehow guilty for the violence, and society can make atonement only by giving in to all of the demands of the violence-prone prisoners.

The Attica syndrome, of course, causes further victimization inside our prisons. Those who are violence-prone believe that they can get away with anything or, at least, that they will receive a most sympathetic response to their crimes from those on the outside whose only concern is with the prisoners' rights.

In addition to the Attica syndrome, a good deal of victimization inside the walls results from ultralenient and permissive policies. These are either instituted by some corrections officials or imposed on them by outside "experts" including the courts and pressure groups.

Finally, although most correctional administrators carry out their awesomely difficult tasks with due regard for the safety of society, there have been some who have utterly failed. They have placed patently dangerous individuals at liberty to victimize others, *outside* the prison, through unduly permissive policies on parole, conditional release, furloughs, and escapes. Society has placed prisoners inside the walls precisely because they were believed dangerous. All of this is undone if they are foisted back onto the streets by those whose duty is to keep them so isolated.

Victimization Behind the Walls

Those who rail the loudest at the "excesses" committed in the retaking of Attica Prison in 1971 conveniently forget, or dismiss as "unfortunate," the fact that *before* the prison was retaken one corrections officer and three inmates were murdered by rebel prisoners. A prisoner who was present during the revolt describes additional activities of the rebels over whose "plight" so many tears have been shed: ". . . the rebels brutally and repeatedly raped two young white kids (not homosexuals) at knife point. They held knives at their throats and forced them to submit to oral and anal sodomy at the same time."[82]

Examples of the manner in which correctional personnel and inmates have been victimized are common in our prison system:

● The California Department of Corrections released a report in January 1974 on violence behind the walls of that state's prisons for a four-year period:

YEAR	STABBINGS	DEATHS	
		Inmates	*Prison Staff*
1970	66	9	2
1971	110	17	7
1972	168	35	1
1973 (thru Nov.)	150	19	1
TOTAL	494	80	11[83]

● According to Warden L. S. Nelson of San Quentin Prison in California, there were in that institution alone forty-one stabbing attacks (seven fatal) committed by inmates against other inmates and seventy-one assaults by inmates against prison personnel, in the first nine months of 1973.[84]

● In Arizona's maximum-security prison at Florence two guards were stabbed to death by inmates in June 1973 in an assault which the warden described as having been carried out ". . . deliberately, wantonly and very viciously."[85]

● In August 1972 in Norfolk Prison near Boston a convicted murderer killed two prison employees, his wife, and himself in an escape attempt. The prisoner's wife was believed to have smuggled the guns used in the killings into the visiting area by concealing them under her skirt. She had not been searched when she entered the prison.[86]

● Officials in Massachusetts reported that during 1972 more than thirty inmates had been stabbed, twelve fatally, in that state's prison system. A federal anticrime official charged that convicted organized-crime figures ran the prisons and ordered some of the killings on a contract basis. He noted: "It's easier to kill somebody inside a prison than it is on the outside. When you've got somebody enclosed in a certain boundary you know where your victim is."[87]

● During a riot at the Oklahoma State Prison at McAlester in July 1973, at least four inmates were murdered by other inmates. During the same week one guard was murdered and five other guards injured in a prison riot at Leavenworth, Kansas.[88]

This senseless wave of killings, assaults, and riots is a direct result of overlenient policies towards prisoners in the view of at least one group of individuals in a position to know: corrections officers. In case after case, correctional officers have threatened strikes and work stoppages unless prison security was tightened. A case in point, described by columnist William Raspberry of the *Washington Post*, arose in December 1973. Mr. Raspberry described the feelings of the guards at the Lorton Correctional Complex of the District of Columbia Department of Corrections: "The prison keepers, no less than the imprisoned, have their fears, outrages and feelings of neglect, and being on the "right" side of a locked cell door is no guarantee that these emotions won't get all confused and impossible to convey."[89]

The Lorton officers were understandably upset because a guard was found murdered inside the prison the week before. They threatened a walkout unless the prison authorities permitted a full-scale shakedown, for weapons and contraband, of the inmate's cells. The shakedown was finally approved, although the prisoners were forewarned that it would take place, thus undoing much of the effectiveness of the search. The walkout was averted. However, prior to the authorization for the shakedown, some of the officers expressed their frustrations in a letter to Mr. Raspberry: "The present administration of the Department of Corrections has continuously worked against the officers within its institutions. It has repeatedly set up programs and procedures which undermine security and jeopardize the safety of officers and inmates."[90] Another officer told Mr. Raspberry: "It looks as though the institution doesn't want to offend the inmates."[91]

Guards at the Walpole, Massachusetts, maximum-security prison did walk out in March 1973 in a protest over the permissive policies of then corrections commissioner John O. Boone. A representative of the guards stated flatly: "Inmates are running the institution and until the situation is changed, the men aren't going to work. Some have already been threatened by prisoners released from the segregated maximum-security section."[92] One of the main complaints of the guards was over the permissiveness shown to the inmates, permissiveness that included ordering the release of about one third of the prisoners in segregation and permitting outside observers to interfere with the prisoners' routine and to enter the prison after visiting hours.

Eventually the views of the guards prevailed over the permissive policies of Commissioner Boone, who was dismissed by Governor Francis Sargent, himself a liberal, in June 1973.[93] Pressure on Boone and his policies had increased because two weeks prior to his dismissal two inmates had been murdered at Walpole, one of whom was doused with inflammable liquid and burned to death in his cell. Permissiveness towards violence-prone inmates had resulted in just too much victimization behind the walls.

There are several reasons for the recent wave of permissiveness towards prisoners. There are, in the first place, the individual philosophies of some few corrections administrators. But, even those administrators who wish to run institutions with a due regard for the safety of prison employees and nonviolent inmates have found their discretion to do so impinged upon by outside sources.

The courts, both federal and state, have interjected themselves into the area of prison administration to a great extent. This is, of course, entirely proper when real abuses such as beatings or degrading treatment take place. But many courts have gone much further, literally dictating to the corrections administrators, from the lofty eminence of the bench, the manner in which they shall run their prisons. Restrictions on inmate disciplinary proceedings, limitations on access of visitors, inspection of mail, keep-locking* unruly prisoners and other methods of maintaining internal security have been imposed on the administrators by the courts in the name of the rights of prisoners. In many of these decisions, the rights of nonviolent inmates and members of the correctional staff *not* to be outraged by the violence-prone inmate have been ignored.

And the same judges who set up these restrictions against enforcing prison security are not hesitant to enforce them against the administrators by holding them liable, in their *personal* capacity, for outlandish amounts of money damages in favor of inmates who sue them. One

*This is the precaution of making unruly prisoners stay in their cells when others are let out for recreation.

federal judge in Virginia assessed $26,000 in damages personally, against a warden in favor of three prisoners. The judge, in a patently unfair decision, set certain standards for running the prison and then applied them *retroactively* to the warden, holding him liable for acts that had taken place years before.[94]

In addition to the courts, our prison administrators now feel enormous pressure from various "prisoners' rights" groups that have taken it upon themselves to tell the administrators how to run their institutions. Many of these groups are well meaning in their concern for prisoners' rights. But they, like the courts, appear sublimely unconcerned over the possibility that their efforts will result in opportunities for the violent criminals to victimize others inside the walls.

Governor Meldrim Thompson of New Hampshire, commenting upon a report made by District Attorney George D. Burke of Norfolk District, Massachusetts, concerning the prison upheaval in the Bay State, noted the effects of such prisoners' rights groups on Walpole Prison:

> In short, the inmates ran Walpole.
>
> Helping them destroy the institution and wreck all semblance of security were the citizen observers—one of whom was Gene Mason, political science professor at Franconia College, Franconia, N.H., where he helped to form a New England Prisoner Association—and the National Prisoners Rights Association, which was recognized by former Corrections Commissioner John O. Boone as the "exclusive authorized representative of inmates for the purpose of resolving all grievances."[95]

Warden Russell Lash of the Indiana State Penitentiary has commented rather pungently upon the efforts of self-appointed prison reformers:

> One of the nice things about prisons and prison reform is that anyone can be an expert on the subject—from "ex-cons" to Supreme Court justices. Most prison "experts" have one common denominator, that they have never worked in today's prisons for an appreciable amount of time. Few, if any, have ever taken the time to read current correctional research.[96]

A particularly disturbing aspect of the prison "reform" movement is the current attempt by militant leftist groups, which are not even slightly well intentioned, to radicalize the prison population of this country. On December 18, 1973, the Internal Security Committee of the U.S. House of Representatives released a report entitled "Revolutionary Target: The American Penal System," which focuses in detail on the way radical and militant groups like the Black Panther Party, the Communist Party, U.S.A., and the National Lawyers Guild are attempting to politicize American penal institutions according to their views.

Concerning the problems of the activities in the legal area of the prisoners' rights groups and especially the involvement of the radical elements in such activities, Warden L. S. Nelson and Associate Warden J. W. Pack of California have stated:

> . . . institutions were besieged by attorneys who demonstrated an enthusiastic interest in their clients. . . . Wardens found, to their dismay, that instead of being regarded as protectors of society, they were now considered oppressors of the poor and underprivileged. . . . The seemingly endless flow of allegations, charges, exposes, and investigations has kept wardens on the defensive. Much of their day is spent in answering accusations, many of which are either untrue or based on distorted segments of the truth.
>
> More serious problems arise for the warden from those few attorneys who profess to be advocates for radical-social political movements. These doctrinaire, rigid, violently oriented individuals use the prisoner and his discontent in the pursuit of their political philosophies, the actual welfare of the man being a secondary consideration.
>
> Not content to merely criticize the prison system, nor to help particular prisoners, activists have inspired prison rebellions. San Quentin staff believes that the incident of Aug. 21, 1971, which resulted in the death of three officers and three inmates, was caused by the intervention of Marxist revolutionaries, among whom there was at least one attorney.[97]

These are the views of professionals, men who must confront the problems of running a penal institution on a day-to-day basis; men who are charged with the awesome responsibility of securing not only the safety of society, but also the rights of their employees and the vast majority of their inmate charges who do not wish to commit acts of violence upon one another.

The interested, and generally well-meaning, amateur prison reformer may spend a day or two wandering about a prison, talking to inmates, and then retire to his home, an instant expert on penology. Men such as Wardens Nelson and Pack *live* with the problem and that is precisely why they *are* experts. Their views should be heeded.

Prison reform is vital if our criminal justice system is ever to be effective. But prison reform that gives a license to violent prisoners to prey upon others, or prison reform that is a product of the Attica syndrome—"It's our fault that you were forced to riot and kill"—is surely not the answer. Those who weep and wail over the fate of our violent prisoners could well take a leaf from the book of Mike Royko, the brilliant columnist—not noted for his conservative views—for the *Chicago Daily News*.

September 1973 witnessed a revolt at Stateville Penitentiary in Illinois. Ten guards were held hostage and eventually released. Two leaders of the revolt, George Carney and Sam Early, became instant celebrities in the local media, telling one and all that they were the victims of social injustice. Carney stated that prison had brutalized him to the extent that he could now "kill any human being and not feel anything."

Royko did a little digging into the records of Carney and Early, noting that most of the stories about them had said little or nothing about why they were in prison. Royko pointed out that Carney

> says prison turned him into a person capable of harming other humans.
>
> That probably surprises a couple a gas station attendants in Peoria who met Carney before he spent even one day in prison.
>
> One of the attendants didn't move fast enough when Carney robbed him in 1959. So Carney belted him on the head with a blackjack, hard enough to put him in a hospital.
>
> Carney was caught and was let out on bond to await trial.
>
> While he was out, he went to another gas station. This time he had a gun. He not only robbed the attendant, but he forced the terrified man into his car, apparently as a hostage. When state police chased him at high speeds, he finally turned the car over and wrecked it.
>
> For these robberies and the assault, Carney spent the next seven years in prison. He would have been there longer, but the state gave him a parole.[98]

Royko went on to point out that Carney, after his parole, was arrested for assault and child molesting and finally given twelve years for manslaughter.

Royko then researched Early's record, which consists of convictions for forgery, attempted murder, and armed robbery and a host of other arrests. He summarized: "And that's why Early is in prison. He runs around with a gun in his hand, shooting and beating and robbing people."[99] Not afflicted with the Attica syndrome, Royko ended his column with the following tough-minded admonition:

> I'm all for prison reform, as long as society can afford it. From a practical point of view, it makes sense. If some prisoners can be reformed, then we'll save money and maybe lives. And while some convicts might be even worse than animals, we shouldn't treat them as such because it degrades us.
>
> But spare me the hand-wringing.
>
> As far as their "rights" go, the only "right" they have is to be kept alive. Anything else is extra. Had they been treated in prison the way they treated people outside, Early would have bullet holes in his head and Carney would be dead. Both of them are ahead of the game.[100]

It is precisely this sort of realistic attitude, coupled with a desire to do something constructive about our very real corrections problems, that is needed if we are to find worthwhile solutions to the problems.

Victims of Correctional Leniency

Even worse than crimes committed by those behind prison walls are the countless crimes committed on the outside by persons who should have been behind prison walls, but who were not because of leniency granted them while in the corrections system. As a result, numerous innocent citizens have been victimized because some person or group of persons, again, erroneously decided to take a chance on freeing an inmate.

In addition, we have the problem of unnecessary escapes. These are occasioned by situations in which the convicted criminal has not been formally released but the security arrangements for him are so lax that with little or no effort he unilaterally frees himself.

In each event the onus of further victimization of innocent people rests squarely upon the particular system of corrections involved.

PAROLE ABUSES

Parole is the conditional release of a prisoner before his sentence has been completed. It is undoubtedly a useful device when an individual who has served part of his sentence *really* indicates that he has rehabilitated himself and that he is ready to return to society. The problem with parole is the same problem found in cases dealing with other types of release such as bail or probation: those who make the decision as to release far too often err on the side of leniency in the *hope* that the criminal at liberty will not victimize again. It is the same old story of those of a permissive bent being willing to risk the safety of society.

Today, estimates indicate that sixty percent of all adult felons are released on parole before their sentence has expired and placed into an unsuspecting society.[101] Far too many of them victimize again. A recent study of parole practices in New York indicated that the rearrest rate of those granted parole was about the same as for those who had served out their sentences. This finding indicates that those who are in the position to make decisions as to early release were not able to predict with any certainty whether the parolees, as opposed to those denied parole, were rehabilitated.

Statistics from California and Washington, D.C., bear this out.[102] The California Governor's Select Committee on the Problems of Law Enforcement found that, in a selected sample of cases, persons released on parole had a rearrest rate of 53.6 percent, ranging from one rearrest for thirty-six percent of those released to six or more rearrests for five percent of those placed on parole.[103] A survey of persons released on parole from all types of sentences in Washington, D.C. in 1970 indicated that

40.2 percent of them had had warrants issued against them for other crimes.[104]

Obviously some of the rearrests of parolees will be for minor offenses. But many times the rearrests may be for serious crimes—crimes that *would not have been committed had the parolees not been released into society before their sentences expired.*

State senator H. L. (Bill) Richardson of California compiled data on five murders committed in that state in a *two-month period* by individuals on parole:

Case A) Sentenced in 1971 for four years for Grand Theft, paroled after seven months. He shot and killed another man who was attempting to protect the parolee's own sister from being savagely beaten by the parolee.

Case B) Convicted of First Degree Robbery and Manslaughter, sentenced to two terms of eight years each to run consecutively, paroled after 13 years. He shot and killed another during a heated argument while he was on parole.

Case C) Sentenced to five years for Possession of Dangerous Drugs, paroled after 13 months. While on parole, he shot and killed a store employee and wounded three others in an attempted robbery.

Case D) Convicted of Burglary, paroled after two years on condition that he totally abstain from liquor. He stabbed to death another during a drunken brawl in a saloon.

Case E) Convicted of possession of marijuana and an illegal sawed-off shotgun, sentenced to six-year and five-year terms to run consecutively. He was paroled after serving three years and shot and killed his girlfriend during an argument in a bar.[105]

Cases like these are not confined to California. In East Lansing, Michigan, a parolee from the Michigan State Penitentiary was arrested for sexually assaulting three Michigan State University coeds. He was paroled after serving four years in Michigan for armed robbery, having been previously convicted in Mississippi for rape.[106]

In 1970 a thirty-nine-year-old man was released by the Georgia Parole Board from a burglary conviction, despite the fact that a prison psychologist had warned the board that "he may be dangerous to himself and others." He now faces charges in the murder of seven people.[107]

Perhaps the number of murders, rapes, and other violent crimes by parolees bears a direct relationship to the *attitude* of those who are in a position to grant or deny parole. In chapter one I discussed the case of William P. Sweeney, who was paroled after serving two and one-half years of a seventy-five-year sentence for murdering an Iowa police chief. The Iowa Parole Board was convinced, wrongly as matters turned out, that Sweeney was rehabilitated. Not wishing under any circumstances to punish him further, the board freed him. This clearly demonstrates that any thought about the safety of society was decidedly secondary in the Iowa Parole Board's attitude.

A corrections officer from the Illinois Department of Corrections (Juvenile Division) wrote this author to express his frustration over the attitude of a "member of the high tribunal of the Illinois Industrial School for Boys," apparently the parole-granting authority for whom the officer worked. This corrections officer, who from his correspondence was obviously an intelligent and dedicated—albeit frustrated—man, stated that the parole authorities told him they were not going to "discriminate" against any of the young criminals under their jurisdiction. That, in fact, "the rapist, the murderer, the severely aggressive, could get a furlough as easily as the youth with a mild criminality, *and that they could get parole in three or four months.*"

Ernest Rocco Infelice, a high-ranking Chicago mobster, was sentenced in 1973 to ten years in prison for selling heroin. In February 1974 Infelice, with the blessing of U.S. District Court judge Prentice Marshall who had released him on bail pending the appeal of his conviction, left Chicago for the sunny climes of Florida. Despite a long criminal record, Infelice was on parole from a five-year federal conviction at the time of his heroin-peddling conviction. He was immediately taken into custody for parole violation, but three weeks later the U.S. Parole Board released him.[108] Apparently a conviction for the sale of heroin by a convicted racketeer was not sufficient grounds to revoke his parole in the eyes of the parole board.

The attitude of the Iowa Parole Board: "We must not punish our convicted murderers"; the attitude of the Illinois juvenile parole authorities: "It discriminates against our murderers and rapists if we do not parole them as quickly as we do our minor offenders, so we must parole them too"; the attitude of the United States Parole Board: "A conviction for the sale of heroin by a major organized crime figure already on parole from a previous offense, nonetheless requires his release"—these attitudes are far too common and contribute to our climate of permissiveness. So long as they remain the credo, the law-abiding citizen can expect to be victimized by the beneficiaries of such leniency.

THE "OVER THE FENCE GANG"—FURLOUGHS, WALKAWAYS, AND ESCAPES

Finally, leniency or laxity, or both, often results in dangerous criminals being released or permitted to escape into society while still serving their sentences. This is generally accomplished in three ways: intentionally furloughing a prisoner or placing him on work-release programs—that is, letting him out of prison on his own devices, with little or no supervision; allowing a prisoner out of the walls under such loose supervision that he is in a position simply to walk away; and relaxing the security of a prisoner technically in custody to the extent that he can escape almost at will.

The concepts of furloughs and unsupervised work-release programs (in the latter the convict usually leaves the institution during the day to work and returns at night) are based on the theory that such a temporary return to the community, especially to work therein, will prepare him for his final return to the community when he is eventually released. Usually there are restrictions upon the discretion of correctional administrators to grant furloughs, such as the requirement that the furloughed or released prisoner must be close to parole eligibility.

The idea of permitting prisoners to leave the walls under minimal supervision, or to be placed in a facility from which escape is pretty much just a matter of walking away, derives from the theory that maximum security should be reserved for the dangerous few and that the "warehousing" concept should apply only to those who are truly dangerous.

Such concepts, based on modern penal theory, have considerable merit but they are also prone to the grossest sort of abuse. When a criminal has proven by his crimes that he is in fact dangerous, then the wholesale release of such criminals constitutes a clear danger to society. When the discretion to release a prisoner or put him in a walkaway position is abused, the innocent in society are placed in the position of having in their midst a dangerous person who can victimize again.

Unfortunately this abuse of discretion in prison security and release programs is not rare. California state senator H. L. Richardson, for example, announced in November 1972 that in the preceding twenty-one months in that state there had been 1,518 escapes from release programs and minimum-security facilities.[109]

That persons placed on release status will commit other crimes is demonstrated by statistics compiled for the four-and-one-half-month period from mid-February 1971 to June 30, 1971, by the Major Violators Branch of the Metropolitan Police Department of Washington, D.C. During that time 213 persons who had been released by the District of Columbia Department of Corrections committed further crimes, including such serious felonies as rape and armed robbery.[110]

Cases of prisoners who were patently dangerous individuals but who were placed in positions to escape, abscond, or walk away, exist in every part of the country.

● In 1973 in Columbus, Ohio, Franklin County prosecutor George C. Smith criticized prison officials for permitting a convicted murderer, who had beaten a fourteen-year-old girl to death with a brick, to walk away from a visit to a Columbus shopping center.[111]

• In Chicago a man convicted of murder in 1971 walked away from a guard while attending the funeral of his mother.[112]

• In Stormville, New York, in January 1974, another convicted murderer walked away from a work detail at the warden's residence outside the walls of the maximum-security Green-Haven State Prison.[113]

• A New York assemblyman charged in November 1973 that New York City's Jennings Hall, a temporary shelter for boys, "was a place from which youngsters easily sortie to commit muggings and return 'bedecked' in stolen finery and from which youths once left to perpetrate a rape and a murder."[114]

• On November 2, 1973, a prisoner who was serving time for the murder of a New Jersey state trooper walked away from a work detail outside the prison walls. He was killed on November 18 by New York City detectives after he tried to run them down with his automobile.[115]

• In October 1973 a prisoner serving a life term for murder failed to return from a nine-hour furlough, which had been granted to attend a seminar on prison reform.[116]

Any person who escapes while on release status is potentially dangerous. The very fact of his escape indicates clearly that he was not rehabilitated to the extent that the leniency of release status should have been accorded to him. On occasion the grimmest tragedy of all occurs. Convicted murderers escape, walk away, or are put on furlough only to kill again.

• In October 1973, in New York, a convict who had been sentenced to a five-year term for manslaughter was furloughed "to improve his family ties." He failed to return. He was arrested in January 1974, after a high-speed chase, by police officers who were seeking him for questioning in another murder.[117]

• In 1973 a convict serving a prison sentence for manslaughter in Trenton, New Jersey, wrote to the local newspapers: "The chances of most murderers repeating the offense are quite low." Some two months later he was given a weekend pass from the prison. On the Sunday of that weekend he was accused of killing a sixty-six-year-old man with a hatchet in a dispute over a woman.[118]

• In Sarasota, Florida, in September 1972, a prisoner who was serving a twenty-year sentence for the 1971 murder of his wife, and who had been granted a weekend furlough, was accused of killing his late wife's brother in a barroom brawl.[119]

Two recent cases also illustrate that those who are shown excessive leniency through release programs will often abuse this leniency and commit other crimes. In these two cases, two murders and one attempted murder occurred. There is, however, an extra element in these cases: the next of kin of the two murdered victims and the victim of the attempted murder have attempted to do something about *their* rights by suing those responsible for freeing the prisoners.

The first case involved one Arthur St. Peter, who in 1972 was serving a life term in the state prison at Walla Walla, Washington. Despite his record of forty felonies and seventeen escapes and escape attempts, he was described by one guard as a "model prisoner."

Warden Bobby J. Rhay had instituted at the penitentiary a "Take-a-Lifer-to-Dinner" program, whereby persons serving life sentences were authorized by the warden to go outside the walls to have dinner with selected persons. "Model prisoner" St. Peter was permitted to leave the prison to have dinner with a prison baker. He escaped through a bathroom window of the baker's home and disappeared.

On May 3, 1972, during an armed robbery, St. Peter murdered shop-owner Robert Taylor and wounded Taylor's wife, Lorraine. Mrs. Taylor sued the state of Washington and Warden Rhay on the theory that he had no legislative authority to permit lifers to leave the walls and that he was negligent in the exercise of his administrative discretion when he permitted St. Peter to go out to dinner. This negligence, Mrs. Taylor's attorneys argued, caused the death of her husband and her injuries at St. Peter's hands. The jury agreed and on May 20, 1973, awarded Mrs. Taylor $186,000 in damages. Should this verdict be allowed to stand on appeal, it may well be a landmark case for the rights of victims. Surely such a verdict will make officials think twice before they risk loosing dangerous criminals.[120]

The verdict in the Taylor case may have motivated the father of a slain gas station attendant. He also sued the state of Washington, for $275,000, on the grounds that it was negligent in releasing a prisoner who bludgeoned to death his son while on a work-release program in Tacoma. The prisoner, convicted of the robbery-murder of the plaintiff's son, committed the crime while on work release from prison at a state hospital. The suit contends that the state acted negligently and carelessly in permitting the convict to remove himself from an institution.[121]

These two cases are important. They reveal encouraging attitudes. Two victims believe they should not be obliged to sit in aggrieved silence when they have been victimized as a result of excessive leniency shown dangerous criminals by state officialdom. Perhaps if it is made clear to those who are willing to take a chance with the safety of society that the chance entails some risk to *themselves as well,* we might see far fewer victims of such leniency.

6
The Killers vs.
the Victims:
The Death-Penalty
Argument

No OTHER SINGLE ISSUE BRINGS INTO FOCUS the current climate of permissiveness toward criminals better than the issue of capital punishment. Likewise, no others more clearly display an utter disregard for the victims of crime than the advocates of the abolition of the death penalty.

The abolitionists speak for the killer. The pro-death-penalty forces speak for the victims. The lines are drawn. The abolitionist argument runs something like this:

—Capital punishment is cruel and unusual.

—It cannot with mathematical certainty be proven that the death penalty deters people from murdering others; therefore, we must not be "cruel" to our murderers by executing them.

—Human life is sacred.

—Executing the killer will not bring the victim back to life.

—We might execute an innocent man.

—Capital punishment is arbitrary and discriminates against racial minorities.

The pro-capital-punishment argument runs as follows:

—Capital punishment is neither cruel nor unusual.

—There is evidence that capital punishment is, in fact, a deterrent. But even if this cannot be proven with certainty, neither can it be proven that capital punishment does *not* deter potential murderers from killing innocent victims. Capital punishment should be utilized, then; if the threat of death deters even one potential killer from claiming the life of his victim, then its use is worthwhile. The victim rather than the killer should be the principal object of our concern.

—Human life is indeed sacred. So sacred in fact that he who willfully, wantonly, or feloniously takes the life of another should forfeit his own life.

—The victim may be dead but the value of his life and society's abhorrence of the crime of murder will be vindicated if we deal severely with the victim's killers.

—The chances of executing an innocent man are, to say the least, remote under our system of criminal justice, which erects more procedural safeguards around the criminal accused than any other system in the world.

—If capital punishment is applied in an arbitrary and discriminatory manner, the solution is to apply it in a nonarbitrary and nondiscriminatory manner. As for the argument that more minority members are sentenced to death, it should also be remembered that minorities are disproportionately the victims of murder.

—Finally, if a murderer has been executed, we can be absolutely certain that he will never kill again.

Thus, two opposing views of the death penalty: one a victim-oriented position, the other a criminal-oriented position. The purpose of this chapter is to set forth the more important aspects of the victim-oriented view.

In March 1972 the California Supreme Court legislated the death penalty out of existence in that state. It held that it was "cruel or unusual" punishment under the California Constitution.[1] In June of that year a five-justice majority* of the U.S. Supreme Court, in *Furman* v. *Georgia*[2] and its companion cases, decided that, the legislatures of thirty-four states and the Congress of the United States notwithstanding, capital punishment was unconstitutional.

*Brennan, Douglas, Marshall, Stewart, and White. Dissenting were Burger, Blackmun, Rehnquist, and Powell. Each justice wrote a separate opinion.

Questions of the propriety of capital punishment aside, this was one of the most arrogant usurpations of the legislative function of government that the U.S. Supreme Court had ever engaged in. Rarely has it had the temerity summarily to strike down so many state and federal laws in a single case—and by a 5 to 4 majority at that. One of the truly disturbing aspects of the majority opinion is that most of the states whose death-penalty laws were struck down *were not even represented* before the Court. Death sentences in only three states—Georgia, California, and Texas—were under review by the Court, yet capital-punishment legislation in thirty-one other states and in the federal system was also cast out by the Court.

Perhaps supremely exemplifying judicial arrogance is the majority opinion of justice William J. Brennan. He based his decision upon sociological considerations:

> In sum, the punishment of death is inconsistent with . . . four principles: Death is an unusually severe and degrading punishment; there is a strong probability that it is inflicted arbitrarily; its rejection by contemporary society is virtually total, and there is no reason to believe that it serves any penal purpose more effectively than the less severe punishment of imprisonment. The function of these principles is to enable a court to determine whether a punishment comports with human dignity. Death, quite simply, does not.[3]

Justice Brennan's "four principles" should be considered together and then one by one. Taken together, Justice Brennan's four points might be in their proper place if stated in a position paper presented by, say, the ACLU, to a legislative body considering capital punishment. His position expounds a completely sociological viewpoint and has no business in an opinion of the Court whose function is to interpret the law. Many of us are in favor of the death penalty and Justice Brennan is not, but he has no more right to impose his *personal* predilection on us than we on him. Yet he (with Douglas and Marshall, who also based their decisions on sociological abstractions) has done just that. Our Constitution recognizes capital punishment in its wording, and until *Furman* it was well settled by the Supreme Court itself that the death penalty was not unconstitutional.[4] If the death penalty is socially unacceptable to Justices Brennan, Marshall, and Douglas, they are, of course, free to speak out against it in their personal capacities. But it does grave disservice to our system of justice when three men impose their personal feelings upon society in the threadbare guise of "interpreting the law."

Consider now Justice Brennan's four principles one by one, from the point of view of victims of crime:

"Death is an unusually severe and degrading punishment." To the vic-

tim, murder is a severe and degrading punishment and, incidentally, a totally undeserved punishment. If one makes the fairly safe assumption that none of the victims of Richard Speck, Charles Manson, and the 700-odd other murderers on death rows across the nation (at the time *Furman* was decided) wished to die, it can be accurately stated that their deaths were severe and degrading and certainly constituted a deprivation, without due process of law, of every right they had. But Justice Brennan evidences no regard for them. He is concerned solely that the convicted killers not be punished in too "severe" or "degrading" a manner.

"There is a strong probability that it is inflicted arbitrarily." This may or may not be true, but there is an absolute certainty that death is often inflicted arbitrarily on the victims of murderers. The fatal shooting of little Joyce Ann Huff as she played in her yard was about as arbitrary an act as one can imagine. Justice Brennan is concerned about arbitrariness in the law towards convicted killers and supremely unconcerned about the thousands of innocent people murdered in this country every year in an arbitrary manner.

"[The death penalty's] rejection by contemporary society is virtually total." This statement is simply not true and Justice Brennan knew it or should have known it. It is bad enough when judicial arrogance seeks to impose a single man's opinions upon an entire nation. But it is completely intolerable when statements having no bearing in fact are used to support the imposition. As late as March 1972 a Gallup poll had shown that fifty percent of those polled favored the death penalty while forty-one percent opposed it.[5] In 1970 the voters of Illinois elected to *retain* capital punishment by a count of 1,217,791 to 676,302—almost 2 to 1.[6] While this may not indicate a uniform acceptance of capital punishment, it is a far cry from "virtually total" rejection. Brennan's statement is so inaccurate that it strains one's credibility that a Supreme Court justice would make it.

"There is no reason to believe that [death] serves any penal purpose more effectively than the less severe punishment of imprisonment." There may be no reason for Justice Brennan to believe that capital punishment serves any penal purpose, but there are a great many people—the million-plus voters of Illinois and the respondents to the Gallup poll cited above—who evidently *do* believe it serves a useful purpose, whether incapacitation, deterrence, or punishment. It certainly has never been proven that the death penalty does *not* accomplish these ends. Again, we see Brennan's complete preoccupation with the convicted killers: they must not be as "severely" punished for their murders as capital punishment would entail, despite the fact that they "severely" punished their victims.

Finally, Justice Brennan's four principles lead him to the conclusion that capital punishment does not "comport with human dignity." This is a flimsy-to-nonexistent basis upon which to base an opinion supposedly grounded in the law. If fifty people, selected at random, were asked to define so nebulous a term as "human dignity," fifty different responses would emerge. And none would have any more right to force his definition on the nation than does Justice Brennan.

This aside, the jurist's statement that capital punishment does not "comport with human dignity" is callous, a cynical expression of contempt for the victims of crime. Anyone who has ever seen, in the flesh or in photographs, the body of a murder victim knows that the victim's loss of human dignity is complete and final. To engage in judicial hand-wringing about the human dignity of murderers is to mock the meaning of the lives of their victims.

Despite the decision in the *Furman* case, capital punishment is far from a dead issue. Four members of the Court (Burger, Powell, Rehnquist, and Blackmun) held that capital punishment was not unconstitutional at all. Justice Harry Blackmun stated: "I yield to no one in the depth of my distaste, antipathy and indeed abhorrence for the death penalty . . ."; yet, in striking contrast to Justices Brennan, Marshall and Douglas, Justice Blackmun *refused* to impose his personal views on the nation, stating that it was a matter for legislative or executive action and not a "judicial expedient."[7]

Justices Potter Stewart and Byron White joined the majority, in the thought not so much that capital punishment is unconstitutional, as that it was applied in an arbitrary manner. These two justices did not address themselves to the way murder is applied to its innocent victims, and it is difficult to see how the application of the death penalty to such mass murderers as Richard Speck and Charles Manson could, by any stretch of the imagination, be called "arbitrary." But, Justices Stewart and White did at least leave the door open for the states and the federal government to enact legislation applying the death penalty in a manner that is not arbitrary, that is, by making the death penalty mandatory for some crimes.

Several approaches have been taken in an effort to restore the death penalty in the United States. Congressman Lowell Wyman of New Hampshire, a former attorney general of that state, has introduced a constitutional amendment that would restore the death penalty across the nation—at least for those states that wished to restore it. As of this writing twenty-nine states have by legislation restored the death penalty for certain crimes, legislation which one hopes will pass muster with the Supreme Court. In other states similar bills have been introduced. The supreme courts of two states (Delaware and North Carolina) have held that the laws in their states met the objections of the Supreme Court majority and that capital punishment is validly in effect in those states. At a December 1972 meeting of the National Association of State Attorneys General, a resolution was passed by a vote of 32 to 1 recommending that the states reinstate the death penalty for "murder during the commission of certain felonies—armed robbery, rape, burglary, arson, kidnapping, and perhaps other felonies; murder of a police officer or a public figure; murder by explosive devices; multiple slayings; contract killings; [and] killings for personal gain."[8]

The public is apparently in favor of reinstating the death penalty. A Gallup poll taken in November 1972, after the Supreme Court's decision outlawing it, indicated fifty-seven percent favoring the death penalty and thirty-two percent opposing it,[9] and a Harris poll of June 1973 showed fifty-nine percent support with opposition down to thiry-one percent.[10] These figures indicate a sharp increase in favor of the death penalty and a decrease in those opposed to it, compared with the poll in March 1972 (noted above) in which fifty percent favored capital punishment and forty-one percent opposed it. The Harris poll noted that the increase was apparently "due in considerable measure to widespread fear concerning personal and family safety."

Buttressing the contention that the public generally supports the death penalty for murderers (and completely undermining Justice Brennan's assertion that rejection of it is "virtually total") is the result of a special referendum held in California during the national election on November 7, 1972. In this referendum the voters were asked whether the death penalty should be restored in that state. The outcome was that restoration of the death penalty won by a 2-to-1 margin.

In the *Furman* case the abolitionists may have won the battle and yet lost the war. As crime continues to rise, law-abiding citizens are reacting strongly to the permissiveness towards murderers embodied in *Furman*. There may be an equally strong reaction among state and national legislators to having the laws that they had in good faith enacted for the protection of the innocent, rendered impotent by the whimsical and judicial legislation of Justices Brennan, Douglas, and Marshall.

We'll now consider the case for the death penalty from the point of view of crime's victims; in addition, the way abolitionists snub the same victims by their tender solicitude for the lives of the murderers.

Abolitionists argue that capital punishment is "cruel and unusual." This argument can go round and round and little that is useful will be gained by lengthy discussion of it. Six justices of the U.S. Supreme Court have refused to characterize capital punishment itself as cruel and unusual, and the question remains open. Other than this, however, the question of whether something is cruel and unusual depends entirely on the point of view of the observer. To the devoted abolitionist, any executed death sentence is by definition cruel and unusual; nothing will change his mind. The more generally held view, however, is that if the manner of execution is such that it does not entail unusual or unnecessary suffering on the part of the condemned, then it is not cruel and unusual punishment. Surely execution in the gas chamber of the state of California would be far less cruel and unusual for the murderers of Joyce Ann Huff than was the manner in which they slew her.

The most critical argument insofar as capital punishment is concerned is really whether the death penalty deters would-be murderers. This cannot with mathematical certainty be proven one way or the other, even though, as will be seen, there is considerable evidence that capital punishment does deter criminals from killing in the course of their criminal acts. Abolitionists use the argument that homicide rates are, in some cases, lower in states that do not have capital punishment than in states that do. This argument begs the question. No one would argue that the threat of death deters *all* murderers. But, just because it does not deter *all* killers, does not for a moment mean that it does not deter *any* killers. It may very well deter a given number of potential murderers about whom we will never know simply because, being deterred, they did not kill. It is easy enough for either side to state categorically that capital punishment does or does not deter; it is a great deal harder to back up such statements.

The question remains, however, since we are not really sure about the deterrent effect: Whose side are we to err on, that of proven and convicted killers or of innocent potential victims? If capital punishment is in truth no deterrent to a would-be killer and we still retain it, then our "error" is made on the side of executing convicted murderers, many of whom are cancers in society that should be removed anyway. If, however, capital punishment *is* a deterrent and we retain it as such, then for each potential killer deterred an innocent victim's life is spared. It seems fair to say that most people would rather take the chance that by executing murderers, we will be sparing innocent victims of other would-be killers who are deterred. That is to say most people, if given the option of protecting murderers from the consequences of their acts or of protecting their potential victims, would doubtless choose the latter.

The abolitionists are simply not victim-oriented (except as they view a convicted murderer as the victim of the state). They evidence an unrealistic and lofty disregard for (a) the plight of the actual victims of countless murderers, and (b) the safety of the *potential* victims of future killers. But past and future victims of crime *are* deserving of our consideration, especially in view of the fact that our racial minorities and ghetto dwellers are unquestionably the principal victims of violent crimes, including those crimes for which the death penalty is provided. In 1971 Illinois state senator Raymond Ewing, a black, refused to vote for a moratorium on the death penalty in Illinois: "I realize that most of those who would face the death penalty are poor and black and friendless. *I also realize that most of their victims are poor and black and friendless and dead.*"[11]

Concern for the victims of murders leads inevitably to the abolitionist response that executing killer A will not bring victim B back to life. This is of course true. But this argument ignores two things: (1) the execution of A may well deter C, D, and E from following A's example, and (2) *it will* make absolutely certain that A will never kill again.

If capital punishment were a real rather than an imagined threat, potential murderers in many cases would be deterred from killing. Evidence to support this contention is found in a study conducted by the Los Angeles Police Department in 1970 and '71 to measure the deterrent effect of the death penalty. The study embraced a compilation of statements by persons arrested for crimes of violence. Those interviewed had been unarmed during the commission of their crimes, or had been armed but did not use their weapons, or had carried inoperative weapons. Of ninety-nine persons who gave a statement as to why they went unarmed or did not use their weapons the results were classified as follows:

1. Deterred by fear of death penalty from carrying weapon or operative weapon, 50 (50.5%).
2. Unaffected by death penalty because it was no longer being enforced, 7 (7.07%).
3. Undeterred by death penalty, would kill whether it was enforced or not, 10 (10.1%).
4. Unaffected by death penalty because they would not carry weapon in any event, primarily out of fear of being injured themselves or of injuring someone else, 32 (32.3%).[12]

Thus we see a 5-to-1 ratio of deterrence over nondeterrence as reported by individuals who were in the best position to make such a judgment: the perpetrators themselves.

The adoption of an *effectively enforced* death-penalty system would be a deterrent in the prevention of homicides. Although the death penalty had not, at the time of the study, been removed from the statutes in California, seven percent of the questioned suspects believed that, in reality, no death penalty existed because it was not being enforced; consequently there was no deterrent. Some suspects, while realizing that the California death penalty existed in name only, disclosed that the *certainty* of an executed death-penalty sentence would deter them from arming themselves or using their weapons while committing crimes.

The report also notes: *"If this study contained only one and not the 50 documented cases supporting the fact that the death penalty is a deterrent, there should be no question of its retention and enforcement.* In 1970 in the City of Los Angeles, 394 innocent people were victims of an unlawful execution without the right of due process of law."

Additionally, Justice Marshall McComb of the California Supreme Court (the sole dissenter in the case in which the California Supreme Court held the death penalty to be "cruel or unusual") had in an earlier case cited, as evidence of the deterrent effect of the death penalty, another series of examples of violent criminals who did *not* kill because of the threat of death involved for capital crimes.[13]

From Justice McComb's opinion here are examples that demonstrate clearly the true deterrent nature of capital punishment. In these cases lives were *actually saved* because a would-be killer, *by his own admission,* was deterred by the death penalty from murdering others in the course of violent crimes.

(i) Margaret Elizabeth Daly, of San Pedro, was arrested August 28, 1961, for assaulting Pete Gibbons with a knife. She stated to investigating officers: "Yeh, I cut him and I should have done a better job. *I would have killed him but I didn't want to go to the gas chamber."*

(ii) Robert D. Thomas, alias Robert Hall, an ex-convict from Kentucky; Melvin Eugene Young, alias Gene Wilson, a petty criminal from Iowa and Illinois; and Shirley R. Coffee, alias Elizabeth Salquist, of California, were arrested April 25, 1961, for robbery. They had used toy pistols to force their victims into rear rooms, there the victims were bound. When questioned by the investigating officers as to the reason for using toy guns instead of genuine guns, all agreed that real guns were too dangerous, *and if someone were killed in the commission of the robberies, they could all receive the death penalty.*

(iii) Louis Joseph Turck, alias Luigi Furchiano, alias Joseph Farino, alias Glen Hooper, alias Joe Moreno, an ex-convict with a felony record dating from 1941, was arrested May 20, 1961, for robbery. He had used guns in prior robberies in other states but simulated a gun in the robbery here. He told investigating officers that he was aware of the California death penalty although he had been in this state for only one month, and said, when asked why he had only simulated a gun, *"I knew that if I used a real gun and that if I shot someone in a robbery, I might get the death penalty and go to the gas chamber."*

(iv) Ramon Jesse Velarde was arrested September 26, 1960, while attempting to rob a supermarket. At that time, armed with a loaded .38-caliber revolver, he was holding several employees of the market as hostages. He subsequently escaped from jail and was apprehended at the

190

Mexican border. While being returned to Los Angeles for prosecution, he made the following statement to the transporting officers: "I think I might have escaped at the market if I had shot one or more of them. *I probably would have done it if it wasn't for the gas chamber.* I'll only do 7 or 10 years for this. I don't want to die no matter what happens, you want to live another day."

(v) Orelius Mathew Stewart, an ex-convict, with a long felony record, was arrested March 3, 1960, for attempted bank robbery. He was subsequently convicted and sentenced to the state prison. While discussing the matter with his probation officer he stated: "The officer who arrested me was by himself, and if I had wanted, I could have blasted him. *I thought about it at the time, but I changed my mind when I thought of the gas chamber.*"

(vi) Paul Anthony Brusseau, with a criminal record in six other states, was arrested February 6, 1960, for robbery. He readily admitted five holdups of candy stores in Los Angeles. In this series of robberies he had only simulated a gun. When questioned by investigators as to the reason for his simulating a gun rather than using a real one, he replied that *he did not want to get the gas chamber.*

(vii) Salvador A. Estrada, a 19-year-old youth with a four-year criminal record, was arrested February 2, 1960, just after he had stolen an automobile from a parking lot by wiring around the ignition switch. As he was being booked at the station, he stated to the arresting officers: "I want to ask you one question, do you think they will repeal the capital-punishment law. *If they do, we can kill all you cops and judges without worrying about it.*"

(viii) Jack Colevris, a habitual criminal with a record dating back to 1945, committed an armed robbery at a supermarket on April 25, 1960, about a week after escaping from San Quentin Prison. Shortly thereafter he was stopped by a motorcycle officer. Colevris, who had twice been sentenced to the state prison for armed robbery, knew that if brought to trial, he would again be sent to prison for a long term. The loaded revolver was on the seat of the automobile beside him, and he could easily have shot and killed the arresting officer. By his own statements to the interrogating officers, however, *he was deterred from this action because he preferred a possible life sentence to death in the gas chamber.*

(ix) Edward Joseph Laplenski, who had a criminal record dating back to 1948, was arrested in December 1959 for a holdup committed with a toy automatic-type pistol. When questioned by investigators as to why he had threatened his victim with death and had not provided himself with the means of carrying out the threat, he stated, *"I know that if I had a real gun and killed someone, I would get the gas chamber."*

(x) George Hewitt Dixon, an ex-convict with a long felony record in the East, was arrested for robbery and kidnapping committed on November 27, 1959. Using a screwdriver in his jacket pocket to simulate a gun, he had held up and kidnapped the attendant of a service station, later releasing him unharmed. When questioned about his using a screwdriver to simulate a gun, this man, a hardened criminal with many felony arrests and at least two known escapes from custody, indicated his fear and respect for the California death penalty and stated, *"I did not want to get the gas."*

(xi) Eugene Freeland Fitzgerald, alias Edward Finley, an ex-convict with a felony record dating back to 1951, was arrested February 2, 1960, for the robbery of a chain of candy stores. He used a toy gun in committing the robberies, and when questioned by the investigating officers as to his reasons for doing so, he stated: *"If I had a real gun and killed someone, I would get the gas, I would rather have it this way."*

(xii) Quentin Lawson, an ex-convict on parole, was arrested January 24, 1959, for committing two robberies, in which he had simulated a gun in his coat pocket. When questioned on his reason for simulating a gun and not using a real one, he replied that *he did not want to kill someone and get the death penalty.*

(xiii) Theodore Roosevelt Cronell, with many aliases, an ex-convict from Michigan with a criminal record of 26 years, was arrested December 31, 1958, while attempting to hold up the box office of a theater. He had simulated a gun in his coat pocket, and when asked by investigating officers why an ex-convict with everything to lose would not use a real gun, he replied, *"If I used a real gun and shot someone, I could lose my life."*

(xiv) Robert Ellis Blood, Daniel B. Gridley, and Richard R. Hurst were arrested December 3, 1958, for attempted robbery. They were equipped with a roll of cord and a toy pistol. When questioned, all of them stated that they used the toy pistol because *they did not want to kill anyone, as they were aware that the penalty for killing a person in a robbery was death in the gas chamber.* [Emphasis in the original.]

These are cases in which the existence of the death penalty *did* deter killings. Soon after the *Furman* case was decided, an incident in New York City clearly demonstrated that, with the death penalty no longer in effect, some people felt that a significant deterrent to killing was gone. One John Wojtowicz and another held eight bank employees as hostages and threatened to kill them before FBI agents captured Wojtowicz and killed his companion. In threatening to kill the hostages, Wojtowicz was explicit:

> I'll shoot everyone in the bank. The Supreme Court will let me get away with this. There's no death penalty. It's ridiculous. I can shoot everyone here, then throw my gun down and walk out and they can't put me in the electric chair. You have to have a death penalty, otherwise this can happen every day.[14]

Thanks to the aggressive action of the FBI, Wojtowicz and his companion were not able to kill any hostages, but they were certainly encouraged by the Supreme Court's leniency in *Furman*.

In March 1973 five men robbed the warehouse of the Canteen Corporation located in Landover, Maryland. They shot five of the employees and pistol-whipped eleven others after herding them into a men's room. A female employee had been shot in the throat by one of the robbers. She later testified that the robber who shot her threatened to blow all of them up with a hand grenade because there was no death penalty, so that the worst that could happen to him would be that he would be taken care of for life in prison. No hand grenade was found, but the fact that the robbers shot five people clearly indicates that since there was no death penalty for murder they were quite willing to kill.[15]

Prior to *Furman* the abolitionists often argued that the ever-increasing murder rate in the United States indicated that capital punishment, then in effect in most states, was not a deterrent. This argument might have some validity if capital punishment had for the past few years constituted a *genuine* threat. However, it was common knowledge that, because of judicial, legislative, and other legal maneuvering against the death penalty, there had been no executions in this country since 1967 and very few executions before then. As a result, the threat of capital punishment was not taken seriously by many killers. If in certain carefully delineated classes of crime (premeditated murder, felony-murder, killing of law-enforcement officers and prison guards, murder for hire, and multiple murder) the death penalty for the convicted perpetrator were swift and sure, the number of murders of innocent victims would likely decline. On this point Glen D. King, director of the Information Service Division of the International Association of Chiefs of Police, testified before a congressional subcommittee in May 1972. Noting that there had been no executions in the United States since 1967, King said, "We have in effect become a nation in which capital punishment does not exist and I am convinced that part of the results of this has been a very great increase in capital offenses."[16]

Of interest in the deterrent argument is Great Britain, where capital punishment was abolished in 1965. Homicides in England and Wales increased by almost twenty-five percent from 1970 to 1971.[17] In Canada, where capital punishment was abolished in 1966, the murder rate rose from 1.5 per thousand in 1966 to 2.3 in 1971.[18]

Sheriff Daniel F. McMahon of Westchester County, New York, testified before a committee of the New York State Assembly in October 1972 about the rise in homicides in that state since it abolished the death penalty in 1965:

> Since the abolition of the death penalty in our state, we have had a continuous increase in the homicide rate. As a matter of fact, over the past two years, we have had one record after another broken with the

number of murders. New York City had 1,466 murders in 1971, an increase of 31 percent over the previous year. During the first five months of 1972, New York City had a record of 614 homicides and an unprecedented number of 57 homicides for the first week in July of this year. It is noteworthy that this one-week record came immediately following the announcement of the U.S. Supreme Court decision.[19]

Abolitionists are quick to point out all sorts of *other* reasons for the fact that the homicide rate rises when the death penalty has been abolished. Nevertheless, the fact remains that significant increases in homicides have taken place when there is no longer any provision for capital punishment. Again, it cannot be proven that the climb in the number of murders was directly attributable to the abolition of the death penalty, but certainly that inference can be fairly drawn.

Abolitionists tell us that we should not execute murderers if there is only a *chance* that potential victims would be saved. Proponents believe the chance is well worth taking and that the rights of potential victims who might not be victimized far outweigh those of convicted killers.

A murderer executed for his first crime will not kill again—this is axiomatic. On the other hand, as we saw in the preceding chapter, a convicted murderer who has not been executed may (a) be paroled and kill again, (b) escape and kill again, or (c) kill someone in prison, either a guard* or a fellow prisoner. These "second murders" could, of course, have been prevented if the murderer had been executed after his first crime. The innocent victim of the second murder is the victim not only of the slayer himself but also of the misguided leniency and permissiveness shown to the killer in the first place.

In a brief filed in a capital-punishment case in 1972 the state of California cited to the U.S. Supreme Court a series of second murders in that state. These cases are worth pondering for they prove that a man or woman who has killed once will likely kill again.

People v. *Purvis*, 52 Cal. 2d 871, 346 P.2d 22 (1959)
In 1950 defendant was convicted of second-degree murder of his wife and sentenced to prison. In 1954 he was paroled. In 1957 he murdered a woman and was convicted with the death penalty imposed. The California Supreme Court affirmed judgment but ordered a retrial on issue of penalty.

---

*The safety of corrections officers and prison inmates is a key issue in the capital-punishment debate. If a prisoner is serving a life sentence, what possible deterrent other than death is there to keep him from killing a corrections officer or another prisoner? Corrections officers are in constant contact with dangerous men and they, if anyone, deserve the protection which capital punishment can give.

People v. *Gilbert*, 63 Cal. 2d 690, 408 P.2d 365 (1965)

Gilbert was convicted in 1947 of second-degree murder for killing a fellow prisoner at San Quentin. He was released on parole in 1959 and convicted of burglary in 1960. He escaped in 1965 and committed a series of armed bank robberies. In 1964 he killed a police officer while committing a bank robbery. Gilbert was convicted of first-degree robbery and kidnapping and received the death penalty.

People v. *Robles*, 2 Cal. 3d 205, 466 P.2d 710 (1970)

Robles was serving life sentence for first-degree murder. He had a prior conviction for assault with intent to commit murder. While in prison, he murdered an inmate by striking him on the head and cutting his throat from ear to ear. Robles was convicted of first-degree murder and received the death penalty. The California Supreme Court reversed the penalty.

People v. *St. Martin*, 1 Cal. 3d 524, 463 P.2f 390 (1970)

Defendant was serving a life sentence for second-degree murder and robbery in the first degree. While a guard was trying to restrain him, defendant plunged a knife three times into an inmate's chest killing him. Defendant was convicted and given the death penalty. The California Supreme Court reversed the judgment.

People v. *Peete*, 28 Cal. 2d 306 (1946)

Defendant was convicted of murder in 1921 and after eighteen years was released from prison. In 1944 defendant murdered another person and this time received the death penalty.

People v. *Hall*, 199 Cal. 451 (1926)

Hall escaped from prison while serving a life sentence for murder. Subsequently he committed another murder and was convicted and received the death penalty. The California Supreme Court reversed judgment.

People v. *Morse*, 70 Cal. 2d 711

Morse, serving a sentence of life imprisonment for two murders, garroted a fellow prisoner who owed him some cigarettes. Sentenced to death for this murder, Morse had the judgment reversed by the California Supreme Court.

Incapacitation takes on even greater importance when we consider the increasingly permissive parole laws and attitudes of parole boards in this country—even for convicted murderers of the worst kind. The case (described in chapter one) of the murderer of the Iowa police chief who was freed by the Iowa Parole Board after serving two and one-half years of a seventy-five-year sentence, and the case of Richard Speck's parole eligibility in five years, after a new corrections code went into effect in Illinois in January 1973, indicate that permissiveness to the killers rather than a decent concern for society could return the like of Speck, Manson, or James Earl Ray to the streets—perhaps to kill again. In one California case a woman was convicted of burning her husband alive in her car. She received a life sentence, but upon her automatic parole eligibility in seven years, was promptly freed by the California parole authorities.

Cases like these make urgent the restoration of the death penalty for murder because the forces of permissiveness will, most assuredly, try time and again to have the foulest of murderers freed.

There are those in our society whose total lack of concern for the victims of crime is such that they will reject any consideration of what potential harm a convicted criminal could do if released. With a desire to serve *only* the interests of the criminal, they will release him in the vague hope that he will not kill, rape, rob, or steal again.

Three cases that arose in Colorado in 1969 illustrate the ease with which murderers are put in a position to kill again:

● On January 14, 1969, Douglas Becksted, then serving a life sentence for murder, simply walked away from a luncheon in Denver that he was attending with the warden. Two days later Becksted and two companions were stopped by Denver police and U.S. Secret Service agents. Becksted attempted to shoot Denver police officer Tangye, but his companion Moore jerked his gun arm down, whereupon Becksted put his gun in his own mouth and killed himself. In 1960 Becksted had escaped from the Colorado Reformatory at gun point. He was returned in 1964 to resume his life sentence.

● On October 1, 1969, Jerry Stilley and William Cardwell were permitted to leave the penitentiary and come to Denver with an *unarmed guard*, for the purpose of promoting a prison theatrical performance. Stilley was serving a life sentence for the 1962 murder of Denver police officer Darrell Suer, and Cardwell an eight-to-nine-year sentence for robbery. He had entered the penitentiary in 1968. Cardwell had escaped once before, in 1968, from the confinement ward of Denver General Hospital. Cardwell and Stilley assaulted and overcame their unarmed guard, tied him up, and took the $300 they had collected for the prison play. Within hours they were captured attempting to charter a plane to Albuquerque.

● James Sherbondy, on October 10, 1969, walked away from the minimum-security Buckley Honor Farm. What sort of record had Sherbondy that he was placed in a position where he could walk away from captivity? In 1937, wanted for robbery, Sherbondy murdered an Eagle County deputy sheriff who attempted to arrest him. He was sentenced to life imprisonment for this murder. In 1947 Sherbondy escaped from the penitentiary, slugging two guards in the process. Recaptured, he attempted to escape in 1962, slugging three guards in the attempt. He was captured before he could get over the wall. Sherbondy was later paroled but his parole was revoked when he was convicted of robbery in Illinois. He was returned to Colorado State Penitentiary. He was placed on the honor farm, returned to the penitentiary in January 1969 and returned again to the honor farm. On October 10 he walked away. On November 29 he was stopped by Denver police detective Dowd and shot Dowd six times. Dowd killed Sherbondy in turn. Two dynamite bombs were found on his body. This is the man who was placed on the honor farm from which he could walk away as it pleased him.[20]

In each of these incidents a convicted criminal, three of them murderers, two of them murderers of policemen, was permitted, through official leniency, to walk away from confinement or from unarmed guards. As a result of this leniency one policeman was critically injured and one was almost killed. So long as this sort of official permissiveness exists, society quite simply needs the death penalty for its own protection.

At the present, there is no way these lofty theorists can be held accountable if the object of their concern victimizes others. So long as there are those who subordinate the rights of potential victims of crime to official coddling of dangerous criminals, these victims need the protection that incapacitation by capital punishment will ensure.

Any argument over capital punishment will eventually reach the point where the abolitionists invoke the sanctity of human life as a major basis for their thesis. That human life is sacred is beyond doubt. But how the abolitionists can plead sanctity in urging that the killer of a family of five not be executed while ignoring the sanctity of his victims' lives is a feat of mental gymnastics that never ceases to amaze. The basic abolitionist argument that the victims are dead and executing the murderer won't bring them back to life has in it the almost plaintive request that, since they are dead, we should simply forget about the victims and concentrate on the rights of the killers.

When the proponents of capital punishment refuse to drop the point that one or more human beings lie dead at the hand of the murderer, there is, on the part of the abolitionists, a sort of irritable intimation that the proponent is talking about irrelevant matters. On occasion, those speaking for victims are accused of using "scare tactics." This is an unfair accusation. The overall picture of murder in this country and the specific ultrahorrible killings such as that of Joyce Ann Huff are grim facts. The abolitionists most assuredly wish not to be reminded of them. But they are a vital part of the proponent's case that we must *never* forget the value of lives such as Joyce Ann's and society's duty to prevent such wanton slayings.

It is necessary to deal with the abolitionist argument that if we utilize capital punishment, we run the risk of executing an innocent man. The risk is of course there. But, first, it is not a grave risk, given the elaborate safeguards surrounding the criminal accused under our criminal justice system. Next, the possibility of convicting and executing an innocent man must be put in perspective: that possibility is remote to say the least. What is *not* remote, but hard fact, is the rising number of murders in this country. If, as the proponents of capital punishment firmly believe, the death penalty is a significant deterrent to many would-be killers, then the lives saved through the restoration of capital punishment would more than counterbalance the remote possibility of executing an innocent man.

Finally, we turn to the question whether capital punishment discriminates against minorities. First, minorities are far more likely, proportionately, to be *victims* of murderers than are whites. Blacks make up about twelve percent of our population and fifty-five percent of our homicide victims. Thus, whether or not capital punishment, as applied before *Furman*, discriminated against racial minorities, it is quite clear that the crime of murder did, and does, discriminate against them.

If indeed there was discrimination in applying the death penalty, then, obviously, this is intolerable. The answer is to make certain that such discrimination no longer takes place. The current laws in the states that have already reinstated or are considering reinstatement of the death penalty have been drafted to meet the guidelines laid down by the Supreme Court in the *Furman* case. As a result, they have been structured to avoid discrimination in the application of the penalty.

In chapter one we were introduced to Myron Lance and Walter Kelbach, the pair of criminals who murdered six people in Utah and who described their exploits in a television interview. This was the pair who got such a kick out of the way one of their victims "squirmed" as they stabbed him to death.

The case of Lance and Kelbach raises the question of the sanctity of human life. Lance and Kelbach are beneficiaries of the permissiveness embodied in the *Furman* ruling and of the efforts of the abolitionists which culminated in that ruling. The six victims of the two, whose lives were just as sacred, are simply not considered by those who talk about the sanctity of lives or of human dignity in the context of confessed killers.

Another example of the "sanctity of human life" is Dalton Williams, who, in August 1974, escaped from the Colorado State Penitentiary and set out for Texas with several other escaped convicts for the specific purpose of murdering an otherwise inoffensive rancher, W. T. Baker, who had testified against him. According to Bob Glasgow, District Attorney of Erath County, Texas, Williams and his companions, hidden in the grass of Mr. Baker's yard, waited until he appeared and then shot him four times with a .308 Magnum rifle. After Williams shot Baker he went up to the front porch where he lay, looked at him, and asked him if he recognized him [Williams]. "Mr. Baker," said Williams, "do you recognize me?" Baker nodded. Williams said, "I want you to know why I killed you. I told you I was going to do it." Williams and his cohorts then killed Baker's wife.[21]

In New York City, on September 8, 1974, Supreme Court Justice Bernard Dubin sentenced Allen King to a 25-years-to-life term for the murder of a Roman Catholic priest. King's response to the judge was: "I'll do you too." In sentencing King, the judge noted that the priest had offered no resistance, yet "his life was destroyed." Defendant King retorted: "Want a handkerchief? It's so bad."[22]

Lance and Kelbach, Dalton Williams, and Allen King have chosen to make their own mockeries of the "sanctity of human life." Is there really any reason why society should let such men live? And if Lance, Kelbach, Williams, and King are *not* executed, who can say with certainty that remorseless murderers such as these will not someday—through escape or overly lenient parole decisions—be back on the streets? It most assuredly *could* be said with certainty if these worthless killers were executed, as they deserve.

This is the picture of capital punishment from the point of view of potential murder victims. When the murderer approaches his terrified victim with gun, knife, hatchet, or other weapon, the ACLU and anti-capital-punishment forces are not there to plead for mercy for the victim or to defend his civil right not to be killed. So the victim is killed by a murderer who might have been deterred by the sure and certain knowledge that he would in turn be executed if he killed his victim. It is only *after* the murderer is caught and convicted that the weeping and wailing over *his* "rights" and the sanctity of *his* life begins. This cannot be tolerated. We must place the sanctity of human life in its proper context—that of the innocent victim. If the life of *one* such victim can be saved through the deterrent effect of the death penalty, then its usefulness has been established—except perhaps to those whose philosophy shuns the victims of crime completely.

7
The Antivictim Forces
vs. the Victims

WE HAVE SEEN THE WAY the more formal components of the criminal justice system have created and cultivated the current climate of permissiveness toward criminals. Other, less official forces in our country are also at work to foster the same climate of permissiveness. These are, for purposes of this analysis, the antivictim forces.

The term "antivictim forces" was arrived at after considerable thought. The first appellation that came to mind was more stark: "victim haters." This term may go too far. Super-civil-libertarian groups and individuals often take a course of action that is calculated to smooth the path for criminals to victimize others. For example, they may appear in our courts and legislatures seeking to reduce drastically the power and effectiveness of police officers in some major aspect of law enforcement. They take this action knowing fully that if they are successful, more innocent people will be victimized because the ability of the police to protect the innocent will have been sharply curtailed. This philosophy, of course, ignores the victims. But it cannot be said, in fairness, that its proponents actually *hate* those who will be victimized as a result of their activities in the behalf of the criminal.

The antivictim philosophy and its disregard for the victims has been summed up rather succinctly by Clarence M. Kelley, the director of the Federal Bureau of Investigation:

We hear very little about the victims of crime. The reports of their loss too often are the sole accounts of their plight or their demise. This is in puzzling contrast to the frequently prolonged, hand-wringing appeals made in behalf of those who commit crime. There seems to be no scarcity of spokesmen who will concoct any rationale from any platform to excuse persons accused or convicted of crime.[1]

The antivictim forces, then, are those who take a course of action, or express an opinion, that they expect to be taken seriously, and one that will materially benefit a criminal or group of criminals, will result in more criminally inclined individuals being at liberty to victimize the innocent, or will make the task of the peace forces to protect the law-abiding more difficult.

This is not to say that the efforts of the antivictim forces are usually illegitimate or illegal. The ACLU has an absolute right to file a brief in court urging the restriction of police powers or to lobby against legislation favorable to law enforcement. That such efforts will materially assist criminals by making them harder to apprehend does not in the slightest make the efforts themselves criminal; but they are antivictim.

Similarly, a defense attorney is obligated to use any legitimate* means at his disposal—for example, the suppression of the truth as allowed by the Exclusionary Rule or the *Miranda* decision—to obtain for his client an acquittal. The acquittal of a defendant whose guilt is obvious, but who benefits from the suppression of the truth of his guilt, is certainly antithetical to the rights of the victim of that defendant and of society in general. Nevertheless, so long as these legal tools are available to the defense attorney, he is obligated to utilize them.

The defense attorney who in good faith takes advantage of, say, the Exclusionary Rule to free his client is not really a member of the antivictim forces. Rather, the antivictim forces are those who have bent all of their efforts to foster and maintain the climate of permissiveness that has engendered the suppression of the truth and the freeing of the guilty.

Who then, specifically, are the antivictim forces in our society who have carried (or wish to carry) the climate of permissiveness to exces-

---

*The word "legitimate" is important here. Trial tactics like those used by William Kunstler and others in the defense of the "Chicago Seven" are clearly not legitimate and, indeed, have been held to be criminal in themselves.

sive lengths. First of all, they are not those who believe, as do true libertarians, that a balance must be struck between the rights of society and the rights of individuals. It is useful to look again at Dr. Sidney Hook's definition of a "liberal," noted in chapter one, and to read "libertarian" for "liberal" in the context: "Liberalism in social life may be defined as devotion to human freedom pursued and tested by the arts of intelligence." But, he says, not all of those who call themselves liberals meet this test. There are "those who think they can be liberal without being intelligent." For example, any number of libertarians in New York City might well have been concerned that a fair trial was accorded to a group of Black Panthers there, who were charged with plotting to bomb several buildings and police stations. (They were acquitted.) But composer Leonard Bernstein and his wife invited their supporters to an avant-garde, jet-set soiree that, as the *New York Times* commented editorially, mocked the aspirations of decent law-abiding blacks. Author Tom Wolfe, probably the greatest satirical writer in this country, dissected the Bernsteins' little affair in a devastating article.[2] Parties for the Panthers abruptly ended. Bernstein and his wife, by lionizing a group that has called specifically for the murder of policemen and Jews, among others, were, in Dr. Hook's words, being "liberal without being intelligent." They idolized a group of racists, many of whom advocated criminal activity, and in so doing clearly typified the antivictim forces.

Libertarians, as such, then, are not, for the purposes of this book, considered as the "antivictim forces." The definition of the latter encompasses those who do not *wish* a balance between the victim's rights and the suspect's rights, those for whom "individual rights"— meaning the rights of criminals—are the *only* consideration. The antivictim individual or group as defined here is simply that individual or group that would bring to its knees all of the protective responses society has set up against the lawless.

Turning now to specific antivictim groups, first and foremost are the American Civil Liberties Union and its state affiliates. This group, to do it justice, is an effective organization in its single-minded pursuit of undermining all legally constituted authority that conflicts with its views of what the rights of the individual should be. It has won some extremely significant victories, especially in the areas of national security laws, antisubversion laws, the death penalty, and any type of legislation or court action that in any manner strengthens the hand of law enforcement in dealing with the criminal element.

In its supreme lack of concern for the rights of the law-abiding, the ACLU has evidenced a totally antivictim attitude. This can be illustrated by the fact that the Exclusionary Rule and the *Miranda* decision have resulted in as much or more victimization of innocent individuals as any two court decisions in our history. The ACLU, of course, thoroughly supports both. In a 1972 case in which the Supreme Court had agreed to review the entire scope of the Exclusionary Rule, the ACLU filed a brief urging the Court to continue the rule in its full effect.* The ACLU has also lobbied vigorously against any attempts by Congress to cut back the scope of the Exclusionary Rule and *Miranda*.

In two important criminal cases, *Terry* v. *Ohio* (1968)[3] and *Adams* v. *Williams* (1972),[4] the U.S. Supreme Court had before it questions involving the constitutionality of the police practice generally known as "stop and frisk." Now, this practice is nothing more than a law-enforcement procedure that permits a police officer to take aggressive preventive action against street crime by stopping and questioning persons who he reasonably believes may be committing, may have committed, or may be about to commit a crime, and to protect himself by patting down or "frisking" the persons for weapons. Basically, the purposes of the stop-and-frisk practice are protecting innocent people from being victimized by preventing crime, and protecting the police officer or officers involved in the all too common dangers of performing these preventive actions.

Each of the two Supreme Court cases dealing with the stop-and-frisk practice illustrates perfectly its preventive and protective nature. In *Terry* v. *Ohio*, an experienced police officer observed the actions of three men, who he reasonably believed were "casing" a store for a robbery. He stopped and questioned them and, receiving no intelligible reply to his questions, patted the men down for weapons. *Two of the men had pistols.* The officer's preventive stop clearly saved the storeowner from being victimized by a robbery or worse, and the protective frisk may have saved the officer's life.

In *Adams* v. *Williams* a police sergeant received a tip from an informer that a man, sitting in a car in a high-crime area at about 3:00 A.M., had a gun in the waistband of his trousers and heroin in his possession. The officer, believing that this tip gave him reasonable grounds to suspect that at least a weapons violation was being committed, approached the suspect, removed a pistol from his trousers, and then searched the man and the car. He found another gun, a quantity of heroin, and a machete. The stop likely prevented several sales of heroin to victims and perhaps prevented innocent people from being shot or robbed with the suspect's weapons. And again, the frisk may have saved the officer's life.

In each of these cases the U.S. Supreme Court upheld the practice of

*After agreeing to review the case, the Court rejected it on a procedural ground.

stop and frisk as a constitutional and effective means of preventing crime and of protecting police officers. In each case the ACLU filed a brief urging the Court to hold the practice to be in violation of the rights of the two armed criminals involved.

This was a completely antivictim position. The ACLU's position was that *its* concept of individual rights superseded any decent view of the rights of the potential victims, and of the rights of police officers, who might have been killed or injured. In both cases the Court based its decision in part upon the number of police officers killed or injured in the line of duty, a consideration that has never greatly bothered the ACLU.

The ACLU has lobbied against almost every piece of anticrime legislation that has appeared in Congress. It has filed briefs in case after case opposing any strengthening of law-enforcement powers. And it has every right to do so, but the way it exercises this right is patently antivictim. Every time its position in behalf or proven or potential criminals is successful, the result is, usually, victimization of more innocent citizens.

The ACLU engages in activities also on state and local levels. You will recall (see chapter one) that when the accused murderers of nine people were held for forty-eight hours without a bond hearing, the Illinois chapter was "outraged." It never occurred to the ACLU lawyers and staffers to be outraged over the nine human beings executed without due process of law. But when it thought the "rights" of the accused were being brushed against, its ire was thoroughly aroused.

The ACLU has also busied itself with civil suits against police officers and law-enforcement agencies, suits that appear to have as their purpose the weakening of law-enforcement authority and making individual officers afraid to do their jobs for fear of having harassment suits filed against them. This type of activity will be detailed later in this chapter, under collateral attacks against the police, but here suffice it to say that no greater antivictim activity can be found than this type of attack on the police power and the policemen. For if these collateral attacks ever succeed in any measure, they may well drive every good policeman in the country off the job. The criminals will then not need the ACLU to set up legal safeguards for them. The streets will be theirs, and innocent citizens, particularly the poor and the minorities, will find themselves many more times likely to become victims.

Even some thoughtful civil libertarians have expressed a growing disillusionment with the ACLU. Professor Joseph Bishop of Harvard University Law School wrote in *Commentary* a scathing analysis of how the extreme leftist trend and politicization of the ACLU had left its members disenchanted.[5] A true civil libertarian would be as concerned with the violations of civil rights and liberties of the innocent victims of crime as with those of criminals. The ACLU cares not a whit about the rights of the law-abiding.

This attitude was also scored by liberal Democratic assemblyman Andrew Stein of Manhattan. He condemned the "dogmatism" of the New York Civil Liberties Union, which had deplored Governor Rockefeller's hard-line plan calling for mandatory life sentences for drug pushers. Said Mr. Stein, in a statement issued by his office: "People are fed up with knee-jerk liberal reaction against the measures to deal with drugs. It's not antiliberal to be concerned with the growing drug cancer that threatens to destroy our city and the lives of our children."[6]

There are other antivictim organizations that take positions similar to those of the ACLU. (A few take stances even more radical.) The Center for Constitutional Rights in New York, the Emergency Civil Liberties Committee, the Lawyers Committee for Civil Rights Under Law, the Chicago-based Alliance to End Repression, and the Committee for Public Justice (whose main aim seems to be to put the FBI out of business) are but a few of ACLU's brethren. The ACLU, however, has been in business since 1919, and is today the dominant organization in the field of antivictim activities.

Antivictim individuals are similar to antivictim organizations; they are of some prominence and believe, as the antivictim organizations, in total permissiveness for criminals while totally disregarding the rights of law-abiding citizens. A brief description of a few such individuals will suffice to describe the class.

There are of course firebrands. These—radical attorney William Kunstler, for one—claim headlines almost daily by championing some new kind of lawless nonsense or by attacking respected public figures. An instance: Kunstler stated that then Governor Rockefeller of New York "should be indicted for murder" because of the incidents that occurred during the suppression of the Attica prison riots. Rhetoric wins few cases, however, and relatively few intelligent people are really impressed with the mouthings of the Kunstlers. There is probably no other individual alive today that is more antivictim than William Kunstler. Fortunately, however, his influence, except with starry-eyed law students and frowsty revolutionaries, is nowhere nearly as large as his mouth.

More influential by far than Kunstler and his ilk is a man who qualifies as one of the preeminent leaders of the permissivists: Tom Wicker. A columnist for and an associate editor of the *New York Times*, Mr. Wicker has long been the voice of permissiveness for that permissive newspaper. He and his antivictim crusade doubtless gained the summit when in his column he eulogized George Jackson, a prisoner at San Quentin who was killed in an escape attempt, which he apparently engineered and in which two prison guards and two prisoners were also slain.[7] Wicker's diatribe against society and its right to protect itself by holding dangerous persons in prisons (Mr. Wicker is against prisons) was sufficiently intemperate that he was chastised by an editorial in his own newspaper.

Mr. Wicker stated that minorities *and* "whites in low economic status know what it means to be powerless and hopeless before an uncaring and oppressive law." A lady tartly responded, in a letter to the editor:

> "To be powerless and hopeless before an uncaring and oppressive law" is to be an elderly lady walking on the streets of New York. Even if a criminal is caught in the act, the chances are he will walk away laughing because the laws are stacked in his favor and he knows it.[8]

Although Mr. Wicker probably received the most attention of his writing career (much of it critical) for his piece about George Jackson, it is another statement he made, in a different article, that makes him the dean of American permissivists. The article was a sort of requiem for the Bill of Rights, because the Senate had passed a bill that permitted police officers having a search warrant to enter premises without knocking and announcing their purpose, if the judge issuing the warrant was convinced that knocking and announcing would endanger the officers or others, or would result in the destruction of evidence. This "no-knock" law, which is in effect no more than a codification of the realities of search and seizure—which is not a sort of game, but a serious and often dangerous business—seems to hold a morbid fascination for permissivists. No other issue evokes greater wails about "burning the Constitution" and "trampling the Fourth Amendment."

The no-knock law and its application were put into context by Mike Mansfield (D.-Mont.) and Hugh Scott (R.-Pa.), the Senate majority and minority leaders respectively. Neither one can be regarded as a hard-line conservative, but both endorsed the bill. Senator Scott stated that narcotic dealers "are contributing to murder and suicide and the destruction of a person's personality. We are encountering a certain amount of 'sob-sisterism' from people who tend to weep somewhat excessively about the rights of the drug pusher and minimize the effects of their dreadful trade."[9]

Senator Scott did not convince Tom Wicker. In his article about the evils of the no-knock bill, Wicker viewed with alarm that provision and other pieces of anticrime legislation. He then quoted Senator

Roman Hruska of Nebraska, who spoke for the majority after the 79-1 Senate vote passed the legislation, as saying that it is necessary because "we are grappling for survival in the battle against crime."[10] This really threw Wicker, because,

> What we are really grappling for a survival against is those who think that the rights of criminals can be suspended or diluted without endangering the rights of all Americans. *The rights of criminals ARE the rights of all Americans* and the inescapable truth is that if they are taken away from criminals they are taken away from all of us.[11]

Ponder the italicized portion: "The rights of criminals ARE the rights of all Americans. . . ." There we have the credo of the permissivists and the antivictim forces. And we also have a piece of utter nonsense.

The rights of criminals are *not* the rights of all Americans because most Americans are not, and do not plan to become, criminals. True, law-abiding citizens and criminals have in common certain fundamental rights under the Constitution. But one of those rights is not the right to victimize others and get away with it because hypertechnical restrictions on the police and prosecution make it difficult or impossible to convict. Law-abiding citizens neither want nor need such "rights," and it is crystal clear from the broadest samplings of public opinion that the law-abiding want these "rights," agonized over by Wicker, *taken away* from the criminals.

A far more accurate statement, to paraphrase Mr. Wicker, would be: "The rights of *victims* ARE [or should be] the rights of all Americans. . . ." This statement is definitely true. All Americans have the right to be left alone, to go about their business without being murdered, raped, robbed, assaulted, stolen from, or otherwise victimized. In short, the right to be safe. This is the first and fundamental right of every citizen in a free society, and it should be accorded to him without any question. Unfortunately, as we have seen, that right in this country is now largely an illusion—particularly for the poor and powerless. The reason: the climate of permissiveness, in large measure fostered by the acts and writing of Tom Wicker and the antivictim forces.

If Mr. Wicker is the dean of these forces, the title of prophet and public relations front man must be accorded to Ramsey Clark, former attorney general of the United States. After leaving that office he wrote the bible of American permissiveness, *Crime in America*,[12] a monumental collection of slogans and inanities. Mr. Clark's fame as a permissivist is such that no great amount of space is here needed to elaborate on it. This author reviewed Clark's book in December 1970 for the *Chicago Tribune*. What was said then is still true (except, perhaps, that Clark has drifted rather more sharply to the Left). That review, printed here in part, will suffice to show why Ramsey Clark must rank high in the hierarchy of the permissive anticrime forces:

There are two basic attitudes towards crime in this country. One holds that crime is caused by criminals. The other—the apologist attitude—seeks to blame our crime problems on anything and everything except those who actually engage in lawlessness and violence. Ramsey Clark, while attorney general of the United States, became, to many, the symbol of permissiveness. His book, *Crime in America*, undoubtedly will become the bible of the apologists for crime.

The book deals in generalities. There can be no doubt, for instance, that inhuman ghetto living conditions breed crime. Likewise, speedier trials and rehabilitation of offenders are absolutely essential to the success of our criminal justice system. These propositions are obvious, but the book offers us nothing new about them; the need for reforms in these areas is talked about, but nothing by way of tough-minded, clear-thinking solutions to the problems raised is given.

In 1968 Congress passed, overwhelmingly, a tough anticrime law containing strengthened crime-fighting provisions for federal officers in such areas as confessions, lineups, and electronic surveillance. With consummate arrogance, then Attorney General Ramsey Clark informed Congress that he would not use these laws because *he* believed them unconstitutional. The same arrogance permeates his book. He treats with contempt the decent concern of most of our citizens, black and white, for law and order instead of lawlessness and chaos.

Every poll taken indicates that our citizens favor tougher action against crime. This, Clark informs us, is wrong. He states that tough police action is "basically a bullying technique, implying force, even unfairness." Instead of vigorously enforcing the law, Clark says that we must "create a reverence for life and seek gentleness and tolerance and a concern for others." To a nation deeply disturbed by the realities of crime, such slogans can appear as plain mockery.

The permissiveness espoused in this book invariably subordinates the rights of the law-abiding to those of the lawless. In a rather amazing sentence we are told that during riots, untrained guardsmen should not be used because their use "involves risks to the rioters of excessive use of gunfire" and, secondarily, risks to the public due to the Guard's failure to stop further rioting. Here the risks to the rioters are the primary concern. By the same token, the author places the rights of campus revolutionaries above those of law enforcement, since "police should not be armed in confrontations with students and troops should never carry rifles."[13]

Far and away the most candid antivictim individual in the United States is Professor Vern Countryman of Harvard University Law School. In a two-day conference at Princeton University in October 1971, called by the Committee for Public Justice to attack the FBI and then Director J. Edgar Hoover, Countryman and this author engaged in a colloquy that brings the antivictim mentality sharply into focus. The following conversation concerns the right and duty of the FBI to use infiltration techniques to prevent or solve bombings, specifically the bombing by the Ku Klux Klan of several school buses in Pontiac, Michigan.

> *Countryman*: Well, my judgment would be that if the only way to detect that bombing is to have the FBI infiltrating political organizations, I would rather the bombing go undetected.
> *Carrington*: No matter whether somebody was killed?
> *Countryman*: *Yes. Yes, there are worse things than having people killed.* When you have got the entire population intimidated, that may be worse. We put some limits on law enforcement in the interests of preserving a free and open society or at least we try to, and every time we do that—things like the privilege against self-incrimination, things like the Fourth Amendment—every time we do that, that involves a judgment that even though some crimes and some crimes involving the loss of life will go undetected, it is better in the long run to have a society where there is some protection from police surveillance.
> *Carrington*: I'm not really that sure that the family of Robert Fassnacht, who was blown up at Wisconsin, or the families of the kids that were killed in the Birmingham church bombing would agree with that.
> *Countryman*: I'm sure that the families of the victims would not agree in any of the instances that I've mentioned but I don't believe that most of us would say that for that reason we should repeal the Fourth and Fifth amendments.[14]

If Professor Countryman seems incredibly callous about the deaths of the victims of bombers, equally callous were the "peace" activists who took it upon themselves in September 1973 to plead with a Wisconsin judge to mitigate the sentence of Karl Armstrong. Armstrong had pled guilty to bombing the mathematics building at the University of Wisconsin in August 1970. He had admitted a series of antimilitary bombings, but his plea was entered to a charge of second-degree murder and arson in the bombing of the math building, in which Robert Fassnacht, a thirty-three-year-old physicist and the father of three children, was killed.

The attitude of the apologists for this wanton murder is typified by a statement of Daniel Ellsberg, the admitted thief of the Pentagon Papers. Ellsberg, little concerned that Mr. Fassnacht was a totally innocent victim, called for a movement toward a "just society" and said that "the place to start is not by punishing the action of Karl Armstrong."[15] This is an antivictim attitude with a vengeance.

Kunstler, Wicker, Clark, Countryman, and Ellsberg are spokesmen for the lawless in our society. All more or less express contempt for the victims of crime. Why are they like this? What has caused men and organizations to take a stand evidencing such a heartless attitude towards the victims of crime? One premise of permissiveness is that the individual must be protected from the government. Whether the individual would *rather* have protection from being hit on the head by some thug is beside the point to the permissivists. In attempting to protect the law-abiding, the government is, to them, the enemy. Governmental acts are by definition repressive. Repression—the repression syndrome—is a major motivating force of permissiveness. The fact that most law-abiding Americans would like to see some *real* repression of criminals is no part of the thinking of the antivictim forces.

The repression syndrome is a state of mind, held and fostered by those who are oblivious to the real and terrible impact of crime upon others, and who are obsessed with abstractionist views of the rights of criminals. The spokesmen for the repression syndrome postulate a topsyturvy world in which, as the number of criminal acts increases, the enforcement function by which society protects itself from crime must decrease. Does the number of bombings double in a given year? Then by all means, say the permissivists, we must find some means to prevent the police and federal agents from investigating, apprehending, and prosecuting bombers, lest the bombers—actual and potential—feel repressed. Is violent street crime on the rise? Then, we should strive for new restraints on law-enforcement officers to hamper their efforts to deal with such crimes, lest, again, such efforts appear repressive to those who are criminally inclined and to those who apologize for them.

The entire repression syndrome is contemptuous of crime's victims. The "rights" of those who victimize, or who are inclined to victimize, are preeminent. We must never, *never* do anything to cause them the slightest concern, no matter how many innocent people suffer.

A most succinct and devastating refutation of the repression syndrome was made by Lewis Powell, before his elevation to the U.S. Supreme Court. In an article in the *Richmond Times-Dispatch* of August 1, 1971— later reproduced in the *FBI Bulletin*—Mr. Powell minced no words:

> At a time when slogans often substitute for rational thought, it is fashionable to charge that "repression" of civil liberties is widespread. This charge—directed primarily against law enforcement—is standard leftist propaganda. It is also made and widely believed on the campus, in the arts and theater, in the pulpit, and among some of the media. Many persons genuinely concerned about civil liberties thus join in promoting or accepting the propaganda of the radical left.
>
> The charge of repression is not a rifle shot at occasional aberrations. Rather, it is a sweeping shotgun blast at "the system" which is condemned as systematically repressive of those accused of crime, of minorities, and of the right to dissent.

The purpose of this article is to examine, necessarily in general terms, the basis for the charge of repression. Is it fact or fiction?

There are, of course, some instances of repressive action. Officials are sometimes overzealous; police do employ unlawful means or excess force; and injustices do occur even in the courts. Such miscarriages occur in every society. The real test is whether these are episodic departures from the norm, or whether they are, as charged, part of a system of countenanced repression.

The evidence is clear that the charge is a false one. America is not a repressive society. The Bill of Rights is widely revered and zealously safeguarded by the courts. There is in turn no significant threat to individual freedom in this country by law enforcement.

Solicitor General Griswold, former dean of the Harvard Law School and member of the Civil Rights Commission, recently addressed this issue in a talk at the University of Virginia. He stated that there is greater freedom and less repression in America than in any other country.

In the general assault on law enforcement, charges of police repression have become a reflexive response by many civil libertarians as well as by radicals.

Examples are legion. Young people are being incited not to respect law officers but to regard them as "pigs." Black Panther literature, in the vilest language, urges the young to assault the police.

Those who charge repression say that dissent is suppressed and free speech denied. Despite the wide credence given this assertion, it is sheer nonsense. There is no more open society in the world than America. No other press is as free. No other country accords its writers and artists such untrammeled freedom. No Solzhenitsyns are persecuted in America.

What other government would allow the Chicago Seven, while out on bail, to preach revolution across the land, vastly enriching themselves in the process?

What other country would tolerate in wartime the crescendo of criticism of government policy? Indeed, what other country would allow its citizens—including some political leaders—to negotiate privately with the North Vietnamese enemy?

The rights of accused persons—without regard to race or belief—are more carefully safeguarded in America than in any other country. Under our system the accused is presumed to be innocent; the burden of proof lies on the state; guilt must be proved beyond reasonable doubt; public jury trial is guaranteed; and a guilty verdict must be unanimous.*

In recent years, dramatic decisions of the Supreme Court have further strengthened the rights of accused persons and correspondingly limited the powers of law enforcement. There are no constitutional decisions in other countries comparable to those rendered in the cases of *Escobedo* and *Miranda*.

*In 1972 the Supreme Court ruled that jury verdicts in criminal cases need no longer be unanimous. Guilty verdicts of 10-2 and 9-3 were upheld as constitutional except, perhaps, in capital cases.

211

Rather than "repressive criminal justice," our system subordinates the safety of society to the rights of persons accused of crime. The need is for greater protection—not of criminals but of law-abiding citizens.

America has its full share of problems. BUT significant or systematic government repression of civil liberties is not one of them.

The radical Left—expert in such matters—knows the charge of repression is false. It is a cover for leftist inspired violence and repression. It is also a propaganda line designed to undermine confidence in our free institutions, to brainwash the youth, and ultimately to overthrow our democratic system.

It is unfortunate that so many nonradical Americans are taken in by this leftist line. They unwittingly weaken the very institutions of freedom they wish to sustain. They may hasten the day when the heel of repression is a reality—not from the sources now recklessly defamed but from whatever tyranny follows the overthrow of representative government.

This is the greatest danger to human liberty in America.[16]

So much for repression. Now to one final and insidious aspect of the activities of the antivictim forces, one that undermines the entire criminal justice system: collateral attacks on the police.

Collateral Attacks on Law Enforcement

In chapter two, I described three types of attacks currently being waged against our law-enforcement forces. The first two involved assaults against the policeman's physical safety: *direct attacks,* an actual physical attack against a law-enforcement officer; and *targeting attacks,* actions by individuals or groups that pave the way for the criminal physically to attack an officer. Discussion of the third classification, *collateral attacks,* I deferred until this chapter, because the usual source of collateral attacks is the antivictim forces.

Collateral attacks are those activities that are designed to demoralize, discredit, neutralize, or control law-enforcement agencies and individual law-enforcement officers. The late J. Edgar Hoover, writing in the *FBI Law Enforcement Bulletin* of June 1970, described some collateral attacks:

Groups have been established to gain community control over police departments. Some, receiving financial support from well-meaning but misled organizations, have set up "police watching" programs. Some spokesmen advocate that each city ghetto be given public funds and authorization to form its own racially segregated police force. Others say college youth should not be subject to contacts by police officers and that specially trained, highly paid, unarmed, elite police forces should be used to handle "civil demonstrations." If these ideas and techniques seem half-baked, it is because they are. But the intent to foster such schemes is clear. They want to negate the rule of law. To do this they must first create public distrust of, and ill will towards, those who enforce the law.

And the police surely do not need this ill will and distrust. A study released in April 1974 by the National Institute of Occupational Safety and Health indicates that, in addition to the physical dangers that confront the policeman, the stresses of his job make him more prone to suicide and heart problems than most of us.[17]

Four areas of stress, cited by William Kroes, chief of stress of the institute, were:

● The courts, where a policeman faces criticism from defense attorneys or judges and sees cases dismissed on technicalities.

● The community, where he is called derisive names and is routinely obstructed in the performance of his duties.

● The negative values of law and order held by groups the officer must deal with.

● The regular exposure to danger and to inhumane treatment of victims of crime.[18]

Mr. Kroes defined the problem:

> People don't like income taxes, but they don't go to the Internal Revenue Service office and yell at the clerk. The policeman is just doing a job, a tough job, and he shouldn't have to face unnecessary abuse.
>
> If we, the people, were more tolerant and took a closer look at the difficult work he is performing, we might help him live a longer and happier life.[19]

Indeed. But many in the forefront of the collateral attacks against the police not only refuse to take such a tolerant look at the problems faced by the policeman, but also go out of their way to demoralize him further.

The importance of collateral attacks and the need to respond to them cannot be overstated, because if they succeed, they will drive the best and most professional law-enforcement officers from their jobs. Their places will either not be filled or be taken by those unfit to engage in law-enforcement work under the demanding standards of today.

Collateral attacks take many forms but the general thrust of all of them is the same: 1) to control the police by political elements, so that an officer who exercises his discretion may be held accountable, not for what he did, but for the political consequences of his acts; 2) to make the policeman literally afraid to act through the tactic of a constant barrage of complaints of misconduct and frivolous harassment-type civil suits; and 3) to destroy the morale of the police through unjustified criticism and attack.

The question is asked: Why are collateral attacks so important? The answer is quite simple. If a policeman is made afraid to perform his duty because he knows that all of his actions will be judged by politically motivated groups like civilian review boards or so-called community-control groups, or that he will be constantly harassed by complaints, civil suits, or even criminal accusations, then he will do one of three things: he will refuse to act at all; he will quit the jurisdiction where the collateral attacks occur and go elsewhere; or he will leave police work entirely. If these are the conditions under which a given policeman quits, then a qualified and professional replacement for him will be very difficult to find. An illustration: in 1971 a radical city council was elected in Berkeley, California. The council's unremitting pressure on the police department has caused thirty-one of the 190 police officers to quit, many of them complaining bitterly about what they described as an antipolice campaign in Berkeley.[20]

Likewise a competent police administrator will be deterred from properly performing his job if he is continually haled into court to defend police practices he knows are constitutional and necessary to enforce the law.

Indeed, if such restrictions on police conduct as the Exclusionary Rule or the *Miranda* requirements were modified so that technical errors in police procedures would not automatically result in the suppression of evidence and the freeing of the guilty, these modifications would benefit neither society nor the victims of crime if the police have through outside pressures been made afraid to do their job. Likewise, if a police administrator, because of similar pressure, is afraid to administer his department, then only the criminal element will benefit and only the victims of crimes will suffer.

Precisely what is envisioned by collateral attacks? The exertion of *outside* pressure, despite the fact that no such pressure should normally be imposed upon the legitimate functions of law enforcement agencies and officers. Such pressure would, for example, be found in a politically established and politically motivated civilian review board; in a system of community control of the police; or in the constant harassment of police departments and officers by *unwarranted* civil suits or complaints.

Now I reemphasize that no police officer in our country is above the law and that we cannot tolerate willful, malicious, or wanton abuse of police authority. If an officer who has subdued and handcuffed a suspect deliberately and without cause beats him, there is certainly no outside pressure upon that officer if, in addition to departmental disciplinary proceedings, a civil suit for damages or even a criminal action in state or federal court is brought against him. But if every police officer who has to subdue a belligerent suspect, a drunk, or an armed felon has a complaint filed against him; or if he is sued simply because he had to resort to the use of such force as was necessary to defend himself, or to arrest an offender—then those making the complaints or filing the suits are exerting outside pressure that cannot be tolerated. The difference is one of degree, depending largely upon whether or not the police officer acts willfully and wantonly, but the incidence of complaints and civil suits against police departments and officers is rising at a rate that clearly indicates these devices are being used as collateral attacks.

By the same token, if a police chief has ordered his men to stop and search every person they happen to see on the street, or if he knowingly condones brutality by his men, then no outside pressure is placed upon him if he is sued to enjoin this conduct. However, if suits are brought to restrain his officers from engaging in patently constitutional police practices, which just happen to be effective, or if suits are brought to place his department under "referees" or "special masters" depriving him of control of that department, then this is indeed outside pressure and it constitutes a collateral attack. If such collateral attacks succeed in making either the chief executive of the agency or the individual officers so "gun shy" that they will refuse to take action, then the only ones who will suffer will be the victims of crime.

Let us examine some of these collateral attacks.

Civilian Review Boards[21]

In recent years increasingly shrill demands have been made in our cities for civilian review boards to review complaints against police officers. Louisville, Kentucky, presents a recent and all too typical example. In May 1972 a coalition of groups that included the Louisville branch of the American Civil Liberties Union, the Louisville Urban League, the Kentucky Women's Socialist Caucus, the Community Action Commission, and the Louisville chapter of the NAACP, attempted to pass a city ordinance creating a civilian review board.[22]

The proposed board in Louisville would have had the power to "accept and look into complaints of brutality or poor performance of duty against police officers and would be authorized to mete out punishment," according to one of the organizers, Rev. Terrence H. Davis.

The Louisville case illustrates nationwide attempts to wrest the control of police discipline from police management and to place law enforcement under the control of politically appointed and motivated civilian boards. Fortunately, the Louisville Board of Aldermen rejected this proposal by a vote of 8 to 2.

Advocates of civilian review boards base the need for these boards upon charges that police "brutality" and other misconduct have increased in recent years. These charges are simply not substantiated. There doubtless has been an increase in the *allegations* of police brutality, but substantiation has in most cases been lacking. In fact, the President's Commission on Law Enforcement and Criminal Justice in 1967 reported that physical abuse is not as serious as it was in the past and it recommended against the establishment of such boards.[23]

Although there is little substantiation of charges of police brutality, there is unquestionable evidence that crime has in recent years risen out of all proportion and that "citizen brutality" against the police (murders of and assaults against police officers) has increased at a rate paralleling or even exceeding the rise in crime. In all of this, the victims of crime in general and the police victims of direct attacks against them are, as usual, ignored by the antivictim forces who, in their single-minded efforts to neutralize the police through such collateral attacks, continue to agitate for the creation of civilian review boards.

Civilian review boards would irreparably damage the effectiveness of law enforcement. This is a fact well known to every police officer in the country. Resistance to any sort of politically inspired outside pressure is virtually unanimous in the police community. Police opposition to civilian review boards (opposition also shared by the majority of law-abiding citizens) is based upon the deeply held conviction that the *real* problem today is not that society needs protection from the policeman. Rather, our law-abiding citizens (and law-enforcement officers themselves) need protection from the lawless in society and, to a lesser extent, from the antivictim forces who advocate total permissiveness for criminals. Against this background let us examine the primary arguments against civilian review boards.

1. *Civilian Review Boards Are Political and Usurp the Rightful Function of Police Management*

To be legally effective civilian review boards must be set up through the political process, that is, they must be created by statute, ordinance, or executive order. For example, in 1965 John V. Lindsay, running for mayor of New York City, promised to create a civilian review board for the New York City Police Department. This was a flagrantly political act, as was his actual creation of the board by executive order after his election. Although Mayor Lindsay's board was voted out of existence in a citywide referendum in 1966 by a 2-to-1 margin, this case illustrates the inherent political nature of civilian review boards.

In addition to the politics behind the *creation* of civilian review boards, their *makeup* must also reflect the influence of politics. J. Edgar Hoover summed this up succinctly, stating that in many cases, "Appointments will be made for political expediency rather than merit, and every faction, clique, group, and organization which has an axe to grind will demand representation."

This becomes obvious when one examines the nature of the groups currently agitating for civilian review boards. Most of these groups are special-interest pressure groups (for example, the American Civil Liberties Union, various civil rights groups, legal-aid societies, and Left-oriented organizations generally). It strains the imagination to believe that if those seeking to establish civilian review boards should succeed, they would not immediately begin equally extensive pressure to dominate such boards.

Given, then, the politics behind and the membership of civilian review boards, the result is inevitable: subordination of both the police executive control of internal management, and the discipline to sheer pressure politics. The law-enforcement establishment in this country has made significant and generally successful efforts to professionalize itself in recent years. But very few professional police executives could, or would, remain long in office once their powers became subordinate to political pressure groups.

The responsibility for the overall administration of a given police department must lie in the chief executive of that department, subject to duly and lawfully constituted supervisory control through such entities as police and public safety commissions and city executives. To remove the punishment of wrongdoing by officers—one facet of the police administrative process—from the police executive and to place it into the hands of politically motivated civilian boards would undermine the entire process. The position of the International Association of Chiefs of Police, which represents most of the professional police executives in the United States, has been well stated:

The external board champions advance the argument that public confidence will be restored and maintained so long as the task of punishing the police is in their hands. It may be true that some citizens may take solace in the spectacle of punishment, but the community cannot hope to achieve a better level of police service simply by administering punishment. Negative discipline is only one minor aspect of police administration. More training, supervision, direction, and incentive are other parts of the overall process. Where misconduct becomes apparent, all of the basic processes by which the department is operated must be examined. Clearly this is the responsibility of the duly appointed and empowered public officials. The Police or Public Safety Commission, which is, in fact, a broad policy setting group, combines all of these diverse but related aspects of administration and thus becomes the responsible focal point of leadership. The review board, devoid of both responsibility and authority for the basic functions of administration, represents a superficial attempt to deal with more complex problems. Outside review boards represent a direct reflection upon inadequate police leadership, since they can exist only where the police leaders fail, for whatever reason, to adequately discharge their responsibility to impartially investigate and deal with complaints by citizens against department personnel.[24]

Most police executives in this country sincerely desire to maintain fair and effective internal discipline and to remove the corrupt, the inefficient, and the brutal officer from their agencies. In a situation as

217

unique and complex as the enforcement of the criminal law, perfection in police disciplinary matters is not attainable, but this does not mean that the power to discipline should be taken from the police executive and given to outside political forces. To do so would seriously weaken the authority of the police executive and would be ruinous for police morale.

2. *The Effect of Civilian Review Boards on Law Enforcement and Thus on the Victims of Crime Would Be Disastrous*

Police officers in the United States, almost to a man, and police organizations—from management associations like the International Association of Chiefs of Police to line associations like the Fraternal Order of Police and the International Conference of Police Associations— are unalterably opposed to any form of the civilian review board. There are valid reasons for this. The most important follow:

a. *Civilians who have no experience in police work are not qualified to sit in judgment on police officers.* Police work is unique. It requires the officer to place his life and safety on the line every time he leaves the station, as the casualty statistics cited in chapter two amply prove. Police work is dirty, difficult, demanding, and dangerous. Few of the extremely vocal "police watchers" and critics would undertake the job themselves. yet they are always ready and willing to second-guess the policeman's every act.

It is this second-guessing aspect of civilian review boards that probably enrages the professional policeman the most. When an officer confronts a suspect in an alley at 3:00 A.M.; when a belligerent drunk advances upon a policeman; when a sniper's bullet comes out of a window somewhere in a dark tenement; or when an officer walks up to a curbed car that fits the description of one used in an armed robbery, the policeman is, literally, on his own. Society demands that he take action to prevent crime and to apprehend criminals, and in many cases he must make a split-second decision as to what action to take in the heat and tension of the moment. It is easy to sit in an air-conditioned hearing chamber, months after the act, and tell a policeman what he *should* have done in a given case, but it is terribly unfair to the officer who was *there*, on the street, facing the danger without benefit of hindsight.

Civilian review boards are by their very nature not only political, but also established for the express purpose of engaging in the sort of second-guessing that the policeman feels, quite properly, they are unqualified to do. The policeman's complaint over such second-guessing is valid. He is willing to take the risks his job entails but unwilling to have to justify his actions in dealing with such risks to those who have never known the realities, problems, and dangers of police work.

b. *Law-abiding citizens cannot afford to have law-enforcement of-*
ficers handcuffed through the fear of being second-guessed by civilian
review boards. The crime rates in this country and the extent to which
violent crime preys on minority victims have been discussed. It is indeed ironic that as violence and lawlessness escalate as never before,
the self-appointed critics of the police, the advocates of civilian review
boards, have never been more vocal. At this juncture *society* simply
cannot afford to have its peace forces hamstrung by threats of political
civilian review of police actions.

The policeman on the street is the front line of defense against
crime. He is expected, of course, to respond to calls for help and to apprehend perpetrators. Perhaps more important, he is also expected to
prevent crime by aggressive street patrolling. Such aggressive police
action has been sanctioned as constitutional by the U.S. Supreme Court—
for example, in recent cases allowing the police to "stop and frisk"
criminal suspects. It is doubtful, however, that many civilian review
proponents would have similarly sanctioned such action. When a
policeman observes a figure in an alley at 3:00 A.M.; when an officer
observes two suspects who are apparently "casing" a store for a robbery;
when an officer receives a tip that an individual is carrying a gun, the
policeman involved has a duty to take action to prevent a crime from
taking place. This sort of aggressive action is the only effective way of
dealing with street crime.

But when an officer is aware that he may be called before a civilian
review board to justify his actions, then he may very well refrain from
taking action in those critical areas in which aggressive, preventive
police conduct is called for. This hesitancy to act is an attitude that
society simply cannot afford.

We have no need for policemen who are calculatedly and willfully
brutal, or who are for no reason abusive to law-abiding citizens. But
such policemen are a small minority of our peace forces today. The professional policeman—the officer who is willing to act, at considerable
personal risk to himself, to prevent crime from happening—is absolutely
necessary to the restoration and maintenance of order in society,
especially in the higher-crime areas of the ghetto. If we permit the
threat of civilian review boards to scare off the good cops, to paralyze
them when they should be aggressive, then the innocent victims of
crime will be the losers.

c. *Complaints against policemen are used, in many cases, by wrong-
doers to avoid the consequences of their acts.* Policemen are well aware
from experience that the criminal commonly utilizes charges of "brutality," "excessive force," "false arrest," or other misconduct against an
arresting officer to divert attention from his crime. A civilian review

board, with its built-in antipolice bias (most boards, by their very nature, have such a bias), serves as a mechanism for criminals to utilize in order to escape the consequences of their acts. An armed robber whom a policeman has been forced to shoot or subdue can, by filing a complaint against the officer with a civilian review board, place the officer on the defensive merely for doing his duty.

In Philadelphia, which had a civilian review board until it was nullified by court order, just such tactics by complainant criminals caused the resignation of a board member. A Lutheran minister, who served about two and a half years on the board, testified that he resigned because most cases up for review were picayune. "Most cases involved criminal elements bringing in policemen in an attempt to have their record expunged," declared the Reverend W. Carter Merbrier, pastor of Messiah Lutheran Church. "I resigned because I believed it accomplished no good purpose."[25]

3. *Civilian Review Boards and the Rights of Law-Enforcement Officers*

Proponents of civilian review boards are, almost invariably, those individuals or groups of individuals that profess a deep concern for "individual rights." However, when the question of civilian review boards is raised, the proponents—perhaps cynically, perhaps naively—disregard such rights as a policeman might have and relegate the police officer to the status of a second-class citizen.

Basically, the areas in which civilian review boards impinge on the rights of policemen can be summarized as follows:

a. *Civilian review boards subject police officers to a kind of "double jeopardy."* A policeman should be accorded the basic right of having to answer but once for his civil or criminal misconduct. This, however, is not the case with civilian review boards. A case in point arose under the now defunct civilian review board in Philadelphia. An off-duty white Philadelphia officer was accused of severely beating a Negro porter. The officer was acquitted by the criminal court and by the Police Trial Board, yet the civilian review board persisted in hearing the case. The following statement, from the board's annual report of September 1959, describes its attitude: "We were concerned as to whether we could still hear the complaint against the police officer, but in light of the strong recommendation for *punitive action* on the part of the police investigator and our belief that the complaint might have substance, we decided to hold *public hearings* which will be scheduled shortly."[26]

Public hearings were held in this case and the policeman was again acquitted by the civilian review board. The point is, however, that *after* acquittal by both the criminal court and the police department, this officer was forced to be pilloried publicly by the civilian review board in an attempt, to judge from the board's own statement, to take "punitive action" against him. This is a clear violation of our concept of double jeopardy, in effect making the policeman's rights subordinate to the board's desire to air the case.

b. *Civilian review boards have been and can be used to solicit complaints against the police.* An example of this sort of callous disregard for a policeman's basic rights is contained in a proposed ordinance for a civilian review board drafted by ACLU's affiliate in Los Angeles. Section 7.g(1) of the ordinance authorized an award of up to $500.00 to a complainant if the proposed board made a finding of police misconduct, while section 10 provided that a complainant before the board could not be prosecuted or punished for making a complaint, nor could *he be prosecuted under the section of the municipal code that made it an offense to make a false report to the police.*[27]

Taken together these two sections literally placed a bounty on anti-police complaints by offering a reward to the successful complainant; at the same time, a complainant before the board would have been granted immunity from a perjured complaint or perjured testimony.

This incredible piece of legislation was unanimously defeated by the Los Angeles City Council but it well illustrates the lengths to which some will go to deny to policemen rights that are taken for granted by the average citizen.

c. *Civilian review boards can be used for public attack upon the reputations of police officers.* Any civilian review board created by legislative action or executive order will bear, at least in part, the imprimatur of the governing body that created it. Thus, policemen who are haled before such boards may have their reputations smeared publicly by governmental or quasi-governmental bodies. As we have seen, the Philadelphia board held such public hearings even after the officer in question had been acquitted by a criminal court.

Policemen are constantly in the public eye and are as jealous of their good reputations, and that of their departments, as the next person. If a policeman is guilty of wrongdoing, obviously he should be brought before the proper civil or criminal tribunal and suffer the attendant bad publicity. But the civil and criminal courts are duly constituted arenas where aggrieved individuals or society itself can seek redress from a wrongdoer. No policeman is above the law, but it is a totally different matter to single out policemen for *additional* public exposure before some politically oriented civilian review board. Too, in this day when "leaks" to the news media are the rule rather than the exception, it is not difficult to imagine members of a civilian review board leaking the most confidential information about a policeman to the press, regardless of accuracy.

d. *Civilian review boards can deny due process of law to a police officer.* Such basic rights as trial by jury and appeal through the proper legal channels, the protections inherent in the rules of evidence used in civil and criminal trials, the right to confront one's accusers, the protection against self-incrimination, and others, can often be lost in the civilian review board procedure. Civilian review boards are, by nature, exceptional bodies, created most often for political expediency at the insistence of pressure groups. The antipolice bias of the ACLU, for example, is well known. Yet the ACLU has been in the forefront of those agitating for civilian review boards. It is difficult to imagine a police officer receiving a "fair trial" before the aforementioned board the ACLU proposed in Los Angeles, a board that solicited complaints through the device of rewarding successful complainants but that granted immunity to such complainants for the use of perjured testimony.

We have been dealing in this section with basic and fundamental rights of police officers. Of more practical effect and perhaps of equal importance is the number of hours a policeman consumes preparing for and appearing before civilian review boards. Not to mention the expense to individual officers should they be forced to retain private counsel to represent them at civilian review board hearings.

Finally, a policeman should be accorded the basic right to go about his sworn duty of protecting the public without fearing that he may later be publicly and unjustly smeared by quasi-governmental superagencies. Again, no policeman is above the law and the wrongdoing officer must be brought to book. But he should be answerable only to public authority lodged in *properly constituted tribunals* and based on *established principles of law.* The accused policeman must defend his actions in the civil and criminal courts and he must be accorded the same rights and safeguards our system accords to any accused. Civilian review boards of a political nature are a far cry from our orderly courtroom processes, and policemen have the basic right not to be singled out to answer to such extraordinary bodies.

4. *Civilian Review Boards Have Not Worked and the Majority of Law-Abiding Citizens Do Not Want Them*

The record of civilian review boards in this country is something less than outstanding. To date civilian review boards have been created in Philadelphia; Rochester, New York; New York City; and Washington, D.C. The boards in Philadelphia and Rochester were by court action closed down as unlawfully created and, significantly, as violative of policemen's rights. More dramatically, the civilian review board in New York City, the political creation of Mayor Lindsay, was voted out of existence in a popular referendum by a crushing vote of 1,307,738 to 768,492.[28]

Attempts to create civilian review boards in other cities have fared

222

no better. In 1960 the Los Angeles City Council unanimously voted down an ACLU-inspired city ordinance that would have created a civilian review board. The Cincinnati City Council refused to consider a civilian review board, again urged by the ACLU. As mentioned, the Louisville City Council rejected a board by an 8-to-2 vote in 1972.

These incidents are instructive and point out one salient fact: the great majority of law-abiding citizens simply do not *want* their peace-keeping forces encumbered by politically inspired civilian review boards. These facts are, of course, in sharp contradistinction to the claims of the board proponents, who would have us believe that there is an all-consuming desire in our citizens for the creation of civilian review boards. Evidence is singularly lacking. The vote in New York City, rejecting a civilian review board by a nearly 2-to-1 margin, is typical of the sentiments of our law-abiding citizens nationwide. New York City is, after all, regarded as the most liberal city in the country, yet it overwhelmingly rejected a civilian review board.

The major concern of our citizens is with crime and violence, not with that bogeyman "police brutality," Even though our policemen are not perfect, the preponderant majority supports them and rebels at the notion of politically oriented superagency control of its peace-keeping forces.

5. *Adequate Remedies Exist in Our Legal System for Redress Against Police Misconduct*

Perhaps no system of justice in the world is as concerned with the rights of individuals as that in the United States. Our system for example, protects the criminal accused with a shield of procedural safeguards that often result in patently guilty offenders being freed. This same solicitude over individual rights is at the disposal of one who has been injured by police misconduct, and civilian review boards can add nothing useful to the remedies available to the injured party.

If an officer's behavior is criminal in nature there are both state and federal statutes under which he can be prosecuted. State laws such as those punishing assault and battery, extortion, manslaughter or murder are available for prosecution, and there are federal statutes that make it a felony for a law-enforcement officer willfully to deprive anyone of his constitutional rights. In the rare cases of police misconduct in which state officials, for whatever reason, refuse to act, federal prosecution can be undertaken. For example, when state prosecution failed against law-enforcement officers who beat or killed civil rights workers in the Deep South in the 1960s, the officers were successfully prosecuted in the federal courts.

Grand juries in almost every state have the power to investigate cases of police brutality, including the power to subpoena witnesses and to compel testimony, even from reluctant witnesses, through grants of immunity. The argument is sometimes heard that prosecutors are reluctant to prosecute policemen for brutality or that juries are unwilling to convict. This may have been true in the past, but with our current concern over minority and human rights, this is simply no longer the case. If a policeman is definitely in the wrong, public opinion, backed by the media, can force a reluctant prosecutor to act. It is, moreover, a slur on the entire system to state that no fair-minded jury will convict a police officer whose conduct is found willfully violative of the law.

Civil remedies of every nature are additionally available to one who has been injured as a result of police misconduct. State actions in tort, such as assault and battery, invasion of privacy, libel and slander, and malicious prosecution, lie against the erring policeman and the number of such suits is increasing dramatically. The federal Civil Rights Act grants a remedy in our federal courts to anyone who believes that his constitutional rights have been violated by law-enforcement officers. And in 1971 the U.S. Supreme Court greatly expanded the scope of this act as it related to law-enforcement officers.

The argument is sometimes made with regard to civil suits against policemen that the courts are the province of the wealthy and that the poor are denied recourse there. While this was perhaps true years ago, the current proliferation of legal services for the poor—community legal centers, legal-aid societies, groups like the ACLU and the NAACP— makes it reasonably certain that the poor person who is aggrieved by alleged police misconduct will have the same access to the civil courts as his more affluent neighbor.

Finally, despite a good deal of clamor to the contrary, the greatest majority of our police departments and police administrators do desire to punish those officers who are guilty of wrongdoing. Police internal affairs divisions and similar police disciplinary bodies have made great strides in recent years to deal with misconduct by members of the force. No professional police executive today doubts that if he is to run an effective department, he must have effective internal discipline. Tremendous efforts are being made nationwide to implement firm, fair, and responsible grievance procedures for the handling of civilian complaints.

This panoply of remedies available to those aggrieved by errant policemen makes the idea of civilian review boards superfluous. The boards would be an extralegal appendage to the system; they would add little to the chances of punishment for the few bad policemen. Rather, they would inevitably become tools for use in harassing the majority of good, dedicated policemen who ask nothing more than to be able to go about their jobs properly.

These arguments have been dealt with at length because of the importance of the issue. If politically motivated outside pressure is placed on law enforcement, in effect neutralizing its aggressive action in fighting crime, obviously the ones who will suffer will be the victims of crime.

Community Control of the Police

Another collateral attack sometimes launched on law enforcement is agitation for "community control of the police." What this boils down to is that each "community" within a city be placed in control of the police forces that work in that community. Usually an additional requirement is that all policemen who work in the community must live in that community. The idea of community control has not caught the fancy of as many collateral attackers as has that of civilian review boards. This is probably because the concept is so obviously unworkable. On one occasion in 1971 a group of radicals in Berkeley, California, placed on the ballot a proposal for community control of the police whereby the city would be divided up into three communities: roughly, the black community, the white community, and the university community. Each community would have and control its own police force. Despite the fact that in the same election a radical majority was elected to city council, the community-control proposal was voted down by a wide margin.

The subsidiary proposal that a policeman must live in the community where he works is patently ridiculous. Those who advance this surely must do so with tongue in cheek. First of all, in a large city an officer would have to move his residence each time he was transferred from one district or area to another. Secondly, it is an inescapable fact that no police officer, black or white, is going to move from a suburban home or more affluent part of a large city into the ghetto just because he happens to be assigned there. Most police officers work one, sometimes two extra jobs to support their families because their salaries are so low. To ask them to move into areas not of their choice is to ask them to quit their police jobs—at once.

Community control, unlike civilian review boards, has not thus far been a major collateral attack on the police. It may, however, have a future. If so, it obviously would result in many good policemen leaving whichever jurisdiction is putting community control into effect; as usual, the victims of crime would suffer from their loss.

Harassment-Type Civil Suits Against Police Officers

One of the major objections to civilian review boards developed above was that aggrieved parties had adequate remedies at law against that minority of policemen that willfully engages in brutality, false arrest, or other violations of individual rights in our courts. This is true. Legitimate suits against willfully wrongdoing officers are a necessary part of our criminal justice system. We simply cannot permit the bad cop to act with impunity. Recently, however, the number of civil suits against policemen has risen steeply. The evidence is fairly clear that in a great majority of these cases the suits were filed (a) for harassment purposes, (b) to revenge an arrest or to attempt to use the suit as a means to prevent prosecution for a crime, or (c) to attempt to force the police officer-defendant, or his insurance carrier, to settle the suit for its "nuisance value"—some minor fraction of the amount claimed which is cheaper to pay than going to the expense of litigating the claim.

Congressman Richard Ichord (D.-Mo.) has described the effect of such suits on law enforcement nationally. In an article entitled "Lawsuits That Handcuff Our Lawmen," in the November 1972 issue of *Nation's Business*, Ichord wrote:

> Lawsuits . . . filed to harass law enforcement officers, were once rare. But no longer.
> The number of frivolous suits is growing rapidly. They have become an increasingly serious impediment to efficient, vigorous law enforcement.
> No one objects, of course, to filing suits for false or improper arrest, when there is justification for such action.
> But I believe that altogether too many such suits are being filed these days as a ploy to delay prosecution, to create publicity, or to try to win sympathy for a patently guilty defendant.
> I believe that officers are increasingly more hesitant to perform their duties diligently because of the fear of such suits.
> This result is easily understandable when it is realized that many lawmen must rely on their own financial resources in defending against such litigation. Law officers, particularly policemen in our smaller communities, usually are not paid well enough to finance, on their own, expensive legal defenses. They can be plunged deeply into debt, or even reduced to poverty.[29]

Congressman Henry Gonzales, a liberal Democrat from Texas, echoed the concern of Mr. Ichord in a speech on the floor of the House:

> A short time ago a lawsuit was brought against one of my constituents who is a police officer which launched him and his family into poverty, even though he was proven innocent of the charges brought against him for actions taken during his line of duty. The family was forced into serious debt due to the legal fees incurred and they lost their home after having to mortgage it during those trying times. We can only imagine the tremendous amount of pressure and sufferings the officer and his family had to endure. This is an incredible situation and a very sad one.

Mr. Ichord, in the last session of Congress, brought to the attention of this House facts which indicate that the case I posed is not an isolated one by any means. He documented the increase in the number of "frivolous" suits being brought against law enforcement officers, prosecutors, and others in the field of law. The excuses for bringing these suits are endless. It may be that is a ploy to delay prosecution, to create publicity, to gain sympathy, or even to "get back" at those who were only performing a duty on behalf of the citizenry at large.

Since these suits must be defended with the lawman's own resources, it can but have ill effects on their performance for fear that they will be brought to trial themselves.[30]

The two congressmen are in no wise overstating the problem. A United States Circuit Court of Appeals judge has viewed the problem from the judicial vantage:

As one of some experience in such matters, I am well aware that a favorite ploy of the law violator is to discourage law enforcement officials by suing them on some pretext or another, false arrest or malicious prosecution or something else, if an officer dares arrest one of them or has to hurt him in the line of duty. This ought not to be encouraged beyond the requirements of due process, especially in a case admittedly without merit unless something can be turned up by fishing files presently confidential.[31]

A survey released in 1974 by Americans for Effective Law Enforcement, Inc., and the International Association of Chiefs of Police documented the rise in civil suits against the police. Law-enforcement agencies employing over ten sworn officers were surveyed to determine the number of civil suits filed against the agencies and their officers.[32] Replying were 1,604 agencies, employing 202,022 officers. Between 1967 and 1971, 5,663 suits were filed. The breakdown by year shows the increase in the number of suits filed:

Year	Suits
1967	762
1968	820
1969	1,047
1970	1,325
1971	1,709

The number of cases filed against individual police agencies indicates the increase in the number of suits being filed each year. For example, in Los Angeles in the five-year period 1967-71 a total of 768 civil suits were filed against the Los Angeles Police Department, the number of suits rising from ninety-five in 1967 to 186 in 1971.[33] In Detroit during the same period 878 civil suits were filed against the police, the number increasing from 130 in 1967 to 232 in 1971.[34]

In 1971 alone, fifty suits were filed against the District of Columbia Police Department and thirty-nine against the relatively small Charlotte (North Carolina) Police Department.[35]

Additionally, there is every indication that most of the suits are in fact frivolous, brought only to harass the police department or police officers. The 1974 survey of the Americans for Effective Law Enforcement and the International Association of Chiefs of Police indicates that of 1,230 suits which came to judgment between 1967 and 1971, only 225 (one in five) were decided in favor of the party suing.[36] For example, in one week in 1971 the Charlotte Police Department defended seven civil suits in court. Six of the suits were resolved in favor of the police. In the seventh, the jury brought in a total verdict of $10.00 against two police officers, primarily because the judge, in effect, ordered them to. This order was appealed and reversed and the suit was not refiled.[37]

The civil suits filed take two basic forms—suits against law-enforcement agencies and suits against individual officers. The former usually are filed in federal district courts and ask the courts to take such extraordinary steps as to supervise all or part of the agency's function, to place the agency in receivership, to forbid the agency from taking certain law-enforcement actions, or to find the agency and its officers to be involved in some sort of massive conspiracy to violate the rights of groups or individuals.

In his article Congressman Ichord described one such suit, which indicates not only the type of suit filed but also the frivolous nature of the suits and the tremendous burden on the police department:

> In 1968 the Western Center on Law and Poverty filed a suit against the Los Angeles police chief, and others, claiming there was a conspiracy to violate the civil rights of all Negroes in the south-central portion of the city. The suit was later expanded to include all Negroes in Los Angeles County.
>
> The Center is financed with federal funds by the Office of Economic Opportunity.
>
> An investigation was launched and it soon became evident that the Center could not sustain its complaint with the persons named as plaintiffs because of their activities in various militant organizations. Then, through a series of legal maneuvers, the militants were replaced in the lawsuit by persons not connected—or at least not known to be connected—with militant groups.
>
> The city of Los Angeles went on to conduct extensive discovery proceedings and the Center eventually was ordered to write a pretrial order. It was unable to do this for several reasons, among them an inability to find its plaintiffs. *Faced with either dismissal or bringing the case to trial, the Center, on its own motion, asked that the case be dismissed.*

That is the legal background to the Los Angeles incident. Now let us examine what all this futile, expensive and frivolous maneuvering cost the taxpayers in the city and county of Los Angeles.

The city police department paid more than $61,000 in salaries for investigators whose work was confined to this case alone.

Another $40,000, it is estimated, was spent in additional investigator's time and the time other police officers spent in court proceedings, gathering testimony, obtaining depositions and so on.

Clerical time involved in the effort is estimated to have cost more than $16,000.

Thus what amounted to no more than a nuisance suit cost the taxpayers more than $117,000 in man hours alone.[38]

Other examples: In Baltimore in 1971 the Black Panther Party, through its attorney William Kunstler, brought suit in federal district court. The suit asked the court to prohibit the prosecution of an attorney charged with complicity in the torture-murder of a police informant and to prohibit the Baltimore City Police Department from "infiltrating, surveilling or otherwise interfering with the activities of the Black Panther Party." The court dismissed the case.[39]

In Richmond, Virginia, the Virginia Civil Liberties Union sued to prohibit the Richmond Police Department from taking photographs at demonstrations and protests. The court ruled in favor of the police department and this decision was upheld by the United States Court of Appeals.[40]

The impact of such suits is evident. If those filing them should succeed to any significant degree, we would see the phenomenon of police departments being run by federal district courts or by special receivers appointed by the courts. Or we might witness the spectacle of a police department—based on the interpretation of a single judge—being prohibited from using perfectly legitimate law-enforcement techniques, such as infiltration, surveillance, and the like. This would undermine the authority of the police chief or agency head completely, and in fact many professional police administrators would probably resign under such circumstances. The effectiveness of law enforcement would be completely destroyed and the law-abiding would suffer.

The other class of suits is filed against individual officers. These suits allege some form of misconduct—brutality, false arrest, false imprisonment, violation of civil rights, etc. They have a devastating effect on the officers involved because of adverse publicity when the suit is filed and because officers must often pay for their own defense—an expense they can ill afford on the salary they receive. Even if an officer is insured, his insurance may not cover the acts charged (for example, civil rights violations or malicious damage to property), in which case the officer must pay for his own attorney to defend against these charges.

229

These cases are particularly frustrating to the officer, especially when he knows that the suit is filed for harassment purposes. Congressman Ichord described one such suit.

Missouri's Highway Patrol had been on William Howard's trail a long, long time.

The 22-year-old Missourian was known to be pushing drugs. But it was hard to catch him red-handed.

Now, officers felt they had him cold. Acting on a tip, they tailed him from Ft. Leonard Wood, a giant Army post in the Missouri Ozarks. They followed him uphill and down, around the sweeping curves of Interstate 44, as it wound through the pine-clad hills.

Suddenly, his car came to a screeching halt at a diner just west of Rolla, county seat of rural Phelps County.

He and "horse"—an attractive blonde accomplice who usually carried his narcotics supply in her bra—made a dash for the rest rooms. Highway patrolmen nabbed them before the drugs could be flushed away.

Howard later pleaded guilty to possession and transfer of drugs. He was sentenced to five years in the Missouri Penitentiary.

It may sound like a happy ending to one battle with crime. It wasn't.

Instead, it was the curtain raiser to a campaign of harassment that plagued—among others—Rolla's Assistant Chief of Police Gene Roluffs and Phelps County's Prosecuting Attorney Zane White.

Both were sued by Howard for conspiring to coerce him into pleading guilty!

As often happens, they were stuck with the expense of defending themselves.

"Fortunately, the suit was dismissed by a federal court in St. Louis," says Mr. White. "If it had gone to trial, it could have cost us plenty."[41]

Cases such as these are numerous and a common form of collateral attack. They demoralize the police officers involved and other officers who learn of the suits. The real danger of these attacks lies in the effect they can have on law enforcement by making officers afraid to act for fear of civil suits or unfounded complaints. Police officers are, for the most part, brave men, or they simply would not take the job with all of its inherent dangers. Most willingly hazard their lives by facing the dangers that abound in police work. But it is quite another thing to ask a police officer to risk the financial security of himself and his family—a security usually precarious at best—in civil suits filed against him simply for doing his job as best he knows how. As Congressman Ichord noted: "I believe that officers are increasingly more hesitant to perform their duties diligently because of the fear of such suits."[42]

If the officer is afraid to do his job because of this kind of collateral attack, the greater will be the danger to the innocent citizen.

Other Collateral Attacks

J. Edgar Hoover, as noted earlier, referred to certain types of collateral attackers who "create public distrust of, and ill will towards, those who enforce the law." Those who do this, either deliberately or unwittingly, are indeed collateral attackers. In most cases, I reiterate, the collateral attackers are within their rights in making these assaults. It is perfectly legal to advocate civilian review boards, file civil suits (unless the attorneys or parties to the suit know that their allegations are untrue), or disparage law enforcement in articles and speeches. My purpose in this section is not to quarrel with the *right* of the antivictim forces to make collateral attacks, but to point out the gravity of the situation, the potential adverse effect on law enforcement contained in such attacks, and the concomitant adverse effect on victims of crime.

A vicious collateral attack designed specifically to disparage the police is contained in an article by Byron F. Lindsley in the spring 1969 edition of the *Civil Rights Digest*. Under the topic "The Quality of Law Enforcement," Lindsley launches a virulent attack, replete with generalities, on all of this nation's policemen:

> Most policemen are not suited by their education, training, cultural background or attitude to cope effectively, or relevantly, with the complex law enforcement and crime prevention needs of a society going through the throes of broad, fast moving and dramatic cultural evolution. . . .
> The majority of white Americans and a still larger majority of white policemen equate poverty and human misery, and in some peculiar way even skin color, with sin and evil. . . .
> Not only does [the policeman] reflect America's racist thinking, but he tends to be even more racist, with more opportunities to express it, and is more forceful and openly debasing in the ways he displays his racism in his daily work. . . .
> The police are the great single initiating force confronting the upward struggling minority with daily indignity.[43]

Now here is a real collateral attack against the police. It utilizes the unfair device of generality to debase an entire class of people: the police. What makes this particular collateral attack so disturbing is that its author is a judge of the California Superior Court at San Diego. Certainly, a San Diego police officer appearing in a case before Judge Lindsley would have every right to demand that the judge disqualify himself for "extreme prejudice."

Judge Lindsley's collateral attack was a deliberate effort to create public distrust of, and ill will towards, the police. An example of a nondeliberate collateral attack, nevertheless inexcusable, was the readiness of a large segment of our media to accept as unquestionably true

231

the statement made in December 1969 by Black Panther attorney Charles Gary that the police of this country had murdered twenty-eight Black Panthers. This assertion, from a source that is questionable at best, was reported as fact by the *New York Times,* whose news service encompasses some two hundred newspapers. *Time* and *Newsweek* repeated the story as fact. Through this coverage the story had reached most of this nation's readers whose opinions about such things count.

The charge was, of course, a lie. Ronald Koziol, a crack investigative reporter for the *Chicago Tribune,* branded it as such shortly after it was printed, but nobody paid much attention to him. It took Edward J. Epstein, a liberal, writing in the ultraliberal *New Yorker* of February 13, 1971, to skewer the lie. Mr. Epstein proved conclusively that in only two cases could there possibly have been an intent to murder Black Panthers and in those cases it was by no means certain.[44]

Now none of the media giants who fostered the lie of a nationwide police-directed extermination campaign against the Black Panther Party would consider *directly* attacking the police (that is, shooting a policeman). But the *collateral* attack via this shoddy journalism demeaned and disparaged the police before millions of Americans. Many policemen believe that the liberal media giants ran the story as a fact because they *wanted* to believe it and it would take a good deal to prove this thesis wrong. Lewis F. (now Justice) Powell went even further. He accused the media of perhaps contributing to the danger of police officers. He observed that although the *New Yorker* had proven the charge to be a lie, "the truth rarely overtakes falsehood—especially when the latter is disseminated by prestigious newspapers—millions of young Americans, especially blacks, now believe these false charges. There is little wonder that assaults on police are steadily increasing."[45]

Whether deliberate, as Judge Lindsley's, or through the intolerable negligence marking the "genocide" story, these collateral attacks *can* damage the police in the eyes of others.

Part III
What Can Be Done

8
Recognition and Representation for the Victims

UNTIL COMPARATIVELY RECENTLY THE TREND IN THIS COUNTRY was pretty much to ignore the rights of minorities. "Jim Crow" laws in the South and job and housing discrimination nationwide are examples of this. The trend now is, quite properly, away from this. Equal rights laws, affirmative action programs, and court decisions striking down discrimination against racial minorities are now an integral part of the law of this country. Many, indeed, believe we have gone overboard in this direction. Antidiscrimination activities, they feel, as presently interpreted and implemented, are actually resulting in reverse discrimination against those not of a minority.

Whatever, the fact remains that we are at least attempting to guarantee the rights of minorities. Essential to this was a gradual awakening in this country that there were racial minorities, that they had rights, and that they were entitled to have these rights enforced. Groups like the National Association for the Advancement of Colored People helped this country realize that among our minorities were many whose rights were being ignored.

The victims of crime in the United States occupy, as a class, the same position that the racial minorities did years ago. To date few have recognized that these victims do constitute a class that has rights and that is entitled to have them enforced.

Patrick V. Murphy, former New York City police commissioner and now the head of the Police Foundation, described the nonstatus of the victims of crime: "The way crime victims are treated in many jurisdictions from their first contact with the police to their final hours in the courtroom is often insensitive. Rarely are their needs considered to any degree."[1]

Echoing these thoughts, Donald E. Santarelli, former administrator of the Law Enforcement Assistance Administration of the Department of Justice, was even more specific about the status of the victims in our criminal justice system: "Put yourself in the shoes of a crime victim—who finds himself to be a pawn on the criminal justice chessboard, who has to suffer all sorts of indignities, and then sees, as the final straw, the accused offender walking out free."[2]

The need, then, is to move from these excellent statements toward doing something constructive about the grisly situation. The first step, obviously, is to reorient our thinking about the victims. Today each victim is largely regarded as an individual statistic, if he is regarded at all. We must recognize that crime's victims are a class of people with rights that must be protected.

There are, as a matter of fact, two groups that constitute the class of victims: the actual victims of crime and the potential victims. The first group can be numbered with reasonable certainty, at least with regard to reported crime. For example, the 19,500 murder victims, the 51,000 forcible-rape victims, the 382,680 robbery victims, and the 416,207 victims of aggravated assaults in 1973—when these are added to the *millions* of victims of other crimes in that year and in preceding ones, a fairly definable group emerges.

The second group within the victims class, the potential victims, can be defined quite simply as everyone; we are *all* potential victims of a criminal act. This admittedly makes up a pretty large group of people to recognize as a class. This does not mean, however, that the class cannot or should not be recognized as such. Nor does it for a moment mean that effective action cannot be taken in behalf of the class. If we recognize the class of actual victims of crime—which is pretty sizable as it is—then any constructive action we take in their behalf will by definition redound to the benefit of the potential victims also.

To illustrate. Suppose an official or quasi-official body is set up whose function is to protect the rights of the victims of crime. Suppose also that because of unwarranted leniency, a murderer and known escape artist is allowed his freedom from confinement and kills again. Now if an organization concerned with the victim's rights should file a suit on behalf of the murdered victim's family, against those responsible for his being freed, or if the victims' rights organization should hold hearings to find out just why the killer was freed, it will obviously be acting in behalf of the known victim.

If the suit is successful, or if the hearings result in bringing enough public pressure to bear upon the delinquent authorities so that they will think twice before freeing another dangerous man, then this state of mind will obviously benefit the potential victims who might have suffered at the hands of others similarly freed. In short, such actions will have a prospective effect that will benefit the potential victims, in addition to a retrospective effect in behalf of the actual victim.

The first step towards doing something in behalf of the victims is recognizing the victims of crime as a class. There will be little use, however, in even the fullest kind of recognition unless machinery is set in motion to *represent* the victims as a class so as to enforce their rights.

Justice White, in his dissenting opinion in *Miranda* v. *Arizona*, characterized the victims of crime as being, among other things, "unrepresented." This is largely true. Except in those rare cases where a victim hires a lawyer to vindicate his personal rights against a criminal, the victims *as a class* are unrepresented.

This statement does not in the least reflect upon the constant and dedicated efforts of our law-enforcement agencies, charged with apprehending criminals, or of our prosecutors, who must prosecute criminals. Under our system of criminal justice the police and the prosecutors represent the authority of the state. Criminal cases are invariably styled *State* v. *Smith, People* v. *Brown,* or *United States* v. *Jones.* And this is perfectly proper. The prosecutor, for example, is an officer of the state, elected by the people. His duty is to represent the state by trying and convicting the individual who has transgressed that state's laws.

If the prosecutor secures a conviction and perhaps a properly harsh sentence against a criminal, he will have vindicated the right of the state to capture and punish criminals. He will also have vindicated the rights of the victim, but this vindication will have been *incidental* to the prosecutor's duty to represent the state.

The difference between the two types of representation is illustrated in the following manner. Suppose that in a state a law or a court decision makes proving rape extremely difficult, if not impossible, and that as a result of this law, prosecutors are required to dismiss or reduce many otherwise valid rape charges. Now the prosecutors of that state might seek, in the legislature or the courts, to change the particular law, but they will be doing it to be able to represent the state more effectively.

A victim-oriented organization might also, perhaps in conjunction with the prosecutors, perhaps independently, petition the courts and the legislatures to change the law, but in that instance it would be representing, specifically, the *victims* of the crime: the actual victims who have been raped and who have seen their assailants freed or convicted of much reduced charges, and potential rape victims.

Assuming, then, that crime victims as a class are recognized and that there is a desire that they be represented to enforce their rights, what form might such representation take? First of all, it would be necessary to decide whether the representation would be governmental or from the private sector, or both. Optimally, such representation should come from the government *and* the private sector.

There would be clear-cut advantages to governmental activity in this area. Principally because the government, if it desires to do so, could place virtually unlimited financial and supportive resources at the disposal of such a project. Additionally, a governmental entity would have the power to enforce compliance with its decrees (subject, of course, to constitutional limitations), and would be able to obtain information and testimony that might well be denied to a private organization.

One disadvantage attaching to a governmental entity is that as part of the bureaucratic structure, the organization established to protect victims' rights would, unless exceptional, spend much of its resources in paper shuffling. Another point is that a governmental agency would generally reflect the philosophy of the appointing authority; hence, members of a state victims' rights commission would likely mirror the outlook of the appointing governor. Obviously, if a victims' rights commission were to be useful, it would have of necessity to comprise people who believe that *at least* a balance should be struck between the rights of the victim and those of the criminal accused.

If a victim-oriented commission were created by a moderate-to-conservative governor and then a new, liberal governor replaced its members with, say, ACLU types, then such an entity not only would become useless but could actually prove inimical to the rights of its clientele: the victims.

Finally, another disadvantage would be spending taxpayers' dollars. Not all taxpayers feel the same about a given issue, although the public opinion polls cited in chapter one clearly indicate that most people would heartily welcome an official organization that would enforce their rights as actual or potential victims of crime. This contention can be answered by pointing out that in most governments today— federal, state, and local—there are such things as civil rights and human rights commissions that are, quite frankly, liberally oriented, and not all of the taxpayers agree with the activities of these commissions either. A governmental victims' rights commission would merely serve as a balance to other entities whose concern is with individual rights, as opposed to the collective safety of society.

With regard to victim-oriented organizations from the private sector, in their favor is the fact that such organizations of concerned citizens can be extremely effective, as we'll shortly see. Citizen groups can, in large measure, avoid the bureaucratic stumblingblocks inherent in a governmental structure. "Citizen power," if responsibly applied, can unquestionably work wonders towards attaining its goals. Witness, for example, the extraordinary effectiveness of citizen influence in the environmental movement.

Citizen groups have the advantage of not being subject to the vicissitudes of political change to which a governmental agency would always be subject. Citizen organizations would ordinarily be more flexible in their positions.

The disadvantages to a citizen effort are that it would lack the power of the government as to both financial resources and capability to enforce anything. A citizens' group could, for example, hold public hearings, but it would not (and should not) have any authority at all to compel anyone to appear.

From the foregoing it is reasonably clear that the most effective protection of the victim's rights would be found in the coexistence of a governmental body and a citizens' group, created for and dedicated to the protection of the rights of the law-abiding citizens who have been victimized and who are potential victims.

Before proceeding to an examination of models for victim-oriented organizations, one important point must be raised as to their scope. Legislation is pending that would monetarily compensate innocent victims of crime. Similar legislation is also pending in some states. Moreover, proposals have been made to provide therapy and counseling to the victims of crime.

Such activities are important and reflect a due concern for the rights of the victims. But one factor is common to all or most of them: they would assist the victim only after the fact—that is, after he becomes a victim. The proposals herein have a much broader scope. If implemented, they not only would compensate and assist the victimized, but also would attempt, by representing the victims of crime, to identify and deal with situations that cause innocent people to be victimized and that cause criminals to go unpunished or be released despite the fact that their liberty endangers the community.

This broader scope is what sets apart the proposals made here from any other victim-oriented proposal familiar to me. The organizations I propose, at least those involving government, are frankly patterned after various effective civil rights, human rights, and human relations commissions that operate as governmental entities across the nation. These commissions do not, for the most part, sit back and wait until a person has been discriminated against, or has had his civil rights violated, and then compensate or counsel him. They act, rather, extremely aggressively to weed out potential discrimination. They act through public and executive hearings and in the courts and legislatures to *prevent* violations falling within their jurisdiction and to deal generally with the entire area of the problem, as opposed to taking a mere after-the-fact approach.

There is no reason in the world why a body as concerned with victims' rights as others are with the rights that they were created to protect, should not be set up and be equally effective. An aggressive victims' rights commission, which would direct its energies to the entire scope of victimization, could accomplish an amazing amount of good for the actual and potential victims of crime.

A Victims' Rights Commission— Government Model

A victims' rights commission could be set up by any governmental entity at any level. The authority to create such a commission would naturally depend upon the law of the jurisdiction. The executive— governor, mayor, county executive—may have authority to establish it on his own, or the legislative branch may have to do it. In any event, funding the commission would almost certainly have to be by legislation or ordinance.

Membership on the commission would generally be by executive appointment. The commission would consist of those in the criminal justice field, responsible persons in the lay community, and a substantial number of persons who have themselves been the victims of crime, *particularly* persons of minority races who have been victimized. One of the criteria for appointment should be that the members must, by past activities, have evidenced a responsible concern over the rights of crime's victims.

This does not mean that the commission should consist entirely of the most hard-line law-and-order conservatives in the jurisdiction.

240

But it should be made up of those who have the interests of the law-abiding as their primary concern. Just as human and civil rights commissions are made up of those who have provably devoted past efforts to the values embraced by these commissions, so should a victims' rights commission be made up.

The commission should have an executive director and staff, as funding would allow. Compensation to the members and staff would follow along the lines of similar bodies in the jurisdiction.

The mandate of the commission would contain first a statement recognizing that innocent actual and potential victims of crime constitute a class of persons whose rights the commission is duty-bound to represent. The commission should possess sufficient powers to perform this duty, including the power of subpoena; the right to make recommendations to lawmaking and policy-setting bodies in the criminal justice field; the right to hold hearings, both public and private; the right to represent the victims of crime by filing court cases or briefs, or both, in matters concerning their rights; and the right and duty to do all else necessary, subject to constitutional and statutory limitations, to enforce the rights of the victims of crime.

Through its members and staff the commission could then:

● Inform itself, through hearings, investigations, and analyses, on the amount of victimization in its jurisdiction, particularly the victimization of minorities.

● Inform itself of the causes of such victimization—whether legislative or court-ordered restraints on law enforcement and the prosecution, or excessive leniency toward criminals in any part of the system, or other.

● Make recommendations for changes (again, within constitutional limitations) in the criminal justice system, changes that would help prevent victimization of the innocent.

● Appear in court on behalf of the victims of crime both at the trial and at the appellate levels.

● Take action to support *proper* and *responsible* law enforcement.

● Protect the victims of crime from unnecessary and personally traumatic media coverage.

● Assist the victims in receiving compensation, from the state, or the perpetrator, or other lawful sources.

● Aid and counsel the victims of crime.

● Take action to ensure some sort of accountability either in the courts or in the eye of public opinion for those whose unwarranted leniency toward dangerous criminals has caused victimization of the innocent.

● Work closely with the law-enforcement and the prosecutive forces within the jurisdiction.

This listing is not exhaustive but it gives an idea of what a responsible government body, dedicated to the representation of the victims of crime, could accomplish.

There are, of course, certain things that the commission should *not* be:

● A shelter or haven for the truly brutal or corrupt law-enforcement officer. Should, for example, a police officer or police department be sued, the commission could, within its guidelines, enter the case on behalf of the officer or department. *But only* after a most thoroughgoing investigation has determined that the allegations are groundless and that the effectiveness of law enforcement will be impaired if the adverse party prevails.

● A champion for changes in the law that would be truly repressive, changes like allowing the police to hold suspects for overlong periods before bringing them before a judge, allowing "third-degree" tactics on suspects, and similar violations of fundamental rights.

● A mindless law-and-order-at-any-price entity. Each position the commission takes in behalf of the victims of crime should be consistent with concepts of fundamental fairness to the accused. But when the thicket of technical safeguards around the accused benefits only the guilty, then the commission should act as forcefully as it can to restore a balance to the system.

If a victims' rights commission like this were established, there would, predictably, be a thunderous outcry by the antivictim forces. They would clamor about there being no need for such a commission, about its unconstitutionality, and about its trampling individual rights under foot.

These contentions are specious and readily answered. All are predicated upon the assumption that the victims of crime, as such, have no right to have their rights represented. No constitution or statute in the country provides any such thing. On the contrary, implicit in the guarantees found in most constitutions are the rights to life and liberty and the right to enjoy these blessings free from the depredations of the lawless and violent. One argument that would likely be made against the formation of a victims' rights commission is that it could, or would, be used as just one more device to repress racial minorities. This can be categorically refuted. The racial minorities are by far the principal victims of crime. Therefore, *any* plan or proposal for representing the victims of crime must seek to represent that great majority of law-abiding blacks and other minorities upon whom the burden of crime is so great.

To be sure, on occasion a position of a victims' rights commission and that of some other state agency would conflict. Suppose, for example, a state legislature was considering a bill to liberalize, in accordance with recent Supreme Court decisions, state restrictions on the right of the police to make certain searches and seizures. Conceivably, that state's civil rights commission might oppose the bill, while its victims' rights commission might support it as a lawful extension of police authority to protect the innocent. Far from being in any way a bad thing, the conflict would be healthy. The legislative body considering the bill would have the opportunity of hearing the conflicting points of view from two state organizations, both having considerable expertise and *both having a legitimate and responsible position on the matter*.

This is the sort of balance an entity speaking for victims could supply—a balance now sorely lacking.

An alternative to the commission proposal would be the creation within a governmental entity of a victims' ombudsman. The ombudsman concept has become more acceptable in recent years. At least one state, Minnesota, has an ombudsman position for prisoners. John P. J. Dussich of the Florida Governor's Council on Criminal Justice proposed a victims' ombudsman for the Sunshine State; however, the ombudsman's duties would be limited to after-the-fact counseling and assistance to the victim.[3]

To be effective the ombudsman concept should be broader than mere after-the-crime assistance. He should, along with his staff, be authorized to engage in all or most of the activities proposed above for the victims' rights commission.

The victims' ombudsman concept has the definite advantage of reposing in one man the powers granted to a more cumbersomely structured multimember commission. It also has the drawback that the single ombudsman may not carry as much clout for his clientele as would a formally created state or local commission. Additionally, there might be problems, depending on local laws, as to just how much power could be granted to a single man. Could he or his office, for example, be legally authorized to hold hearings and compel testimony, subpoena documents, file cases or briefs, or both, in court? If such restrictions were imposed, it would seriously curtail his effectiveness.

Both concepts—a victims' rights commission and a victims' ombudsman—are novel. For implicit in them is the recognition by government for the first time, that the victims of crime have some rights too and that it is proper to set up the machinery whereby these rights may be represented and enforced. This recognition would be a major forward step and have a tremendous impact on the criminal justice system's current failure to do much of anything for the victims.

Representation of the Victims—
Citizen Action Models

Citizens' groups can have tremendous impact on our national life. There is to most people something very appealing in the idea of ordinary citizens giving—sometimes lavishly—of their time and money to support and advance a cause in which they believe.

In the criminal justice system, with certain notable exceptions, unfortunately, there has been little citizen concern or input insofar as victims' rights are concerned. Citizen impact in behalf of the criminal accused has, on the other hand, been enormous. In chapter seven the activities of the American Civil Liberties Union, which does everything in its power to restrict even the most legitimate and necessary law-enforcement activities, were described. In chapter five we noted the position of the National Council on Crime and Delinquency that *no one*, except those with a proven pattern of dangerous behavior, should ever be imprisoned.

Groups like ACLU and the NCCD are supported by well-meaning people who are obviously in sympathy with their goals. But these goals can have (though not intended) only the most adverse impact on the rights of the victims of crime.

There are, however, some citizens' organizations that are established to, and do, devote all of their efforts to battle crime. Citizens' crime commissions in various cities—for example, Chicago and New Orleans—have been quite successful on the local level in their anti-crime activities, directed primarily against organized crime.

There are two victim-oriented citizens' organizations in existence, one national and one local (but with the potential of growth to state-wide influence). Both devote their entire efforts to making the criminal justice system more responsive to the needs of the victim by assisting the victims directly, by supporting proper law enforcement, and by opposing unwarranted leniency for the criminal at every level of the system.

The national citizens' organization is Americans for Effective Law Enforcement, Inc. (AELE), a not-for-profit corporation headquartered in Evanston, Illinois.* AELE was founded in 1966 by Fred E. Inbau, professor of law at Northwestern University and an internationally known expert in criminal law and criminology; the late O. W. Wilson, also renowned in criminology, and at the time the superintendent of the Chicago Police Department; James R. Thompson, then a Northwestern law professor and currently the United States attorney for the Northern District of Illinois; and Richard B. Ogilvie, former governor

*This writer is the executive director of AELE.

of Illinois and then the president of the Cook County Board of Commissioners.

AELE was founded in the belief that while organizations such as the ACLU were extremely vocal in behalf of the criminal accused, no responsible national citizens' group was speaking out for the law-abiding citizen. In the opinion of the founders, the rights of the law-abiding to be free from victimization by the lawless and violent could best be represented by responsible and effective support for law-enforcement officers nationwide, that thin blue line between the citizens and the criminal.

AELE has, in its seven years of existence, become a force to reckon with in the criminal justice system. Its most effective program has been the filing of *amicus curiae,* or friend of the court, briefs in important criminal-law cases, primarily in the U.S. Supreme Court. These briefs buttress the legal arguments made by the party representing the law-enforcement side of the issue by presenting to the court empirical data and other arguments as to why the law-enforcement side of the issue should be sustained. The briefs have, AELE believes, assisted the courts in deciding in favor of law enforcement in sixteen out of the eighteen decided cases in which AELE has filed.

In the cases in which AELE has participated as a friend of the court, it has argued that law-enforcement officers must be granted proper legal authority in order to protect the law-abiding. In several of its briefs AELE pointed out to the courts the manner in which restrictions on reasonable police investigations would work to the detriment of the victims of crime, thus making a specific, and generally successful victim-oriented appeal.

AELE also operates the only legal center in the country dedicated to defending policemen who have been sued in frivolous or harassment-type civil cases. As noted in chapter seven, most of the suits filed against police officers are frivolous, designed to make the average policeman afraid to do his job for fear of being haled into court. Nothing else could have a more adverse impact on the victims of crime if the purposes of those who utilize the device of civil suits succeed. Thus, again, AELE's Law Enforcement Legal Defense Center (LELDC) has a victim-oriented emphasis.

AELE's participation in support of policemen who have become the target of civil suits is exemplified in a case recently decided by the court of appeals of Missouri. A St. Louis police detective had arrested a seventeen-year-old youth for the unprovoked shooting of a man. While the youth was being booked at the station, he crashed through a plate-glass window and fled. The detective and an officer gave chase. After warning the fleeing felon to stop, the officer shot and killed him.

In a wrongful death suit, the jury exonerated the officer but assessed $1,000 damages against the detective because he had not informed the officer that the suspect was a juvenile. This unfair verdict was appealed to the Missouri Court of Appeals. AELE filed a brief in the case in support of the detective. This brief cited a case on which the appeals court relied as authority to reverse, unanimously, the jury verdict, and the court ordered the case against the detective dismissed.

This successful brief was written by Wayne W. Schmidt, an outstanding attorney and former law-enforcement officer who directs AELE's Law Enforcement Legal Defense Center. In addition to entering civil cases in support of police officers, the LELDC provides, free of charge, advice on the law and on those trial techniques that have been used in successfully defending police officers. This centralized research service is available to every law-enforcement agency in the country. Literally hundreds of such agencies have taken advantage of it.

The most recent trend in AELE's activities has been toward direct representation of the victims of crime. It is currently involved in filing a civil suit, on behalf of the parents, against a man who brutally murdered a young girl, and is preparing a definitive legal blueprint on the rights of the victims of crime.

As AELE is a tax-exempt organization it cannot and does not lobby. However, members of its legal staff have testified personally or presented written testimony before the Congress of the United States and state legislative bodies on such matters as support for capital punishment and support for more severe sentences for convicted criminals.

Some measure of the success of AELE's victim-oriented program is perhaps indicated by the fact that AELE, since 1970, has received well over a million dollars in contributions and pledges *entirely from the private sector.* Certainly, AELE's record reveals that representation of the victims of crime through citizen involvement can be highly effective.

The scope of AELE's program is national. AELE has chapters in ten states and is expanding rapidly. The record of an organization located in Northern California indicates that citizen action against crime on the local level can be equally effective. The group is Citizens for Law and Order (CLO), headquartered in Oakland (Alameda County) and run by an energetic businessman named Earl W. Huntting.

CLO takes a very hard line against crime and has been enormously effective in doing so. Its stated aims are: "to educate and inform the silent majority of business, professional men, women and homeowners who want to become involved through lawful means in active support of law and order in our nation, our state, and our local community." It lobbies in the California legislature for bills that support proper law enforcement and opposes legislation that would weaken it.

Far and away the most effective program of CLO is its "court watcher" program. Volunteers from the organization go into the courts and record the sentences given to convicted criminals by various judges. A box score on leniency is published in CLO's weekly news-letter with the names of judges who have granted excessively lenient sentences to criminals prominently mentioned. This program has sparked some controversy, but judges and prosecutors in the area have conceded its effectiveness. Statistics seem to bear this out; in 1970 CLO began its watchdog activities, and prison sentences for convicted felons rose from 11.5 percent in that year to 15.6 percent in 1972.[4]

Representation for the victims of crime by citizen groups is an important aspect of the overall picture concerning what can be done for the victims of crime. Representation for victims at *both* the govern-ment and the private sector levels could work to the tremendous advantage of the hitherto unrepresented victims.

Other Victim-Oriented Activities

The only major area in which the criminal justice system has paid more than meagre lip-service to the victims of crime is in the area dealing with compensation for their injuries. Of course, in most instances the victim, or his family, can file a civil suit against his assailant for wrongful death or for such common-law torts as assault and battery. The problem with this approach is that most criminals are "judgment proof," that is, they simply do not have the money to pay a judgment that a victim might obtain against one. As one writer pointed out, "Crimes of violence are not ordinarily committed by the rich."[5]

Compensation of victims may take several forms. Illinois, for example, has enacted legislation whereby innocent victims of crime who have cooperated with law-enforcement officers investigating the crime, and "good Samaritans" who are injured while coming to the aid of victims of crime or of law-enforcement officers, may make a claim in the state's Court of Claims Division for up to $10,000 com-pensation for those medical or funeral expenses and loss of earnings and support not otherwise paid for by insurance or other compensation plans.[6]

New York, in 1966, created the Crime Victims' Compensation Board, similar to the Illinois legislation, but with higher limits on compensation. By March 1973, $3.77 million had been paid to 1,609 crime victims.[7] Similar legislation is pending in other states and in the U.S. Congress. Compensation directly from the state is, of course, extremely helpful to those victims who would otherwise have to bear alone the financial burden of their victimization. Such schemes are based on the sound logic that the state has failed in its duty to protect, through its police powers, the law-abiding from the lawless.

Other methods of compensating victims that have been suggested include a public insurance system—analogous to our current welfare system and funded through general taxation—and devices whereby part of the fine levied against a defendant able to pay it, be given to his victim.[8]

There are certain mechanical problems with methods of compensation that are dependent upon the processes of the state for their efficacy. First, it is difficult to make known to all of the victims of crime, particularly the poor and uneducated, that compensation is available. Next, as with every bureaucratic system, there will be considerable red tape involved in proving and collecting a claim, although members of the staff of a victims' rights commission or a victims' ombudsman could be helpful here.

These drawbacks are, however, only mechanical in nature; they can be overcome. Two very serious philosophical problems are involved in the question of compensation for the victims of crime. First, there is the risk that if the victim is compensated, those who now engage in inordinate leniency towards the convicted criminal will utilize this fact as justifying even further leniency. This would result in the monstrous situation wherein A victimizes B, someone else—almost assuredly the taxpayer—compensates B for what A did to him, and then A is let off with little or no penalty because B was compensated.

Such a conjunction of events destroys any deterrent to future misconduct by A. He is assured that, whatever he does, the consequences of his crimes, as to himself, will be "bought off" by the fact that B will be compensated. Thus A can do as he pleases knowing that society's laudable concern for the economic impact of his crime upon his victim has ransomed him from any *personal* liability therefor.

If some sort of publicly financed compensation for crime's victims is to achieve general acceptance, then it must be made clear that the criminal will still be punished *even if* his victim is compensated for his economic loss. Certainty of punishment must never be made conditional upon the fact that society has compensated the victim— the criminal must still be punished in order to deter him, and others like him, from future crimes.

The other philosophical problem regarding the concept of compensating victims is even more important. Compensating victims must always be regarded as only a stopgap measure. The aim of a victim-oriented criminal justice system must be to *prevent,* to the extent humanly possible, victimization in the first place.

If an innocent citizen has been hit on the head with a lead pipe and hospitalized for three weeks, it is a fine thing to compensate him for his financial losses (he can, of course, never be compensated for his pain, suffering, and outrage). But chances are, this victim, even though given a certain sum of money for his losses, would rather not have been hit on the head to begin with. If at any time the compensating of victims should build into the criminal justice system the smug self-assurance that it has thereby done its duty to the victim and that there is no longer a need to bend every effort to prevent crime in the first place, then the worthy theory of compensation will have perverted the system beyond belief.

To summarize: compensation of the victims of crime should be encouraged, but only if it coexists with a firm intention to punish the criminal and to make every attempt, through aggressive deterrent action, to prevent other crimes from happening.

Analogous to the concept of compensating the victims of crime is that of requiring the criminal to make restitution to the victim—that is, paying the victim for his losses either out of prison earnings or as a condition for putting the criminal on probation. So long as the earnings of inmates remain as low as they now are in most states, the concept of restitution through such earnings is theoretically good but of little practical value.

The idea of restitution as a condition of probation or parole has been adopted in Iowa. There a plan for restitution is required if a defendant is to be considered for probation. The criminal, if he wishes to be placed on probation, must meet with his probation officer and make a plan for restitution to the victim, including a schedule of payments.[9]

Two problems are immediately apparent. First, it is patent that such a plan will only be effective if it is enforced. A convicted criminal who, naturally enough, does not want to go to jail may make all sorts of promises to pay his victim in order to receive probation. But, human nature being what it is, once on probation, the promise to pay may not be kept. Now, if any defaults on payments are rigorously followed up by the probation officer, upon the complaint of the victim, and the criminal knows that his probation will be revoked if he defaults, then this system might work. If, however, probation officers, who are generally considerably overworked, are unable or unwilling to take action against restitution defaulters, then we have a situation in which the criminal has his freedom and the victim an empty promise.

The other problem with the restitution-as-a-condition-of-probation concept is that it is at variance with the idea of certainty of punishment as a deterrent. If every criminal knows that he can avoid any sort of confinement by paying off his victim in small installments, then he may well be willing to commit crimes for profit—that is, theft, burglary, and armed robbery—knowing that if caught, he will face only the inconvenience of "working off" the consequences of his crime.

Additionally, in the area of crimes against persons—particularly rape—there may well be very little actual monetary loss to the victim. A woman, not a virgin, who has been raped may spend only one night in the hospital, if that, and lose only a little time off from work. But the crime remains a very serious one and the trauma to the victim simply cannot be calculated. To grant probation to the rapist provided only that he make good the minimal monetary loss to his victim mocks the victim's rights.

In short, making the criminal make restitution to his victim is, if enforced, a wholly worthy concept. But, if the idea of restitution is carried to the extent that any criminal can "buy his way out" of the consequences of his acts by his promise to repay, then the concept has been seriously perverted. A system of deterrence through punishment *and* restitution to the victim would be of extreme benefit to the victims generally. However, a system that substitutes restitution for *any* punishment will, through its lack of any deterrent at all, be of little or no benefit to the victims.

With the exception of the emerging concepts of compensation and restitution for the victims of crime, little consideration has been given to the victims by the criminal justice system. Even these concepts fall far short of what should be the *primary* concern of the system: the prevention of victimization in the first place.

The proposals in this chapter would, if ever implemented, admittedly cause an upheaval in a system that up to now has focused its concern so single-mindedly upon the rights of the criminal. Such an upheaval is absolutely necessary, however, if we wish to do anything useful for the victims of crime who have for so long been so grievously neglected.

9
Specific
Victim-Oriented
Activities

LET US ASSUME FOR A MOMENT that the United States has, by some happy chance, become a victim-oriented society. Assume that this nation has developed a consciousness that the victims of crime, both actual and potential, do indeed constitute a recognizable class of people that have certain rights and that are entitled to have these rights enforced. Assume that our society now seeks a reordering of the priorities of a criminal justice system that has reached a point at which the lawless and violent are fairly well convinced that they may prey upon others with relative impunity. What, then, *specifically* can be done to ensure that this newfound victim orientation will become truly effective in its efforts to vindicate the rights of the victims?

The answer to this question is of enormous importance in any analysis of the question of what of a useful nature can be done to assist the victims. For, obviously, any concept of victim consciousness and orientation that exists only in theory will be as useless to the interests of the objects of its concern as would any other theoretical concept. There must exist, along with theory, a concrete plan of action geared toward doing something about the rights of crime's victims.

251

This chapter deals with such a plan. It presents something of a blueprint for change that must be implemented throughout the criminal justice system if we are ever to make the concept of a victim-oriented society a reality.

If the criminal justice system is to be the target of a victim-oriented call for change, away from the current preoccupation with the rights of criminals, who should become the spokesmen for such a change? Who will go out front in the assault against those elements in the system that through their permissive attitudes have given the criminal the edge over the law-abiding citizen?

Consider some sources of spokesmen for the victims. In the preceding chapter I suggested that something really constructive could be done about the rights of the victims of crime if government at every level would set up victims' rights commissions along the lines, and with the powers, of the various active civil rights and human rights commissions currently in existence. If bona fide victims' rights commissions should be set up, bearing the imprimatur of the government entity under whose authority they are formed and truly concerned about the rights of the victim, then such commissions would be one of the most potent spokesmen for the victims rights.

The very existence of these commissions would be clear evidence that the government had recognized that the victims of crime had rights that must be enforced. If vested with the proper authority, the commissions would be in an enviable position to speak in the courts, in the legislatures and to the general public. And with the force of goverment behind them, they could effect changes in the criminal justice system that are so necessary to enforce the rights of the victims of crime.

Another source of representation for the victims' rights lies in victim-oriented citizens groups such as Americans for Effective Law Enforcement (AELE) and Citizens for Law and Order (CLO), both of which were described in chapter eight. While both are admittedly small—AELE has about 20,000 members and contributors, CLO some 3,000—they have demonstrated an effectiveness in acting as spokesmen for victims' rights far out of proportion to their size. Active in the courts and legislatures and in focusing public opinion upon the rights of the victims, AELE and CLO are prime examples of the way victim representation by the private sector can be an extremely potent force for change in the system.

Law-enforcement and corrections officers—attorneys general, prosecutors, police chiefs, sheriffs, other law-enforcement agency heads, and wardens and superintendents—know firsthand the problems in the criminal justice system and they know the impact of these problems on the victims. Many law-enforcement officers—FBI director Clarence Kelley, Los Angeles County sheriff Peter Pitchess, and Cook County corrections director Winston Moore, for example—have been highly articulate and vocal spokesmen for a return to common sense in the criminal justice system. This articulation should continue and increase. Who can better know how to alleviate the plight of the victims than those charged with the administration and enforcement of criminal laws and correctional responsibilities that are designed to protect the law-abiding from victimization.

Additionally, there are umbrella organizations that represent groups of law-enforcement officers and agencies. Some represent law-enforcement officers at the executive level: the National District Attorneys Association (NDAA), the International Association of Chiefs of Police (IACP), the National Sheriffs Association (NSA), and various state and local associations of prosecutors, police chiefs, and sheriffs. Other organizations represent the line officers: the International Conference of Police Associations, the Fraternal Order of Police, and, again, state and local police officers' associations. Such organizations also form a cadre of potential representatives for the rights of the victims. Many of these organizations have already been heard from. For example, the NDAA, the IACP, and the NSA have each, at one time or another, joined in the friend of the court briefs filed in the U.S. Supreme Court by Americans for Effective Law Enforcement. In each of these cases the Court was successfully urged to take a realistic attitude toward the law-enforcement problems and to grant to the law-enforcement agencies involved the proper legal tools to enable them to perform their function of protecting the innocent. It is obvious that law enforcement at both the operational and the associational levels must become a spokesman for the victims in any victim-conscious society.

Statements of our nation's leaders who are deeply concerned with the failure of our criminal justice system have appeared throughout this book. We have heard from judges, legislators, businessmen, academicians, and journalists, in short, leaders from every segment of the community. All of these are voices for the victims, spokesmen for the victims' rights. Obviously, if we are to attain a victim-conscious society, these voices must continue to be heard—and heeded.

Finally, and most important, the key to an effective victim orientation lies in that most potent force in all of our society: an educated and aroused citizenry—the law-abiding majority—calling out, through the ballot box and the various outlets that shape public opinion, for an end to the permissiveness that has caused the inordinate amount of present victimization.

In 1972 the voters of California restored the death penalty in that state by a 2-to-1 margin. In 1965 the voters of New York City defeated a politically motivated civilian review board for the police, also by a 2-to-1 margin. These are examples of the public expressing its opinion that criminals should pay for their crimes and that the police should be able to go about their business of enforcing the laws without political harassment. Each case, and there are many others, is an example of the law-abiding majority becoming, through its vote, a spokesman for the victims of crime.

There is, then, a potentially enormous reservoir of spokesmen for the victims of crime. If these spokesmen can get their message across to the permissive elements of the criminal justice system at every level—executive, legislative, and judicial—and to those antivictim forces, outside the formal boundaries of the system, whose sole preoccupation is with the criminal and his rights, that victims' rights are *at least* equal to those of the lawless and that they must be enforced, then we will be well on the way to having the victim-oriented society.

Now for the specifics in our blueprint for change in the criminal justice system. The following sections contain suggested ways for accomplishing two basic ends by which the system can fulfill its duty to the law-abiding: (1) swift apprehension and conviction of those guilty of crimes; and (2) sure and certain punishment for those who have been convicted.

The suggestions made herein will be specific; they cannot, of necessity, be lengthy. The call is for a basic change in the permissiveness of the system. This, in turn, requires a basic change in laws, court decisions and the attitudes of criminal justice policymakers in which such permissiveness is countenanced. Our criminal justice system is so fragmented that it is impossible to go into detail over every suggestion made, for this would require an analysis of the laws, court decisions, administrative rulings, and attitudes of policymakers of the federal system, the several states, and even the local government entities. Such a detailed analysis is simply not possible within the scope of this work. The suggested changes merely state what should be done if we are to restore a balance to the system.

The same considerations foreclose any discussion at length of the implementation of the suggested changes, for this implementation will be a function of the source of the original imbalance in the first place. If, for example, a change is needed in a decision of the United States Supreme Court, then only that Court, or in some cases an act of Congress, can bring about the change. Implementation of the change will obviously lie in persuading the Court to reverse or modify its former ruling or in persuading the Congress to make the necessary change. In either case this will be a long and cumbersome process, one which may not even be capable of realization. Similarly, a suggested change in a state's laws would be entirely dependent upon whether the legislature of that state was disposed to make the change. In sum, the changes suggested herein are those that *should* be made in order to vindicate the rights of crime's victims. Whether they are made or not will determine whether we see the beginnings of a victim-oriented society.

Finally, before turning to specific suggestions, it is perhaps necessary again to emphasize that the changes suggested herein merely seek to establish a *balance* between the conflicting rights of the victim and the criminal accused. It is obvious that we must always ensure fundamental fairness to the accused in the criminal justice process. However, the system is now so unbalanced in favor of the accused that the concept of fundamental fairness is perverted. Far too many of the safeguards around the accused are so contrived and artificial that they benefit *only* the guilty. These so-called safeguards can well be modified or done away with without doing the slightest damage to the concept of fundamental fairness. Likewise a balance is sought herein between undue harshness in the punishment process and the current theory of undue leniency which is being so ardently championed by so many. We have, in this book, seen case after case of innocent people being victimized because criminals, whose totally dangerous nature has been demonstrated by their prior acts, were placed into society due to the excessive leniency shown to them by a system which has been only too willing to take a chance that they will not victimize again. This is an intolerable situation and one in which a restoration of some sort of balance is obviously necessary.

SPECIFIC RECOMMENDATIONS FOR A
VICTIM-ORIENTED CRIMINAL JUSTICE SYSTEM

1. *We Should Take a Long Hard Look at the British System of Criminal Justice*

None of the countries in the British Empire can, by any stretch of the imagination, be called a police state. Yet justice in these countries is reasonably swift and sure.

There are basically three reasons for this happy state of affairs in these countries, with which we share a common legal heritage. First and foremost, the criminal trial in the British system is a search for the truth: did the accused commit the crime with which he is charged? As an English barrister noted, a barrister's duty as advocate is "closer to that of serving justice than simply one's client, as in America."[1] Such devices for the suppression of the truth as the *Miranda* ruling, which often requires the exclusion of a completely voluntary confession (or, in some cases, prevents the police from questioning a suspect at all), and the

Exclusionary Rule, which requires the exclusion of any physical evidence if the police obtained it by "illegal" means, simply do not exist in the British system. Relevant and competent evidence that leads to a finding of the truth about the matter in question is routinely admitted in criminal trials.

Next, the British criminal justice system is infinitely more speedy than that of the United States. Trials take a fraction of the time that they do in our system. Juries are generally impaneled in as short a period as a half an hour.[2] Courts are much less liberal in granting adjournments and postponements. And trial delays caused by defense attorneys for their own tactical purposes are simply not tolerated. British solicitor David Napley crisply sums up the situation thus: "[In England] it is unthinkable that delays are in any way attributable to deliberate tactics of defense lawyers. Any lawyer guilty of such conduct would soon find himself without a profession."[3]

Appeals in the British system take months rather than years. The right of appeal is restricted to a far greater extent than in the United States. Such appeals as are granted are handled with dispatch; often they are decided after oral argument on the same day that the appeal is heard.

Finally, in British courts, courtroom disruptions, like delay tactics, are not tolerated. The disruptive attorney or prisoner is dealt with quickly and firmly and most trials are conducted in a decorous manner with proper respect being shown all parties. The circus atmosphere of the notorious Chicago 7 trial in the United States would not be condoned for a moment. Nor can one imagine the like of Chicago 7 attorney William Kunstler or the convicted defendants traveling the length and breadth of England being lionized by radical groups—including many law students—as they describe how they tried (for the most part successfully) to bring the system of orderly justice to its knees.

In short, the British system of criminal justice works. It strikes a proper balance between the rights of the accused and the rights of the law-abiding. It is justly famous as being perhaps the most completely fair system in the world. In fact, it is not uncommon for convicted defendants, after sentence, to thank the court for the fairness shown to them.

Those who are interested in establishing a victim-oriented criminal justice system in this country would do well to take a long hard look at the British system. As a matter of fact, Senator James L. Buckley, Republican-Conservative of New York, who is probably as concerned with the imbalance in our criminal justice system as anyone in the country, suggested in 1972 that a Presidential commission be set up to study the British system and to compare it with that of the United States.[4]

Senator Buckley's point is well taken. The vehicle he suggests for the study, a Presidential commission, is less so, for a very good reason. The fact is patent: for the past seven years or so, Presidential commissions dealing with the issue of crime, violence, lawlessness, public morals, or individual responsibility under the law, have vied with each other to see which could come up with the most permissive sort of nonsense.

Washington, D.C., is a haven for liberal to radical young bureaucrats who gravitate to the staffs of such commissions with unerring speed and accuracy. After looking at the conclusions in the reports of the Kerner Commission on Civil Disorders (riots are the fault of everyone except the rioters), the (Milton) Eisenhower Commission on the Causes and Prevention of Violence (violence is the fault of everyone except the violent), and the Commission on Pornography and Obscenity (a *carte blanche* for the pornographer), we can be fairly certain that a study of the British criminal justice system by these Washington-based professional staffers would result in a paean of praise for *our* permissive system; the British system would be dismissed as "repressive" or "unresponsive to the needs of our criminals," despite the fact that it seems to work.

This does not mean that Senator Buckley's suggestion should be lightly cast aside. On the contrary, if such a study were made by a qualified body, with an open mind, it is all but certain that the result would be devastating to our system, which is failing in precisely those areas in which the British system succeeds. That is to say, in the latter, the criminal justice process is a search for the truth and a balanced process; it is not wholly preoccupied with sociological notions of excessive and unwarranted leniency towards the criminal. Such balance in the British system accomplishes its primary purpose of protecting the law-abiding far better than our system.

In the preceding chapter, where I discussed the idea of the creation of victims' rights commissions, I emphasized that these commissions should *not* consist entirely of the most hard-nosed law-and-order conservatives to be found. Rather, their makeup should be of persons who seek a balance in the system. So it is with any proposed study of the British system. Should a group of men and women make an honest and objective comparison of the two criminal justice systems, the results would startle and almost assuredly favor the balance and fairness inherent in the British system.

Thus, we seem to have reached an impasse over Senator Buckley's meritorious proposal. It would certainly be a major undertaking requiring rather lavish financing. The only entity likely able to finance it would be the federal government. Its track record in similar undertakings, however, leaves one relatively certain that this worthy enterprise would result in a costly report, with dozens of young bureaucrats happily and expensively ensconced on the shores of the Potomac, and with a conclusion demonstrating that *our* method of dealing with the victims of crime—that is, subordinating their rights to overwhelming concern with the criminal—is vastly superior to the rather victim-oriented British system.

Perhaps, if we begin to develop a victim-conscious system, those who are concerned and who recognize the potential of the comparative study, would be able properly to finance the study. This, however, for the time being, must wait. Now we can only envy the British system from afar.

2. *The Criminal Justice Process Should Return to a Search for the Truth*

As opposed to the British criminal justice system, in criminal cases in our system the truth is far too often completely suppressed, to the advantage of no one except the guilty party. A fundamental change in our system is thus imperative.

The principal doctrines upon which the suppression of the truth is predicated are the Exclusionary Rule and the *Miranda* decision. Both should be eliminated or modified.

ELIMINATION OF THE EXCLUSIONARY RULE

The case against the Exclusionary Rule has been set forth in chapter four. The rule requires the suppression of all evidence against an accused that was obtained in violation of his rights. The stated purpose of the rule is to deter unlawful police conduct, but it is doubtful if it accomplishes this. The rule does nothing whatever to protect innocent persons aggrieved by unlawful search or seizure, or both, and against whom no incriminating evidence has been found. Finally, the application of the rule has resulted, and will continue to result, in the freeing of countless criminals, whose factual guilt of crime is clearly indicated, because relevant and probative evidence of their guilt has been suppressed.

Elimination of the Exclusionary Rule is an absolutely necessary first step in a program to return our criminal process to a search for the truth. How can this be done? First of all, since the U.S. Supreme Court imposed the Exclusionary Rule as a constitutional requirement upon the entire criminal justice system of this country, only that Court can give a final sanction to its elimination. This the Court could do only if a case involving the question of whether the rule should be retained, eliminated, or modified should be presented. The Court has evidenced a willingness to hear such a case. Twice it has agreed to hear cases involving, among other issues, the continued viability of the rule, but in each instance it decided the case on one of the other issues.[5] Nevertheless, it is likely that within the next year or two the Court will squarely confront the issue.

The question of the Exclusionary Rule could reach the Court in the case of the U.S. Congress or a state legislature enacting a law that purports to modify or eliminate the rule. Such legislation would be certain to be challenged by proponents of the rule and the issue would then be squarely before the Court. As a matter of fact, legislation that would modify or eliminate the Exclusionary Rule in federal trials has been introduced in the United States Congress by Senator Lloyd Bentsen (D.-Tex.) and Congressman Sam Steiger (R.-Ariz.). Senator Bentsen's bill modifies the Exclusionary Rule by applying it generally only to willful and substantial violations.[6] Congressman Steiger's bill does away with the Exclusionary Rule entirely, making all evidence admissible.[7] Both bills provide a remedy in civil damages against the government for persons aggrieved by search-and-seizure violations by federal agents. A bill, similar to the Steiger bill, on the state level was introduced by state senator (now U.S. congressman) Robert Lagomarsino.[8]

In any event, whether it accepts a case involving the Exclusionary Rule of its own accord, or whether a case arises through a request for review of legislation eliminating or modifying the rule, the U.S. Supreme Court will have the final say on the matter. Attempts to predict which way the Court will rule are always risky, but in view of the strong views against the Exclusionary Rule expressed by Chief Justice Burger and in view of the current conservative makeup of a majority of the Court, it is not unlikely that the Court would eliminate or modify the rule, if a proper case were presented to it.

A case decided by the Court in 1974 gives some evidence to support this contention. In the *United States* v. *Calandra*,[9] the Court held that the Exclusionary Rule could not be invoked to suppress illegally seized evidence that was used to question before a grand jury a witness who had been granted immunity from prosecution. Justice William J. Brennan, dissenting in the *Calandra* case, unhappily predicted the demise of the Exclusionary Rule at the hands of his more conservative brethren: "I am left with the uneasy feeling that today's decision may signal that a majority of my colleagues have positioned themselves to reopen the door and abandon altogether the exclusionary rule in search and seizure cases. . . ."[10] Those who desire a return to a search for the truth in our criminal justice system doubtless crave that Justice Brennan's prediction comes true.

One critical aspect of the question of the Exclusionary Rule, should it come before the Court, would be whether or not there was an effective alternative method of redressing the rights of persons aggrieved by illegal searches and seizures. Such methods of redress are built into each of the three laws, noted above, dealing with the elimination or modification of the rule; their presence might be determinative of the outcome of the case.

The Exclusionary Rule, then, should be eliminated, or at least modified. No evidence that is relevant or probative as to a suspect's guilt should be suppressed. At the same time there must be a remedy available to those whose rights have been violated by illegal searches and seizures. This remedy can easily be supplied by permitting aggrieved parties to sue the public entity—federal, state, or local—for monetary damages caused by the violation of rights by the officers employed by that public entity. Only if an officer's violation was *clearly* willful, malicious, and intentionally oppressive, should he be personally liable (as of course he is under the present system). The onus for nonwillful violations by police officers should be confined to the entity that employs him. And, of course, compensation would be based solely upon the theory of violation of rights. No one could or should be compensated for the consequences of his guilty acts, such as costs of a criminal trial in which he was convicted, loss of contraband, or time spent in jail. In other words, a guilty party aggrieved by an illegal search and seizure would be compensated only to the extent that an innocent party would likewise be compensated.

This would give *any* aggrieved citizen an enforceable right against a federal, state, or local government, which would be able to pay a judgment to an aggrieved party (as opposed to most police officers, who, because of their financial situation, would not have the resources to pay such a judgment). At the same time the suppression of the truth embodied in the Exclusionary Rule would be ended, competent and relevant evidence would be admitted against the accused, and many more guilty criminals would be convicted and, we hope, punished. The benefits of this change to the victims of those criminals who would have been freed by application of the Exclusionary Rule are obvious.

MODIFICATION OF MIRANDA

Miranda v. *Arizona* requires the suppression of the confession of a criminal suspect if a litany of warnings is not given, letter perfect, by the police prior to interrogation. This even if there is overwhelming evidence that the confession was otherwise voluntarily made. The effects of *Miranda* upon law enforcement and, as a result, upon the victims of crime have been discussed in chapter four and need no repetition here.

Now no one who is concerned with the fairness of the criminal justice system wishes to have a suspect convicted on the basis of a confession that is involuntary—one obtained by force or threats or unwarranted promises of leniency. Obviously, such a confession might be untrue. *Miranda*, however, goes much farther in suppressing the truth. The perfectly proper concept of voluntariness as the standard for the admission into evidence of confessions made by suspects has been perverted by the *Miranda* decision into an absolute rule of suppression if a court should find that the police in any manner ran afoul of the rigid requirement of the warnings. Countless criminals have been freed because of the rigidity of this decision.

As in the Exclusionary Rule, the final say on the continued viability of *Miranda* will be up to the U.S. Supreme Court because *Miranda* was decided on the basis of our Constitution. It is true that Congress, in Title II of the Safe Streets Act of 1968, purported to "overrule" *Miranda* by providing that in federal criminal cases, the trial judge could admit a confession he had found to be voluntary, after all the circumstances surrounding the confession were considered, even through the *Miranda* requirements had not been literally complied with. This provision, however, has rarely been invoked, and because of the constitutional basis upon which *Miranda* was decided, the Supreme Court will almost assuredly have to rule upon the constitutionality of the provision.

Michigan v. *Tucker,* described in chapter four, dealt with the question whether the prosecution might call as a witness against the accused a third party whose existence was learned of only through the statements of the accused who had not been given the proper *Miranda* warnings. In June of 1974 the Supreme Court held that such third-party witness evidence *could* be used, despite the fact that the witness had been discovered through a *Miranda* "violation."[11]

Justice William H. Rehnquist wrote the majority opinion in the *Tucker* case. He held that while *Miranda* applied to the situation insofar as the actual statements made by the accused himself were concerned, the requirements of *Miranda* nevertheless were not so absolute that competent evidence given by third parties must also be excluded even though the evidence of the third party was a "fruit" of a *Miranda* violation.

The *Tucker* case is a complicated one, made more so by the fact that the statements of the accused were made before *Miranda* was decided. The Court refused in *Tucker* to consider the much broader issue of whether *Miranda* should be overruled in its entirety; as a consequence, *Miranda* still applies, in all of its rigidity to statements made by the accused: if the police run afoul of the required warnings in the slightest, even the most patently voluntary confession may not be used against him. The Court in *Tucker* dealt only with evidence other than the actual statements made by the suspect.

This does not mean, however, that the Burger Court has forever foreclosed the issue. Since *Tucker* did not squarely present the question of the admissibility of the suspect's own statements, that question is still alive. Some of the language used by Justice Rehnquist in *Tucker* gives hope that, if the issue is presented to the Court, the rigidity of *Miranda* may yet be greatly modified. Justice Rehnquist called for a rule of reason and common sense when police practices in obtaining statements from the accused are under scrutiny. He stated:

> Just as the law does not require that a defendant receive a perfect trial, only a fair one, it cannot realistically require that policemen investigating serious crimes make no errors whatsoever. The pressures of law enforcement and the vagaries of human nature would make such an expectation unrealistic. Before we penalize police error, therefore, we must consider whether the sanction serves a valid and useful purpose.[12]

In view of this, the *Miranda* question is far from over. As in the case of the Exclusionary Rule, we may yet see, from the Court, a return to a search for the truth.

In any event, until the Court faces the issue squarely, *Miranda* stands as a monument to the principle of the suppression of the truth, and it certainly should be modified to permit the admission of voluntary confessions. This would work no unfairness on the criminal suspect, for if his confession was in fact voluntarily made, then no injustice is done if it is used against him. If, on the other hand, his confession is found to be involuntary, then it would still be inadmissible even under any modification of *Miranda* that the Court might make. In other words, an innocent man, who had been coerced into making a false confession, would still receive the protection of having it suppressed; but the rigidity of the *Miranda* requirements would no longer be a shield to the guilty party that had voluntarily confessed to his crime.

Were the Exclusionary Rule eliminated and *Miranda* modified, our criminal process would largely be returned to a search for the truth. The question before the courts would no longer be whether the police have erred in some slight manner but, more fundamentally, whether the accused committed the crime with which he is charged. A search for the truth is precisely what the goal of any criminal justice system should be. It works pretty well in England and the other countries with a legal system similar to ours; and, except in the view of those whose concern is solely with the criminal accused, it would work pretty well here. Certainly, a return to the truth in this country's criminal justice system would spare the victims of crime the sight of those who had victimized them walking out of court as free men, at liberty to victimize again.

3. We Should Make Justice Swift and Sure

JUSTICE MADE SWIFT—DEALING WITH COURT DELAYS

The point has been made in chapter five that one of the most corrosive aspects of our criminal justice system is the unbearably slow manner in which justice is dispensed in this country. Part of the problem—a large part in fact—is that we have so many crimes being committed that their weight breaks down the entire court system. This fact becomes a part of the vicious cycle whereby crime is made so attractive to the criminal, because it is so unlikely that he will have to pay for it that he is tempted to commit more and more crimes; when he *is* caught, he is able to take advantage of the delays caused by the sheer volume of criminal cases, which volume in turn is caused by his activities and those of people like him.

This vicious circle will be stopped, or at least slowed, only when the entire criminal justice system devotes itself to convincing the criminal that crime does *not* pay. Until then, there are certain measures that can be taken to speed up the process of justice.

First, court delays can be cut by more efficient administration of the criminal courts. Chief Justice Burger has led the effort in this area and the utilization of professional court administrators, computerized operations, and modern management techniques give promise that at least those delays that are caused by inefficiency in the judicial process can be reduced significantly.

Second, the use of continuances and postponements of criminal cases for the purpose of delay must be drastically curtailed. Criminal cases should be given an official precedence over civil cases in our court systems, and an attorney who has been assigned a trial date in a criminal case should be made to appear despite the fact that the criminal case may conflict with a more lucrative civil case.

Continuances should be the exception rather than the rule. This should be rigidly enforced with heavy fines for contempt for attorneys, parties, or witnesses who cause a trial to be delayed except for reasons that clearly indicate the delay is absolutely necessary. In this context computers would be of significant benefit, being used to store information about trial dates and to put out information far enough in advance of the trial date so that all parties are notified in plenty of time to appear and be ready.

Third, more judges, prosecutors, defenders, and courtrooms should be provided. The expense of doing so would be well worthwhile—no matter the cost—when measured against the chaos now caused by court delays.

Fourth, the process of presenting every felony case to a grand jury is extremely cumbersome and adds immeasurably to delays in the criminal justice system. Under the grand-jury system, each felony defendant not waiving this right must have his case presented to a grand jury and the grand jury must vote to indict him before his case can be presented for trial. This is enormously time-consuming, when compared with the system, operative in several states, that permits the prosecuting attorney to file a criminal information—that is, a formal, written complaint against the defendant—and then to proceed directly to trial, sometimes after a preliminary hearing.

Our Constitution states that in federal cases involving felony charges, an indictment by the grand jury is mandatory.[13] There is no such restriction on the states, however;[14] and one method of expediting the criminal process would be to abolish, by statute or constitutional amendment, the requirement that felony cases be presented to a grand jury in those states now requiring it.

Fifth, the proliferation of procedural motions, which now consume so much time, should be ended. If the Exclusionary Rule were eliminated and the rigidity of the *Miranda* requirements modified, then the time consumed by motions to suppress physical evidence and confessions would also be eliminated. In any event, the motion process could be streamlined so that all procedural motions *must* be presented at the same time; if not so presented, they would, in the absence of exceptional circumstances—such as newly discovered evidence—be deemed waived.

Sixth, legislation or court rules, or both, in some jurisdictions require that a defendant be brought to trial within a certain period of time or the charges against him must be dismissed. The basic theory embodied in such provisions has considerable merit because it forces the dilatory prosecutor to go to trial or risk losing his case. Such provisions, however, should have some built-in flexibility; if the prosecutor can show that he has failed to meet his "deadline" through no fault of his own but simply because of the sheer volume of cases before the courts, then no dismissal should result.

It would be terribly unfair to the prosecutor to require the dismissal of an important criminal case when the delay in bringing the case to trial had been caused by conditions in his jurisdiction totally beyond his control, such as congested court dockets or lack of his own staff resources. Only when it is clear that an unwarranted delay was caused by the prosecutor, as the representative of the state, should dismissal be required. Any other construction of such forced dismissal provisions would make society suffer for a condition beyond its control; only the criminal stands to benefit if he must be freed because the activities of so many other criminals have so congested the criminal justice process that he cannot be brought to trial within a rigidly fixed time.

Seventh, when the defendant is brought to trial, no inordinate amount of time should be permitted to be consumed in the jury selection process. The trial judge alone should have the responsibility for questioning prospective jurors and his questions should be strictly limited to an evaluation of whether they can fairly try the case. The currently fashionable process of permitting attorneys to question jurors *ad infinitum,* in effect to try the case in its entirety through the questioning of each prospective juror, should be eliminated.

Eighth, evidence in criminal trials themselves should be limited to the central question of whether the defendant committed the crime. Only such evidence as is material, relevant, and competent with regard to that central issue should be admitted. Any delays in the trial itself caused by the misbehavior of any attorney or defendant should be dealt with by heavy fines and imprisonment for contempt of court. A study of criminal trials in England would be helpful in this area. There criminal cases are tried expeditiously and with exemplary fairness, usually in a matter of days or, at most, weeks.

Ninth, the Supreme Court of the United States ruled in 1972 that non-unanimous jury verdicts in criminal cases—that is, verdicts of 10 to 2 and 9 to 3—were constitutionally permissible.[15] Implementation of this procedure could materially speed up the criminal justice process and bring about an end to those cases in which one or two jurors can, because of stubbornness or eccentricity, exercise a veto over the responsible judgment of their fellow jurors. Such cases result in hung juries, which necessitate another criminal trial from beginning to end, thus contributing to the backlog of cases. States now requiring unanimous jury verdicts in criminal cases should implement a nonunanimous system.

Tenth, once convicted the accused should be granted a single appeal through the appellate structure of the jurisdiction, and to request review by the Supreme Court of the United States. All points on appeal should be raised in this appeal or must be regarded as waived (except, of course, in extraordinary circumstances such as when new evidence, which would materially change the outcome of the case, has been discovered). The process of collateral review by writs of habeas corpus of state criminal court decisions by federal courts should be abolished by federal legislation in all cases, except those in which the alleged violation of the defendant's federal constitutional rights by the state courts is flagrant and substantial and the questions raised go to the matter of the defendant's actual guilt or innocence.

It is probably too much to ask our criminal justice system to switch over to the British system, in which most appeals are heard on oral argument, without written briefs, and in which the judges usually return a final decision at the time the case is heard. We might, however, experiment in some jurisdictions with this expeditious concept to see whether it would work here, at least in the less serious cases.

Obviously, not all of the suggested solutions for speeding up the court process will work, or even be legal, in all jurisdictions. But even if *some* of them were adopted, or attempted, on an experimental basis, they could have a considerable impact upon the entire process and make justice a lot more swift than it is now.

JUSTICE MADE SURE—DEALING WITH LENIENCY
TOWARD THE CONVICTED CRIMINAL

a. *The Sentencing Process*

As we have seen, there is currently afoot in the criminal justice system a concerted effort to structure the entire system so that only in the rarest case will we incarcerate criminals. Leniency towards them is to be the principal goal of the sentencing and corrections process.

From the criminal's standpoint, this trend could not be more encouraging. However, from that of actual and potential victims of crime, the leniency-at-any-cost theory has the most serious drawbacks.

It is of course frustrating to the victim of an actual crime to be told, in effect, that his rights are of so little consequence that the one who has violated them need not be punished. Those wailing for nursery treatment for the criminal appear to ignore this aspect of the matter completely.

The leniency enthusiasts also ignore the fairly well established fact that certainty of punishment is a deterrent to criminal activity, not to mention its corollary, that the certainty of nonpunishment reduces the deterrent factor to precisely zero.

Finally, two important questions must be raised: How many criminals, who have been shown leniency, will use it to victimize again? And if we cannot be sure of the answer, who should be required to take the risk?

A victim-oriented approach to each of these questions suggests that the actual victim is entitled to have his rights vindicated through punishment of the individual who has violated them; that potential victims of crime are entitled to have would-be criminals deterred through the certainty of punishment; and that if there is a risk that a criminal who has been shown leniency will victimize again, then the law-abiding citizen should not be forced to assume that risk.

The suggestions made herein, then, are oriented against *carte blanche* leniency and towards a more balanced approach. This does not mean that leniency should never be utilized. Obviously it should be, in certain cases. But leniency for its own sake, which appears to be the current trend, is dangerous for it ignores the rights of the victims of crime.

The concept of deterrence of crime through the certainty of punishment should certainly be recognized in the criminal justice system. So should the concept of isolation of those who are dangerous. Thus, in certain instances, when the crime is relatively minor and involves a first offense, the severity of punishment need not be great. But when serious crimes are committed or repeat offenders are involved, certainty of punishment should be combined with severity of punishment. In effect, the factor of isolation—that is, severity—should be added to the factor of certainty. And the skyrocketing rates of violent crimes committed by juveniles dictate that in cases of violent and serious crimes, juveniles should receive much the same treatment as adults—there is really no difference to the victim if she has been raped and beaten by a sixteen-year-old or a twenty-one-year-old.

This combination can be accomplished by a system of fixed-term sentences, set by statute, which could not be increased or lowered by the sentencing judge. Terms of probation, available *only* after some minimum fixed term has been served in all but minor offenses, should also be set by statute, with certain criteria—including the nature of the crime, the amenability of the convict to rehabilitation, his prior record, and the impact of the crime upon its victims—that *must* be considered by the court in its determination whether to grant probation.

The most serious crimes—crimes involving loss of life, serious personal injury or the threat of it, those in which a dangerous weapon was used, and repeat crimes—should provide for no probation at all or for probation only after a fixed minimum term had been served.

Less serious crimes would provide for immediate probation, but only if statutory criteria designed to protect the public were met. In any case, the state could appeal a grant of probation if it felt that the public safety was jeopardized or that the judge improperly applied the criteria for granting probation.

Such a scheme would not guarantee absolutely the certainty of punishment, but it would go a long way towards achieving this end. It would have the additional advantage of enforcing uniformity in the sentencing process, so that inordinately harsh or inordinately lenient sentences could not be handed down based upon the particular philosophy of the judge. Most important, such a system would be based upon the determination of the legislative body, which is directly answerable to the people, that the safety of the law-abiding was the primary concern of the sentencing and corrections process.

In those systems in which no such predetermined certainty of punishment exists, and in which sentencing judges have an almost absolute discretion as to whether to grant leniency to criminals, the only means of attempting to deal with undue leniency, particularly that which results in further victimization, is to establish a basis for accountability. Sentencing judges are almost universally immune from the direct legal consequences of their dispositions. They are thus answerable only to public opinion, which could be brought to bear upon them through publicity generated by organizations like Citizens for Law and

Order, which employs volunteer court watchers to report on the sentencing policies of various judges.

The theory of accountability for overlenient sentencing policies through the force of public opinion is anathema to some judges and to those who share their permissive philosophy. The cry ascends that any sort of public scrutiny will destroy the independence of the judge in the sentencing process. The response to this attitude is that no one, not even a judge, should be so absolutely isolated from the consequences of his acts that he could in no way be called to account for them. A judge is a servant of the public as are prosecutors or policemen. In the sentencing process, the judge has the responsibility of making dispositions that take into consideration the safety of the community as well as what might be best for the convicted criminal. If a judge engages in an overly lenient sentencing policy that results in criminals, who should be locked up, being released time and again to continue to victimize the community, then it is not only appropriate, but absolutely necessary, for the community to know what is going on and to attempt to change either the attitude of that judge or the judge himself.

Because the force of public opinion is such a powerful thing, it should be handled with care. Certainly, in the instant context, public opinion should not be used to second-guess a judge every time he makes a sentencing disposition that turns out badly. A judge may, in all good faith and with due consideration for the public safety, impose a very lenient sentence or grant probation to a criminal because he honestly believes the criminal will be amenable to rehabilitation and commit no further crimes. If that criminal then makes use of the leniency shown him to commit another crime, or series of crimes, it would be horribly unfair to the judge to launch a campaign against him on the basis of an infrequent error. Just as sentencing judges should not be held absolutely unaccountable for their acts, they should not be called to account because, in exercising the enormous responsibility the sentencing process imposes upon them, they occasionally err on the side of leniency.

But when a *pattern* of permissiveness begins to evolve, when a judge indicates by his dispositions in case after case that his concern is solely for the convicted criminal and that the rights of the law-abiding members of the community not to be victimized are of no importance, then the full force of public opinion can legitimately, and should, be brought to bear upon him. For this basic reason: whatever his motivations might be, that judge is failing in his duty to consider the safety of the community in the sentencing process.

Just how much good the pressure of such public opinion will do will depend on many factors. Some judges (federal judges, for example) are appointed by the chief executive of the jurisdiction, face confirmation by the legislative branch, and then serve for life or for very long terms. Others are elected and terms vary from jurisdiction to jurisdiction. Thus many, if not most, judges are fairly safe in their positions, at least for a matter of years, and they may feel relatively safe from the force of public opinion.

Nevertheless, no one, not even a judge, unless he is so committed to the policy of permissiveness that he simply doesn't care what *anybody* thinks, can remain aloof for very long when he knows that his dispositions will be reported to and scrutinized by a public that expects him to consider its rights. Add to this that most judges are honest, conscientious men who desire to perform their function with due regard for all of the interests they are charged with protecting, and it is obvious that public opinion can be for them a very potent factor.

Despite the fact that some judges may be impervious to public opinion, the forces of permissiveness, who are not sentencing judges themselves, but who urge upon the courts the most lenient sentencing policies imaginable, are not. Consider, for example, the position of the National Council on Crime and Delinquency (NCCD) that no criminal except one with an established record of violence should be locked up. Now, what this permissiveness means is that no burglars, thieves, shoplifters, or embezzlers should ever be sent to prison. Surely, those who are concerned with the rights of the victims of such crimes—people who have been stolen from in various nonviolent ways—should take a stand against the NCCD position.

No one who consciously sets out to commit a crime, even if the crime is nonviolent, should be encouraged by the fact that he knows that certain groups are making every effort to ensure that he is not punished. On the contrary, he should know that the provictim forces are conducting a countercampaign in the courts and legislatures to make sure that, except in unusual cases, he does go to prison for his crime. This sort of countereffort can be made *before* the permissivists are able to influence the sentencing courts.

In any event, the question of criminal sentences is one of the most important aspects of the criminal justice system so far as victims are concerned. If the current wave of leniency in the sentencing process continues, the avenue of approach seems to be legislatively enacted mandatory minimum sentences; failing that, public opinion must be rallied to convince sentencing judges that victims have rights too.

b. *Parole and Corrections*

The sentencing process deals with putting criminals into some form of incarceration. Little will be accomplished, however, if realistic sentencing policies that take into consideration the safety of the community are implemented only to be rendered ineffective because a criminal can be released by a parole board or similar institution after serving the most minimal portion of his sentence. In chapter five we saw how overly lenient parole practices result in continual victimization of the innocent because of a decision to take the chance that a convict would not commit other crimes.

The solutions to this problem are similar to those suggested for dealing with overly permissive sentencing policies. First of all, if mandatory minimum sentences were in effect, the public would not be victimized by undue leniency in the parole process; the parole boards would not have the power to free a criminal sentenced under such fixed-term sentences. In fact, the parole aspect of the issue would for all practical purposes be foreclosed. The function of release would lie almost exclusively with the courts through grants of probation in accordance with previously set legislative standards.

The fact remains that in many jurisdictions parole boards have the authority to release criminals from prisons almost any time they want to. In these jurisdictions the remedy for inordinate leniency becomes, as in the sentencing process, a question of accountability.

The first type of accountability could be financial liability to those who have been victimized by criminals who were freed by parole boards under circumstances indicating *gross negligence* or a *complete disregard* for the rights of the law-abiding. Here we can make at least a partial analogy to the suggested alternatives to the Exclusionary Rule advanced earlier in this chapter. One alternative to the suppression of evidence is to make the governmental entity that employs a law-enforcement officer liable in monetary damages to those whose rights have been violated by that officer, the theory being that the state should compensate those who have been damaged by the mistakes of its policemen.

Suppose, now, a state parole board engages in unwarranted leniency by releasing prematurely a criminal when that board knew or should have known that the release of the criminal would threaten society with criminal acts. Why should not the state that employs that parole board set up some means of compensation for the victims of the board's negligence?

Obviously, the state should not be liable for the acts of every parolee. In certain cases the release of a convict on parole will be completely warranted by his record in prison and his apparent rehabilitation. In these it would be as unfair to second-guess the parole board for an occasional mistake in ordering a release as it would be to second-guess a judge who errs in a sentencing disposition. If, however, it can be shown that a parolee has used his freedom to victimize, that the board either violated statutes or administrative regulations that govern it, or that it acted with a gross disregard of such factors as a long and violent prior record, attempts to escape, a record of misconduct while incarcerated, or recommendations against release by medical or correctional staff personnel, then the victim of the released prisoner has been victimized because of the negligence of the board or because the board acted with total disregard of the consequences of its leniency. No reason exists why any state should not set up a mechanism for compensating the victim if such negligence could be shown.

Such a proposal would make those of a highly permissive bent on state parole boards less willing to give *all* of the benefit of the doubt to a prospective parolee and less likely to be quite so generous in risking the safety of the law-abiding in their decisions, particularly if the liability extended to the parole board members personally in those cases where gross negligence could be proven. A plan of this kind should hold no terrors for those conscientious public servants who now sit on our federal and state parole boards, those who weigh the rights of society along with the rights of the convict. This suggestion specifically excludes the concept of liability of any sort for the kind of good-faith mistakes that will invariably occur in making the important decision about releasing convicts. Liability should arise only when the parolee's victim can show that the board acted with total disregard for the consequences of its permissiveness and that his victimization was a direct result of the board's negligence. The discretion of a parole board should not lightly be tampered with. But when that discretion is clearly abused and some innocent citizen is victimized as a result, then the state should at least compensate the victim.

A system of state compensation to the victims of unwarranted parole leniency would undoubtedly take legislation to implement. Doubtless this would be fought tooth and nail by the permissivists, who as a rule are more than happy to require all sorts of legal accountability for law-enforcement officers but who raise the roof at the thought of accountability for those who share their permissive bent for criminals. Notwithstanding, spokesmen for victims should push for such legislation, but until it is enacted, they will, as in sentencing leniency, have to fall back on the force of public opinion.

Concededly, the opinion of the townspeople of Bellevue, Iowa, did not count for much with the state's parole board when it freed the murderer of their police chief after he had served but two and a half years of a seventy-five-year sentence. Their concern over such leniency met with a condescending parole board spokesman who delivered a little lecture on his theories of modern penal thinking. Nevertheless, public opinion can have an effect in this area, at least on those who wish to do a conscientious job. Additionally, in many states parole boards are appointed by the governor. If any sort of politician at all, he will listen if enough community members make it known that they do not wish to have their rights trifled with to vindicate the modern social theories of permissive parole board members. A responsible and articulate call for a little more realistic application of the parole-granting process would hardly go unheeded.

The corrections aspect of the problem deals with those who have been sentenced to some form of incarceration but who are placed in positions where they may easily escape (sometimes by simply walking away) from the corrections facility, or who are permitted to roam free in the community through such devices as work release or furloughs. The law-abiding public has a right to expect that those convicted of crimes, particularly violent crimes, will be isolated from society with reasonable security precautions so that they do not return to society at will, free to victimize again. When such security precautions are not taken and a criminal is allowed into the community, the fault lies with the corrections process if he victimizes innocent people. This happens with intolerable frequency in today's society, and the problem is one of major concern to the victims of crime.

This problem was discussed in some detail in chapter five. The solution, parallel to that regarding sentencing and parole abuses, lies in a victim-oriented response to end the abuses. At the same time, the obvious benefits that some prisoners (and society as a whole) receive from work release and furloughs should be retained.

Where a given corrections administrator has unfettered discretion to release anyone he chooses, legislative or administrative standards should be established for protecting society. Surely no real harm would be done to the concept of rehabilitation if convicts with records for violent and dangerous crimes, repeat offenders, and escape artists were denied the privilege of release, which might safely be accorded to the more tractable offenders. In many jurisdictions the number of violent crimes committed by criminals freed through the permissiveness of the corrections process clearly demonstrates that legislative action is necessary if this state of affairs is to be corrected.

Those permissivists willing to risk public safety by releasing patently dangerous individuals are not directly answerable to the public. Legislators are, and the provictim forces should spare no effort to have a legislative brake applied to the social tinkerers and their theories.

Accountability is also of major importance in this context. Accountability at law, in damages to be awarded to the victims of those who have been accorded unwarranted leniency in the corrections process, is an absolute necessity if we are to restore balance to the system. The previously mentioned theory of negligence, based on the willful disregard for the consequences of leniency shown to a dangerous criminal, is equally applicable in the corrections field. The caveat that under no circumstances should we second-guess the good-faith acts that result in occasional mistakes is equally applicable. *Only* when circumstances demonstrate clearly that a criminal was at liberty to victimize another because the official who released him acted with total disregard for the public safety should liability attach to the state or, in the most flagrant cases, to the official personally. When these circumstances can be proved, the victim is surely entitled to recover. Too, the threat of liability will help prevent such victimization because the officials in question will think twice before releasing a convict who presents a danger to the public.

As before, legislation permitting the state to be sued and held liable in such cases would be necessary. Pending this, we should resort to public opinion. The force of public opinion, when brought to bear upon issues of permissiveness in the correctional system, could be extremely effective. In Massachusetts recently, Governor Francis Sargent dismissed a corrections commissioner whose liberal policies, particularly regarding releases, had caused a storm of protest. Likewise in Illinois, in 1972, the state senate refused to confirm Governor Daniel Walker's first nominee for director of corrections because he came to that state with a reputation of being one of the most permissive penologists in the country. In both instances, leniency towards convicted criminals, with a corresponding disregard for the rights of the law-abiding, became the issue—and the forces of permissiveness lost.

The foregoing is directed at those in the corrections field whose permissiveness has scorned the rights of victims. I have already expressed my admiration for the job being done by the majority of correctional administrators and officers in this country. Their attitude is characterized by a progressive professionalism tempered with a desire to fulfill their responsibility to protect the public at large.* The difficulties that confront these people are awesome; they deserve the fullest possible support that the public can give them. There is no contradiction in calling for an aroused public opinion against that minority of corrections officials who seem heedless of the consequences of their permissiveness, and, at the same time, in calling for public support for the professionals in the field.

*In fact, Americans for Effective Law Enforcement, of which I am executive director, prepared a friend-of-the-court brief in defense of a penitentiary superintendent who had unjustly been held liable in civil damages for the alleged violation of several prisoners' constitutional rights.

The professionals need this support. They are under attack from every quarter: the courts, the militant Left, and the misguided groups and individuals ever nagging them about "prison reform" but without the slightest idea of the problems confronting them. Violence in prisons is escalating to such an extent that retired warden Louis S. Nelson of San Quentin has flatly predicted that penitentiaries will be unmanageable in ten years. He blamed lawyers and judges for much of the trouble, giving as an example the judge who ordered him to make two books available to a convicted burglar. One dealt with how to make a bomb, the other described how to pick locks.[16]

Such rulings, which boggle the mind, are not uncommon. Courts throughout the country have interjected themselves at every level of prison administration. They often order correctional officials to take actions that materially increase the potential for violence and disorder in the correctional facilities involved, thus endangering lives of correctional officers and nonviolent prisoners.

Prisons are today hotbeds of revolutionary rhetoric and violence, abetted by court decisions invoking "freedom of speech" and "freedom of expression." This is evidenced by the established fact that the roots of the terrorist Symbionese Liberation Army took hold in California's superpermissive prison system, which permitted, and perhaps encouraged, the formation of radical groups within prison walls. Most professional prison administrators deplore this trend. They want nothing more than to run the facilities entrusted to their charge as humanely as they can and with due regard to the security of their staffs, the nonviolent inmates, and the general public. Yet they are increasingly unable to do this because of the concerted efforts of certain courts and self-appointed prison "reformers" whose single-minded desire is to accord prisoners their "rights." Warden Nelson's prediction that the prisons will become unmanageable in ten years may come true years in advance.

The U.S. Supreme Court has entered the area of prisoners' rights. It has brought a good deal more common sense to the problem than have those many lower courts that have taken an absolutist view of the rights belonging to prisoners. The Supreme Court ruled in 1974 that prison officials may read ingoing and outgoing mail of the inmates, although they may only censor it when there is some certainty that the contents will produce disorder.[17] The test, stated Justice Lewis Powell, is whether censorship can be justified by a substantial government interest in security, order, and rehabilitation.

Likewise the Court took a realistic view of prison discipline problems. In another 1974 case, *Wolfe* v. *McDonnell*,[18] the justices held that while a prisoner is entitled to a hearing if he is threatened with disciplinary measures, correctional administrators are not to be so restricted that they are unable to maintain order in their institutions. Thus, prisoners who are brought up on charges do not have an absolute right to have outside counsel or to confront their accusers.

Finally, the Court held that prisoners' rights are not violated by regulations prohibiting inmate interviews with designated media representatives, provided that alternative means of communication with family, friends, clergy, and the media generally are afforded. The Court upheld regulations that prohibited "special" interviews with media representatives if the regulations were adopted to protect legitimate correctional goals of deterrence, rehabilitation, and prison security.[19] In this case Justice Potter Stewart, in an opinion that may well be a barometer of the Court's common-sense approach to the question of balancing the rights of prisoners against the legitimate needs of correctional personnel, defined the basic theory of corrections:

> An important function of the corrections system is the deterrence of crime. The premise is that by confining criminal offenders in a facility where they are isolated from the rest of society, a condition that most people presumably find undesirable, they and others will be deterred from committing additional criminal offenses. This isolation, of course, also serves a protective function by quarantining offenders for a given period of time while, it is hoped, the rehabilitative processes of the corrections system work to correct the offender's demonstrated criminal proclivity. Thus, since most offenders will eventually return to society, another paramount objective of the corrections system is the rehabilitation of those committed to its custody. Finally, central to all other corrections goals is the institutional consideration of internal security within the corrections facilities themselves. It is in the light of these legitimate penal objectives that a court must assess challenges to prison regulations based on asserted constitutional rights of prisoners.[20]

Indeed. It is hoped that this common-sense mandate will be heeded by those lower courts that have heretofore made a practice of ignoring the realities of the problems with which correctional administrators are faced. It is time that the law-abiding majority informs itself about such problems and that some support is shown for the vast majority of professional correctional officials who are attempting to perform their difficult, and often dangerous, function: the humane and secure custody of those who have victimized society.

Until now, most of those who have concerned themselves with prison reform listened only to an unending list of "grievances" of the prisoners. Thus fortified, they have then entered into campaigns of sniping at the professionals in the field without the slightest recognition of the problems they face. Correctional administrators are justifiably angered at such an unbalanced approach. They know the problems involved in corrections because they live with them on a day-to-day basis. Their voices should be heeded. No more provictim activity can be imagined than that of a responsible and vocal public support for those correctional officials who are doing their jobs with a concern for the rights of society as well as for their charges.

4. *The Bail Problem*

In May 1974 a Cicero, Illinois, man was robbed. At the time of the robbery the two assailants told their victim, "Don't tell the police or you'll regret it." He did, however, tell the police. The two robbers were arrested and then released on bond. The day before the victim was to testify against the robbers, a dynamite bomb blew a hole in the side of his house.[21] Fortunately no one was injured.

This incident illustrates the problem of the liberal bail policies in effect in most jurisdictions in the United States: criminals more often than not are released on little or no bail and are accorded total freedom to intimidate their original victim, to prey upon others, and generally to continue their criminal activities. Evidence of this was documented in chapter five.

The problem of pretrial release is one of the most acute in the criminal justice system. By legislation, court decision, or constitutional mandate, in most jurisdictions, the right to bail has become so absolute that, as the California Supreme Court has held,[22] the safety of society *cannot even be taken into consideration* in the decision as to setting bail or the amount thereof. This is a lovely situation for the criminal, but a sorry one indeed for the innocent victims of criminals set at liberty through ultrapermissive bail policies. Granted that the presumption of innocence is not to be taken lightly, the number of such crimes calls for a toughening of the procedure if the rights of the law-abiding are to be accorded any weight at all. This can be accomplished in various ways.

First, the concept of preventive detention, albeit anathema to the antivictim forces, should be implemented. In most jurisdictions this could be accomplished only by statute[23] or constitutional amendment; this would be, concededly, difficult. Nevertheless, it should be considered. Preventive detention simply means that when there is clear and convincing evidence that a criminal accused is so dangerous to the community that he should be confined before trial, then a bail-setting court should have the authority to do so.

Obviously, procedural safeguards for the accused should be set up so that he would not be confined at the whim of the magistrate who must rule on his release. But in those cases where there is clear and convincing evidence that the defendant will victimize again and where the proof of the crime of which he is accused is great, he should be detained for the protection of the community and then tried as expeditiously as can be—perhaps before those who have been accused but who have been admitted to bail. The cry is always raised that it is impossible for a judge to predict with any accuracy whether the accused will repeat his crime. While there is some validity to this point of view, it seems clear that the application of a little common sense to the problem will enable courts to act with essential fairness.

A person without a previous criminal record who is arrested for purse snatching is entirely different from a person accused of rape who has two prior rape convictions and against whom the evidence clearly indicates guilt. Other circumstances absent, a judge would almost invariably grant bail to the former, whereas the latter might well be a candidate for preventive detention. No system will work perfectly. Undeniably there will be an occasional injustice if someone is detained prior to trial. But if we balance *that* injustice against the total injustice visited upon innocent, law-abiding citizens who are victimized time and again by those out on bail for serious crimes, then a case for some limited form of preventive detention can be made.

Statistics are helpful in this area. For example, a survey released in May 1974 by the U.S. Drug Enforcement Administration showed that 47.5 percent of those arrested on federal drug-trafficking charges, and then released on bond, were implicated in postarrest drug-trafficking activities.[24] This percentage is certainly high enough to make a bond court judge ponder carefully whether to release a defendant with a long record for narcotics offenses.

The constitutionality of preventive detention has not been directly decided by the Supreme Court. Pretrial detention was enacted into law in the District of Columbia Court Reform and Criminal Procedure Act of 1970, but the constitutionality of this act has not been before the Supreme Court. Should the concept of preventive detention be held unconstitutional by the Court, the matter would be effectively disposed of. Until then the idea of keeping dangerous criminals off the streets merits serious consideration in any victim-oriented scheme of things.

The victims of crime can take some encouragement from the Arizona Constitution. It permits the denial of bail to those who commit a felony offense when they are already on bail for a separate offense, provided that the proof is evident or the presumption of guilt of the second offense is great.[25] The Arizona Supreme Court has upheld this provision as constitutional.[26] The common sense inherent in it is obvious. Such laws or constitutional provisions should be enacted *and enforced* in other jurisdictions.

The victim-oriented state of Arizona has, in addition, enacted a law that makes it a separate felony to commit a felony while on bail.[27] This, together with laws that make bail-jumping a crime, plus severe penalties imposed for any violation, can result in a tightening of overly liberal bail policies and will surely have a beneficial effect on the victims of crime.

Certainly the theory, oriented wholly to the rights of the criminal, that the *only* purpose of bail is to assure the presence of the defendant at trial embodies the idea that the safety of the law-abiding is of negligible concern, and expresses an antivictim point of view. There is simply no balance in it at all. The law-abiding in our society are entitled to protection from criminals. Any system that insists on placing dangerous individuals on the street time and again via ultralenient bail policies, heedless of how much they may threaten the innocent, has no regard for the victims at all.

5. Countering the Antivictim Forces

Chapter seven described the antivictim forces in the United States—groups and individuals to whom certain abstract concepts are of such fanatical importance that they support them utterly disdainful of the fact that if implemented, these concepts will cause untold victimization.

In any victim-oriented society the spokesmen for the victims *must* be aware of the works of the antivictim forces and counter them with every means available. It is essential that those making the law and implementing policy in the criminal justice system be aware of the effect that certain actions they may be asked to take in the name of such high-minded concepts as "freedom of speech," "freedom from repression," and "protection of personal privacy," will have on the victims of crime.

AN EXAMPLE of ANTIVICTIM ACTIVITY: THE "PRIVACY LOBBY"

The need for a concerted effort in behalf of the victims can be illustrated by a potentially disastrous campaign currently being waged by the antivictim forces in the name of privacy. If this campaign is successful, the impact on the victims simply cannot be calculated. The "privacy lobby," an outgrowth of the repression syndrome of the antivictim forces, is composed of most of the antivictim organizations. Spearheaded by the ACLU, antivictim individuals, segments of the media, highly influential legislators, and Washington bureaucrats, the lobby is currently seeking to hamstring law enforcement in the areas of investigation and indentification of those involved in organized crime, terroristic crime, and street crime generally. All of this is being done in the name of privacy. Indeed, privacy has become an all-consuming end. The privacy lobby treats contemptuously the fact that its efforts may well lead to an era of victimization such as has not been seen before.

The impetus for the privacy lobby was, of course, Watergate. The supreme irony of that sorry mess may well be that the criminal acts of a few highly placed men will, through the efforts of the antivictim forces, be the greatest single boon to the criminal since the Warren Court decided to revolutionize the criminal law. Watergate set the stage for those to whom the concept of privacy is an absolute to move to have their views institutionalized. If they succeed, the criminal will be so shielded as to be nearly immunized from investigation by law-enforcement authorities.

Now there is nothing wrong with the concept of privacy as such. We all cherish our personal privacy. But this does not mean privacy should be so elevated that law-enforcement officials are powerless to investigate crimes and to identify and apprehend criminals. Yet this is exactly what the privacy lobby is attempting to accomplish, primarily in four specific areas.

First, the privacy lobby wants to insulate financial records from effective examination by law-enforcement officers by requiring that anyone so examined must be given notice that the examination is taking place. If this effort is successful it may cripple investigation into organized crime, dope peddling, and white-collar crime forever. Organized crime is one of the major problems facing law enforcement today, and it is one of the most difficult areas of criminal activity to investigate because of the deep veil of secrecy about it. Top- and middle-level syndicate figures rarely if ever participate in the actual criminal transactions upon which they thrive: sales of illicit narcotics, prostitution, gambling, and contraband. Only the money goes to the top. This is accomplished by various complicated financial transactions involving fronts to conceal such transactions and to infiltrate legitimate businesses.

In many cases the *only* way federal and state agents are able to unravel these transactions and make criminal cases against major syndicate figures is by examining, without the suspects' knowledge, their financial records held by banks and other commercial institutions. The law currently requires that such institutions keep copies of third-party financial records and make them available to law-enforcement officers.[28] This law has been upheld as constitutional by the U.S. Supreme Court.[29] There are, of course, limitations upon government access to such records: the investigating agency must show that the inquiry is material to its investigation and must have some sort of authority to make the inspection.

279

The critical aspect of the entire matter is that when a government agency now inspects such records in a criminal investigation, there is no duty upon that agency or upon the financial institution to notify the subject of the investigation about the inquiry. If such a duty were imposed, it would in many cases render the investigation fruitless by tipping off the subject.

Two of the nation's top authorities on organized crime, Eugene T. Rossides, former assistant secretary of the Treasury for Enforcement, and William S. Lynch, chief of the Organized Crime and Racketeering Section of the Criminal Division of the Department of Justice, testified before the Senate Subcommittee on Financial Institutions of the Committee on Banking, Housing and Urban Affairs, on August 11, 1972, about the impact of notice requirements on criminal investigations. Mr. Rossides stated:

> The provisions for notice to the subject are at best cumbersome if not totally impracticable. In numerous instances where bank records are sought, it is crucial that the subject of the investigation not be made aware of the matter under inquiry. The notice requirement would enable the suspect, in effect, to follow the progress of the investigation. As a result, the life of an informer or undercover agent may be jeopardized, records may be falsified or destroyed, funds may be concealed, and the subject may disappear. [Rossides statement, pp. 20, 21.]

Mr. Lynch concurred:

> I submit to the Subcommittee that . . . giving notice to an account holder that law enforcement officials desire to review his bank records will sabotage the ongoing criminal investigation. Since financial records are commonly an initial means of developing a criminal case, exposure of the government's interest in bank records will allow a suspect to alter his operations, to falsify or destroy evidence, or even to flee the jurisdiction before an indictable case can be developed. This notice will serve as a red flag to the criminal that the authorities are on his trail. [Lynch statement, p. 13.]

Thus, requiring the government to tell the subject that he is under investigation will often defeat the purpose of the investigation. This is apparently what the privacy lobby wants. There are now bills in both houses of Congress that would require, under civil and criminal penalties, notice to the party under investigation before financial records could be obtained. The ACLU and others are pushing hard for such legislation. If their concepts of privacy render law-enforcement agencies powerless to uncover and prosecute organized-crime figures, major drug suppliers, embezzlers, corrupt officials, swindlers, and other white-collar criminals, so be it; the ACLU et al. are quite willing that the victims of such criminals pay this price.

Second, the privacy lobby wants a ban on all wiretapping. Senator Lowell Weicker has called for such a ban. The ACLU has been single-mindedly doing the same for years. It matters not to the lobby that the great majority of law-enforcement officers agree that electronic eavesdropping is absolutely necessary effectively to fight organized crime, narcotics smuggling, gambling, and, in some cases, kidnapping and extortion. Nor does it matter that under our federal and state laws the use of wiretapping is rigidly controlled and can be done only with a court order. The privacy lobby wants it stopped. If stopping it means that criminals must go undetected or unprosecuted to continue victimizing others—or, in the case of organized crime, to continue victimizing our entire society—the lobby cares little.

Third, the privacy lobby wants rigid controls on dissemination of criminal information among law-enforcement agencies. Led by Senator Sam Ervin, the privacy lobby has introduced legislation that would drastically restrict the exchange of information among criminal justice agencies. The legislation is so extreme that in many cases it would prohibit, under the threat of civil and criminal penalties, one law-enforcement agency from giving to another information vital to solving a crime or apprehending a criminal. Now there is no disagreement among law-enforcement officers that criminal justice information is sensitive information and that it should not be bandied about in an unrestricted manner. But the privacy lobby wants to go much further. It would restrict criminal justice agencies from exchanging information that is crucial for them to do their jobs.

The two most critical areas involve proposed prohibitions on dissemination of critical records of suspects (sometimes called "sealing" of records), even *among criminal justice agencies* in certain cases: if the suspect was convicted but a certain period of years has elapsed, and if the suspect was arrested but no conviction was obtained through either an acquittal or a dismissal of the charges. These proposals, enthusiastically supported by the privacy lobby, could, in the words of Clarence M. Kelley, director of the FBI, "severely restrict or preclude the effective use of criminal justice information by law enforcement to investigate and prosecute criminal activity."[30]

Behind the proposed restrictions on dissemination of arrest records that do not result in a conviction is the theory that since a man is presumed innocent until proven guilty, no one, not even law-enforcement agencies, should have access to information unless there was a conviction. This theory breaks down, however, when we consider that our criminal justice system is geared towards suppressing the truth in criminal cases and countless numbers of patently guilty individuals are freed through such devices as the suppression of physical evidence and confessions; that victims and witnesses are often terrorized into refusing to testify, or simply get disgusted and refuse to testify because of inordinate trial delays; and that victims often refuse to testify in cases such as rape and child molesting because the system makes a defendant out of the victim. The mere fact that a given criminal defendant was acquitted, or that the charges against him were dropped, does not in our system mean that he did not commit the crime with which he was charged.

The exchange of information among criminal justice agencies is absolutely essential to the effectiveness of law enforcement. Consider the following two examples of how restrictions upon the dissemination of information of arrest records, not resulting in a conviction, would hamstring law enforcement:

Detective Jones in Detroit is investigating a series of rapes by a white male of a certain description. The rapist consistently uses a modus operandi of, say, tying his victims up with their stockings. Jones calls Detective Smith in Kalamazoo to ask whether he knows anything about such a rapist. Now Smith may know the name, even the address, of a man who fits the description, who uses the same modus operandi, and who has been positively identified as the rapist of two women in Kalamazoo. But because the women had refused to testify against the suspect on account of the adverse publicity and the attendant mental trauma that rape victims face at trial, he was never prosecuted. Under the right-of-privacy-for-criminals theory, Detective Smith would incur civil and criminal penalties if he mentioned the name of the rape suspect to Detective Jones because that suspect had not been convicted.

The second example. Police in Chicago are investigating a conspiracy to smuggle narcotics into that city from Toledo. They call the Toledo narcotics officers to find out whether they know anything about such a plot. The Toledo officers had in fact apprehended X in possession of a large quantity of heroin in a car with Illinois plates in Toledo some six months before. But because the search by the Toledo police of X's car was held to be illegal, the heroin was suppressed and the case against X dismissed. As in the prior example, the Toledo police would be prohibited from advising the Chicago police of X's arrest.

In addition to hampering law enforcement by prohibiting the exchange of badly needed information between law-enforcement agencies, the unrealistic restrictions proposed by the privacy lobby could materially increase the danger of police work for law-enforcement officers and bystanders. If an officer was going out to arrest a man for a nonviolent offense—a traffic warrant, for instance—and the man had a record of arrests but no convictions for violent crimes, the lack of this information could materially increase the risk to the safety of that officer.

Despite the obvious need for the exchange of criminal information among criminal justice agencies, the privacy enthusiasts would like to ban it. The rights of the victims and the safety of police officers are of little consequence to the privacy lobby.

Fourth, the privacy lobby is mounting an all-out effort to destroy the effectiveness of domestic intelligence-gathering activities by law-enforcement officers. What makes this so amazing is that terrorism by United States citizens is clearly on the rise. On June 5, 1974, W. Raymond Wannall, assistant director of the FBI's Intelligence Division, told the House Committee on Internal Security:

> As an indicator of the extent of the violent activities which occur across the nation, during the period 1971-73, there was a total of 573 incidents of violence attributed to terrorists. This figure breaks down to 114 fire-bombings, 21 arsons, 45 snipings, 114 shootings, 23 ambushes, 27 other physical attacks, 59 incidents of weapon stockpiling, 43 criminal acts in support of terrorist endeavors, and 127 bombings.
>
> During the same period, terrorists were known to be responsible for *152 police woundings and 43 deaths and 53 civilian woundings and 22 deaths.*
>
> As can be seen from these statistical data, the police officer has been and continues to be a prime target of terrorist and subversive elements engaged in urban guerrilla-type activity.[31]

Current events reinforce this. Terrorist attacks abound. "Urban guerrilla" bands like the Symbionese Liberation Army have been engaged in violent crimes, including murders in many parts of the country. The theft from the Compton (California) National Guard Armory, in July 1974, of enough weapons and ammunition to equip an army unit is an ominous indicator that such terrorism will continue to increase.

Nevertheless, the privacy lobby is doing all that it can to put those elements of our law-enforcement agencies out of business. Kidnappers, murderers, arsonists, bombers, and bank robbers are, to the privacy-at-any-price advocates, merely "political dissidents." Court cases have been filed and legislation introduced to require the police to obtain a search warrant before infiltrating or surveilling "political" groups; to prohibit the dissemination of computerized intelligence information among law-enforcement agencies; to set up "watchdog" committees over domestic intelligence gathering; and to prevent the police from stopping and questioning persons who fit the description of terrorist killers.

Phrases like "political spying" and "domestic snooping" are constantly used—and dutifully echoed in the media—by the privacy lobby to denigrate the legitimate efforts of law-enforcement intelligence agencies to gather information on and prevent further activities by terrorist groups. Unfortunately, the excesses of the Watergate principals gave some credence to the antivictim attacks on intelligence gathering; it will probably take a wave of terrorism, something like the violence in the late sixties, to awaken people to the fact that despite the Watergate chicanery, which was mostly politically motivated, a nation does have the right and the duty to protect itself from domestic subversion. But before this realization again takes hold, there will assuredly be numerous victims—many of them law-enforcement officers—who will be killed, maimed, burned, robbed, or otherwise outraged by terrorist activities. Thanks largely to the privacy lobby.

The privacy lobby and its antivictim activities demonstrate the compelling need for some sort of countereffort in behalf of the victims. The necessity is unquestioned. If the path of organized crime, major narcotics smugglers, and other criminals is smoothed by the efforts of the privacy lobby, the result will be a given number of victims. If the police cannot exchange information necessary to enforce the law effectively, there will be more victims. If a "climate of freedom" for terrorists is created by restricting legitimate efforts to deal with terrorism, there will be even more.

Some response has already been made in behalf of the victims. Law enforcement has been heard from in the person of the highly articulate FBI director Clarence Kelley and through other spokesmen. Americans for Effective Law Enforcement has testified in Congress and appeared in the courts in opposition to the theory that privacy is an absolute end in itself, and that the rights of the victims of crime should be totally subordinated to that end.

Francis B. Looney, deputy commissioner of the New York Police Department and president of the International Association of Chiefs of Police, has presented the case for law enforcement (and by implication for the victims of crime) against unreasonable restrictions upon the police in the name of privacy. Commissioner Looney, in a lead editorial in *Police Chief* magazine, presented the issue of privacy and its impact upon police effectiveness:

> The issue of the individual's right to privacy has become very prevalent in recent months. Americans are becoming concerned that massive, interconnected computer data systems, not to mention sophisticated electronic surveillance devices, are posing a significant threat to their ability to lead lives free of government snooping and interference. Several bills designed to deal with this problem have been introduced in Congress, and they have caused great concern among law enforcement officials.

Much of this concern is justified. But I feel that legislation harmful to law enforcement must be approached cautiously, with complete awareness of the very legitimate concerns that underlie these bills. The fact is that individual privacy *is* under attack. Schools, employers, and credit bureaus maintain detailed files on millions of Americans. Incorrect information in these files can seriously affect an individual's ability to get a job, establish credit, and continue to earn a living. Electronic bugging equipment can be built or purchased by practically everyone. Already, there have been numerous instances of the criminal misuse of such spy gadgetry.

Clearly, much of the proposed privacy legislation, if passed, would do great harm to the cause of law enforcement. Most of the proposed bills would provide for the purging or sealing of criminal records after a specified number of years. Not only would this prevent the police from making use of vital information, it would also destroy the central concept that second offenses should be punished more harshly than first offenses. After a certain period of time, the slate would merely be wiped clean.

Several bills would require that police obtain access warrants in order to obtain certain kinds of criminal information. The drafters of this legislation obviously did not know that such information is often needed on very short notice, *perhaps to help the capture of a fugitive.* The warrant procedure would simply serve to hamper investigations, and would present an impossible hardship for rural police departments hundreds of miles from the appropriate courtroom. Finally, several of the bills would flatly ban the computerization of criminal intelligence information.

What police administrators must do in order to oppose these bills is to point out that it is not computerization per se that is the villain, but the misuse of computerized information. The police must be allowed to maintain free internal communications. They must be allowed to use all the tools at their command to protect society from crime. At the same time, they must show their continued willingness to guard this information zealously against those who would use it for their own purposes. In this way, both the right of the individual to protect his personal privacy, and the right of society to protect itself against criminal acts, can be safeguarded.[32]

Others too have been heard from as spokesmen for the victims. But the provictim forces are not nearly as organized, coordinated, and vocal as the antivictim forces. To protection of privacy from government, a great many more Americans prefer protection of privacy from a bomber at liberty to operate because of the restrictions on law-enforcement intelligence-gathering efforts; from a narcotics addict or pusher supplied by an organized-crime syndicate that is effectually immunized from federal investigation or from court-ordered wire-tapping; and from an unconvicted rapist not identified to the local police because exchanging information is prohibited, despite several arrests.

However, the privacy lobby is able to drown out such provictim articulation simply because it is so well organized, coordinated, and vocal. Achieving an effective victim-oriented society will depend in large measure upon whether the provictim forces can become sufficiently articulate so as to counter effectively those concerned solely with the criminal.

COUNTERING COLLATERAL ATTACKS AGAINST THE POLICE

America's law-enforcement officers—policemen, sheriff's deputies, federal agents, state troopers, and anyone else who wears the badge— are the single line of protection between society and the criminal. Most people realize this and appreciate the dirty, dangerous job done by these dedicated men and women. Yet the vocal antivictim forces, those who single-mindedly continue to launch collateral attacks designed to demoralize and degrade the police and their function, continue to dominate the scene.

As is true with most of the antivictim forces, the collateral attackers are skillfully organized. Those who support the police are not. And so the collateral attacks continue—cries for civilian review boards, constant harassment of law enforcement via frivolous civil suits, and attacks against every facet of law enforcement by criticism, carping, and general faultfinding.

No clearer example of this exists than the reaction of certain elements after the Los Angeles Police Department engaged in a shootout with the Symbionese Liberation Army that resulted in the death of four of the terrorists. Now it is unquestioned that the SLA members were guilty of any number of violent crimes, that they were armed with an arsenal of firearms including automatic weapons, and that they had made every effort to kill the policemen who had demanded that they surrender.

Immediately, the American Civil Liberties Union in Southern California launched an attack against the police officers for "overreacting"—in effect, for shooting back when they were fired on. National network carried a press conference of a local ACLU staffer condemning the policemen and promising legal reprisals against them for their actions. One fatuous minister from Des Moines, Iowa, wrote the *Chicago Daily News*: "It will take a vigorous congressional inquiry to make it clear whether or not the best interests of the nation, and the rights of individuals, are being properly served by such action on the part of our law-enforcement agencies."

This sort of lunacy was too much for Pat Oliphant, the brilliant cartoonist for the *Denver Post*. He responded with a depiction of a fanatical female with the letters ACLU across her enormous buttocks sitting astride the shoulders of a police sergeant and beating him on the head with her pocketbook. The sergeant is explaining to a file of long-suffering officers: "She wants to know why you men overreact so nastily towards terrorists who use cyanide bullets and .50-caliber machine guns."

Mr. Oliphant's cartoon probably summed up the feelings of most people, but the fact remains that the antipolice attacks received the widest possible publicity. The antivictims had engaged in a virulent collateral attack against the Los Angeles Police Department and had, as usual, won the media battle hands down. Letters and telephone calls to the department overwhelmingly supported the police's actions, but there appeared to be little or no demonstrable, organized, articulate public support that would counter the charges of the ACLU and its adherents.

This incident, plus countless others, demonstrates conclusively the need for an organized force of spokesmen in behalf of the law-enforcement officers. This is in no way a call for the approbation of "the police—right or wrong." If the Los Angeles police *had* gunned down innocent parties, then such a response would be as bad as the attacks by the ACLU. But the fact remains that in this instance, the policemen were acting entirely correctly. They had every right to use the force necessary to capture the armed terrorists who refused to surrender. Any other action by the policemen would clearly have been dereliction of duty. But for doing their duty, at considerable risk to themselves, they were subjected to the most vicious attacks by those to whom any police action is wrong, attacks that received nationwide exposure via the media.

On occasion the law-abiding majority does join forces to counter collateral attacks against the police. This happened in 1965 when the issue of the civilian review board was placed before the voters of New York City in a special referendum. The civilian review board, created by Mayor John V. Lindsay, was defeated by a margin of 2 to 1. A sizable number of individuals, including some of that city's most prominent citizens, worked to secure its defeat. But such examples of support for law enforcement are far too rare. As a general rule, we hear only from those who attack the police. If they are heard from long and loud enough, they will probably prevail, simply because they are free to carry on their campaigns without any kind of countervailing effort. If they succeed, many good policemen will quit, many others will go elsewhere, and those who remain will be so afraid to act that the criminals will be able to act with relative impunity. The antivictim forces will have won. The victims will suffer.

The law-abiding then have every reason to support law-enforcement when it comes under collateral attacks. To reemphasize, this support should be responsible. Policemen, like everyone else, can and do

287

engage in wanton, brutal and corrupt acts. When they do they should be punished. Likewise, policemen can make mistakes and these should be corrected. No one would advocate that a policeman should not be called to account no matter what he has done. But when policemen *are* acting properly and are objects of collateral attacks simply because the attackers resent the authority that the law-enforcement officer represents, then the provictim forces should become vocal in support of the right of society to protect itself, and let it be known that they will not stand idly by and watch as the thin blue line is broken.

One of the most effective collateral attacks against the police is the harassment-type civil suit. Such suits are easy enough to file against policemen. There are any number of antivictim groups and individuals who are willing, even eager, to file them. Presently no real check exists on the filing of even the most unfair suits. Two Democratic congressmen, Richard Ichord of Missouri and Henry Gonzales of Texas, have each introduced bills that would require that parties bringing suit against any law-enforcement officer in federal court file a surety bond with the court in which the action is brought in order to guarantee the payment of legal fees and costs of investigation if the defendant officers prevail.

This legislation is eminently fair to all concerned. It guarantees to the officers that they will not be broken financially by harassing civil suits. It ensures that only those potential plaintiffs who believe their case sufficiently meritorious to prevail will bring actions. The legislation, in a word, will not deter legitimate lawsuits but will mightily prevent frivolous lawsuits, now on the increase.

In addition, Rep. William D. Ford, Democrat of Michigan, introduced in 1972 a bill that authorizes the attorney general of the United States to reimburse law-enforcement officers for legal fees and costs of investigation incurred in civil suits that arise from the performance of their official duties and that they win. Regarding the need for such legislation, Congressman Ford stated:

> While I would be the first to agree that the law-enforcement officer must not use his position of authority to commit acts outside the scope of his official duties, my basic concern is for the law enforcement officers who are being forced to spend their own time and money defending themselves against lawsuits which are primarily frivolous in nature—or suits which have little or no basis for being filed in the first place.
>
> The effect of this type of lawsuit can be very detrimental to effective law enforcement. One consequence is that an officer and his family may suffer substantial hardship in terms of time, money, and mental anguish while he is defending himself. Another undesirable result is that the continuing threat of civil liability hanging over the heads of police officers tends to increase the anxieties associated with their very difficult

and complex job. It is my opinion that unless we can devise a means of indemnifying individual officers for the cost of defending frivolous and ungrounded civil actions, they will continue to live in constant fear that the security of their families may someday be jeopardized.

Some are, finally, beginning to recognize the problems caused by harassment suits against the police. In addition, the Law Enforcement Legal Defense Center of Americans for Effective Law Enforcement, Inc. (described in chapter eight) now operates the only citizen effort in the nation designed to assist law enforcement in countering such frivolous actions. Any consideration of a victim-oriented society must face the fact that the antivictim forces have in the harassment suit a potent weapon with which to make the police afraid to do their jobs. Legislation like that introduced by Congressmen Ichord, Gonzales, and Ford deserves the fullest support of all who are concerned about the victims.

6. *Specific Provictim Activities*

In 1973 sixteen-year-old Valerie Smith* and two of her teenage friends were walking home from a basketball game in Oak Park, Illinois. They were stopped and robbed at gunpoint by three men. The victims obtained the license number of the robbers' car, reported it to the police, and the criminals were apprehended. The three victims identified their assailants in a lineup; the latter were subsequently bound over for trial.

The case seemed routine until, in 1974, Valerie was presented by U.S. deputy marshals with a complaint summoning her to appear in federal district court in Chicago. The robbers had filed a civil suit *against their victims*. They alleged that the victims "conspired" with the police and prosecution to "violate the rights" of the accused robbers because they were black.

To the sixteen-year-old robbery victim and her family, this turn of events was unbelievable. They frankly wondered if our criminal justice process had become so perverted that criminals were now suing their victims. The answer was yes. They must defend the action or risk a default judgment against them. And it appeared they must defend it alone. The prosecuting attorney in Cook County genuinely wanted to help them but had no authority to defend them in the suit. The homeowners policy owned by Valerie's father would not cover such an action. They were, it seemed, on their own.

The first assistant to the state's attorney contacted Americans for Effective Law Enforcement (AELE), which at the time was beginning to implement a program of assistance to the victims of crime. AELE

*Not the victim's real name. However, the case as reported here is real.

attorneys filed a motion to dismiss the complaint. The motion was granted. In this case, at least, the victim did not have to stand trial for having been robbed. The defense of the victim was undertaken by AELE at no expense to the family; they were spared some rather substantial attorney's fees. More important, this case illustrates the need for specific victim-oriented responses when the system becomes as topsy-turvy as it obviously has.

Consider the ramifications of the case. It is, even now, difficult enough to motivate the victims of and witnesses to crimes to testify. Time-consuming trial delays, the threat of reprisals by criminals, and the general atmosphere of a criminal justice system that seems to subordinate the rights of the victim to those of the accused, have disillusioned victims and witnesses alike. The case of Valerie Smith adds a new dimension: if you are victimized and you cooperate with the police, *you*, the victim, will face a lawsuit at the whim of the criminals. The difficulties involved in obtaining the testimony of *anyone* would be materially enhanced if the robber's lawsuit had succeeded.

The immediate impact of a case like this is, of course, felt by the victim, who is astounded and outraged at being sued because she was robbed. A far greater impact would be felt if such actions should become relatively common. The victims of the criminals would become fair game for utterly frivolous civil suits by those who had originally victimized them.

Now if Valerie's father had hired an attorney to represent him, that attorney would likely have also been able to win the dismissal of the case. But Mr. Smith would have suffered the additional outrage of having to pay legal fees for defending his daughter against the allegations of the men who robbed her. AELE's participation indicates the need for victim-oriented organizations that are able and willing to step in and represent the victim without cost to him or his family. Victims' rights commissions, created along the lines of those suggested in chapter eight, or perhaps a victims' ombudsman, could likewise have entered the case on behalf of Valerie. Whatever, without specific assistance to the victims of crime, they must, in many cases, face alone a system that not only holds *their* rights in complete contempt, but also permits the criminal actually to sue his victim.

Another area of provictim activity just beginning to receive a little attention is the filing of lawsuits, on behalf of the victims, against those who have victimized them or against those who through negligence have caused them to be victimized.

Sueing the average murderer, rapist, or armed robber will be of little practical value to the victim. The majority of such criminals are generally "judgment-proof," that is, they simply have no assets out of which a judgment against them could be satisfied. In those cases in which the criminal does have enough material wealth to make a lawsuit worthwhile, however, this avenue of approach should be followed. In criminal cases the accused is protected by a system that is extraordinarily solicitous of his rights. The case against him must be proven beyond a reasonable doubt, and, as noted, laws and court decisions often exclude entirely relevant evidence of guilt.

In civil cases, however, where the victim is sueing the defendant for damages, the plaintiff-victim need only prove his case by a "preponderance of the evidence." That is, to win, he must present only enough facts to the jury to make his case, on balance, more believable than that of the person he has sued. Thus a case that might not have been prosecuted in the criminal courts might well be a strong case in the civil courts because the burden of proof is so radically different.

There are, of course, reasons why the victims are reluctant to sue their assailants. Expense is the main factor. Also, trial delays in the civil court system are equal to or longer than those in the criminal courts. And not least, the natural victim is naturally reluctant to expose himself further to publicity or to the criminal.

Nevertheless, this is a fertile field of exploration for the provictim forces. A few test cases, after careful screening, might successfully be brought in the civil courts against those who have victimized others. This could well result in a body of law that would in turn spark a general turn-around in thinking, so far as victims' rights are concerned. Say a young hoodlum member of a motorcycle gang beats an innocent citizen just for kicks. He either receives a slap-on-the-wrist sentence or is not prosecuted because there is not sufficient evidence to prove the *criminal* case beyond a reasonable doubt. Thus nothing prevents his going right back out and beating someone else for kicks. But suppose this hoodlum sees the sheriff cart his motorcycle off to be sold in order to satisfy a *civil* judgment for assault and battery in favor of his victim. The hoodlum may think twice about doing it again. And the victim's rights are vindicated.

The concept of civil suits against those whose negligence actually caused an individual to be victimized is also relatively new. A successful action, described in chapter five, was filed against the state of Washington and the warden of the state penitentiary who let a convicted murderer and escape artist out as a part of a "take a lifer to dinner" program.

In New York, suits were filed against landlords by tenants who alleged that they were victimized because of lax security on the premises, and that the landlords were negligent in providing proper protection for them.[33]

A rape victim in Washington, D.C. won a jury verdict of $33,000 from delivery firms whose employee attacked her while delivering a mattress.[34]

These cases raise interesting and sometimes disturbing questions. Just as law-enforcement officers should not be harassed by frivolous lawsuits because of an occasional mistake in judgment, neither should everyone who hires a person who commits a criminal act, or upon whose property an attack takes place be held liable. The essential question in such cases is negligence. Was the defendant so negligent that his action or inaction resulted in the victimization of the plaintiff? Clear-cut lines are difficult to draw here. Surely the victim's rights should be accorded consideration, but to what extent should a third party be liable because *someone else* commits a crime.

Perhaps the only definitive statement that can be made at this point is that the concept of vindicating victims' rights via the civil process warrants careful examination. Certainly this is an area in which the pro-victim forces can take an active interest. AELE, for example, has been engaged in research along the lines set forth. If victims' rights can be enhanced by civil suits against criminals and those whose negligence materially assists the criminal, surely this will contribute favorably toward recognition and effective enforcement of these rights.

This country's prosecutors, by definition, represent primarily the interests of the state rather than those of victims. A particularly victim-oriented program, however, has been instituted by Harl Haas, the district attorney for Multnomah County (Portland), Oregon. Currently his office is engaged in a Victims Assistance Project that could well serve as a model for other prosecutors nationwide. Mr. Haas defined the problem in general terms:

> Although the police departments, the courts and other criminal justice agencies were designed to protect citizens from the lawless acts of others, hundreds of thousands of Americans are victims of crime and violence yearly. In Portland and Multnomah County alone, more than 65,000 crimes were reported to law enforcement officials in 1972.
>
> When society fails to protect its citizens and crime occurs, the major resources of the criminal justice system are then focused upon the offender. Too often the victim of crime is taken for granted and the only concern for him at this stage is that he or she be present at certain stages of the proceedings. Once the victim has fulfilled his duty by reporting the crime and fulfilling his prosecutorial function, the criminal justice system is through with him, often without even a simple thank you.

He then turned to specifics:

> 1) The scheduling of cases for trial and other court appearances is most frequently done to meet the scheduling problems of the defendant

and his attorney. Other than the prosecuting attorney, no one can speak to the convenience or inconvenience of a particular time and date for the victim. A rather tragic example of this problem occurred in Multnomah County in 1973. In the case in question, the defense attorney had requested several setovers of the case because he was going to be out of town. Both setovers were granted. The case was rescheduled but this time the victim (a man who was beaten practically to death by his assailant) could not be present. The state requested a setover but instead the judge dismissed the case. It is not difficult to understand the frustration and bewilderment of the victim in a circumstance such as this.

2) Upon finding of guilt and before the judge imposes sentence, the prosecuting attorney often recommends to the judge that a condition of probation include restitution to the victim. The difficulty here is that an accurate assessment of the loss is not always available. Without this information the judge cannot include restitution as a part of the sentence. Staff of this project, particularly the investigator, will determine the actual dollar loss to victims and see that that information is available to the prosecutor for recommendation.

3) Victims, and other citizens, often have complaints and problems that cannot be resolved by the District Attorney's office but must be handled by either the courts or an enforcement or corrections agency. Rather than redirect these people from one intake office to another only to retell their story one more time, there is a need for an individual in the system who can act as a liaison on behalf of the victims and see that the right agency and the right person within the agency are contacted.

4) Lack of adequate staff makes it an impossibility to go through each file at the closing of a case and determine if everything is in order and if all property involved in the case has been returned. Often months later the victim will call the District Attorney's office and ask to have property returned. Having personal property tied up during the court process is an inconvenience and can cause frustration that will prevent cooperating with the system in the future either as a complainant or as a prosecution witness.

5) It is not unusual for the citizen to come into brief contact with some component of the criminal justice system, do what he is told and exit the system again without ever gaining an understanding of how the process works, how it affects him or why his cooperation was so important. At the very least, each contact with the criminal justice system should have some meaning and understood purpose in it for the citizen/taxpayer involved. The consequence of unpleasant, frustrating contacts with the criminal justice system is a disgruntled citizenry unwilling to pay the bills to keep the system operating.

The goals of Mr. Haas's Victims Assistance Project are to:

1) Assist victims in the recovery of their property through prompt release of property used as evidence and through sentencing recommendations of restitution.

293

2) Assist victims and other witnesses for the state with their scheduling conflicts.

3) Notify victims of the outcome of their case.

4) Thank the victims and other witnesses for their assistance and co-operation in the preparation and presentation of a case.

5) Prepare and distribute pamphlets and/or brochures about how the criminal justice system functions so that witnesses will understand how their participation fits into the overall system.

6) Develop effective procedures for advising the victim of the status of his case at every stage in the process.

7) Ensure that victims are not abused during the process of investigation and prosecution.

8) Explore the advisability and possibility of involving the victim in the pretrial plea bargaining process and perhaps the sentencing process.

9) Conduct preliminary research into the scope of victim loss due to crime for the information of the legislative committee developing Victim Compensation Legislation.

To implement these goals, the project engages in the following specific activities:

1) Answer telephone calls of victims and witnesses and resolve their problems whenever possible.

2) Assist the Public Information Officer in the preparation and distribution of literature which explains in lay terms how the criminal justice system works.

3) Assist the Police Liaison Officer by providing up-to-date information regarding the outcome of cases of concern to arresting and investigating officers.

4) Send letters daily to the victims and witnesses in cases which have been adjudicated informing them of the outcome and thanking them for their assistance in the trial.

5) Assist the pretrial and trial attorneys in assessing how the victim feels either about a negotiated plea or the sentence if the case is resolved by a finding of guilt.

6) Act as ombudsperson for the victim in setting trial dates and other appearances and in providing information to the prosecutor and the court regarding victim's loss due to the criminal act.

7) Assist the Assistant District Attorney who tries negligent homicide and other homicide cases in notifying the victim's next of kin at time of sentencing.

8) Examine each case file at the close of the case to be sure that all property held by the court has been returned to the rightful owner and that all witnesses and police officers have been notified of the outcome and thanked for their assistance.

This is a very comprehensive, victim-oriented project. It may be a landmark of sorts concerning what a prosecutor's office can do for the victims.

Certainly it reflects a genuine recognition by Mr. Haas of the rights of the victims and a desire to do something constructive for the victims.

The foregoing examples of specific, calculated provictim activities seem to have emerged sporadically as various individuals and groups first recognized, then attempted to enforce victims' rights. This sporadic emergence is perhaps itself a measure of the sorry situation today. That is, the antivictim forces are so well organized and their efforts so skillfully orchestrated and so widely publicized that the provictim forces are, by comparison, but an army scattered in a wilderness, leaderless and in complete disarray. The activities of the latter are thus uncoordinated, the accomplishments haphazard—the influence minimal. Until the provictim forces can begin to approach the effectiveness of their adversaries' coordination and organization, it is doubtful that useful and constructive victim orientation can be achieved.

So we have the problem and as yet the unreached solution. We live in a society where an inordinate number of people—especially the poor and powerless—are victimized, many atrociously. The criminal justice system should, ideally, *secure* the rights of the law-abiding. Not only does it fail to protect these rights; in many cases it actually encourages victimization of the law-abiding. An intolerable imbalance unquestionably exists in the system. The forces of permissiveness weigh heavy in the scales, and the interests of the victims scarcely register.

What can be done? Very little, it appears, unless our society develops victim consciousness. Then, and probably only then, will we undertake the specific tasks needed to restore the balance, to make the right to be safe and reasonably free from criminal harm a reality, rather than the cruel farce it is now. If this book generates among the actual and potential victims of crime an abiding awareness that *they* have enforceable rights and that something should be done about them, it has accomplished its purpose.

✦ Appendix

"Tonto, We Have Been Doing Things All Wrong"
Edwin A. Roberts

[Edwin A. Roberts, a writer for the *National Observer,* is one of our country's most incisive commentators on the criminal justice system. This article, which appeared in the June 3, 1972, issue of the *National Observer,* is a classic. It pillories the permissiveness shown criminals today and sardonically underscores every cliché that underlies it. Reprinted by permission of the *National Observer.*]

Life is different now from the way it was 100 years ago when law and order in the American West was the responsibility of the masked rider of the plains and his faithful Indian companion. In those days of yesteryear, crime and punishment tended toward the plain and simple.

That is why Americans cling to the fantasy of the Old West with its striking absence of court delays, endless appeals, Constitutional niceties, inventive sociologists, and high-flown theories about crime and its causes. What, one wonders, would the Lone Ranger have done had his efforts been circumscribed by the restraints and social values of today?

Return with us now . . .

The Lone Ranger and Tonto are seated by a campfire. As they have been for many hours, they are reading books that fell off a stage back there where the trail makes a sharp turn. The masked man speaks:

297

"Tonto, we have been doing things all wrong. These new books on sociopolitical commentary from the East suggest we have functioned essentially as hardliners. We have failed to realize that criminals are caused by society.

"I have been reading a number of daring and progressive works, Old Friend. This, for instance, is *My Heart Is on the Left* by Dorcas Sweeney, president of the Ladies League for Kindness Toward Thugs and Hooligans. The other volume is *Hired Killers Are People Too* by J. Markham Tootle, professor of criminology at a great Eastern university. And this other tome, notable for its thickness, is *How to Win the Hearts and Minds of Mad-Dog Murderers* by Herbert Hemple Highgate, chairman of the Beacon Street Philosophical Society."

"What them say?"

"They say, Tonto, we must change our approach in championing justice."

"Moon high now," Tonto observed. "We get going after Bart Slade gang?"

"Yes. We must find poor Slade and talk him into surrendering. Then we must consider how best to rehabilitate him."

"That not easy. Slade kill 126 men, women and children in bloody march from Lincoln County to Kansas. His men kill 235 more. Women and girls all raped. Men tortured to death. Slade gang rob 14 banks, 31 general stores, 18 stagecoaches, and 2 trains. They shoot dogs and horses. They set fire to six cats. They tough cookies."

"You're right, Tonto. And that's why we must try all the harder to help Bart and his friends see the error of their ways. Remember that Bart Slade is a victim of his environment. He is merely the product of a society that doesn't care. He was raised in a sod house not far from here, and he had few chances to find his true identity."

Tonto turned thoughtful. "But thousands of pioneers make new life in West by first living in sod houses. Slade family not richer or poorer than others. Most others don't turn out criminals. We catch Slade and Slade hang."

"No, no, Tonto. Capital punishment is cruel and unusual . . ."

"But Bart Slade is cruel and unusual."

"That doesn't matter, Tonto. Just a moment ago I was poring over a monograph on the death penalty by Mary Elizabeth Bonkers, a sociology major at Sarah Loveland College. Miss Bonkers has convinced me that capital punishment doesn't discourage murder."

"But it discourage murderer."

"That's vengeful thinking, Indian Companion. No, I want to catch Slade, not because I wish him ill, but because the sooner he is apprehended the sooner he will be back on the path of righteousness. I want to salvage him so that he may one day be a credit to the society that made him what he is."

"But Slade swear to kill you. He say he chop off your head and stuff it so far down in your ribs you think you in jail."

"That is just criminal rhetoric," remarked the Lone Ranger. "Now saddle Silver and Scout and don't go on talking like a reactionary Indian. And you can leave the guns here. We won't be needing them. The fewer guns around the fewer people will get hurt."

Tonto scratched his head. "But then just bad guys have guns and good guys don't. That very strange way to bring law to West. How you shoot Slade's gun out of hand if you got no gun?"

"I am going to treat him with the respect he deserves. He is a human being and entitled to a sense of dignity. I'm going to say, 'Hello there, Bart. I am the Lone Ranger and I want to help you. I know you are only the victim of your environment. Lay down your arms and let us talk like brothers.' "

"He blow your head off," said Tonto.

"Tonto, if I weren't a liberal and a progressive, I'd tell you what I think of savages. Fortunately for you, I am laden with guilt feelings for being a member of the white race, and I plan to spend the rest of my life thinking up new ways to suffer for the collective guilt of all white men."

"But you and Tonto old friends," said Tonto. "You never cheat Indians or hurt them. You treat Indians as equals. Why you feel guilty?"

"Because if you are liberal and progressive you must feel guilty for things you didn't do. It's right here in all these books. Now let's pick up the trail of the Slade gang."

"All right," Tonto said glumly. "Maybe we never catch Slade. Maybe he outwit us. Shouldn't be too hard."

◆ Notes

Chapter 1: The Victims

1. 384 U.S. 436 (1966).
2. *Ibid.*, p. 542.
3. *Ibid.*
4. 384 U.S. 436, p. 543.
5. H. L. Richardson, "The National Conference on Criminal Justice, Blueprint for the Felon," Richardson Special Report, State Capitol, Sacramento, California, no. 6, February 6, 1973, p. 2.
6. James J. Kilpatrick, "Equal Rights for Victims of Crime," *Chicago Daily News*, January 18, 1973, p. 8.
7. Article by Winston Moore reprinted from the *Houston Chronicle* in *The Grapevine* (American Association of Wardens and Superintendents, 13930 S. 1700 West, Riverton, Utah 84065) 5, no. 9, p. 4.
8. "Police Arrest 3 for Shotgun 'Joy' Killing of Girl, 4," *Chicago Tribune*, July 5, 1972, p. 1.
9. 408 U.S. 238 (1972).
10. *People* v. *Anderson*, Calif. Supreme Court, 493 P. 2d 880 (1972).
11. Peter Jefferies (producer), "Thou Shalt Not Kill," NBC News, July 28, 1972 (script, pp. 14-16).
12. Carolyn Colwell, "Mitford Scales the Prison Walls," *Chicago Today*, September 18, 1973, p. 29.
13. Thomas Ryder, "Paroled in '69 Killing; Jailed," *Des Moines Register*, December 22, 1972, p. 1.

14. Timothy S. Robinson, "Convicted Murderer Freed, U.S. Prosecutor Bewildered," *Washington Post,* November 28, 1973, p. C-1.
15. Charles Mount, "Handling of 6 Accused Hit," *Chicago Tribune,* October 16, 1972, p. 2.
16. *Ibid.*
17. Robert Wiedreich "Tower Ticker," *Chicago Tribune,* October 17, 1972, p. 18.
18. *Ibid.*
19. *Ibid.*
20. Tom Fitzpatrick, " 'Pleas' Electric Chair . . . and a Joint," *Chicago Sun Times,* October 19, 1972, p. 44.
21. Linda Greenhouse, "Ruppert, Jailed in Deaths of 12, Ordered Freed by Appeals Court," *New York Times,* June 11, 1971, p. C-23.
22. Karlyn Baker, "She Felt Like a Defendant," *Washington Post,* December 3, 1972.
23. Richard Wood, "Children's Code Is Still Controversial Issue," *Rocky Mountain News* (Denver), July 21, 1969.
24. *In Re Underwood,* Calif. Supreme Court, *Criminal Law Reporter* 13, 1254, p. 1255 (4/18/73).
25. This information was obtained from the Baltimore City Police Department and from the then States Attorney Charles E. Moylan of Baltimore.
26. "Colorado Girl Shot, Chum Killed After Birthday Party," *Chicago Daily News,* November 16, 1972, p. 17.
27. "Man Admits Killing His Mother, Her Friend, 6 Coeds," *Chicago Tribune,* April 25, 1973, p. 2.
28. "Coast Man Guilty in Eight Murders," *New York Times,* November 9, 1973, p. C-5.
29. *Uniform Crime Reports 1972,* Federal Bureau of Investigation, Department of Justice, Washington, D.C., pp. 2ff.
30. Bill Kovach, "Study Finds Crime Rates Far Higher Than Reports," *New York Times,* April 27, 1973, p. 1.
31. Peter Schneider, "In Memory of Seymour Schneider," *New York Times,* October 16, 1971, p. 29.
32. "Crime and Its Victims," *Wall Street Journal,* April 11, 1972.
33. George Gallup, "Crime Top Domestic Concern," *Denver Post,* February 28, 1968.
34. *Idem.,* "Crime-in-Streets Fear Prevalent," *Denver Post,* October 9, 1968, p. 72.
35. *Idem.,* "Inflation, Crime Top Problems in 70 Nations," *Chicago Sun Times,* May 2, 1971, p. 96.
36. *Idem.,* "Fear of Walking Alone in Neighborhood at Night Increases," *Washington Post,* April 23, 1972, p. 6.

37. *Idem.*, "51% in Survey Say Crime Is Growing," *New York Times,* January 16, 1973, p. 15.
38. Louis Harris, "Find Fear of Crime Increasing," *Chicago Tribune,* November 16, 1970, p. 1.
39. "Readers Speak Out," *Life,* January 16, 1972, pp. 28 ff.
40. David Burnham, "Most Call Crime Worst City Ill," *New York Times,* January 16, 1974, p. 1.
41. "Justice on Trial—A Special Report," *Newsweek,* March 8, 1971, p. 39.
42. George Gallup, "Public Wants 'Harder Line' to Win War on Crime," *Denver Post,* February 16, 1969, p. 20.
43. *Idem.*, "51% in Survey Say Crime Is Growing," *New York Times,* January 16, 1973, p. 15.
44. *Idem.*, "Public Esteem for High Court Has Fallen in Past Six Years," *Denver Post,* June 15, 1969, p. 18.
45. *Idem.*, "57% in Poll Back a Death Penalty," *New York Times,* November 23, 1972, p. 18.
46. Louis Harris, "New Favor for Death Penalty," *Chicago Tribune* June 11, 1973, p. 26.
47. George Gallup, "67% Back Life Terms for Hard Drug Sellers," *Chicago Daily News,* January 8, 1973.
48. William Claiborne, "Vigilantism Increasing in New York," *Washington Post,* September 16, 1973, p. 1.
49. "Citizen Posses Said Causing Jitters in Pacific Northwest," *Crime Control Digest,* March 25, 1974, p. 10.
50. "Voice of the People," *Chicago Tribune,* April 28, 1973, p. 10.

Chapter 2: The Special Victims

1. Vernon Jarrett, "Strength of Black Families Ignored," *Chicago Tribune,* September 14, 1973, p. 18.
2. *Crime Control Digest,* March 25, 1970, p. 7.
3. Associated Press, "Black Crime Preys on Black Victims," *Denver Post,* August 23, 1970. p. 35.
4. "Psychology of Murder," *Time,* April 24, 1972, p. 58.
5. Associated Press, *op. cit.*
6. Walter Trohan, "Crime Still Rife in Washington," *Chicago Tribune,* February 1, 1972, p. 18.
7. "Sutton Says Harlem Is Prisoner of Few Who Are Criminals," *New York Times,* November 12, 1972, p. 68.
8. Charlayne Hunter, "Harlem Crime Toll Is Put at $2 Billion," *New York Times,* April 27, 1971, p. 1.

9. William Raspberry, "The Poor Pay for Crime," *Denver Post,* January 10, 1970, p. 12.
10. Fred Cook, "Wherever the Central Cities Are Going, Newark Is Going to Get There First," *New York Times Magazine,* July 25, 1971, p. 7.
11. Edwin A. Roberts, "Black Law and Order," *National Observer,* May 1970, p. 1.
12. *Ibid.*
13. "New York NAACP Urges Crime Crack-Down in Harlem," *Criminal Law Reporter,* December 25, 1968, p. 2269.
14. "Justice on Trial," *Newsweek,* March 18, 1971, p. 27.
15. Orde Coombs, "It's Blacks Who Must Control Crime," *Washington Post,* December 3, 1972, p. 1.
16. *Ibid.*
17. Noted in J. A. Parker and Allan C. Brownfeld, *What the Negro Can Do About Crime* (New Rochelle, N.Y.: Arlington House, 1974), pp. 54-55.
18. James Elsener and Rick Soll, " 'Help Us Fight Dope Scum,' Hatcher Begs," *Chicago Tribune,* May 11, 1973, p. 1.
19. "A Challenge for Detroit's Mayor," *New York Times,* January 3, 1974, p. 43.
20. Vernon Jarrett, "The Mayor Who Knows His People," *Chicago Tribune,* January 9, 1974, p. 14.
21. Brief, *amicus curiae,* in U.S. Supreme Court, case of *Terry* v. *Ohio,* p. 28.
22. Editorial, "Urban Warfare," *New York Times,* January 27, 1973, p. 26.
23. Lewis M. Phelps, "On Becoming a Crime Statistic," *Wall Street Journal,* September 9, 1974.
24. Clarence Kelley, *Uniform Crime Reports 1973,* Federal Bureau of Investigation, p. 38.
25. *Ibid.* p. 47.
26. *Ibid.* p. 38.
27. *Life,* November 13, 1970, p. 36.
28. Opinion of the U.S. Supreme Court in *United States* v. *Robinson,* 94 S. Ct. 467, 476. (1973).
29. *U.S.* v. *Robinson,* 471 F. 2d 1082 (D.C. Cir., 1972).
30. *People* v. *Superior Court,* Los Angeles County (Simon, Real Party of Interest), 496 P. 2d 1205 (1972).
31. *U.S.* v. *Robinson,* 94 S. Ct. 467 (1973).
32. *People* v. *Superior Court, Los Angeles County* (Simon, Real Party of Interest), 496 P. 2d 1205, 1220 (1972).

33. Editorial, "A Red-Letter Day of Criminals," *Chicago Tribune*, February 14, 1971.
34. Lawrence Van Gelder, "Murphy Denounces the Granting of Probation to 2 of 'Harlem 5'," *New York Times*, June 11, 1971, p. 1.
35. Gerhard Falk, "The Police Dilemma in England," Papers of the American Society of Criminology (Columbus, Ohio State University), p. 119.
36. Information containing this incident is based upon a letter of June 24, 1970, with supporting documentation, from Chief Francis Keala of the Honolulu Police Department to the author.
37. *Ibid.*
38. *Ibid.*
39. *Stribling* v. *Malliard*, Civ. No. 26863 (Calif. Ct. App., 1st App. Dist., Div. 4), June 10, 1969.
40. *Crime Control Digest*, April 20, 1970, p. 16.
41. *Pomerleau* v. *Black Panther Party*, Baltimore City Circuit Court, April 30, 1970.
42. "Crime Expense Now up to 51 Billion a Year," *U.S. News & World Report*, October 26, 1970, p. 30.
43. Walter Trohan, "Crime Still Rife in Washington," *Chicago Tribune*, February 1, 1972, p. 18.
44. Morris Kaplan, "9 Allegedly in Black Liberation Army Indicted Here," *New York Times*, August 24, 1973, p. 1.
45. "Kidnappers: Who? and Why?" *New York Times*, February 10, 1974, p. 3.
46. "Bombings Continue in September, FBI Director Reports," *National Sheriff* (October–November 1973), p. 33.

Chapter 3: Overview: A Faltering System

1. John Petersen, "New Ghetto Gangs Vie to Prove Who's 'the Baddest'," *National Observer*, December 16, 1972, p. 3.
2. Address by Superintendent James Rochford, Chicago Police Department, before the Illinois Chapter of Americans for Effective Law Enforcement, September 12, 1974, at Chicago.
3. Ridgely Hunt, "After Crime, Victims' Emotional Wounds Remain," *Chicago Tribune*, December 10, 1972, p. 2.
4. "Hanrahan Hits Light Sentence," *Chicago Tribune*, February 17, 1972, p. 3.
5. 384 U.S. 436 (1966).
6. *U.S.* v. *Wade*, 388 U.S. 218 (1967); *Gilbert* v. *California*, 388 U.S. 263 (1967); *Stovall* v. *Denno*, 388 U.S. 293 (1967).

7. *Kirby* v. *Illinois,* 406 U.S. 682 (1972).
8. *Cupp* v. *Murphy,* 412 U.S. 292 (1973).
9. 465 P. 2d 900, p. 905.
10. Leonard Orland, "Human Rights for Prisoners," *New York Times,* September 24, 1971, p. 89.
11. "Judge Releases a Homosexual Rather Than Send Him to Attica," *New York Times,* November 13, 1972, p. 16.
12. Editorial, "Crime and Punishment," *Wall Street Journal,* March 5, 1973, p. 12.

Chapter 4: The Warren Court vs. the Victims: Suppression of the Truth

1. U.S. Senate, *Congressional Record,* August 11, 1969, p. 9565.
2. *Ibid.*
3. *Ibid.*
4. *Ibid.*
5. *State* v. *Bisaccia,* 58 N.J. 586, p. 590 (1971).
6. *Ibid.*
7. See chapter 1.
8. 18 U.S.C. 3501 (1968).
9. Fred Graham, *The Self-Inflicted Wound* (New York: Macmillan), p. 4.
10. *Witherspoon* v. *Illinois,* 391 U.S. 510 (1968).
11. 367 U.S. 643 (1961).
12. *Bivens* v. *Six Unknown Fed. Narcotics Agents,* 403 U.S. 388, p. 413.
13. *Ibid.,* p. 417.
14. *Ibid.*
15. Dallin Oaks, "Studying the Exclusionary Rule in Search and Seizure," University of Chicago Law Review 37, no. 665 (1970); Spiotto, "Search and Seizure: An Empirical Study of the Exclusionary Rule and Its Alternatives," *Journal of Legal Studies* (University of Chicago Law School) 2, no. 1, January 1973: 243.
16. *State* v. *Bisaccia.*
17. *Bivens* v. *Six Unknown Fed. Narcotics Agents,* 403 U.S. 388, p. 416.
18. *Ibid.,* p. 418.
19. Quoted in W. J. Thornton, "Justice in Chains," *National Review,* March 16, 1973, p. 312.
20. *The Queen* v. *Wray,* 11 Dominion Law Reports (3d) 674 (1970).
21. See chapter 1.
22. See, e.g.:
Barrett, "Exclusion of Evidence Obtained by Illegal Searches—A

Comment on People vs. Cahan," 43 *California Law Review* 565 (1955).

Burns, *"Mapp v. Ohio:* An All-American Mistake," 19 *DePaul Law Review* 80 (1969).

Friendly, "The Bill of Rights as a Code of Criminal Procedure," 53 *California Law Review* 929, 951-54 (1965).

F. Inbau, J. Thompson, and C. Sowle, *Cases and Comments on Criminal Justice: Criminal Law Administration* (3d ed. 1968), pp. 1-84.

LaFave, "Improving Police Performance Through the Exclusionary Rule" (pts. 1, 2), 30 *Missouri Law Review* 391, 566 (1965).

LaFave and Remington, "Controlling the Police: The Judge's Role in Making and Reviewing Law Enforcement Decisions," 63 *Michigan Law Review* 987 (1965).

N. Morris and G. Hawkins, *The Honest Politician's Guide to Crime Control* (1970), p. 101.

Oaks, "Studying the Exclusionary Rule in Search and Seizure," 37 *University of Chicago Law Review* 665 (1970).

Plumb, "Illegal Enforcement of the Law," 24 *Cornell Law Quarterly* 337 (1939).

Schaefer, "The Fourteenth Amendment and Sanctity of the Person," 64 *Northwestern University Law Review* 1 (1969).

Waite, "Judges and the Crime Burden," 54 *Michigan Law Review* 169 (1955).

Waite, "Evidence—Police Regulation by Rules of Evidence," 42 *Michigan Law Review* 679 (1944).

Wigmore, "Using Evidence Obtained by Illegal Search and Seizure," 8 *American Bar Association Journal* 479 (1922).

Wigmore, "Evidence" S 2184a *McNaughton Review* (1961).

23. 384 U.S. 437 (1966).
24. *Ibid.* p. 444.
25. *Ibid.* pp. 444, 445.
26. *Orozco* v. *Texas,* 394 U.S. 324 (1969).
27. Graham, *op. cit.,* p. 156, 158, 159.
28. 384 U.S. 539, 540.
29. *Ibid.,* p. 541.
30. *Johnson* v. *New Jersey,* 384 U.S. 719 (1966).
31. Eugene Methvin, "Let's Restore the Fifth Amendment," *Human Events,* February 28, 1970.
32. Fred Inbau and John Reid, *Criminal Interrogations and Confessions* (Baltimore: Williams & Wilkins Co., 1967), p. 124.
33. 384 U.S. 436, p. 460.
34. *Berger* v. *New York,* 384 U.S. 41, p. 73 (1967), dissenting opinion.

35. *Burton* v. *People,* 491 P. 2d 793, (1971).
36. Henry Friendly, "The Fifth Amendment Tomorrow: The Case for Constitutional Change," Robert S. Marx Lecture for 1968 at the University of Cincinnati College of Law, November 6-8, 1968.
37. It is interesting to note that in Canada this commonsense approach to the rights of society, *vis a vis* the rights of the criminal accused, was taken by representatives of a political party which styles itself the "Liberal" party.
38. *Ibid.*
39. 401 U.S. 222 (1971).
40. *Michigan* v. *Tucker,* no. 73–482, U.S. Supreme Court, October term 1973.
41. 406 U.S. 682 (1972).
42. *Spinelli* v. *United States,* 393 U.S. 410 (1969).
43. 394 U.S. 721 (1969).
44. *United States* v. *Katz,* 389 U.S. 347 (1967).
45. *Terry* v. *Ohio,* 392 U.S. 1 (1968).
46. *McCray* v. *Illinois,* 386 U.S. 300 (1967).
47. *Warden* v. *Hayden,* 387 U.S. 294 (1967).

Chapter 5: Permissiveness Continued: Courts and Corrections

1. Wilson, "If Every Criminal Knew He Would Be Punished If Caught . . ." *New York Times Magazine,* January 28, 1973, p. 9.
2. *Ibid.,* p. 9.
3. *Ibid.,* p. 44.
4. *Ibid.,* p. 44.
5. "Controlling Crime in California," Report of the Governor's Select Committee on Law Enforcement Problems, August 1973, p. 66.
6. 384 U.S. 436, pp. 540-41.
7. Wilson, *op. cit.,* p. 46.
8. Isaac Ehrlich, "Participation in Illegitimate Activities: A Theoretical and Empirical Investigation," *Journal of Political Economy* 81 (May-June 1973): 545.
9. " 'Telepathy' Led to Killings," *Washington Star-News,* August 15, 1973, p. 3.
10. Ridgely Hunt, "Loss of Dignity May Live on Long for Robbery Victims," *Chicago Tribune,* December 11, 1972, p. 20.
11. "Controlling Crime in California," Report of the Governor's Select Committee on Law Enforcement Problems, August 1973, p. 65.
12. Information regarding this bill was furnished to the author by Mr. Richard O. Wright of the Wisconsin Bar, and former Associate

Executive Director of Americans for Effective Law Enforcement, Inc. Mr. Wright also did extensive research and formulated the plan for fixed-term sentences described in Chapter 9 of this book.

13. See Edward Ranzal, "2d Judge Revokes Bond in Shooting," *New York Times,* December 26, 1972, p. 18; Ralph Blumenthal, "Grand Jury Gets Police Shooting," *New York Times,* December 27, 1972, p. 1; Lesley Oelsner, "Judges Are Not of One Mind on Bail," *New York Times,* December 27, 1972, p. 25; Diedre Carmody, "Gruttola Freed in Bail of $25,000," *New York Times,* January 4, 1973, p. 44.
14. *Ibid.*
15. *Ibid.*
16. *Ibid.*
17. Lesley Oelsner, "Jumping of Bail Called Rampant," *New York Times,* November 11, 1971, p. 55.
18. Morris Kaplan, "Defendant Calls Judge Before Fleeing," *New York Times,* April 5, 1973, p. 47.
19. William Roe, "Which Road to Bail Reform?" pamphlet (Allied Agents, Inc., 6919 E. 10 St., Suite E-1, Indianapolis, Ind. 46219), p. 7.
20. William Roe, "A Cure Worse Than the Disease: The Illinois System of Cash Bail," pamphlet (Allied Agents, Inc.), p. 6.
21. "Judge Reduces Bail for Convicted Robber," *Rocky Mountain News* (Denver), March 23, 1971, p. 13.
22. Mitchell Locik, "Posting Bail for Ward of State Blasted," *Chicago Tribune,* February 26, 1974, p. 1.
23. "$325,000 Forfeit in Drug Case Here," *New York Times,* July 21, 1973, p. 24.
24. "Pretrial Detention in the District of Columbia: A Common Law Approach," *Journal of Criminal Law, Criminology and Police Science* 62, no. 2, Northwestern University School of Law) (1971): 195.
25. 18 U.S.C. #3141-52 (Supp. II. 1966).
26. "Pretrial Detention in the District of Columbia: A Common Law Approach," (see note 24 above), p. 195.
27. Roe, "Which Road to Bail Reform?" p. 5.
28. Mahlon E. Pitts (deputy chief of police), "Second Quarterly Report of the Major Violators Branch, Criminal Investigations Division, Metropolitan Police Department" (Washington, D.C.), July 17, 1972.
29. Frank Dyson, "The Repeat Offender," *Police Chief,* June 1973, p. 36.
30. "Rapist, Out on Bond, Is Charged in Attack," *Chicago Tribune,* March 19, 1972, p. 22.
31. "LEAA-Funded Study Deplores Lack of Witness Cooperation in Courts," *Crime Control Digest,* February 4, 1974, p. 1.

32. Alfonso A. Navarez, "Murder Defendant Sought in Witness Attack Gives Up," *New York Times,* August 28, 1973, p. 35.
33. "Two Held in Plot on Witnesses," *Chicago Tribune,* March 14, 1974, p. 2.
34. "Warrants Out for 4 in Death of Witness," *New York Times,* August 10, 1973, p. 46.
35. See Robert Wiedreich, "Judge's Bizarre Doubt Benefits a Killer," *Chicago Tribune,* November 20, 1973, p. 18; "High Court Backs Bond for Hood," *Chicago Tribune,* January 24, 1974, p. 8: "Killer's Release Upheld, But Why?" *Chicago Tribune,* January 25, 1974, p. 14; "Witness' Reward: Hide from Killer, *Chicago Tribune,* February 8, 1974, p. 14.
36. "Interview with Chief Justice Warren E. Burger," *U.S. News & World Report,* December 21, 1971, p. 1.
37. Eric Pace, "Murphy Indicts the Courts for Rise in City's Crime," *New York Times,* December 21, 1971, p. 1.
38. *Ibid.*
39. "Interview with Chief Justice Warren E. Burger," *op. cit.*
40. John O'Brien, "Lawyers Blamed for Trial Delays in Criminal Court," *Chicago Tribune,* March 10, 1974, p. 18.
41. George Bliss and Philip Caputo, "Two Strangers Suffer Night Terror, Months of Baffling Court Moves," *Chicago Tribune,* February 7, 1972, p. 5; "How 'Easy' Court Freed Robber to Strike Again," *Chicago Tribune,* February 10, 1972, p. 3.
42. Carol Oppenheim and Meg O'Connor, "Judge Tells Why Suspect Was Free at Time of Slaying," *Chicago Tribune,* August 17, 1973, p. 3; Art Petacque and Hugh Hough, "Admits 4 Slayings in Grant Park," *Chicago Sun Times,* August 15, 1973, p. 1.
43. Winston Groom, "A Major Robbery Case Fizzles," *Washington Star-News.*
44. Roger Simon and Patrick Oster, "Justice—How It Falters," *Chicago Sun Times,* p. 3.
45. O'Brien, *op. cit.*
46. Simon and Oster, *op. cit.,* p. 3.
47. Barry Goldwater, "Ervin Blasts Court Delays," *Human Events,* August 18, 1973, p. 15.
48. "What's Needed to Speed up Justice," *U.S. News & World Report,* September 21, 1970, p. 95.
49. Carrington (not this author; first name unavailable), "Crowded Dockets and the Court of Appeals: The Threat to the Function of Review and the National Law," *Harvard Law Review* 82, no. 542 (1969).
50. Robert C. Finley, "The Appellate System: On a Vulnerable Plateau," *Trial* (November-December 1970).

51. From an address by the Honorable Donald E. Santarelli, then associate attorney general of the United States, at the National College of District Attorney's Seminar on Federal Habeas Corpus and Prisoner's Civic Rights, Williamsburg, Virginia, October 16, 1972.
52. Julian Hanley, "Habeas Corpus Ad Infinitum," *National Sheriff* (December 1973-Jan. 1974), pp. 32, 33.
53. *Ibid.*
54. *Ibid.*
55. "U.S. Commission Says Many Criminals Should Go Free," *New York Times,* October 15, 1973, p. 27; "U.S. Prison Study Urges Light Terms," *Chicago Daily News,* October 15, 1973, p. 8.
56. "The Nondangerous Offender Should Not Be Imprisoned" (Policy Statement of the National Council on Crime and Delinquency), *Crime and Delinquency,* October 1973, pp. 456.
57. "A National Strategy to Reduce Crime," National Commission on Criminal Justice Standards and Goals, Washington, D.C., p. 187.
58. Wayne King, "Children's Crime Rising Across U.S.," *New York Times,* October 4, 1971, p. 1.
59. Norman A. Carlson, "Remarks Before the Correctional Seminar of the University of Miami," February 2, 1973, p. 3.
60. William L. Cahalan, "Certainty of Punishment" (Wayne Co. Prosecutor's Office, Detroit), May 9, 1973, p. 9.
61. "The Deterrent Effectiveness of Criminal Justice Sanction Strategies," Public Systems Research Institute, University of Southern California, Los Angeles (1973).
62. Fred Inbau and Frank Carrington, "The Case for the So-Called 'Hard-Line' Approach to Crime," *The Annals* (American Academy of Political and Social Sciences), September 1971, p. 25.
63. *Ibid.*
64. William Farrell, "District Attorneys Score Rockefeller Drug Penalties," *New York Times,* February 7, 1973, p. 45.
65. Carlson, *op. cit.,* p. 4.
66. "Controlling Crime in California," Report of the Governor's Select Committee on Law Enforcement Problems, August 1973.
67. William Heffernon, "Family Court Hit on Loosing Killers, Rapists, Arsonists," *New York Daily News,* October 29, 1973, p. 5.
68. Cahalan, *op. cit.,* p. 2.
69. "'Soft-Headed Justice' Aids Crime," *Republican Congressional Committee Newsletter,* May 7, 1973, p. 2.
70. John Darnton, "Police Drug Aide Assails Judiciary," *New York Times,* January 15, 1973, p. 14.

71. *First Monday* (Republican National Committee, Washington, D.C.), May 1973, p. 15.
72. Pitts, *Op. cit.*, p. 23.
73. John O'Brien, "Critics Hit Probation System Here—But Criminals Think It's Great," *Chicago Tribune*, October 21, 1973, p. 37.
74. *Ibid.*
75. *Ibid.*
76. "Controlling Crime in California," Report of Governor's Select Committee on Law Enforcement Problems, August 1973, p. 70.
77. *Ibid.*, p. 68.
78. *First Monday*, May 1973, p. 15.
79. "A National Strategy to Reduce Crime," *Report of the National Commission on Criminal Justice Standards and Goals,* p. 169.
80. Russell Lash, *The Grapevine* 5, no. 2: 2.
81. Winston Moore, "Posthaste Need for Prison Reform," *Chicago Tribune*, August 17, 1973, p. 14.
82. Frederick Wiggins, "The Truth About Attica by an Inmate," *National Review*, March 31, 1972, p. 329.
83. Earl Caldwell, "California Planning Tough Measures to Curb Violence in Penal Institutions," *New York Times*, January 14, 1974, p. 30.
84. *Idem.*, "Rise in Violence Stirs San Quentin," *New York Times*, November 23, 1973, p. 19.
85. "2 Guards Are Killed in a Surprise Attack at Prison in Arizona," *New York Times*, June 24, 1973, p. 40.
86. Bill Kovach "2 Slain by Convict in Break Attempt," *New York Times*, August 1, 1972, p. 18.
87. "Crime Bosses Run Prison, Say Officials," *Chicago Tribune*, December 14, 1972, p. 14.
88. Martin Waldron, "National Guard Retakes Oklahoma Prison After New Outbreak," *New York Times*, July 30, 1973, p. 13; "Leavenworth Hostages Freed; One Guard Killed," *Chicago Tribune*, August 1, 1973, p. 1.
89. William Raspberry, "Fear and the Prison Keepers," *Washington Post*, December 19, 1973, p. 25.
90. *Ibid.*
91. *Ibid.*
92. "Guards at Walpole Refuse Work," *New York Times*, March 16, 1973, p. 24.
93. John Kifner, "Prisons Dispute Stirs Bay State," *New York Times*, June 24, 1973, p. 55.
94. *Landman* v. *Royster*, 333 F. Supp. 621 (E.D. Va., 1971).

95. Meldrin Thompson, "How Permissiveness Ruins Prison Systems," *Human Events,* September 22, 1973, p. 20.
96. Lash, *op. cit.,* p. 2.
97. Howard Phillips, "How OEO Has Aided Radical Prison Movement," *Human Events,* January 5, 1974, p. 6.
98. Mike Royko, "Riot Leaders; A hard look" *Chicago Daily News,* September 11, 1973.
99. *Ibid.*
100. *Ibid.*
101. "Reform of Our Correctional Systems," Report by the Select Committee on Crime of the United States House of Representatives, 93d Cong., 1st sess., H.R. No. 93-329, June 26, 1973, p. 43.
102. William Raspberry, "Parole: The Image and the Reality," *Washington Post,* March 6, 1974, p. 27.
103. "Controlling Crime in California," Report of the Governor's Select Committee on Law Enforcement Problems, August 1973, p. 70.
104. Robert McNamara, Jr., "The Federal Youth Corrections Act: Past Concern in Need of Legislative Reappraisal," *American Criminal Law Review* 11, no. 1 (Fall 1972): 259.
105. H. L. Richardson, "A Faltering System of Criminal Justice," Richardson Special Report (State Capitol, Sacramento, Calif.), April 19, 1973, p. 2.
106. "Parolee Held in Assault on 3 MSU Coeds," *Detroit Free Press,* January 28, 1973, p. 2.
107. "7th Victim Is Linked with Slay Suspect," *Rocky Mountain News* (Denver), May 19, 1971, p. 13.
108. "Convicted Hood off to Florida Instead of Jail," *Chicago Tribune,* February 9, 1974, p. 5.
109. H. L. Richardson, "1518 Members of the Over the Fence Gang," Richardson Special Report, November, 29, 1972.
110. Mablon E. Pitts, "Semiannual Report of the Major Violators Branch, Criminal Investigation Division, Metropolitan Police Department" (Washington, D.C.), July 26, 1971, p. 34.
111. "Prosecutor Criticizes Pen Officials for Lax Security with Walkaway," *Columbus Dispatch,* December 1973.
112. "Killer Escapes Guard at Mother's Funeral," *Chicago Daily News,* January 4, 1972, p. 3.
113. "Murderer Escapes from Green Haven," *New York Times,* January 26, 1974, p. 35.
114. Peter Kliss, "City Boys' Home Depicted as Base for Criminal Raids," *New York Times,* November 14, 1973, p. 49.
115. Judith Cummings, "Prison Escapee Killed by Police," *New York Times,* November 19, 1973, p. 37.

116. "A Murderer Flees Prison After Hearing Reform Talk," *New York Times*, October 31, 1973, p. 11.
117. "Furloughed Inmate Caught in Car Chase," *New York Times*, January 16, 1974, p. 45.
118. Joseph Sullivan, "Trusty Gives up in Jersey Murder," *New York Times*, September 5, 1973, p. 41.
119. "Furloughed Prisoner Held on Slaying in Barroom," *New York Times*, September 4, 1972.
120. Jack Pyle, "Guard Testified St. Peter Was 'a model prisoner,'" *Tacoma News-Tribune*, May 1973; "Jury Awards Widow of Man Slain by St. Peter $186,000," *Tacoma News-Tribune*, May 20, 1973, p. 1.
121. "Baker Brothers Guilty of Slaying," *Tacoma News-Tribune*, July 15, 1973; "State Is Sued for $275,000," *Tacoma News-Tribune*, August 29, 1973, p. 3.

Chapter 6: The Killers vs. the Victims: The Death-Penalty Argument

1. *People* v. *Anderson*, Calif. Supreme Ct., 493 P. 2d 880 (1972).
2. 408 U.S. 238 (1972).
3. 408 U.S. 238, p. 305.
4. See e.g.: *McGautha* v. *California*, *Crampton* v. *Ohio*, 402 U.S. 183 (1971).
5. George Gallup, "Death Penalty Favored, 50-41%," *Milwaukee Journal*, March 16, 1972.
6. Illinois secretary of state, Constitution of the State of Illinois and the United States, 13, 15, (1971).
7. 408 U.S. 238, p. 405.
8. "State Aides ask a Death Penalty," *New York Times*, December 7, 1972, p. 30.
9. George Gallup, "57% in Poll Back a Death Penalty," *New York Times*, November 23, 1972, p. 18.
10. Louis Harris, "New Favor for Death Penalty," *Chicago Tribune*, June 11, 1973, p. 26.
11. "Ban Death Penalty, State House Unit Urges," *Chicago Tribune*, April 13, 1971, p. 1.
12. Cited in brief of state of California in *Aikens* v. *California*, No. 68-5027, October term 1971, U.S. Supreme Court.
13. *People* v. *Love*, 56 Calif. 2d 720 (19.1) McComb dissenting.
14. Don Holloschutz, "Gunman Slain, Hostages O.K.," *Washington Star-News*, August 23, 1972, p. A-1.
15. Jim Landers, "4 Guilty in Holdup Sentence," *Washington Post*, December 8, 1973, p. B-1.

16. "Controversy over Capital Punishment," *Congressional Quarterly,* January 1973, pp. 15, 17.
17. "Murder in Britain at Record Since End of Death Penalty," *New York Times,* July 16, 1972, p. 5.
18. *Crime Control Digest,* February 2, 1973, p. 4.
19. Daniel F. McMahon "Capital Punishment," *FBI Law Enforcement Bulletin,* February 1973, pp. 20, 21.
20. These incidents are taken from a study of prison escapes made by the author in November–December 1969 while with the Denver Police Department.
21. "Captured Convicts Tell of Killing Spree," *Chicago Tribune,* August 28, 1974, p. 1.
22. "Murderer of Priest Threatens the Judge Who Sentenced Him," *New York Times,* September 11, 1974, p. 39.

Chapter 7: The Antivictim Forces vs. the Victims

1. Clarence M. Kelley, "Message from the Director," *FBI Law Enforcement Bulletin,* April 1974, p. 1.
2. Tom Wolfe, *Radical Chic and Mau-Mauing the Flack Catchers,* (New York: Farrar, Straus & Giroux, 1970).
3. 392 U.S. 1 (1968).
4. 407 U.S. 143 (1972).
5. Joseph Bishop, "Politics and ACLU," *Commentary,* 1971.
6. Michael Kaufman, "Reaction Mixed on Drug Penalty," *New York Times,* January 8, 1973, p. 19.
7. Tom Wicker, "Death of a Brother," *New York Times,* August 24, 1972, p. 31.
8. "Comments on 'Death of a Brother,'" Letters to the Editor, *New York Times,* August 26, 1972.
9. "Senate Leaders OK 'No-Knock' Provision," *Denver Post,* January 26, 1970, p. 8.
10. Tom Wicker, "Evils of the No-Knock Bill," *Denver Post,* January 30, 1970, p. 24.
11. *Ibid.*
12. Ramsey Clark, *Crime in America* (New York: Simon & Schuster, 1970).
13. Frank G. Carrington, review of *Crime in America,* Chicago Tribune, December 7, 1970, p. 24.
14. Transcript of proceedings, Committee for Public Justice, Princeton University, October 1970; see also, U.S. House, *Congressional Record,* November 9, 1971, p. 10783.

15. William Farrell, "Peace Activists Defend Bomber," *New York Times,* October 25, 1973, p. 9.
16. Lewis Powell, "Civil Liberties Repression: Fact or Fiction?" *FBI Law Enforcement Bulletin,* October 1971, pp. 9 ff.
17. William Griffin, "Be Nice to a Cop; You May Save His Life," *Chicago Tribune,* April 22, 1974, p. 7.
18. *Ibid.*
19. *Ibid.*
20. "Electing of Radicals to City Posts Angers Citizens of Berkeley, Cal.," *Chicago Tribune,* September 30, 1971, p. 20.
21. See generally for information within this chapter: "Counter Arguments to Proposals for Civilian Review Boards," a brief prepared by the Law Enforcement Legal Defense Center of Americans for Effective Law Enforcement, Inc. *AELE Law Enforcement Legal Defense Manual,* pp. 73-75, 1973. Cited hereafter as "Brief, n. 21"; references are to pages therein unless otherwise noted.
22. Brief, n. 21, p. 7.
23. *Ibid.,* p. 5.
24. Resolution, International Association of Chiefs of Police, October 6, 1960; see also Brief, n. 21, p. 6.
25. Brief, n. 21, p. 4.
26. *Ibid.,* p. 9.
27. *Ibid.,* p. 7.
28. *Ibid.,* pp. 4-7.
29. Richard Ichord, "Lawsuits That Handcuff Our Lawmen," *Nation's Business,* November 1972, p. 3.
30. U.S. House, *Congressional Record,* July 25, 1973, p. 6645.
31. *Brown* v. *Thompson,* 430 F. 2d 1214, C.A. 5 (1971), pp. 1217-18, Justice Coleman.
32. "Survey of Police Misconduct Litigation, 1967-1971," conducted by International Association of Chiefs of Police, Inc., for Americans for Effective Law Enforcement, Inc., Evanston, Ill., 1974.
33. Ichord, *op. cit.,* p. 4.
34. "Police Misconduct Litigation Survey," International Association of Chiefs of Police, Gaithersburg, Md., January 1972, p. 3.
35. *Ibid.*
36. *Ibid.*
37. Ichord, *op. cit.,* p. 4.
38. *Ibid.*
39. *Turco* v. *Allen,* U.S. District Court, District of Maryland, No. 71–859 HM (1971).
40. *Donohoe* v. *Duling,* 465 F. 2d 196 (1971).
41. Ichord, *op. cit.,* p. 3.

42. *Ibid.,* p. 4.
43. Byron Lindsley, "The Quality of Law Enforcement," *Civil Rights Digest* (Spring 1969), p. 39.
44. Edward J. Epstein, "The Panthers and the Police: A Pattern of Genocide?" *New Yorker,* February 13, 1971, p. 45.
45. Lewis Powell, "Civil Liberties Repression: Fact or Fiction?" *FBI Law Enforcement Bulletin,* October 1971, pp. 9ff.

Chapter 8: Recognition and Representation for the Victim

1. Patrick Murphy, "New and Continuing Projects Listed in Police Foundations Grants," *Crime Control Digest,* March 25, 1974, p. 7.
2. Donald Santarelli, address before the midwinter meeting of the National Conference of State Criminal Justice Planning Administrators, Williamsburg, Va., January 14, 1974, p. 2.
3. John Dussich, "Victim Ombudsman," Governor's Council on Criminal Justice, Tallahassee, Fla., 1973.
4. Philip Hager, "Oakland 'Judge Watchers' Grow in Stature," *Los Angeles Times,* December 30, 1973, p. 3.
5. LeRoy Schultz, "The Violated: A Proposal to Compensate Victims of Violent Crime," *Saint Louis University Law Journal* 10, no. 2 (Winter 1965): 243.
6. Edith Herman, "Victims of Violent Crime Now Can Get up to $10,000 in Help from the State," *Chicago Tribune,* March 24, 1974, p. 26.
7. Ralph Blumenthal, "State Program to Aid Crime Victims Reaches Only a Few of Those Eligible," *New York Times,* March 15, 1973, p. 41.
8. See Gerhard Mueller and H. H. A. Cooper, "The Criminal, Society, and the Victim," *Selected Topic Digest,* no. 2, Law Enforcement Assistance Administration, U.S. Department of Justice, Washington, D.C.
9. Iowa Laws, Senate File 26; approved July 12, 1973.

Chapter 9: Specific Victim—Oriented Activities

1. Felix Kessler, "British Justice Still Functions with Dignity and Without Discord," *Wall Street Journal,* March 30, 1972, p. 1.
2. David Napley, "A British Solicitor Compares His Country's System to America's," *Nation's Business,* May 1971, p. 76.
3. *Ibid.,* p. 80.
4. Felix Kessler, "U.S. Urged to Study Justice in Britain," *New York Times,* November 24, 1972.

5. *California* v. *Krivda,* 409 U.S. 40 (1972); *U.S.* v. *Robinson,* 94 S. U.S. 467 (1973).
6. S. 2657 (1973).
7. H.R. 10275 (1973).
8. California Senate Bill 1153 (1973).
9. 94 S. Ct. 613 (1974).
10. *Ibid.,* p. 628.
11. *Michigan* v. *Tucker,* 94 S.U.S. 2357 (1974).
12. *Ibid.,* p. 2365.
13. U.S. Constitutional, Fifth Amendment.
14. *Hurtado* v. *California,* 110 U.S. 516 (1884).
15. *Apodaca* v. *Oregon,* 406 U.S. 356 (1972); *Johnson* v. *Louisiana,* 406 U.S. 356 (1972).
16. "Unmanageable Jails in 10 Years Predicted," *Chicago Daily Law Bulletin,* July 5, 1974.
17. *Procunier* v. *Martinez,* 94 S. U.S. 1800 (1974).
18. *Wolff* v. *McDonnell,* 15 Cr. L. 3304 (1974).
19. *Pell* v. *Procunier,* 15 Cr. L. 3202 (1974).
20. *Ibid.,* p. 3203.
21. Dave Jackson, "Cicero Bomb Rocks Home of Witness in Pair's Robbery Trial," *Chicago Daily News,* July 12, 1974, p. 2.
22. See chapter 1.
23. E.g., the District of Columbia Court Reform and Criminal Procedure Act of 1970, which provides for preventive detention in certain cases.
24. "Pushers Return to the Street After Posting Bond," *Crime Control Digest,* May 27, 1974, p. 6.
25. Constitution, State of Arizona, art. 2, sec. 22.
26. *Rendel* v. *Muniment.* 474 P. 2d 824 (1970).
27. Arizona Revised Statutes, 13-1578 (1972).
28. P.L. 91-508, 84 Stat. 1114 (1970). Otherwise known as the Bank Secrecy Act.
29. *Schultz* v. *California Bankers Association, et al.,* 94 S.Ct. 1494 (1974).
30. U.S., Congress, House, testimony of Clarence M. Kelley, Director, FBI concerning H.R. 188, H.R. 9873, H.R. 12574, H.R. 12575 before the Civil Rights and Constitutional Rights Subcommittee, Committee on the Judiciary, March 1974, p. iii.
31. U.S., Congress, House, testimony of W. Raymond Wannall, Assistant Director, FBI, before the Committee on Internal Security, July 5, 1974.
32. Francis Looney, Editorial *Police Chief,* June 1974, p. 4.
33. Gerald Fraser, "2 Crime Victims Suing Landlords," *New York Times,* November 15, 1973, p. 47.
34. Timothy S. Robinson, "Rape Victim Wins $33,000 Suit Against Firms Hiring Attacker," *Washington Post,* March 7, 1974, p. 8.

✦ Index

ACA. *See* American Correctional Association

"Act to Create 973.10 of the Statutes, Relating to Prohibiting the Use of Imprisonment as Punishment and Requiring the Sale of State Prisons, An" (legislative bill), 125-26

ACLU. *See* American Civil Liberties Union

Adams v. *Williams,* 203

AELE. *See* Americans for Effective Law Enforcement, Inc.

Alliance to End Repression, 205

American Civil Liberties Union, 82, 199; as antivictim, 202-5, 222-23, 280-81, 286-87; Baltimore, 54; Chicago, 13-15; Los Angeles, 221; Louisville, 215

American Correctional Association, 6

Americans for Effective Law Enforcement, Inc. (AELE), 45, 227, 228, 252, 292; as victim-oriented organization, 289-90

Amurao, Corazon, 9

antivictims: ACLU among, 202-5; civilian review boards among, 215-25; and community control of police, 225; credo of, 207; described, 200-202; and harassment suits, 225-30; opposition to, 278-89; vs. victims, 200-232

appellate system, U.S.: cumbersomeness of, 72-75

Arizona Constitution, 277

Arizona Supreme Court, 277

Armstrong, Karl, 209

Associated Press, 36

Attica Prison, 76, 150, 151, 170

Attica syndrome, 169, 175

Atwell v. *United States,* 107

Bach, M. W., 31

bail: abuses of, 127-41, 276-78; and ap-

318

peal bonds, 139-41; and California Supreme Court, 17; crimes by those on, 132-38; danger presented by those on, 138-39; jumping, 131-32; New York NAACP on, 41

Bail Reform Act, 1966, 131, 133

Baker, W. T., 198-99

Baltimore Police Department, 54, 229

Barbee (Wis. representative), 125

Becksted, Douglas, 196

Bedell, Jack, 11

Bellevue (Iowa) City Council, 11

Bentsen, Lloyd, 259

Berendes, Earl, 11, 12

Bernstein, Leonard, 202

Betancourt, Anna, 95

Biggerstaff v. *State*, 107

Bill of Rights, 81

Bishop, Joseph, 204

Black, Hugo, 79n, 102, 112

Black Liberation Army, 60

Black Panther Party, 54, 173, 202, 229, 232

Blackmun, Harry, 116, 183n; on death penalty, 186

Blagden, Edward M., 130

Blair, D. Gordon, 114

Blakeney (suspect), 98

Blood, Robert Ellis, 192

BNDD. *See* Bureau of Narcotics and Dangerous Drugs

Boehm, David O., 76-77

Bonacum, William T., 156

Boone, Charles, 43

Boone, John O., 172, 173

Bovi, Alfred Delli, 156

Bowers v. *Coiner*, 93

Brennan, William J., 3n, 79n, 85, 102, 183n, 259; on capital punishment, 8, 184; capital-punishment views of, criticized, 184-86

British criminal justice system, 255-58, 265

Brown, George, 100

Brownfeld, Allen: *What the Negro Can Do About Crime*, 44

Brusseau, Paul Anthony, 191

Buckley Honor Farm, 196

Buckley, James L., 256-57

Buckley, William F., Jr., 58

Buddy's Pool Parlor, 37

Bureau of Narcotics and Dangerous Drugs (BNDD), 95

Burger Court, 84, 114, 186, 261; and *Kirby* v. *Illinois*, 116-17

Burger, Warren E., 72, 87, 116, 142, 154, 183n, 259, 263; on court delays, 141; and Exclusionary Rule, 100

Burke, George D., 173

Burke, Lewis, 17

Burns, Joseph A., 70

Burroughs (suspect), 98

"bystander intervention." *See* vigilantism

Cahalan, William L., 154

California Constitution, 17

California Court of Appeals, 53

California Department of Corrections, 170

California Governor's Select Committee on Law Enforcement Problems, 121, 122, 125, 162, 176

California Supreme Court, 51, 66, 89, 194-95; and bail, 17, 137; death penalty outlawed by, 7, 183; permissiveness of, 113

California Youth Authority, 18

Canteen Corporation, 192-93

capital punishment, 6, 7, 8, 85, 182-99; cruel and unusual, 187-88; as deterrent, 188-99; Harris poll on, 29; and minorities, 198; persons deterred by, 190-92; reasons against, 182-83; reasons for, 183; and Richard Speck, 9-10

Cardwell, William, 196

Carlson, Norman A., 154

Carney, George, 175

Carradine, Georgia, 67-68

Carrington (Frank), 209

Center for Constitutional Rights in New York, 205

Charlotte (N.C.) Police Department, 228

Chicago Crime Commission, 147, 161

Chicago Seven, 211, 256

Chicago Tribune, 31, 43, 161

Cincinnati City Council, 223

citizen brutality, 216

citizen power, 239

Citizens for Law and Order (CLO), 246-47, 252, 267-68

Civil Rights Act, 224

Civil Rights Digest, 231

civilian review boards: as antivictims, 215-25

Claiborne, William, 30

Clark, Ramsey, 82, 209; *Crime in America,* 207-8

Clark, Tom, 3 n, 79 n, 102

climate-of-permissiveness theory, 84-85

CLO. *See* Citizens for Law and Order

Coffee, Shirley R., 190

Colbert (defendant), 94

Colevris, Jack, 191

collateral attacks, 54-55, 149-50, 212-32; by civilian review boards, 215-25; by community control of police, 225; countering, 286-89; by harassment suits, 225-30; by media, 231-32

Colorado Children's Code, 17

Commerce Department Federal Credit Union, 144

Commission on Pornography and Obscenity, 257

Committee for Public Justice, 205, 208

Common Pleas Court of Pittsburgh, 121

Commonwealth v. *Davis,* 107

Commonwealth v. *Goldsmith,* 109

Commonwealth v. *Singleton,* 106

Communist Party, U.S.A., 173

Community Action Commission, 215

community control of police, 225

compensation, victim, 247-50, 271

confessions, 71; involuntary, 24; and *Miranda,* 3, 18, 102-15

Coolidge v. *New Hampshire,* 92

Coombs, Orde, 42-43

Cordova, Robert G., 70

corrections system, 120-27, 167-81, 269-76; parole abuses in, 176-78, 269-76; premise underlying, 75-76; victimization inside, 170-75; victims of, in society, 176-81

Countryman, Vern, 208-9

Court Reform and Criminal Procedure Act of 1970, District of Columbia, 277

court system, 120-67; bail abuses of, 127-41; Burger on delays in, 141; delays in 141-52, 262-66; and Exclusionary Rule, 100-101; and sentencing process, 152-67, 266-69; and swift and sure justice, 127-67, 262-76

Crimaldi, Charles (Chuck), 139, 140

crime: economic impact of, 36-39, ghetto, 34-45; terroristic, 59-60

Crime in America (R. Clark), 207-8

crime statistics: interpretation of, 20; 1973, 19, 60, 236

Crime Victims' Compensation Board, 247

criminal justice system: annual expense of, 20-21; British, 255-58; failure of, documented, 67-68; imbalance of, analyzed, 21-24; permissiveness of, 18-19, 115-19, 120-81; primary function of, 63-69; specific recommendations for victim-oriented, 255-95; and Warren Court, 79-119

Criswell, Loys, 111

Cronell, Theodore Roosevelt, 192

Dallas Police Department, 137

Daly, Margaret Elizabeth, 190

Davis (defendant), 93-94

Davis, Terrence H., 215

De Mau Mau gang (Chicago), 13-15

death penalty. *See* capital punishment

Denver Post, 70

Des Moines Register, 11

DeStefano, Mario, 130-40

deterrence, 145; capital punishment and, 188-99; and swift and certain punishment, 122-23; theory of, 122. *See also* punishment, swift and certain

direct attacks, 50, 51, 212

District of Columbia Code, 16

Hill, Robert B., 35
Honolulu Police Department, 53
Hood (chief judge), 109
Hook, Sidney, 21-23, 24-25, 29, 202
Hoover, J. Edgar, 208, 212, 216, 230
Howard, William, 230
Hruska, Roman, 82, 207
Huff, Joyce Ann, 6-7, 20, 185, 188, 197
Human Events, 72
Hunt, Ridgely, 124
Huntting, Earl W., 246
Hurst, Richard R., 192

IACP. *See* International Association of Chiefs of Police
Ichord, Richard, 226-27, 228, 230, 288, 289
Idaho Supreme Court, 99
Illinois corrections code, 10
Illinois Court of Appeals, 139
Illinois Department of Children and Family Services, 132
Illinois Department of Corrections, 178
Illinois Supreme Court, 139
Inbau, Fred E., 244
Infelice, Ernest Rocco, 178
insanity pleas, 72
Institute for Court Management, 143, 146
Institute for Law and Social Research, 138
Internal Security Committee (U.S. House): "Revolutionary Target: The American Penal System," 173
International Association of Chiefs of Police (IACP), 217, 218, 227, 228
International Conference of Police Associations, 218, 253
Iowa Parole Board, 11-12, 77, 84, 177-78, 195

Jackson, George, 206
Jarrett, Vernon, 35
Jennings Hall (New York City), 180
Johnson, Lyndon, 82

Keala, Francis, 53
Keith, Damon, 43
Kelbach, Walter, 8, 198, 199
Kell, Kenneth, 11
Kelley, Clarence M., 201, 253, 281
Kemper, Edmund E., 18

Kentucky Women's Socialist Caucus, 215
Kerner Commission on Civil Disorders, 257
Kilpatrick, James Jackson, 5
King, Allen, 199
King, Glen D., 193
Kirby v. *Illinois,* 116-17
Kleiman, Alfred, 130
Korfist, Norman A., 143
Koziol, Ronald, 232
Kroes, William, 213
Krumm, Theodore G., 70
Ku Klux Klan, 209
Kunstler, William, 201n, 205, 209, 229, 256

Lagomarsino, Robert, 259
Lance, Myron, 8, 198, 199
Lansden, Merle, 111
Laplenski, Edward Joseph, 191
Lash, Russell, 167, 173
law and order: and blacks, 39-45; as code words, 31, 42, 44-45; and Watergate, 30-32
Law Enforcement Legal Defense Center (LELDC), 245, 246
law-enforcement officers: and civilian review boards, 216-25; collateral attacks on, 212-32, 231-32, 286-89; community control of, 225; in ghetto, 34; harassment suits against, 225-30; liberal charges against, 34; organizations representing, 253; and privacy lobby, 283-86; search-and-seizure problems of, 87-90, 117; second-guessed by Warren Court, 117-18; as special victims, 33, 46-55; statistics on slain, 48
Lawson, Quentin, 192
Lawyers Committee for Civil Rights Under Law, 205
Legal Aid Society, 110
LELDC. *See* Law Enforcement Legal Defense Center
leniency, judicial, 266-76; and bail problem, 127-41, 276-78 (*see also* bail); in parole cases, 176-78, 269-76 (*see also* parole); scored by blacks, 43; and sentencing process, 152-67, 266-69; and targeting attacks, 50-52. *See also* corrections system; permissiveness

Oklahoma State Prison, 171
Oliphant, Pat, 286-87
Omnibus Crime Control and Safe Streets Act, 1968, 82
Oppenheimer, Jerrold, 14
Oregon Court of Appeals, 73, 74, 75, 150
Oregon Supreme Court, 73, 150
Orland, Leonard, 76
Oswald, Russell G., 156
"Over the Fence Gang," 178-81

Pack, J. W., 174
Packer, Herbert L., 35
Padilla, Ramona, 70
Parker, Jay A.: *What the Negro Can Do About Crime*, 44
parole, 176-78, 269-76; in California, 195; in Illinois, 10, 195; and Iowa Parole Board, 11-12, 195; New York NAACP on, 41; in Washington, D.C., 13
Paschen, Herbert, 9
People v. *Gilbert*, 195
People v. *Hall*, 195
People v. *Milton*, 108
People v. *Morse*, 195
People v. *Peete*, 195
People v. *Purvis*, 194
People v. *Robles*, 195
People v. *St. Martin*, 195
People v. *Trudeau*, 93
permissiveness, 7, 16-19, 84, 85, 152-55; and ACLU, 13-15; and Iowa Parole Board, 11-12; and Richard Speck, 9-10. *See also* bail; criminal justice system; leniency, judicial; parole; probation; sentencing process
Phelps, Lewis M., 47-48
Philadelphia Inquirer, 156, 163
Piel, Eleanor Jackson, 15
Pitchess, Peter, 253
police brutality, 35, 215, 219, 223, 229
poverty: crime's relation to, 33-45
Powell, Lewis, 116, 183n, 186, 232, 274; on repression syndrome, 210-12
President's Commission on Law Enforcement and Criminal Justice, 215
privacy lobby, 278-86
probation: abuse of, 18; in California, 162; crimes by those on, 157-61;

New York NAACP on, 41; in Pennsylvania, 16
Public Systems Research Institute (UCLA), 155
punishment, swift and certain, 262-76; as deterrent, 121-23, 154-55; vs. permissivism, 152-67

racism: and law and order, 33
Radunovich, Milan, 150-52
Raspberry, William, 38, 171
Ray, James Earl, 195
Reese (defendant), 94
Reese, Jerome, 161-62
rehabilitation, 11, 12, 105
Rehnquist, William H., 116, 183n, 186, 261-62
repression syndrome, 210; Lewis Powell on, 210-12
"Revolutionary Target: The American Penal System" (House Internal Security Committee), 173
Rhay, Bobby J., 181
Rhode Island Supreme Court, 98
Richardson, H. L. (Bill), 5, 177, 179
Richmond (Va.) Police Department, 229
Roberts, Edwin A., Jr., 39; "Tonto, We Have Been Doing Things All Wrong," 297-99
Robinson, Aubrey E., 13
Rochford, James M., 67
Rockefeller (Nelson), 29, 205
Roluffs, Gene, 230
Root v. *Gruper*, 94
Rossides, Eugene T., 280
Royko, Mike, 123, 174-75

St. Peter, Arthur, 181
San Francisco Examiner, 30
San Francisco Neighborhood Legal Assistance Foundation, 53
Santarelli, Donald E., 236
Sargent, Francis, 172, 273
Schmidt, Wayne W., 246
Schneider, Peter, 20
Scholl, Reginald, 32, 101
Scott, Hugh, 206
Scott v. *State*, 108

vigilantism, 30
Virginia Civil Liberties Union, 229
Von Utter v. *Tulloch,* 96

Wade-Gilbert, 115, 116-17
Walker, Daniel, 273
Wall Street Journal, 23, 47, 77-78
Walpole Prison (Mass.), 171-73
Ward (Wis. representative), 125
Warren Court, 45, 71, 72, 79-119; and death penalty, 85; and Exclusionary Rule, 69, 85-102; Gallup poll on, 28-29; 1960-69 record of, 81; permissiveness of, 115-19; second-guesses law-enforcement officers, 117-18
Warren, Earl, 3, 28, 69, 79, 102
Warren Revolution, 79n, 80, 82
Washington, D.C., Bail Agency, 131, 136, 160
Washington Star-News, 72
Watergate, 30-32
Waters, Parthenia, 36
Weicker, Lowell, 281
Weintraub (N.J. chief justice), 81, 91
Western Center on Law and Poverty, 228
What the Negro Can Do About Crime (Parker; Brownfeld), 44
White, Byron R., 79n, 85, 102, 154,

237; and *Furman,* 7n, 183n, 186; on *Miranda,* 3-5, 18, 104-5, 122
White, Zane, 230
Whiteley v. *Warden of Wyoming State Penitentiary,* 95-96
Whittaker, Charles Evans, 79n
Whownes, Selma, 39
Wicker, Tom, 205-7, 209
Wiedreich, Robert, 14-15, 139-40
Wightman, Paul, 110
Wilkins, Roy, 43
Williams, Dalton, 198-99
Williams, Edward Bennett, 147-48
Wilson, James Q., 121, 122
Wilson, Jerry, 58n
Wilson, O. W., 244
"withdrawal syndrome," 47
Wojtowicz, John, 192
Wolfe, Tom, 202
Wolfe v. *McDonnell,* 274
Woods v. *State,* 98-99
work-release programs, 178-79, 181
Wright, Bruce McMarion (Turn-'em-Loose-Bruce), 129-30
Wyman, Lowell, 186

Young, Coleman, 43-44
Young, Melvin Eugene, 190

Zimbardo, William, 30